Contemporary Studies and Theories in

İrfan Yazıcıoğlu / Özgür Yayla / Alper Işın / Fuat
Bayram / Eren Yalçın (eds.)

Contemporary Studies
and Theories in Gastronomy
and Food Science

PETER LANG

Berlin - Bruxelles - Chennai - Lausanne - New York - Oxford

Library of Congress Cataloging-in-Publication Data
A CIP catalog record for this book has been applied for at the
Library of Congress.

Bibliographic information published by the Deutsche Nationalbibliothek.
The German National Library lists this publication in the German National
Bibliography; detailed bibliographic data is available on the Internet at
http://dnb.d-nb.de.

ISBN 978-3-631-92204-0 (Print)
E-ISBN 978-3-631-92830-1 (E-PDF)
E-ISBN 978-3-631-92831-8 (EPUB)
DOI 10.3726/ b22455

© 2025 Peter Lang Group AG, Lausanne
Published by Peter Lang GmbH, Berlin, Deutschland

info@peterlang.com - www.peterlang.com

This publication has been peer reviewed.

Table of Contents

Ecem Akay[1] and Ilkay Yilmaz[2]

Chapter 1 Food Allergy Knowledge, Attitudes and Practices of Food Handlers and Managers Working in Chain Food and Beverage Business in Turkey

Introduction

With the changing life conditions and developing technology, especially women's being more active in business life and the fact that eating is now a form of communication causes the rapid increase in mass consumption places and the fact that businesses producing food products become chains and serve in different locations day by day. Chain businesses are advantageous in that they are managed from a single center and that all products produced are structured over standard recipes. Standardization is very important as chain businesses are businesses that can be in different cities and locations, as well as outside the country.

This study aims to determine the knowledge, attitudes, and practices of the employees in these businesses in Istanbul, which is the headquarters of most chain food and beverage companies in Turkey, about allergenic foods that are required to be notified. In addition, how food allergy management is carried out is to examine the actions taken by the business.

1   Lecturer, Doğuş University, Faculty of Art and Design, Department of gastronomy and culinary arts, HYPERLINK "mailto:eakay@dogus.edu.tr" eakay@dogus.edu.tr
    * This study in based on the first author's master's thesis.
    **The abstract of this study was presented at the 2nd International Gastronomy, Nutrition and Dietetics Conference Ganud.
2   Assoc. Prof. Dr, Başkent University, Faculty of Arts, Design and Architecture, Department of gastronomy and culinary arts, HYPERLINK "mailto:ilkayyilmaz@baskent.edu.tr" ilkayyilmaz@baskent.edu.tr
    * This study in based on the first author's master's thesis.
    **The abstract of this study was presented at the 2nd International Gastronomy, Nutrition and Dietetics Conference Ganud.

Material and Methods Research Design and Participants

In the quantitative part of this research, the sample is; It consists of 384 people working in chain food and beverage businesses affiliated with the center of Istanbul. Istanbul is the most populated city in Turkey. In this context, a questionnaire was applied to kitchen chefs and kitchen staff, service department staff, and branch managers working in chain businesses. Ethical permission was obtained from Ayvansaray University Ethics Committee, numbered E-31675095-100-2100001336, for the research conducted between June and October 2020.

This study was designed as mixed-method research. The process of collecting, analyzing, and interpreting quantitative and qualitative data together to understand the research problem in research or a series of research is expressed as a mixed-method (Cresswell & Clark, 2011).

In the quantitative part of the study, the descriptive survey method was used, which aims to show a situation as it is without trying to influence it (Büyüköztürk et al., 2016). It was aimed to determine the knowledge level of the participants on current food safety and hygiene through the descriptive survey method. A descriptive survey is a qualitative approach in which the researcher presents a situation description by collecting detailed and comprehensive information about one or more situations (Cresswell, 2016).

Data Analysis

In the analysis of quantitative data, descriptive statistical analysis was performed using SPSS V.21 (IBM, IL, USA) and the arithmetic mean standard deviation, and percentages (%) of the obtained data were calculated (Büyüköztürk, 2016). For knowledge questions, the percentage of correct answers given to each knowledge question is given. Attitude questions, on the other hand, were converted into a score that determines the attitudes of the participants, since there is no right or wrong answer for each item since it is subjective. By taking the average of the answers given to each item, a general level of attitude about that participant's food allergy was determined. Similarly, the person's knowledge level was expressed with a single variable by giving 1 point to each person's correct answers and 0 points to their incorrect answers, and adding these points. The mean, standard deviation, minimum and maximum values of these "knowledge" and "attitude" scores are given. In addition, the Cronbach's Alpha values of these variables, that is, the reliability coefficients, are stated. Participants' gender, age, educational background, etc. The independent sample t-test and one-way analysis of variance tested whether all other demographic data differed according to the knowledge and attitude levels of the participants. The pairwise comparison of the groups with the findings that were significant in ANOVA was made with the Scheffe test, known as the post-hoc test. After the comparison analysis, the relationship between knowledge and attitude levels was tested with correlation analysis. Findings with a p-value <0.05 were considered to be statistically significant.

Analysis of Quantitative Data

Table 1.1. The Percentage of Correct Answers of Each Information Proposition Directed to the Participants

Items (T) True, (F) False	Frequency(n)	(%)
A food allergy is an abnormal response of the immune system to ordinarily harmless food or an ingredient in a food.	297	77.3
Lactose into Lactose and milk and dairy products are the same concept.*	101	26.3
Food allergy is caused by the proteins found in foods.	165	43.0
Food Allergy is a reaction after the food is digested in the body.	62	16.1
Food Allergy can even result in death, depending on the sensitivity of the person.	340	88.5
According to the Turkish Food Codex Labeling regulation, the ingredients that cause allergies are shown on the food packaging labels.	316	82.3
According to the Turkish Food Codex Labeling regulation, allergen components are shown on the menus.	294	76.6
As a result of cooking processes performed at high temperatures (deep frying, oven frying, etc.), allergens in the food are destroyed.*	261	68.0
If a person with an allergic reaction consumes large amounts of cold water, the existing reaction will be alleviated.*	157	40.9
When preparing meals with products containing allergens, different tools and equipment should be used.	319	83.1
While preparing a food allergy-safe meal, other non-allergenic foods may be touched with the same glove.*	269	70.1
Factors in allergenic foods can be destroyed if the products are cooked at high temperatures or stored in the freezer.*	269	70.1
A person with allergic sensitivity may have an allergic reaction even in contact with allergenic foods.	279	72.7

(continued on next page)

Table 1.1. Continued

Items (T) True, (F) False	Frequency(n)	(%)
"When the nuts are collected from a salad prepared with nuts, the salad product can be consumed by an allergic person."	280	72.9

*Statements are incorrect knowledge

According to Table 1.1, it has been determined that there is a lack of knowledge about cross-contact.

Table 1.2. Descriptive Analysis Results on Information Questions on Food Allergens

Most Common Allergens (*)	Frequency	(%)
Peanut*	267	69.5
Milk*	340	88.5
Strawberry	117	30.5
Soy*	270	70.3
Fruits	125	32.6
Egg*	345	89.8
Sea products*	274	71.4
Gluten*	327	85.2
Chinese Salt - Monosodium Glutamate (MSG)	98	25.5
Sesame*	244	63.5
Nuts*	293	76.3

According to Table 1.2, 70.3 % of the participants gave the correct answer to the allergenicity of soy.

Table 1.3. Descriptive Analysis Results Regarding Research Variables

	N	Min	Max	Average	SD	α
Knowledge level about food allergy	384	.00	25.00	15.91	4.25	.778
Attitude about food allergy	384	1.00	5.00	3.92	.57	.785

The reliability of the questions asked about the level of knowledge and attitude was tested with Cronbach's alpha coefficient. As a result of the analysis, the Cronbach's alpha coefficient for the knowledge questions was found to be 778, while the Cronbach's alpha coefficient for the attitude variable was found to be 785. These values show that the reliability of the questions asked is high (Table 1.3).

Table 1.4. Independent Sample T Test and One-Way Analysis of Variance Results for the Relationship between Demographic Information and Food Allergy Knowledge

Level of Knowledge About Food Allergy	N	Ort.	SS	F & t	p
Gender				1.762	0.079
Woman	91	16.59	3.61		
Boy	293	15.70	4.42		
Age				3.912	0.004*
16–19 years old	28	14.11	4.98		
20–24 years old	102	15.18	3.97		
25–30 years old	104	16.19	4.09		
30–39 years old	102	16.98	4.01		
40 years and older	48	15.63	4.72		
Educational status				6.341	0.000*
Literate, primary or secondary school graduate	101	14.66	4.96		
High school graduate	176	15.86	4.10		
Associate degree graduate	62	16.95	3.01		
Undergraduate or postgraduate graduate	45	17.44	3.87		
Mission in the business				8.538	0.000*
Executive	75	17.65	3.47		
Kitchen staff	191	15.32	4.65		
service personnel	118	15.75	3.74		
Working time in the current business				1.647	0.178
less than 1 year	85	15.27	4.11		
1–3 years	185	15.88	4.29		
4–6 years	59	16.86	3.91		
7 years and above	55	15.98	4.62		

As a result of the independent sample t-test performed in Table 1.4, it was found that the level of knowledge about food allergy did not differ significantly according to the gender of the participants. t = 1.762. p > 0.05. In addition, according to the results of the one-way analysis of variance, it was found that the level of knowledge about food allergy did not differ significantly according to the working time of the participants in the current business. $F(0.380) = 1.647$. $p > 0.05$.

Table 1.5. Independent Sample T-Test Results Regarding the Relationship between Knowledge of Food Allergy

Level of Knowledge About Food Allergy	N	Ort.	SS	t	p
Have you received any training on food allergies?				3.858	0.000*
Yes	211	16.65	3.48		
No	173	15.00	4.90		
Has training on Food Allergy been given in your current business?				2.610	0.009*
Yes	197	16.46	3.59		
No	187	15.33	4.80		
Have you done personal research on food allergies?				6.686	0.000*
Yes	246	16.94	3.21		
No	138	14.07	5.18		
Do you think that the actions taken for food allergy in your current business are sufficient?				0.693	0.489
Yes	275	16.00	3.88		
No	109	15.67	5.10		

The values shown as * are statistically significant ($p < 0.05$)

According to Table 1.5, the level of knowledge about food allergy is significantly higher among the participants who received training on food allergy according to the labeling regulation, those who received training on food allergy in their workplace, and who conducted personal research on food allergy.

Table 1.6. Independent Sample T-Test Results Regarding the Relationship between Attitudes about Food Allergy

Attitudes about Food Allergy	N	Ort.	SS	t	P
Have you received any training on food allergies?				3.738	0.000*
Yes	211	4.02	0.56		
No	173	3.81	0.57		

Table 1.6.   Continued

Attitudes about Food Allergy	N	Ort.	SS	t	P
Has training on food allergy been given in your current business?				2.353	0.019*
Yes	197	3.99	0.56		
No	187	3.85	0.58		
Have you done personal research on food allergies?				5.176	0.000*
Yes	246	4.03	0.53		
No	138	3.73	0.59		
Do you think that the actions taken for food allergy in your current business are sufficient?				1.972	0.049*
Yes	275	3.96	0.56		
No	109	3.83	0.59		

The values shown as * are statistically significant (p < 0.05)

As a result of the independent sample t-test performed in Table 1.6, it was found that all of them differed according to the answers given to the questions about the attitude about food allergy, respectively, t = 3.738, 2.353, 5.176, 1.972, p <0.05. Accordingly, it is seen that the attitudes of the participants, who received training on food allergy, were trained in this regard in the business they work, who conducted personal research on food allergy, and who found the actions taken for food allergy in the business they work to be sufficient, were significantly more positive.

Table 1.7.   Pearson Correlation Analysis Results Regarding the Relationship between Level of Knowledge about Food Allergy and Attitudes about Food Allergy

		Attitude about Food Allergy
Level of Knowledge About Food Allergy	N	384
	r	0.371
	p	0.000

Pearson correlation analysis was performed to examine the relationships between Attitudes About Food Allergy and Level of Knowledge About Food Allergy (Table 1.7). As a result of the analysis, a significant and positive correlation was found between the Level of Knowledge About Food Allergy and Attitudes About Food Allergy, r = .371, p

<0.01. According to this result, it can be said that as the level of knowledge about food allergy increases, the attitude about food allergy increases positively.

When the nuts are collected from a salad prepared with nuts, the salad product can be consumed by an allergic person." statement is incorrect and 72.9 % of the participants gave the correct answer. In Tatlı (2019)'s research, 62.4 % of the participants gave wrong answers. Common et al. (2013), on the other hand, it was determined that 13 % of the employees thought that the product would not cause allergies since the allergen product was extracted from a ready-to-eat product. In this regard, it can be said that the level of knowledge of the employees has increased.

Conclusion and Recommendations

Receiving food allergy training and supporting awareness of the issue with in-house training will bring more knowledge and attitude to the operating personnel, and as a result, adequate practice will add value to the brand. Although there is no increase in the level of knowledge and attitude depending on the working time in the enterprises, it has been determined that there is no differentiation according to the education level of the participants. On the other hand, the knowledge level of employees who have not received any training on food allergy before increases after food allergy training. Considering the increasing prevalence of food allergies and the potential threat of people with food allergies, allergen management of chain food and beverage businesses should be improved with plans and policies in their operations. The development of these policies should involve a variety of stakeholders, such as individuals with food allergies, catering staff, food inspectors, and food allergy specialists. Businesses should be inspected by establishing such procedures not only by the brand but also by the relevant authorities. If the applied procedures are found to be insufficient, penal action should be applied. If the business has service personnel, the stewardesses should get information about whether the guest is allergic to any product during the reservation process or the service and should guide their colleagues in the light of this information. In this regard, the participation of state institutions is very important for the development of education campaigns for consumers.

Acknowledgments

The authors thank the participants who participated in this study.

Funding

No financial support was received for this study.

Authorship Contribution Statement

İlkay Yılmaz, Ecem Akay: Conceptualization, Methodology, Data curation, Writing an original draft. Visualizing, Reviewing, Controlling, Writing – reviewing and editing. Data curation

Declaration of Competing Interest

The authors declare that they have no conflict of interest.

References

Borchgrevink, C. P., Elsworth, J. D., Taylor, S. E., Christensen, K. L. (2009) Food Intolerances, Food Allergies, and Restaurants. J Culin Sci Technol., 7(4): 259–284. doi:10.1080/15428050903572672

Büyüköztürk, Ş., Kılıç Çakmak, E., Akgün, Ö.E., Karadeniz, Ş., Demirel, F. (2016). Scientific Research Methods. Ankara: Pegem Akademi.

Christensen, L. B., Johnson, R. B., Turner, L.A. (2015). Araştırma Yöntemleri: Desen ve Analiz. Ankara: Anı.

Common, L. A., Corrigan, C. J., Smith, H., Bailey, S., Harris, S., Holloway, J.A., (2013). How safe is your curry? Food allergy awareness of restaurant staff. J. Allergy Ther. 4, 1–4. https://doi.org/10.4172/2155-6121.1000140

Cresswell, J. W., Clark, V. L. P. (2011). Designing and Conducting Mixed Methods Research. Los Angeles: Sage Publications.

Cresswell, J. W. (2016). Nitel Araştırma Yöntemleri: Beş Yaklaşıma Göre Nitel Araştırma ve Araştırma Deseni. Ankara: Siyasal Kitabevi.

Dalal, H. (2002). Food Allergy is a Matter of Geography After All: Sesame as a Majör Cause of Severe Ige-Mediated Food Allergic Reactions Among Infants and Young Children in Israel. Allergy. 57:362–365.

Radke, M., Taylor, J. (2016). Food Allergy Knowledge and Attitudes of Restaurant Managers and Staff: An EHS-Net Study. Journal of Food Protection. 79(9):1588–159.

Tatlı, M. (2019). Food Allergy Knowledge, Attitudes and Practices of Restaurant Employees: The Case of Istanbul Province. Master's Thesis. Divided. Bolu Abant İzzet Baysal University Institute of Social Sciences, Bolu, Türkiye.

Fatma Koç[1]

Chapter 2 The Use of Food in Children's Books: A Review

Introduction

The healthy growth and development of children should be supported in a healthy environment from the beginning of their lives. Early childhood is one of the most sensitive periods of development and healthy nutrition is of great importance during this period (Merdol, 2017). When nutrition is inadequate or of poor quality, children's rapidly developing brains and cognitive functions can be negatively affected; This may affect their academic success in the following years. Children's academic success affects their future health and social outcomes. Therefore, children's eating habits and behaviors at an early age are of great importance (Prado & Dewey, 2012).

When adequate and balanced nutritional habits are acquired at an early age, they continue into adulthood and it becomes easier to intervene in children's nutritional problems in their later lives (Doğan & Ertem, 2005; Küçükkömürler, 2017). Research on nutritional habits and eating behaviors has emphasized the importance of health professionals and pre-school educators providing nutrition education to children and families in order to give children healthy eating habits and intervene in possible nutritional problems (Kano et al., 2020; Kobak & Pek, 2015; Ray et al., 2019).

In this context, studies such as press and publishing activities featuring heroes who can be the right example for children and the preparation of children's books appropriate for their age and development levels are important (Aktaç, 2016).

Food is a substance that underpins life, shapes civilizations and cultures, and forms the basis of imagination, art and learning. Particularly in children's literature, food stimulates the imagination, with picture and chapter books frequently containing fantasy food scenes. However, studies in the field of children's literature have just begun to be accepted by the scientific community in general, and discussions about the role of food have increased in the last few decades (Stephens, 2013:7).

---

1 Lecturer, Siirt University, Vocational School of Social Sciences, Hotel, Restaurant and Catering Services, Cookery Program, fatma.koc@siirt.edu.tr

Keeling and Pollard (2012) contend that civilizations and cultures are constructed not only on the foundations of art but also on those of nutrition. This assertion extends to the realm of children's fantasy literature, suggesting that even fantastical worlds and stories can find their roots in dietary elements. Food within children's literature reveals intricate connections through the kinds of sustenance exchanged and mirrors the dynamics of relationships between children and other entities.

Children's literature is full of food-related images, concepts, and values. Topics such as hospitality, gluttony, celebration, tradition, appetite and even obesity play an important role in this literature. Food holds a unique and important place in this literary world for reasons that are both obvious and fascinating. Understanding the relationship between children and food offers an interesting perspective on how the world of young people works. This perspective offers a way to understand the sociology of childhood; Examining foods, by whom, when and where they are eaten, paints a picture of children's behaviour, problems and concerns. Food is actually an important representation in children's literature. The aim of this study is to examine children's books and evaluate the social, psychological and economic factors of the ideas they carry.

Green Eggs and Ham

Green Eggs and Ham is a popular children's book written and illustrated by Dr. Seuss in 1960. The book is written in the words of Dr. Seuss's wife, Helen Palmer Geisel. The story revolves around a character, Sam-I-Am, who suggests to another unnamed character to eat green colored eggs in various places and situations. The other unnamed character initially refuses to eat the green eggs, but eventually tries them and discovers that he likes them. The book encourages change, accepting difference and being open to new experiences.

The narrative unfolds with Sam endeavoring to capture the attention of an unidentified character. Throughout the book, Sam persistently presents green eggs and ham to this unnamed character, each time in a distinct setting (in a house, with a mouse, in a box, with a fox). Despite Sam's efforts, the unnamed character consistently declines the offer. Sam repeatedly identifies himself, exclaiming, "I am Sam - Sam I am," in an attempt to engage the unnamed character. However, the unnamed character remains unimpressed by Sam's persistence and harbors a negative attitude towards him. Despite this resistance, after continuous insistence, the unnamed character eventually relents and agrees to sample green eggs and ham only after Sam-I-am ceases to offer them. Ultimately, in the conclusion of the tale, the unnamed character discovers an appreciation for green eggs and ham, expressing gratitude towards Sam (Lord, 2020: 432).

The central lesson gleaned from the narrative of Green Eggs and Ham is the significance of embracing new experiences. Sam, a youthful character, persistently encourages the unnamed individual to try unfamiliar green cuisine. This evolution in perspective is understandable, as individuals tend to develop a reluctance towards new foods as they age, a phenomenon known as neophobia. Both characters exhibit a desire for familiarity with their sustenance. Sam's approach involves presenting green eggs and ham on fourteen occasions, employing varied methods each time to persuade the unnamed character (Oittinen, 2006: 87–95)

The food that Sam-I-am serves to the unnamed character is green eggs with ham. It is as much unknown food for the child reader as it is for the eponymous character. We know that the unnamed character has never eaten this dish, because he ends up tasting it for the first time and liking it. The climax of the plot occurs when the unnamed character, visibly bored by the persistence, says: "Sam! If you leave me alone, I'll try the green eggs and ham. You'll see." (Seuss, 1998: 54). At the end, the unnamed character thanks Sam-I-Am after tasting the green eggs and ham. He then hugs and smiles; This gives the impression that they are friends. The unnamed character expresses his appreciation by saying 'Sam, I like green eggs and ham, thank you Sam-I-am' (Seuss, 1998: 59–62).

Little Red Riding Hood

While modern children's books focus on nutrition and teach children about where food comes from and how the body uses it;. In classic children's books, food is often used as a tool to give advice. Just like in the classic Little Red Riding Hood. In this story, an important message is conveyed to children that they need to be careful. If children do not heed their parents' warnings, they are warned that they may encounter dangers, be eaten by wolves, or be bitten by dogs (Dundes, 1989).

Little Red Riding Hood stands as a significant folktale across diverse cultures, boasting a plethora of versions and adaptations. Within this tale, food elements hold notable significance, often intertwined with the provisions carried by one of the central characters. Little Red Riding Hood embarks on her journey bearing sustenance intended for her mother or grandmother's abode. These comestibles typically carry straightforward yet symbolic meanings, ranging from bread and wine to cake and cookies. As the narrative progresses, these food items assume pivotal roles in later stages of the tale (Perrault, 1996: 2–46).

When the wolf finds out that Little Red Riding Hood is planning to go to her mother's or grandmother's house, he uses these foods to trick them into eating them. Additionally, while the wolf impersonates Little Red Riding Hood's mother or grandmother to hide his own identity, in some versions he is required to eat the food he eats from them in order to avoid being recognized. For this reason, food has an important role in the development of the tale and the expression of the relationships between the characters (Perrault, 1996: 2–18).

However, it should not be forgotten that there are different versions and adaptations of Little Red Riding Hood, so the use of food elements varies according to these versions and adaptations.

Hansel and Gretel

The tale of Hansel and Gretel (1857) recounts the journey of two siblings navigating through adversity. Within this narrative, food serves as a representation of familial unity and the overall family dynamic. Left to fend for themselves by their parents, Hansel and Gretel seek refuge in the forest amidst their struggles with hunger. However, their respite is short-lived as they encounter a house inhabited by a cannibalistic witch. The witch endeavors to deceive the children into consuming her offerings. Yet, it is Gretel's cunning and bravery that ultimately thwart the witch's plans as she ingeniously dispatches the witch, ensuring her and Hansel's survival as they make their way back home.

The story emphasizes how important food and shelter are to people. It also deals with parents' responsibility to care for their children and children's understanding of the difficulties their families are experiencing. The story of Hansel and Gretel reflects the courage and resilience they showed to survive difficult times. This story tells about life and the struggles of people during the difficult times of the 18th century. Therefore, children can understand the difficulties they experience and identify with the characters in the story (Honeyman, 2007).

The story of Hansel and Gretel highlights how food can affect people and the importance of taking control. The siblings are motivated to indulge in the witch's edible home while fighting hunger. However, this story isn't just a warning about controlling your sweet tooth; It also teaches an important lesson about controlling basic hunger. Hansel and Gretel struggle with hunger later in the story, which makes them more willing to eat. Later in the story, they are punished for wasting food (leaving breadcrumbs as a trail instead of pebbles). This shows that they were punished not only for their bad decisions, but also for their indulgence in "non-material gratifications". This means that the story actually emphasizes the importance of fighting basic hunger as well as resisting the temptation of food (Honeyman, 2007).

Charlotte's Web

Food has a deeper meaning in stories written for children aged 6–9. The best example is the storybook Charlotte's Web (1952).

Charlotte's Web narrates the tale of Wilbur, a pig facing the grim fate of becoming Christmas dinner, saved by his loyal arachnid companion, Charlotte. Facing the imminent threat of slaughter at the hands of his owner, Wilbur seeks assistance, leading Charlotte to devise a plan to spare his life. Through the ingenious weaving of words like "pig," "awesome," "sparkling," and "humble" into her web, Charlotte creates the illusion of Wilbur being a miraculous creature. Despite their efforts, Wilbur's owners, driven by their desire for recognition at the fair, ultimately sacrifice his life in pursuit of acclaim.

Throughout the narrative, various animals exhibit distinct dietary preferences and feeding behaviors, mirroring the diversity found in the nutritional customs of individuals across different cultures and religions. Wilbur, being a pig, consumes scraps provided by his caretakers, while Charlotte, a spider, sustains herself by feeding on the blood of other creatures. Their encounter offers Wilbur insight into Charlotte's unique method of hunting and nourishment, as he observes her capture, wrap, and prepare a fly for breakfast during their initial interaction (White, 1968: 1–48).

Food serves as a tool for delineating the distinct personalities of characters within the narrative, including Charlotte, Wilbur, and Templeton the mouse. Charlotte's consumption of food she hunts herself aligns with her portrayal as a resilient, intelligent, and resourceful character, capable of rallying the barn's inhabitants to save her friend from impending doom. Conversely, Wilbur's reliance on leftovers highlights his passive nature; accustomed to having sustenance provided without effort, he demonstrates a sense of entitlement, expecting life to cater to his needs. He defers entirely to Charlotte for his rescue, displaying a lack of initiative even in the face of dire circumstances, such as his inability to save his friend's offspring without Templeton's assistance (White, 1968: 115–248).

Foods mentioned in Charlotte's Web play an important role in the lives of animals on the farm. Milk obtained from the cows on the farm and corn and beets obtained from the soil are mentioned. Feeds specially prepared for pigs such as Wilber are mentioned. These feeds contain the nutrients necessary for pigs to grow and stay healthy. In one scene in the book, it is mentioned that the animals on the farm eat snow. Snow is a source of food, especially for the spider

Charlotte's children. Throughout the story, various foods consumed in the daily life of the farm people are also mentioned. For example, foods such as milk, eggs and bread are consumed for breakfast (White, 1968).

Alice's Adventures in Wonderland

Books targeted at children aged 9–12 often incorporate themes of maturity, psychological complexities, and educational content, much like Alice's Adventures in Wonderland (1865). Throughout the story, Alice undergoes physical transformations each time she consumes food or drink. Carroll's portrayal of Alice depicts her grappling with temptation in various food-related scenarios, yet ultimately reclaiming agency over herself by the story's conclusion. While Alice navigates numerous decisions during her adventures in Wonderland, her interactions with food and drink serve as catalysts propelling her journey forward, ultimately leading her closer to the climactic trial scene (Carroll, 2010).

Food and drink play an important role in the story. Alice is described through her experiences with marmalade and other foods, while drinking changes her size and allows her to enter Wonderland. These experiences form the basis of Alice's adventures and character development (Garland, 2008).

Foods like pie attract Alice and propel her forward in her adventures. However, sometimes it produces unexpected consequences, disturbing and even endangering Alice. Alice grabs a jar of marmalade from the shelves before falling down the rabbit hole. This marmalade is empty, however, showing that Alice loves sweet things and prepares readers for what they will encounter with food throughout the story. In the trial scene, there is a large plate of pie in front of Alice. The sight of the pies makes Alice hungry and distracts her. When Alice meets the Caterpillar, the Caterpillar finds her a mushroom that can change her size. After eating this mushroom, Alice's size changes. In the tea party scene, Alice encounters a variety of foods, but the scene is more about drinking tea. Alice comes across cookies at the Mad Hatter's house. These cookies whet his appetite, but cause various frenzy (Carroll, 2010).

Alice's relationship with food has varied throughout the story. At first, food stimulates his curiosity and adventures, but eventually contributes to his growth and maturation process. In this process, the importance of food and drink plays a decisive role in Alice's character development and the progression of the story.

The Chronicles of Narnia

The Chronicles of Narnia is full of simple yet detailed fare that will draw in teenagers and adults alike. For example, in The Lion, the Witch and the

Wardrobe, the White Witch seductively uses food to recruit Edmund into her service. Lewis's Irish roots and the connotations of famine in Ireland are also felt in Narnia, which affects the atmosphere of the story. The lack of luxury foods helps us understand Edmund's interest in Turkish delight as the novel progresses. These details explain to modern readers Edmund's interest in sweet foods and why such foods were special at that time (Stephens, 2013: 29).

Lucy's initial journey to Narnia and her encounter with Mr. Tumnus create a positive association with food and drink, contrasting sharply with Edmund's experience with Jadis, the White Witch. These contrasting scenes highlight the profound impact of positive and negative culinary experiences on relationships and personal well-being. While Lucy indulges in a delightful tea spread featuring delicacies like brown eggs, sardines on toast, buttered toast, honey toast, and a sugary cupcake, Edmund's encounter carries a darker undertone. Lucy's enjoyment of tea symbolizes her English middle-class background, adding depth to her character portrayal (Stephens, 2013: 29).

The foods that Lucy indulges in during her tea with Mr. Tumnus are notably wholesome, featuring subtle flavors without excessive sugar. While the sugar-topped cake provides a sweet treat, other offerings like honey toast offer nutritional value without overwhelming sweetness. Demonstrating moderation, Lucy refrains from overindulging and stops eating when satisfied, while Mr. Tumnus reciprocates her visit with warm hospitality. In contrast, Edmund's encounter with the White Witch takes a different turn. When asked his preference, he eagerly requests Turkish delight, finding solace and comfort in its taste. However, this initial relief gradually morphs into addiction, highlighting the perilous consequences of indulging unchecked desires. As the Turkish delight dwindles, Edmund's craving intensifies, illustrating the insidious nature of temptation (Stephens, 2013: 31).

There are two important differences that distinguish the scene in which Lucy drinks tea with Mr. Tumnus and the scene in which Edmund is with the White Witch: the type of food served and the success of the seduction strategy. Mr. Tumnus offers Lucy a common drink, such as English tea, while the White Witch offers Edmund a creamy and sweet drink. Edmund desires this presentation because of his interest in rare and sweet foods such as Turkish delight. Turkish delight is associated with Edmund's gluttonous joy and passion for sugar. Edmund initially accepts the meal willingly, but then falls under the Witch's spell. The witch tries to deceive Edmund by promising to give him more Turkish delight. This becomes a source of motivation that causes Edmund to become a passive character (Stephens, 2013: 32).

Conclusion

Because food preferences are determined very early in life, they are not easy to change. It is believed that the foods consumed by the mother during pregnancy and even during breastfeeding determine the food preferences of the child. Pediatricians believe that eating is a learned behavior learned through exposure and repetition (Robinson, 2008: 96).

In the book Green Eggs and Ham, the child teaches the reader that it is very important to try new things and, above all, that it is impossible to say that you do not like something that has not been tried before. Charlotte's Web has become an unforgettable classic for children and offers a time-tested tale of humanity, love and loyalty; It deals with deep themes such as friendship, sacrifice, death and the cycle of nature. Greed is an important theme in the Hansel and Gretel tale, and children succumb to this feeling and are often punished. In such stories, although the food is tempting, children indulge in sweets without considering healthier alternatives and are punished for it.

Themes such as temptation and self-control are recurrent motifs in children's literature, spanning from historical classics to contemporary works. These time-less narratives endure by adapting past values to suit modern contexts. Central to many of these tales is the struggle between good and evil, underscored by the significance of exercising restraint. In Alice's Adventures in Wonderland (1865), Alice's desires are closely tied to food; she envisions magical edibles to fulfill her wishes, altering her consumption to match her shifting desires for size and age. However, her whimsical journey ultimately leads to a realization of the limitations of such unchecked transformations, prompting her retreat to the stability of a simple tea gathering. Contrastingly, The Chronicles of Narnia highlights virtues like loyalty, courage, honesty, and sacrifice. Through the characters' embodiment of these values, readers are inspired as they confront and overcome adversities. These narratives serve as poignant reminders of the enduring importance of moral integrity amidst life's challenges.

In children's storybooks, food is frequently used as part of character development and descriptive elements, as well as adventure elements. It also has functions such as providing reward and consolation, creating fantasy worlds, conveying cultural and historical context, and providing information for educational purposes. In this way, food enriches the atmosphere of the story and creates a strong bond between the characters and the reader.

References

Aktaç, Ş. (2016). Okul öncesi çağ çocuklar için aile katılımı beslenme eğitim modelinin geliştirilmesi ve çocukların beslenme bilgi ve davranışları üzerine etkisinin değerlendirilmesi. Yayınlanmamış doktora tezi. Başkent Üniversitesi, Ankara.

Carroll, L. (2010). Alice in wonderland, 2. Eds. William Collins Publishing, p. 1–176. ISBN: 978-000-735-08-27.

Doğan, D.G, Ertem, İ.Ö. (2005). Bebeklik ve erken çocukluk döneminde yeme sorunları: İ.Ö. Ertem (Ed.), Gelişimsel Pediatri, içinde (s. 229–246). Ankara: Çocuk Hastalıkları Araştırma Vakfı.

Dundes, A. (1989). Little red ridding hood: A case study. Wisconsin: The university of Wisconsin, 1989.

Garland, C. (2008). Curious appetites: Food, desire, gender and subjectivity in Lewis Carroll's Alice texts. The Lion and The Unicorn, 32(1), p. 22–39.

Honeyman, S. (2007). Gingerbread wishes and candy(land) dreams: The lure of food in cautionary tales of consumption. Marvels & Tales, 21(2), pp. 195–215.

Kano, M., Tanı, Y.,, Ochi, M., Sudo, N., Fujiwara, T. (2020). Association between caregiver's perception of "good" dietary habits and food group intake among preschool children in Tokyo, Japan. Frontier in Pediatrics, 7, p. 554.

Keeling, K. K., & Pollard, S. (2012). "The key is in the mouth: Food and orality in coraline." Annual of the children's literature association and the modern language association division on children's literature, 40, pp. 1–27.

Kobak, C., Pek, H. (2015). Okul öncesi dönemde (3–6 Yaş) ana çocuk sağlığı ve anaokulundaki çocukların beslenme özelliklerinin karşılaştırılması. Hacettepe Üniversitesi Eğitim Fakültesi Dergisi, 30(2), p. 42–55.

Küçükkömürler, S. (2017). Okul öncesi dönemdeki çocuğun beslenmesi. M. Arlı., N. Şanlıer., S. Küçükkömürler, M. Yaman. (Eds.), in Anne ve çocuk beslenmesi, p. 171–192. Ankara: Pegem Akademi.

Lord, P. (2020). O direito e "Ovos verdes e presunto". Revista Internacional de Direito e Literatura, 6(2), pp. 431–448.

Merdol, K. T. (2017). Okul öncesi dönem eğitimi veren kişi ve kurumlar için beslenme eğitimi rehberi. Ankara: Hatipoğlu.

Oittinen, R. (2006). "The verbal and the visual: On the carnivalisim and dialogics of translating for children," in The translation for children's literature, ed. Gillian Lathey (Great Britain: Cromwell Press Ltd, p. 87–95.

Perrault, C. (1996). Little red-riding hood (Everyman's Library Children's Classics). Harper Collins Press, p. 5–46. ISBN: 935-277-68-52.

Prado, E., Dewey, K. (2012). Nutrition and brain development in early life. *A&T Technical Brief*, 4, p. 1–14.

Ray, C., Maatta, S., Lehto, R., Roos, G., Roos, E. (2016). Influencing factors of children's fruit, vegetable and sugar-enriched food intake in a Finnish pre-school setting – Preschool personnel's perceptions. *Appetite, 103(1)*, p. 72–79.

Robinson, B. (2008). Role of parents in promoting healthy nutrition in early childhood. In Life Cycle Nutrition, eds. Sari Edelstein and Judith Sharlin. USA: Jones and Bartlett Publishers, p. 96.

Seuss Geisel, T. (1998). Green Eegs and ham. New York: Beginner Books, p. 54, 59, 62.

Stephens, M. A. (2013). Nothing more delicious: Food as temptation in children's literature. B.A., Georgia Southern University, p. 7-29-31-32.

White, E. B. (1968). Charlotte's web. Puffin Classics Publishing, p. 1–272. ISBN: 014-135-48-28.

Ahu Sezgin[1]

Chapter 3 An Organic Transformation Story: Değirmen Farm

Introduction

With population growth, the demand for agricultural products increases. The methods developed to meet this demand cause food-related problems as well as increased production. Efforts to solve agricultural problems constitute the first step of sustainable agricultural systems based on protecting human health and natural resources. Good agricultural practices, such as organic farming, are considered the most common sustainable agricultural systems today. According to the International Federation of Organic Agriculture Movement (IFOAM), organic agriculture is defined as a production system that protects human health and sustains the ecosystem. This system adopts ecological processing processes, biodiversity and adaptation to local conditions by not using inputs that have negative effects (Aydın Eryılmaz, Kılıç & Boz, 2019).

Organic agriculture is a plant and animal production method that rejects the use of pesticides, fertilizers, genetically modified organisms, antibiotics and growth hormones, and offers consumers healthy and uncontaminated foods without toxic residues (Paull, 2023). Organic production, it is a holistic system designed to improve the productivity and fitness of all stakeholders in the agricultural ecosystem, including humans, animals, plants, and soil organisms. Creating sustainable and environmentally compatible businesses is the goal of organic agriculture (Demir & Doğan Demir, 2021).

In this context, the "Değirmen Farm", located on a 2000-decare land in Kuşadası and established by the Tonbul Family in 1995, draws attention as the place where the first organic farming practices were carried out in the region. In this study, organic farming practices, olive oil production, greenhouse farming, cattle and sheep breeding and water consumption in Değirmen Farm, which strives to keep the sustainable agriculture model alive, are evaluated, and the effects of the restaurants on the farm on the sustainability of the local culinary culture are explained.

---

1   Ph.D., Aydın Adnan Menderes University, Kuşadası Vocational School, Culinary Department, ahu.sezgin@adu.edu.tr

Organic Farming

Organic agriculture emerged in the first half of the last century as a potential solution to problems such as deterioration of natural resources due to industrial agriculture, decline in food quality, and decreased livability of rural areas. In accordance with the I(I)nternational f(F)ood s(S)tandards (Codex Alimentarius), organic agriculture is a holistic production system that promotes and improves agricultural ecosystem health, including biodiversity, biological cycles, and soil biological activity. This is achieved by using agricultural, biological and mechanical methods whenever possible, rather than using synthetic materials to perform any specific function in the system (Kristiansen & Merfield, 2006). Organic agriculture, one of the alternative agricultural systems, is expressed as a system that protects the health of living things, approaches all environmental factors from an integrative perspective which does not allow the use of chemical inputs, contributes to the development of the ecosystem and, as a result, aims to maintain ecological balance. However, organic agriculture is a certified production system within the framework of national and international regulations (Ağızan & Bayramoğlu, 2023).

Organic agriculture has four principles, namely "health", "ecology", "justice" and "care", determined by the International Federation of Organic Agriculture Movements (IFOAM), which express the contribution to sustainability and form the basis of development. These principles state that producers and workers work for a fair wage, have access to the tools used in production, and that consumers will have access to high-quality foods they can trust at fair prices and therefore have a healthy diet (Brzezina, Biely, Helfgott, Kopainsky, Vervoort & Mathijs, 2017).

In line with *The Health Principle* of IFOAM (2021), organic agriculture is expected to maintain and improve the health of all living things on earth. This principle states not only fighting against diseases and pests, but also protecting the physical, spiritual, and ecological balance, and it opposes use of the inputs like all kinds of synthetic fertilizers, pesticides, feed, etc. that will affect health negatively. According to *The Principle of Ecology*, organic agriculture should achieve ecological balance through the design of agricultural systems, the creation of habitats, and the maintenance of genetic and agricultural diversity. Those who produce, process, trade or consume organic products should protect and contribute to the shared environment, including climate, habitats, biodiversity, air and water. *The Principle of Justice* emphasizes that those involved in organic agriculture must conduct human relations at all levels to ensure justice towards all parties (farmers, workers, processors, distributors, traders and consumers). Organic farming should ensure a good quality of life for everyone and contribute to food sovereignty and poverty reduction. It also aims to produce sufficient quantities of quality food and other products. Natural and environmental resources used for production and consumption should be managed in a socially and ecologically fair manner and entrusted to future generations. Being fair requires systems of production, distribution and trade that are open and equitable and consider environmental and social costs. The last principle of organic agriculture, *The Principle of Care*, states that care should be taken to select the methods and technologies used to protect public and environmental health, and to transfer existing resources safely to future generations in accordance with the basic principles of organic agriculture.

In terms of high yield stability, improved soil fertility, high profitability, low use of external input, and therefore cost advantage, contribution to economic and environmental sustainability, increase in the quality of life and environment of living things, reclamation of degraded land, improvement of market access and improvement of farmers' agricultural production, organic agriculture holds numerous advantages when compared to conventional agriculture. Also, it enhances the farmers' capacity to use of local knowledge self-confidently in agricultural production (Morshedi, Lashgarara, Hosseini & Najafabadi, 2017; Das, Chatterjee & Pal, 2020). With all these benefits, the added value created in the organic agriculture sector in the supply-production-marketing-consumption stages benefits the country's economy, while contributing to reducing unemployment with the employment created.

Değirmen Range: The Background

When it comes to family farms, we think of farms where a single farmer owns production and all farm assets, including labor assets are controlled by the family. Değirmen Farm, an example of a family farm, belongs to the Tonbul Family and was established in 1995. It has been observed that the traditional agricultural model applied to the land by farm owners in the first few years harms both nature and living creatures. As a result, "Organic Agriculture" practices were implemented on the farm in the early 2000s.

Değirmen Farm's transition to organic farming was quite difficult. It was realized that the high amounts of chemical fertilizers applied to increase plant production pollute water, soil and air to a great extent, and that organic agriculture, which was put into practice, improved the health and productivity of the soil. Değirmen Farm is the first farm in the Aegean Region where organic farming practices are implemented, which not only provides nutrients but also improves the physical, chemical and biological properties of the soil.

All production and sales stages of organic products in the farm are monitored and certified by a control and certification organization authorized by the Ministry of Agriculture and Forestry, within the framework of the laws and regulations regarding the control and certification of organic agriculture. Control and certification organization also provide training services to producers from input supply to the final marketing stage. Thus, organic products with high nutritional value and reliability are offered to consumers in the farm's restaurants and sales areas.

Organic Transformation Story of Değirmen Farm

In Değirmen Farm, one-third of the land consists of olive trees, the majority of which are for oil production and some for-table olives. The farm has orchards and citrus varieties, peach, plum, apricot, quince, pomegranate, fig, blackberry, almond and walnut trees. All fruit varieties that can grow in the Aegean region are grown on the farm. A wide variety of vegetables and grains are also produced in the fields depending on the season. The most important process in organic change for Değirmen Farm is the implementation of the composting system to maintain all this fruit and vegetable diversity in a healthy way. Composting, a process involving bio-oxidative decomposition of organic matter, is one of the most important management strategies for solid organic waste (Pai, Ai & Zheng, 2019). Because composting is cost-effective, easy to use and environmentally friendly, it can produce high-quality products that are effective in agricultural practices (Bian, Hu, Zhang, Lv, Yang, Yang & Zhang, 2019). Applying compost to fields has a huge impact on crop growth and yield. Sufficient amounts of plant material and animal manure are needed for compost production. In the absence of such materials, fast growing legume plants that create a lot of biomasses must be prioritized to plant and, if appropriate, some animals must be raised on the farm for fertilizer production (Scialabba, 2015). Composting on the mill farm is done in a large pit. All nutrients obtained from the soil (cereals, fruits and vegetables) are recycled without waste. First, the aim is to transform these foods into human food. Afterwards, all the outputs that cannot be used as human food are used as animal food. Excess of what the animals will consume is combined with other biological wastes in the compost pit and matured to become compost and turned into nutrient material for the soil.

Animal husbandry is an essential part of organic agriculture. In the sustainable development process, livestock farming and animal production are of great importance in the economic and social development of countries, as well as making great contributions to countries in international competition (Torgut, Amnayev, Türkekul & Örmeci Kart, 2019). On Değirmen Farm, cattle and dairy farming with disease-free herd certification is carried out. A sheep herd produced from Chios lambs, whose origin is known as the island of Chios, whose gene source in Turkey is Çeşme, and whose production is limited in a limited area due to its commercial value not being considered sufficient, is also fed to meet the needs of the enterprise from own resources.chios lambs,a sheep herd, the gene source of which is Çeşme in Turkey and in limited availability due to little commercial value is raised on the farm to meet the enterprise' needs. Although milk and meat are important production elements for the farm, livestock farming is the provider of solid and liquid fertilizer, which is the most valuable input of organic agriculture, in other words, it is the main nutrient source of the soil. The manure of ruminant animals is also used as compost on the farm. Cow manure is ideal for microorganisms, and sheep, goat and horse manure are also used. Due to the natural availability of land required for compost on farms, and the benefits which compost provides to farmers, the composting process is described as a process suitable for livestock activities (Varol, 2017).

The aim of organic agriculture is to ensure sustainability in agriculture by protecting the health of all living things without polluting the environment, soil, water resources, air and agricultural products. In this regard, production in harmony with nature and closed-system practices are among the main principles of organic agriculture. Closed-system businesses use their own resources. In the closed-system preferred on the farm, where agriculture and animal husbandry are combined, the use of the products produced in the enterprise as animal feed and the use of animal manure and, wastes obtained from animals as organic fertilizer in plant production are important in terms of ensuring the cycle in production (Duman, Altındişli & Aksoy, 2011).

On Değirmen Farm, as well as free range and natural reproduction poultry and horses for riding, other farm animals such as donkeys and camels are also raised. The free-swimming swans, geese, and ducks in the small pond on the farm are the stakeholders of a sustainable life based on common benefit and the natural balance where plant, human and animal friendship are established. Rational use and development of water resources are also gaining importance to maintain ecological balance and ensure the sustainable development of the rapidly growing world population. Generally, pressurized irrigation systems with high water transmission efficiency are used throughout the farm. However, dry farming is practised especially in vineyard and olive cultivation. In this way, excessive irrigation is avoided to obtain high efficiency.

There is a factory where finished products are produced to create added value for the fresh fruits and vegetables grown on the farm. Women work exclusively in the organically certified, production permitted factory where conventional production methods are implemented. The basic philosophy of production in the factory is based on collecting the ancient food production knowledge passed down from previous generations on the farm, bringing it together with the physical conditions required by today's health rules, and accumulating and sharing this knowledge to the next generations. Organic products produced on the farm are offered for sale through online channels and at venues on Değirmen Farm. An example of the manufacturing and fully recyclable use of products is tomatoes. The harvested tomatoes that have marketing value are offered for sale in their freshest form. Tomatoes that cannot go to the market, whose maturity level is different or that are outside market standards are transformed into many different and high value-added products, including tomato paste, puree, various tomato sauces, dried tomatoes and tomato powder. Thus, product waste is prevented.

Local Products and Sustainability on the Farm

The Sustainable Restaurant Association (SRA) states, "The choices we make and the food we grow, cook, serve and eat are our biggest impact on the world." It evaluates a sustainable restaurant with its statement. There is no doubt that SRA's approach to sustainability is relevant to the entire food system. This approach, therefore, reflects the importance of developing sustainable kitchen systems, where which aims to demonstrate that a sustainable kitchen system that combines concerns for current and future generations can optimize food output and consumption without compromising the natural capital stock and ecosystem services (Gössling & Hall, 2021).

It is of great importance to implement sustainable practices in agriculture in the kitchen at Değirmen Farm. In addition to growing products, storing them appropriately, reducing pollution and losses resulting from transportation, and supporting ethical labor practices are among the basic principles of the farm. To reduce environmental impacts, sustainable resource use, waste reduction, adoption of renewable energy sources and efficient supply chain management must be implemented (Gedik, 2021). Therefore, effective waste management and recycling practices in the restaurants on the farm also play an important role in maintaining environmental responsibilities. Minimizing food waste, encouraging composting, recycling and reducing packaging waste, significantly reduces the farm's negative environmental impacts.

Efforts to preserve energy and water resources on the farm are vital to sustainability in restaurants. Particularly, in restaurants, organic cleaners (dishes and floors) and air and water - pressurized machines that consume less water are used. A study conducted by Poore and Nemecek (2018) revealed the impact of excess water consumption in food and beverage businesses on land degradation, greenhouse gas emissions and biodiversity loss.

At the Değirmen farm, local and organic products grown on the farm are offered in food and beverage venues that are easily accessible to the public. Adopting sustainable packaging practices for these products is also a critical component of sustainability for farm owners. This includes the use of environmentally friendly materials, reducing packaging waste and promoting recyclability. Research conducted by Ong, Kaur, Pensupa, Uisan and Lin (2018) and Chen, Sujanto, Bui and Tseng (2022) stated the importance of sustainable packaging development in the food processing industry.

Results

Nowadays, people tend to consume organic products with increasing awareness of healthy living and environmentally friendly products. Organic agriculture aims to increase the use of local renewable resources by minimizing external inputs and using appropriate production techniques without harming people, plants, animals and the environment (Erdoğan, 2023). Organic agriculture, which ensures the protection of water resources against synthetic pesticides and chemical fertilizers, not only contributes to the healthy living of people, but also offers a healthy life to future generations (Ahmadova & Akova, 2016).

Known as the place where the first organic farming practices were carried out in the Aegean Region, Değirmen Farm aims to provide consumers with access to healthy food by providing sustainable agriculture with healthy, organic agricultural products. For this purpose, the farm's own resources are used and a closed system (local input) is applied in the farm. As a source of organic fertilizer, plenty of farm manure is obtained from animals on the farm. In composting, fallen leaves, grass clippings, animal manure, fruit and vegetables and kitchen draff are used. In general, water is applied to the soil using pressurized irrigation systems with high water transmission efficiency throughout the farm.

Based on the need to raise public awareness for the development of organic agriculture, farm visitors can experience agricultural lands and animal habitats. In this context, promotion and training activities regarding the importance of organic agriculture are also carried out by business managers.

Thanks via organic farming on Değirmen Farm, the nutrient cycle occurs faster and the soil structure renews itself quickly. Therefore, the interaction between soil management practices and different aspects of production and environmental impact continues to evolve with organic farming.

References

Ahmadova, A. & Akova, O. (2016). Türkiye'de organik ekoturizm çiftlikleri üzerine bir araştırma, *Karabük Üniversitesi Sosyal Bilimler Enstitüsü Dergisi*, 6(1),14–29.

Ağızan, K. & Bayramoğlu, Z. (2023). Capital structures and financial analysis of organic agriculture marketing enterprises. *Journal of the Institute of Science and Technology*, 13(1), 636–650.

Aydın Eryılmaz, G., Kılıç, B. & Boz, İ. (2019). Türkiye'de organik tarım ve iyi tarım uygulamalarının ekonomik, sosyal ve çevresel sürdürülebilirlik açısından değerlendirilmesi, *Yüzüncü Yıl Üniversitesi Tarım Bilimleri Dergisi*, 29(2), 352–361.

Bian, B., Hu, X., Zhang, S., Lv, C., Yang, Z., Yang, W., & Zhang, L. (2019). Pilot-scale composting of typical multiple agricultural wastes: Parameter optimization and mechanisms. *Bioresource Technology*, 287, 121482.

Brzezina, N., Biely, K., Helfgott, A., Kopainsky, B., Vervoort, J., & Mathijs, E. (2017). Development of organic farming in Europe at the crossroads: Looking for the way forward through system archetypes lenses. *Sustainability*, 9(5):821.

Chen, C. C., Sujanto, R. Y., Bui, T. D., & Tseng, M. L. (2022). Sustainable recyclate packaging in Indonesian food and beverage industry: A hybrid decision-making analysis in consumption stages. *Quality & Quantity*, 57, 2053–2089.

Das, S., Chatterjee, A., & Pal, T. K. (2020). Organic Farming in India: A Vision Towards a Healthy Nation, *Food Quality and Safety*, 4, 69–76.

Demir, Y. & Doğan Demir, A. (2021). *Organik tarim uygulamalarinda toprak ve su yönetimi*, İçinde: K. Kökten; H. İnci (Ed.), Türkiye'de Organik Tarim ve Agro-Ekolojik Gelişmeler (pp. 397–418). Iksad Publishing House, Ankara, Türkiye.

Duman, İ., Altindisli, A. & Aksoy, U. (2011). *Organik çiftlik yönetim modeli.* [Model of management organic farm.] Paper at: *I. GAP Organik Tarım Kongresi*, Şanlıurfa, 17–20 Kasım, 2009.

Erdoğan, Ü. (2023). *Organik tarım ve kırsal kalkınma*, İçinde: A. Akkuş (Ed.). Kapadokya Ekonomi Toplantıları VI: Ekolojik Sürdürülebilirlik ve Ekolojik Tarım. (pp. 97–103). Kapadokya Üniversitesi Yayınları, Nevşehir.

Gedik, Y. (2021). Sürdürülebilir tedarik zinciri yönetimi ve sürdürülebilirliğin tedarik zincirleri üzerindeki etkileri: Kavramsal bir değerlendirme, *Uluslararası Yönetim İktisat ve İşletme Dergisi*, 17(3), 830–860.

Gössling, S., & Hall, C. M. (2021). *The sustainable chef: The environment in culinary arts*, Restaurants, and Hospitality. New York: Routledge. DOI: 10.4324/ 9781315187488.

IFOAM (2021). Principles of Organic Agriculture, https://www.ifoam.bio/why-organic/shaping-agriculture/four-principles-organic, Accessed: 25.04.2024.

Kristiansen, P., & Merfield, C. (2006). *Overview of organic agriculture*. In P. Kristiansen; A. Taji; J. Reganold (Ed.), Organic Agriculture a Global Perspective (pp. 1–19). Csiro Publishing, Australia.

Morshedi, L., Lashgarara, F., Hosseini, S. J. F., & Najafabadi, M. O. (2017). The role of organic farming for improving food security from the perspective of fars farmers. *Sustainability*, 9(11), 2086.

Ong, K. L., Kaur, G., Pensupa, N., Uisan, K., & Lin, C. S. K. (2018). Trends in food waste valorization for the production of chemicals, materials and fuels: Case study South and Southeast Asia. *Bioresource Technology*, 248(A), 100–112.

Pai, S., Ai, N., & Zheng, J. (2019). Decentralized community composting feasibility analysis for residential food waste: A Chicago case study. *Sustain. Cities Soc.* 50, 101683.

Paull, J. (2023). *The global growth and evolution of organic agriculture*. In J. N. Bhakta & S. Rana (Eds.), Research Advancements in Organic Farming (Ch.1, pp. 1–17). New York: Nova Science Publishers.

Poore, J., & Nemecek, T. (2018). Reducing food's environmental impacts through producers and consumers. *Science*, 360(6392), 987–992.

Scialabba, N. (2015). *Training manual for organic agriculture*. chrome-extension:// efaidnbmnnnibpcajpcglclefindmkaj/https://www.fao.org/fileadmin/templa tes/nr/sustainability_pathways/docs/Compilation_techniques_organic_agri culture_rev.pdf.

Torgut, E., Annayev, S., Türkekul, B. & Örmeci Kart, M. Ç. (2019). Türkiye'de uygulanmakta olan hayvancılık desteklemelerinin süt sığırcılığı yapan işletmelere etkisi: İzmir ili örneği, *Ziraat Fakültesi Dergisi*, 14(1): 29–45.

Varol, H. (2017) *Hayvancılık işletmelerinde oluşan atıkların işletimi ve olası çevre etkileri; Afyonkarahisar örneği*, Yüksel Lisans Tezi, SDÜ Fen Bilimleri Enstitüsü, Tarımsal Yapılar ve Sulama ABD, Isparta.

*Note: Basic information about Değirmen Farm was given by Mrs. Gürsel Tonbul.

Ayhan Dağdeviren[1] and Yusuf Ziya Akbaş[2]

Chapter 4 Evaluation of Bursa's Geographically Indicated Food Products within the Scope of Gastronomy Tourism

Introduction

Geographical indication is "a sign indicating a product identified with the region, area, region or country of origin in terms of a distinctive feature, reputation or other characteristics". Geographical indication is evaluated in two scopes: "designation of origin" and "mahreç indication". If all or the main qualities of a product originate from natural and human elements belonging to a certain geographical area, geographical indications in this case are expressed as "designation of origin"; while geographical indications that are identified with a certain geographical area in terms of a distinctive quality, reputation or other characteristics and that are the subject of products where at least one of the production, processing or other processes must take place within the designated geographical area are expressed as "mahreç indication" (Turkish Patent and Trademark Office, 2024).

Gastronomy tourism is a type of tourism activity which is characterized by the visitor's experience associated with food and related products and activities while travelling. Gastronomy tourism may also include other related activities such as visiting the local producers, joining in food festivals and participating cooking courses along with authentic, traditional, or modern culinary experiences (United Nations World Tourism Organization, 2024). In other words it is about exploring, meeting society and history through sustenance and nourishment related exercises in the formation of considerable encounters (Kumar, 2018: 1974). Gastronomy tourism can also be related in its many forms to distinct parts of the production-consumption continuity, from sampling the 'raw' product at the farm or vineyard to the gastronomic experiences supplied by restaurants (Richards, 2002: 18).

1 Assoc. Prof. Dr. Cankırı Karatekin University, Ilgaz Tourism and Hotel Management School, Department of Tourism Management, ayhandagdeviren@karatekin.edu.tr
2 Asst. Prof. Dr. Cankırı Karatekin University, Ilgaz Tourism and Hotel Management School, Department of Tourism Guidance, yusufziyaakbas@ karatekin.edu.tr

Bursa, where different cultures blend with its deep-rooted past, draws attention especially with its historical restaurants, food and beverage establishments offering a rich variety of products, culinary culture and gastronomy events. Bursa; located in the northwest of the Anatolian peninsula and in the southeast of the Marmara Sea, is the fourth largest city in terms of population in Turkey (Cengiz, 2012: 13). The city has a total of 33 geographical indication registered products. 26 of these are food products. In this section of the book, the cuisine, geographical indication registered food products, taste stops, gastronomy routes and activities of Bursa, which is in the position one of the prominent cities of Turkey in gastronomy tourism, were discussed. Finally, recommendations regarding Bursa's gastronomy and gastronomy tourism have been developed.

Bursa Cuisine

Bursa, which was fought for in every period of history, was conquered by Orhangazi on April 6, 1326, after a long siege, and became the first capital of the Great World State, the Ottoman Empire. Very few written sources and documents directly related to the culinary culture of Bursa which is included in historical sources and the works of travelers have survived to the present day (Kondakçı, 2021: 264). In 1502, in addition to being the first consumer law in the world, "Kanunname-i İhtisab-ı Bursa", which also went down in history as the first standards was issued by Sultan Bayezid Khan II. With this law, all products had been subject to certain standards. The diversity and abundance of products grown in Uludağ and Bursa plains have shaped the urban texture of Bursa. The inns and marketplaces where these products are sold and stored, the commercial activity in food products and the open and closed spaces such as Galle Han, Pirinç Han, Tuz Han, Kapan Han, Tuz Pazarı, Balık Pazarı, Tavuk Pazarı, Saman Pazarı have been effective in the urban architecture of Bursa. Towards the end of the 19th century, restaurants were opened in the bazaars for the tradesman and merchant classes (Bursa Governorship, n.d.; Kondakçı, 2021: 265).

Due to its geography being suitable for agriculture, especially its climate and fertile soil, many fruits and vegetables are grown in Bursa. Peach, chestnut, black fig, raspberry, blackberry, strawberry and olive are the first ones that come to mind. Soups, olive oil dishes, meat dishes, seafood, desserts are the foods that are carefully prepared in Bursa cuisine and take their place on the tables. İskender kebap, İnegöl köfte, Kemalpaşa tatlısı, kestane şekeri, Mihaliç peyniri, cantık, pideli köfte are among the flavors specific to Bursa. Apart from these delicacies, Bursa has many local delicacies too (Bursa Special Provincial Administration, 2012: 126; Bursa Governorship, n.d.; GotoB, 2024a). (Page 40)

Bursa, which has a heritage of palace dishes due to being the capital of the Ottoman Empire, has further enriched its cultural heritage with the culinary cultures of immigrants (Thessaloniki-Cretan Emigrants, Bosnians, Albanians, Pomaks, Azeris, Laz, Ahıska, Abkhaz, Circassian, Georgian, etc.). Bursa, which draws attention with its richness, has many food products with geographical indication registration (Bursa Governorship, n.d.; Kondakçı, 2021: 266).

Bursa's Geographical Indication Registered Food Products

Bursa's geographical indication registered food products are presented in Table 4.1. As seen in the table, the total of Bursa's geographical indication registered food products is 26 and the first geographical indication registration was made in 2005 for Gemlik Zeytini.

Table 4.1. Bursa's Geographical Indication Registered Food Products

No	Name of the Geographical Indication	Type of Geographical Indication	Registration No	Registration Date	Registrant
1	Bursa Cantık	Mahreç Indication	940	01.11.2021	Bursa Chamber of Commerce and Industry
2	Bursa Cevizli Lokum	Mahreç Indication	942	01.11.2021	Bursa Chamber of Commerce and Industry
3	Bursa Döner Kebabı	Mahreç Indication	1151	17.06.2022	Bursa Chamber of Commerce and Industry
4	Bursa Kestane Şekeri	Mahreç Indication	652	20.01.2021	Bursa Chamber of Commerce and Industry
5	Bursa Kestanesi	Designation of Origin	1514	25.12.2023	Bursa Metropolitan Municipality, Bursa Province Livestock Development Association
6	Bursa Pideli Köfte	Mahreç Indication	930	25.10.2021	Bursa Commodity Exchange

(continued on next page)

Table 4.1. Continued

No	Name of the Geographical Indication	Type of Geographical Indication	Registration No	Registration Date	Registrant
7	Bursa Santa Maria Armudu	Designation of Origin	1290	16.12.2022	Gürsu Chamber of Agriculture
8	Bursa Siyah İnciri/ Bursa Siyahı/Siyah Bursa İnciri	Designation of Origin	391	14.11.2018	S.S. Bursa Region Agricultural Cooperatives Union
9	Bursa Süt Helvası	Mahreç Indication	912	04.10.2021	Bursa Chamber of Commerce and Industry
10	Bursa Tahinli Pide	Mahreç Indication	941	01.11.2021	Bursa Chamber of Commerce and Industry
11	Bursa Üzüm Şırası	Mahreç Indication	838	09.08.2021	Bursa Chamber of Commerce and Industry
12	Bursa Şeftalisi	Designation of Origin	430	03.05.2019	S.S. Bursa Region Agricultural Cooperatives Union
13	Gemlik Zeytini	Designation of Origin	76	03.10.2005	Gemlik Commodity Exchange
14	Gürsu Deveci Armudu	Designation of Origin	454	10.09.2019	Gürsu Chamber of Agriculture
15	Hasanağa Enginarı	Designation of Origin	533	11.09.2020	Bursa Nilüfer Municipality
16	İnegöl Cerrah Kuru Fasulyesi	Mahreç Indication	1373	07.06.2023	İnegöl Municipality
17	İnegöl Çıbrıkası	Designation of Origin	1374	06.06.2023	İnegöl Municipality
18	İnegöl Köfte	Mahreç Indication	78	28.02.2006	İnegöl Chamber of Commerce and Industry
19	İnegöl Sütlü Kadayıfı	Mahreç Indication	1383	09.06.2023	İnegöl Municipality
20	İznik Müşküle Üzümü	Designation of Origin	869	20.08.2021	İznik Municipality

Table 4.1. Continued

No	Name of the Geographical Indication	Type of Geographical Indication	Registration No	Registration Date	Registrant
21	Karacabey Soğanı	Designation of Origin	247	30.11.2017	Karacabey Commodity Exchange
22	Keles Kirazı	Designation of Origin	1394	22.06.2023	Bursa Metropolitan Municipality
23	Kemalpaşa Tatlısı/ Mustafakemalpaşa Peynir Tatlısı/ Mustafakemalpaşa Tatlısı	Mahreç Indication	784	18.06.2021	Mustafakemalpaşa Chamber of Commerce and Industry
24	Orhangazi Gedelek Turşusu	Mahreç Indication	249	04.12.2017	Orhangazi Chamber of Commerce and Industry
25	Yenişehir Biberi	Mahreç Indication	1263	24.11.2022	Bursa Province Livestock Development Association, Bursa Yenişehir Municipality
26	Zeyniler Hınkalı	Mahreç Indication	1540	15.02.2024	Limited Liability Zeyniler Çalıkuşu Women Agricultural Development Cooperative

Below in Tables 4.2–, Bursa's geographical indication registered food products are separated and explained briefly according to their categories.

Table 4.2. Bursa's Geographical Indication Registered Food Products in the Bakery and Pastry Products, Pastries, Desserts Category

Name of the Geographical Indication	Product Description and Features	Photo
Bursa Cantık	It is a pita baked by placing 60–65 g of ground beef mixture on 120–150 g of yeast dough, leaving 2–3 cm of space on the edge. It was introduced into Bursa cuisine by the Tatars who settled in Bursa during the Ottoman-Russian War.	
Bursa Cevizli Lokum	It is a sweet pastry made from yeast dough, filled with walnut filling flavored with various spices, brushed with beaten egg, sprinkled with sesame seeds, and then baked preferably in a stone-based black oven and over a wood fire. Its history dates back to the Ottoman period.	
Bursa Süt Helvası	It is produced by frying the mixture cooked using raw cow milk, butter, flour and sugar in an oven at 250 °C. Optionally, walnuts or hazelnuts and cinnamon can be sprinkled on top. It is a dessert belonging to the Ottoman palace cuisine.	
Bursa Tahinli Pide	It is a pastry known and consumed in Bursa since the Ottoman period. It can be said that the history of Bursa Tahini Pita, which is produced by pouring a specially prepared tahini mixture on yeast dough, has a history of approximately 500 years.	
İnegöl Sütlü Kadayıfı	It is a kadayif dessert produced in the İnegöl district by wrapping, shaping, cooking and syruping kadayif greased with a mixture of butter and sunflower oil. Its sherbet is prepared by using milk, white sugar, cream and water. Wire kadayif has a spiral appearance because it is wrapped by turning inwards. The history of İnegöl Sütlü Kadayıfı dates back to ancient times.	
Kemalpaşa Tatlısı/ Mustafakemalpaşa Peynir Tatlısı/ Mustafakemalpaşa Tatlısı	It is a dessert consumed by baking the dough obtained by using fresh unsalted curd, semolina, flour, egg and leavening agent, shaping it into a hemisphere and then mixing this semi-finished product with syrup. The most important element that gives it its characteristic feature is the fresh unsalted curd it contains. Its history dates back a century. It is rumored that the first production of the dessert started with the cheese dessert that an immigrant woman produced at home for her children.	

Source: Kondakçı, 2021: 287, Turkish Patent and Trademark Office, 2024.

Table 4.3. Bursa's Geographical Indication Registered Food Products in the Meals and Soups Category

Name of the Geographical Indication	Product Description and Features	Photo
Bursa Döner Kebabı	It is a kebab produced by using leaf meat and minced meat obtained from ovine and bovine meat, cooking it over charcoal, then placing it on pita bread and pouring hot butter over it. The nail pita used in the production is greased with kebab meat oil, fried/heated on the barbecue and cut into small pieces. Its service is made on a heated, wide and flat porcelain or metal plate. Optionally, yoghurt, tomato/tomato paste sauce, roasted peppers, sliced tomatoes or eggplants can be served on the side. Its history dates back to the mid-1800s.	
Bursa Pideli Köfte	It is a dish made with pita, meatball, sauce and butter. Onions are not used in meatballs and no other spices are added to the filling except black pepper and cumin. The flour used in the production of pita does not contain additives and is bran-free. It is served by placing at least 8 meatballs weighing at least 10 g on pitas cut into cubes or rectangles. Its history dates back to the 1870s.	
İnegöl Köfte	It is a product prepared by shaping the uncooked meatball dough with molds and then cooling or freezing it. It is a mixture of butchered animal body meats, preferably butchered veal body meats and butchered sheep body meats, butchered lamb body meats, after removing the bones, tendon fascia, cartilage and lymph nodes, nerves and fats when necessary, adding edible salt, pulling and mixing until it becomes homogeneous and then pulling it again or, if necessary, doing this re-extraction process after resting in the cold for a maximum of 18 hours.	
Zeyniler Hınkalı	It is a dish prepared from pastries specific to the Yıldırım district of Bursa province, which is produced by rolling out the dough prepared with special purpose wheat flour, water, eggs and salt, cutting it into circles, putting the filling, handcrafting it, shrinking it, boiling it, cooking it and serving it by pouring melted hot butter over it. In the preparation of the product, minced meat, onion, salt and spices are used as stuffing.	

Source: Turkish Patent and Trademark Office, 2024.

Table 4.4. Bursa's Geographical Indication Registered Food Product in the Chocolate, Confectionery and Derivative Products Category

Name of the Geographical Indication	Product Description and Features	Photo
Bursa Kestane Şekeri	It is a product obtained by peeling the shells of chestnut fruit and sugaring it by cooking in syrup. It is one of the first tastes that comes to mind when Bursa is mentioned, and Bursa is the first place that comes to mind when chestnut candy is mentioned. One of the reasons why Bursa is famous for its chestnut candy is that its chestnuts are large. There is even a folk song that says "The chestnuts of Bursa, only five of them weigh one okka ". Chestnut candy started to be produced in the famous Şekerciler Bazaar in Bursa since the early 1900s.	

Source: Bursa Governorship, 2008: 148; Turkish Patent and Trademark Office, 2024.

Table 4.5. Geographical Indication Registered Food Product in Bursa's Soft Drinks Category

Name of the Geographical Indication	Product Description and Features	Photo
Bursa Üzüm Şırası	It is a non-alcoholic beverage made from black raisins with seeds, drinking water and optionally using white sugar. Black carrot juice is used as a color stabilizer. No spices are used in production. It can be produced in two ways: traditional and fabricated.	

Source: Turkish Patent and Trademark Office, 2024.

Table 4.6. Bursa's Geographical Indication Registered Food Product in the Seasonings/Flavorings, Sauces and Salt Category for Food

Name of the Geographical Indication	Product Description and Features	Photo
İnegöl Çıbrıkası	As a plant, it is also known as "çıbrıka" by its common name among the people in the region. İnegöl Çıbrıkası is a thyme spice belonging to the Satureja (Lamiaceae) genus. The above-ground parts of the İnegöl Çıbrıka plant, which is harvested and processed in accordance with its technique, are used as spices.	

Source: Turkish Patent and Trademark Office, 2024.

Table 4.7. Bursa's Geographical Indication Registered Food Products in the Processed and Unprocessed Fruits, Vegetables and Mushrooms Category

Name of the Geographical Indication	Product Description and Features	Photo
Bursa Kestanesi	It is the fruit of the chestnut tree belonging to the Castanea sativa species, which belongs to the Fagaceae family and grows at altitudes between 400–600 m in the district villages on the foothills of Uludağ. The distinctive feature of Bursa Kestanesi is that it is large and highly productive. Since the soil on the geographical border is volcanic and has a high potassium content, chestnuts have a high starch and protein ratio too. The history of Bursa Kestanesi dates back to ancient times.	
Bursa Santa Maria Armudu	It is a summer pear belonging to the Pyrus communis species that grows in geographical borders. It is a cultivated pear and is produced by grafting onto rootstocks. The sizes of Bursa Santa Maria Armudu vary between large, large-medium and medium. Bursa Santa Maria Armudu first started to be produced in the 1970s. But in a short time it had an important place in the agricultural economy of the geographical border.	

(continued on next page)

Table 4.7. Continued

Name of the Geographical Indication	Product Description and Features	Photo
Bursa Siyah İnciri/Bursa Siyahı/Siyah Bursa İnciri	It is produced from the "Dürdane" variety. It is a fig with a dark purple outer skin, red flesh and large size (55–65 mm wide). Black figs, produced with the influence of the traditional knowledge of Bursa producers, are large in size, smooth-shaped and sweet. Black figs grown in Bursa are larger and darker in color than black figs grown in other regions.	
Bursa Şeftalisi	It is produced from J.H. Hale and Glohaven varieties. The fame of Bursa Peach dates back to old times. According to a research, records dating back to 1848 and 1881 were found in the Ottoman archives. The records in question show that Bursa Şeftalisi was famous for its taste and was sent as gifts to both family members and the palace.	
Gemlik Zeytini	The most important feature that distinguishes Gemlik zeytini from other olives comes from the fact that the olive trees from which the harvest is made are made from olive saplings grown in the Bursa Gemlik region and obtained by processing.	
Gürsu Deveci Armudu	It is a Deveci pear belonging to the Pyrus Cumminus species. The flower pit is deep. Fruit sizes vary between large and very large. Storage time is very long.	
Hasanağa Enginarı	It is a product produced from Bayrampaşa artichoke (Cynara scolymus L. cv. Bayrampaşa) variety. Studies on the folk culture and history of Bursa show that artichoke has a distinct economic meaning for the city of Bursa and Hasanağa neighborhood and has a place in Bursa food culture since the past.	
İnegöl Cerrah Kuru Fasulyesi	İnegöl Cerrah Kuru Fasulyesi, which are among the edible legumes, are produced from beans with dermason properties, whose Latin species name is Phaseolus vulgaris L. İnegöl Cerrah Kuru Fasulyesi are a hot climate plant in the bean group, which can be considered fringe-rooted and relatively dwarf in terms of plant structure.	

Table 4.7. Continued

Name of the Geographical Indication	Product Description and Features	Photo
İznik Müşküle Üzümü	The grains are very large and slightly elliptical in shape, thick-skinned, hazy, transparent and yellow green in color. İznik Müşküle Üzümü takes the characteristic feature of hard, juicy and slightly elliptical grains with the effect of the ecological situation of the geographical border, climate, proximity to the sea, altitude of about 1,000 m, terrain and soil structure.	
Karacabey Soğanı	Although many varieties are grown in Karacabey district, the onions, which have been famous for their quality from the past to the present and are unique to the region, consist of three varieties. These are; Kantartopu, İmralı and İmralı Kırması varieties.	
Keles Kirazı	It is produced in orchards at the geographical border using the cherry variety, whose Latin species name is Prunus avium L. The establishment of Keles Kirazı Orchards on the geographical border, the cultivation of the product and the subject of cherry festivals that have survived to this day date back to the 1950s.	
Orhangazi Gedelek Turşusu	The distinguishing feature of Orhangazi Gedelek Turşusu is that it is a pickle with a long shelf life, produced by using "Gedelek Pınarbaşı Spring Water" from this region, using sea salt (or rock salt) and acetic acid for various fruits and vegetables, without using any unfamiliar chemical additives.	
Yenişehir Biberi	It is a bright-looking, dark green, thin-skinned, 10–25 cm long and thin-structured pepper the thickest part of its diameter is the stem, and the tip becomes thinner towards the tip, with a pointed structure Latin species name is Capsicum annuum var. longum which is produced intensively in the Yenişehir district of Bursa.	

Source: Anadolu Agency, 2022 (Photo); Turkish Patent and Trademark Office, 2024.

Apart from these food products, geographical indication applications have also been made for; *Hünkar Beğendi, Keles Sorgun Peyniri, Keles Çörek Otu Yağı, Tirilye Zeytini, Tosman Helvası, İnegöl Büryanı/İnegöl Mişörizi, İnegöl Hınkal Mantısı, İnegöl Piyazı, İnegöl Pırasası* and *İnegöl Simidi.*

Taste Stops, Gastronomy Routes and Activities

Bursa has an important image with its many historical food and beverage businesses. Some of these businesses are as follows: Kebapçı İskender, Uludağ Kebapçısı, Acı Dayı Cantık, Besler İnegöl Köftecisi, Yeşil Pideli Köfte, Tavukçuoğlu İşkembe Çorbacısı, Akay Çiğbörek ve Mantı, Abdal Simit Fırını, Tarihi Yaşayanlar Börekçisi, Ulus Pastanesi, Uzay Pastanesi, Bağdat Hurma Tatlıcısı, Helvacı Cengiz.

Whereas Bursa's gastronomy routes are as follows (Gotob, 2024c): (Page 50)

- *Central Gastronomy Route:* In Bursa gastronomy, which has been formed by mixing different cultures together for centuries, you can experience the 700-year-old Bursa Kebabı in the city center or taste Pideli Köfte in the Tarihi Kayhan Çarşısı. Cantık in the old Aynalı Pazar or Tuz Pazarı can be included in the list. Süt helvası in Tahtakale, dondurmalı irmik tatlısı in Kozahan, Bağdat hurma tatlısı, a street delicacy that can be seen in mobile carts on the sidewalks and kestane şekeri that can be found every step on Atatürk Street are among Bursa's sweet delicacies. Közde Türk kahvesi can be enjoyed at Kozahan, tea at Ördekli Kültür Merkezi and tahinli pide, Bursa simidi and cevizli lokum can be eaten around Abdal Mehmed Mosque for breakfast, lunch or afternoon snack.

- *Olive and Olive Oil Route:* It consists of four stops. The first stop is the İznik Olive Groves and includes a walk around the olive groves with olive trees over 1000 years old and a visit to the oldest tree (Göllüce Village) which is 1500 years old. The second stop is Olive-Olive Oil Production, Tasting and Shopping and consists of three alternatives (1st Alternative: Oil Mill visit and tasting, Village bread and Olive Soap production (Göllüce), 2nd Alternative: Lake shore and İznik Center local delicacies, 3rd Alternative: İznik Sınırlı Sorumlu İznik Kadın Üreticiler Kooperatifi). The third stop is İznik, the Capital of Four Civilizations and includes the historical axis walk (Lefke Gate-Green Mosque-Hagia Sophia Mosque-Underwater Basilica-Obelisk). The fourth stop is Harvest Tours and consists of olive (October-November-December), cherry and plum (May-June), peach-nectarine-apple-pear-nashi (July-August), freesia plum-Japanese plum (August) and grape-kiwi (September-October) harvest tours.

Bursa has a rich culinary culture and many gastronomic events are organized in Bursa. "Bursa Gastronomi Festivali", "Mudanya Lezzet Şenliği", "Keles Otçu Göçü Yayla Festivali", "Tirilye Zeytin Şenliği", "Karacabey Ihlamur Festivali", "Yenişehir Uluslararası Altın Biber Festivali", "Uluslararası Gemlik Zeytini

Festivali", "Akçalar İncir Festivali", "Gürsu Kültür, Sanat ve Armut Festivali", "Osmangazi Siyah İncir Festivali", "Orhangazi Zeytin Festivali", "Türk Dünyası Keşkek Festivali", "Geleneksel Kahve Sohbetleri Gecesi", "Bursa Kadın Kooperatifleri ile Bursa Mutfağı", "İnegöl Şeftali Festivali", "İnegöl Yaban Mersini Festivali", "Karabalçık Üzüm Festivali", "Orhangazi Gedelek Turşu Festivali", "Hasanağa Enginar Festivali" ve "Nilüfer İncir Festivali"stand out among these events (Bursa Metropolitan Municipality, 2024; Festivall, 2024; GotoB, 2024b; Nilüfer Municipality, 2024). (Page 51).

Results

In this research, food products that received geographical indication registration of Bursa province were evaluated in the context of gastronomy tourism. As a result of the research it has been observed that six items in *the Bakery and Pastry Products, Pastries, Desserts Category* (Bursa Cantık, Bursa Cevizli Lokum, Bursa Süt Helvası, Bursa Tahinli Pide, İnegöl Sütlü Kadayıfı, Kemalpaşa Tatlısı/Mustafakemalpaşa Peynir Tatlısı/Mustafakemalpaşa Tatlısı) four items in *the Meals and Soups Category* (Bursa Döner Kebabı, Bursa Pideli Köfte, İnegöl Köfte, Zeyniler Hınkalı), one item in *the Chocolate, Confectionery and Derivative Products Category* (Bursa Kestane Şekeri), one item in *the Soft Drinks Category* (Bursa Üzüm Şırası), one item in *Seasonings/Flavorings, Sauces and Salt Category* for Food (İnegöl Çıbrıkası), 13 items in *the Processed and Unprocessed Fruits and Vegetables and Mushrooms Category* (Bursa Kestanesi, Bursa Santa Maria Armudu, Bursa Siyah İnciri/Bursa Siyahı/Siyah Bursa İnciri, Bursa Şeftalisi, Gemlik Zeytini, Gürsu Deveci Armudu, Hasanağa Enginarı, Karacabey Soğanı, Keles Kirazı, Orhangazi Gedelek Turşusu, Yenişehir Biberi, İnegöl Cerrah Kuru Fasulyesi, İznik Müşküle Üzümü) have received geographical indication registration including a total of 26 food products.

Whereas the total number of food products for which geographical indication applications have been made is 10. In addition, it has been determined that Bursa has two gastronomy routes, namely "Central Gastronomy Route" and "Olive and Olive Oil Route". It has also been determined that various gastronomy activities are held in Bursa.

According to the results obtained, the following suggestions have been developed regarding Bursa gastronomy:

1. Although there are 10 food products for which geographical indication applications have been made, this number can be increased further considering the potential of Bursa.

2. As mentioned above in the geographical indication registration, gastronomy events in Bursa are insufficient considering the potential of the city. In particular, events should be moved from the local scale to the international level.
3. Awareness activities should be organized for Bursa's geographically marked products, especially for local people. Especially Bursa Governorship and Bursa Metropolitan Municipality can undertake an important mission in the organization of the events.
4. Products such as Etli Düğün Çorbası (Kemalpaşa Çorbası), Kestaneli Lahana Dolması (Kestaneli Kelem Sarması), Keles Güveci, Ciğer Sarma, Cennet Künkü, Sütlü İncir Dolması are candidates for geographical indication application. It would be appropriate for decision makers to take steps in this regard.
5. Based on the fact that all districts of the province have riches in terms of gastronomy, new ones can be added to the existing gastronomy routes.

References

Bursa Metropolitan Municipality. (2024). From: https://www.bursa.bel.tr/etkinlik/3-uluslararasi-bursa-gastronomi-festivali-893 Accessed on: 22.05.2024.

Special Provincial Administration. (2012). Bursa Kent Rehberi.

Bursa Governorship. (2008) Türkiye Cumhuriyeti'nin Seksenbeşinci Yılında Bursa. Ankara: Ajans-Türk Basın ve Basım A.Ş.

Bursa Governorship. (t.y.). Yemek Kültürü Broşürü.

Cengiz, İ. (2012). Yaşayan Müze: Bursa. İstanbul: Stil Matbaacılık.

Festivall. (2024). Bursa Festivalleri. Access address: https://festivall.com.tr/iller/16/bursa-festivalleri/, Access date: 22.05.2024.

GotoB. (2024a). From: https://www.bursa.com.tr/tr/icerikler/bursa-nin-yerel-lezzetleri-132/ Accessed on: 10.05.2024.

GotoB. (2024b). From: https://www.gotobursa.com.tr/tr/mekanlar/festival-ve-senlikler-193 Accessed on: 22.05.2024.

GotoB. (2024c). From: https://www.gotobursa.com.tr/tr/rotalar/gastronomi-kultur-rotalari-215/ Accessed on: 22.05.2024.

Kondakçı, Z. (2021). 81 İlde Kültür ve Şehir: Bursa. Bursa: Bursa Valiliği Yayını.

Kumar, D. (2018). Gastronomy tourism: An overview of lierature. *International Journal of Research and Analytical Reviews*, 5(2), 1974–1977.

Nilüfer Municipality. (2024). From: https://www.nilufer.bel.tr/kategoriler/hizmet/festivaller/ Accessed on: 22.05.024.

Richards, G. (2002). Gastronomy: An essential ingredient in tourism production and consumption?. In: G, Richards., A.M., Hjalager. (Eds.), Tourism and Gastronomy. Routledge, London, pp. 3–20.

Turkish Patent and Trademark Office. (2024). Coğrafi işaret nedir? Access address: https://ci.turkpatent.gov.tr/sayfa/coğrafi-işaret-nedir, Access date: 10.05.2024.

United Nations World Tourism Organization. (2024). Glossary of tourism terms. Access address: https://www.unwto.org/glossary-tourism-terms, Access date: 13.05.2024.

Maksut Özkeşkek[1]

Chapter 5 The Emergence of New Culinary Movements *

Introduction

The technology developing with globalisation has been the harbinger of change over time. In the face of change, people strive to keep up and are dragged towards the uniformisation brought about by globalisation. Rapid changes in all areas of life have also affected people's eating habits (Güven, 2011). Especially in the last few centuries, speed has been a part of people's lives. The concept of speed, which is dominantly seen in all areas of life, has negatively affected people's eating habits. In parallel with this situation, fast food trends have emerged (Yurtseven, 2006). McDonald, the pioneer of fast food trends, was opened in Pasadena, California in 1937. This trend is based on the principles of fast service, large volume and low price. It applied assembly line instead of traditional cooking methods. Instead of trained cooks, they have designed a system that unskilled people can learn very easily. The fast food chain emphasises quantity rather than quality. We can also think of it as the presence of the same standardised products everywhere and the same volume and flavour of these products under the interest of people in fast food chains (Ritzer, 2011).

In 1987, it was stated in the Brundtland Report that industrial activities have some negative effects on the environment and human life. In this report, it is aimed to leave a livable world to future generations by emphasising the importance of nature. In this report, the concept of sustainability was defined for the first time (Gönel, 2002). The concept of sustainable has been implemented by considering social, cultural and environmental aspects.

"The Slow Food Movement" started in 1986 in Cuneo City in the Langhe Region of Italy under the leadership of Carlo Petrini in order to protect the identity of the region, to ensure the continuity of the traditional cooking method and to express some of the negativities of industrial products, adopting a sustainable philosophy, in favour of traditional production (Yurtseven, 2006). This

---

1   Anadolu University, Postgraduate Education Institute, maksutozkeskek@anadolu.
    edu.tr
*   This book chapter is derived from Maksut Özkeşkek's Master's thesis.

movement is known as traditional cuisine. At the same time, local cuisine means local product (Petrini & Padovani, 2012). It aims to repair our connections with traditional products that have been broken with the negative impact of the fast food movement. Thanks to the "Slow Food Movement" it is thought to contribute to building today's cuisine on solid foundations by protecting the local cuisine.

Another positive development related to the kitchen is that chefs act on the philosophy of sustainability and both protect their culinary culture and build the kitchen of the future. The roots of this process, called "New Cuisine Movement", date back to the period called "Nouvelle Cuisine" French cuisine. In the processes that followed, "The Slow Food Movement" contributed significantly to the development of the innovative culinary movement of the chefs due to the movement on the philosophy of sustainability and protecting local products in the slow food movement. Another development that has an impact on the philosophy of "New Culinary Movements" is "Molecular Gastronomy" practices. The concept of "Molecular Gastronomy" and the developments in this field are thought to have influenced the "New Culinary Movement" especially in terms of presentation and material diversity. Spanish chef Ferran Adrià, a pioneer in the formation of the "New Culinary Movement", has transferred the techniques developed by two scientists (Nicholas Kurti and Hervé This) on the chemical and physical dimension in gastronomy from theory to practice. In the light of these developments in gastronomy, contemporary cuisine has been effective in changing the chefs' perspectives on cuisine. This situation has contributed to the formation of "New Culinary Movements". In this book chapter, how the "New Culinary Movements" emerged and the change processes they have undergone in the historical process are discussed. In addition, the basic philosophy and dimensions of "New Culinary Movements" are emphasised and their differences from traditional culinary culture are explained. When the "New Culinary Movements" are considered chronologically, it is seen that they are based on the "Nouvelle Cuisine" French cuisine. For this reason, the change in the cuisine from the historical process of French cuisine to the present day is explained.

In addition, the basic characteristics of the pioneer chefs of these culinary movements are also discussed.

French Cuisine

The geographical location of France, surrounded by the Atlantic Ocean, the Mediterranean Sea and the English Channel, is effective in having a rich product range. The division of agricultural areas in the country by three large rivers (Seine, Loire and Rhône) contributes to the formation of fertile agricultural areas. It can be concluded that French cuisine is one of the best places for the development of gastronomy due to its geography. In addition, the cultural inter-action with neighbouring Germany, Spain, Italy and Switzerland and reflecting this interaction to the cuisine has been extremely important in the development of French cuisine (Le Cordon Blue, 1998). In addition, French chefs have con-tributed a great deal to French cuisine in the international arena. The historical development of French cuisine can be categorised under four main headings; French Cuisine in the Middle Ages and Renaissance period, Classic French Cuisine-Marie Antonie Caréme (1738–1833) period, Haute Cuisine-Georges Auguste Escoffier (1846–1935) period and Nouvelle Cuisine-Fernand Point (1897–1955) period.

French Cuisine in the Middle Ages and Renaissance

The kings of the period made important contributions to the development of French cuisine during the Middle Ages. The interest of French monarchs in the palace cuisine has carried French cuisine forward. The acceptance of French cuisine as an international cuisine today has been realised in parallel with the important events in the past.

The marriage of the French heir Henry II to Catherine, one of the leading aristocratic families of Italy, is recognised as the turning point of French cuisine. Catherine brought a team of Italian chefs to the palace and brought the influ-ences of Italian culinary culture to French cuisine. French cuisine gained a differ-ent dimension with the introduction of Italian culinary culture (Özdemir, 2001).

Louis XIV and Louis XV made efforts for the development of French cuisine. Louis XIV organised splendid banquets at the Verseilles palace during his 72-year reign. He took a close interest in the palace kitchen and fulfilled the requests of the chefs. Louis XIV also opened schools to train cooks for French cuisine (Maviş, 2003). François Pierre de La Varenne (1618–1678) (real name François Pierre), who was assigned to the palace as the chef de cuisine of Louis XIV (Tez, 2012), collected and published the food recipes in the French cuisine in a book called Le Cuisiner Français in 1651 by order of the king. Varenne's systematic handling of French cuisine in the books he published later guided the chefs of the future periods (Le Cordon Blue, 1998).

The period between the 16th and 18th centuries is known as the period of the Ancien Régime (old regime) in the French Empire. During this period, restric-tions were imposed by the administration of the period, especially on important elements such as culture and activity. It is known that this form of government allowed certain food businesses to operate in designated areas. In France, it is known that by restricting certain gourmet specialists to assigned regions, it prevented the progress of culinary arts in this field (www.ecpi.edu.tr). In Paris and other cities of France, there were few restaurants throughout France at that time due to the restrictions imposed by the administration (Drouard, 2008, p. 273).

With the fall of the old regime in France, the whole culinary system and the role of chefs changed. Chefs declared their independence with the fall of the old regime and opened their own restaurant businesses. The chef as an artisan became an artist and as a restaurant owner became an entrepreneur. While the production of cuisine was transformed from a trade into a profession and an art, consumption became a status in itself. The chef has also come to be recognised as an artist or gourmet serving his own art or knowledge (Clark, 1975).

Classic French Cuisine-Marie Antonie Caréme Period

Marie Antonie Caréme pioneered the modernisation of French cuisine from the old regime. She reorganised the dishes in French cuisine according to the cuisine she created. Her ideas spread rapidly in the kitchens of Paris restaurants and in the rest of France (Ferguson, 1998 cited in Rao, Monin & Durand, 2003). Caréme also categorised sauces under five main headings because he knew the importance of sauces in French cuisine and thought that they would contribute significantly to the consistency, aroma and flavour of the dish. These are: "Espagnole", "tomato", "béchamel", "veloute" and "Hollandaise" (Tez, 2012). He paid attention to the colour harmony between the shape of the main dish on the plate and the garnishes (Maviş, 2003). He reinterpreted "consommé", which has an important place in French cuisine (Gürsoy, 2013). In addition, by making some changes in fasting dishes, he contributed to the re-popularisation of these dishes and proved that good dishes can be made without meat (Drouard, 2008). Caréme soon gained fame and became a sought-after chef for nobles and well-known gourmets. Caréme was called "both the cook of kings and the king of cooks" and he was recognised as the best cook of his time (Maviş, 2003). Caréme had a great share in the recognition of French cuisine as an international cuisine by other countries, especially in Europe (Ferguson, 2000).

Haute Cuisine-Georges Auguste Escoffier Period

After Caréme, French cuisine was marked by George Auguste Escoffier (1846–1935). Escoffier is the founder of "elite cuisine, in other words, haute cuisine" (Ferguson, 2014). Escoffier created the contemporary cuisine of the period by simplifying the complex recipes prepared by Antonie Caréme and making some changes in the kitchen organisation inherited from Caréme (Tomkies, 2010). Escoffier was sent to work as an apprentice in his brother's restaurant in Nice. After completing his apprenticeship period here, Escoffier settled in Paris to improve himself (Gürsoy, 2014). At the age of 19, Escoffier started to work at Petit Moulin Rouge, one of the famous restaurants of Paris. In 1870, he was called to the army due to the Franco-Prussian war (Escoffier, 1979). Escoffier managed the kitchen of Marshal Mazaine during the war in 1870. He organised the catering service of the German Emperor Wilhelm II. Wilhelm II was impressed by Escoffier's cuisine and nicknamed him "The Emperor of Cooks" (Larousse Gastronomique, 2005). After the end of the war, Escoffier returned to the Petit Moulin Rouge as chef (Escoffier, 1979). Although it is thought that the elite French cuisine created by Escoffier appealed to kings and the upper class, in fact, since he spent most of his career in hotels, ordinary people also had the opportunity to taste the dishes he prepared. Escoffier's reinterpreted cuisine is considered as a revolution by most authors (Myhrvold, 2011).

Nouvelle Cuisine – Fernand Point Period

In the first half of the 20th century, two important innovations emerged in French cuisine. The first one is the discovery of French regional cuisines by chefs and the second one is the new dimension of French cuisine by an innovative group of chefs in the 1970s. Against the "Classic French cuisine" representing Escoffier, a brand new culinary movement

called "Nouvelle Cuisine" was introduced under the leadership of chef Michel Guerard and food critics Henri Gault and Christian Millau (Samancı, 2016). In 1972, food writers named Gault and Millau put forward the movement in order to change some of the negative situations they saw in the kitchen, and it has been accepted by many cooks over time. One of the factors that triggered this situation was that French chefs who went to Japan for high fees started to apply the practical knowledge in Japanese cuisine when they returned (Gürsoy, 2013, p. 80). In 1973, it was defined by the food critic Henri Gault in a manifesto called "10 basic principles of Nouvelle Cuisine" (Myhrvold, 2011).

Fernand Point (1897–1955), known as the founder of modern cuisine in France, adopted the ten basic principles established by Gault and Millau as the founder of Nouvelle Cuisine, in other words, contemporary French cuisine. Point, the chef who shaped the world of gastronomy through the "New Cuisine Movement", modernised the "Classic French Cuisine" from the Escoffier period.

The modern cuisine movement created by Point has been adopted by many segments, especially French chefs. The new trend created by Point, who is regarded
as the teacher of gastronomy in the gastronomy community, influenced famous
chefs of the cuisine such as Roger Verge, Raymond Thuillier, Alain Chapelle,
Paul Bocuse and Troisgros brothers (Gillespie, 1994).

In the new trend, classic cooking methods (boiling, steaming, etc.) are used.
In this trend, unlike the "Classic French Cuisine" the cooking times of the dishes
are shortened. Vegetables are cooked with steam instead of being boiled for a
long time. Thus, the taste, vitamins and natural colour of the vegetable are preserved. Very little starch, egg yolk or cream is used instead of flour in soups
and sauces. It has been decided to cook meat at a point (neither too much nor
too little). This is thought to preserve the nutritional value of the meat. Spices,
wine and liqueurs are used in a different way compared to the past and to create
unique flavours (Mussman & Pahalı, 1997).

"Nouvelle Cuisine" has led to radical changes in the cuisine of most French
chefs and helped chefs to become more modern. While French chefs were unable
to showcase their talents due to the standardised recipes in "Classic French
Cuisine", the creativity of the chefs was at the forefront with "Nouvelle Cuisine".
Chefs have created new flavours by adding their own interpretations to the
dishes. The sauces in the dishes have become lighter, unlike the "Classic French
Cuisine". The dishes are

not overcooked compared to the past (Goldstein, 2013, p. 31). "Nouvelle
Cuisine" is the modern version of haute cuisine. Thanks to this trend, new flavours were created by allowing the reinterpretation of all dishes (Levy, 1984)
and by combining the culinary techniques of Caréme and Escoffier with the
visuality of Japanese food (Gürsoy, 2013). The related literature review shows
that "Nouvelle Cuisine", which can be said to have started in the late 1890s in
French cuisine, was founded on values such as freshness, simplicity, naturalness,
creativity and originality as basic principles. These principles not only defined
"Nouvelle Cuisine" but also contributed to its differentiation from "Classic
French Cuisine" (Mallory, 2011).

Since the concept of "Nouvelle Cuisine" was first seen in French cuisine in the
historical process, the concept has been examined primarily within the framework of this chronological flow within the scope of this study. However, there
are other elements that have been effective in the spread of the "New Culinary
Movements" concept worldwide. Since these elements are "Slow Food" and
"Molecular Gastronomy", these elements are also briefly mentioned in the book
chapter.

Slow Food

Western countries, which pioneered the emergence of the industrial revolution or adopted this revolution, have tried to dominate the world by taking advantage of the advantages of technology. Especially in the second half of the 20th century, developing and undeveloped countries have tried to impose Western culture in various ways in order to adopt "global culture". Global culture erodes and even destroys people's national cultures. Global culture has replaced local culture and interacted with people in every field (Mahiroğulları, 2005). Especially in the last few centuries, speed has been a part of people's lives. The concept of speed, which is dominantly seen in all areas of life, has negatively affected people's eating habits. In parallel with this situation, the fast food trend has emerged. "Fast Food" has now entered our homes (Yurtseven, 2006). The founders of the McDonald chain, the pioneer of the "Fast Food Movement", the brothers "Richard and Maurice McDonald" opened their first restaurant in Pasadena, California in 1937. They built this restaurant on the principles of fast service, large volume and low price. They also offered a limited menu for customers to order food in minimum time. It applied assembly line instead of traditional cooking methods. Instead of trained cooks, they have designed a system that unskilled people can learn very easily. The fast food chain emphasises quantity rather than quality (Ritzer, 2011). With this situation, the widespread use of processed and frozen products by people has caused local cuisine to fall into the second plan.

The "Slow Food Movement" started in 1986 in Cuneo City in the Langhe Region of Italy under the leadership of Carlo Petrini in order to protect the identity of the region, to ensure the continuity of the traditional cooking method and to express some of the negativities of industrial products. At the opening of McDonald's in Piazza di Spagna in Rome, the community that adopted this movement (Yurtseven, 2006) protested by throwing pastries. The basis of this movement is that fast food restaurants negatively affect the local flavours of Italy, that these products threaten human health and that people should enjoy their lives with slow movements as opposed to fast living conditions (Güven, 2011). The foundation of this movement started with Associazione Amici del Barolo, an association founded in Bra, Italy. The aim of this association is to raise awareness about local products, to awaken people hypnotised by fast food and to enjoy food and wine (Petrini, 2003). The symbol of this movement is the snail. The snail moves slowly and steadily throughout its life. At the same time, it leaves its mark in the places it passes. Petrini, the pioneer of the slow food movement,

travelled from country to country to publicise the basic philosophy of this movement. Petrini left traces like a snail, the symbol of his movement, in the countries
he visited (Yalçın & Yalçın, 2013). In the following period, authorised persons
from 15 countries signed the slow food manifesto at the Opera Comique in Paris
(Petrini & Padovani, 2012).

Molecular Gastronomy

Nicholas Kurti (1908–1998) was a professor of physics at the University of
Oxford, where he also held the chair of physics. Kurti gave the "Physicist in the
Kitchen" lecture at one of the annual meetings of the British Royal Institution.
In this lecture, he discussed the physical aspect of cooking. In this lecture, Kurti
said, "As a science, we know the temperature inside the stars, but unfortunately
we do not know the temperature inside a soufflé". In 1990, Kurti met with the
chemist Hervé This. They worked on the physical and chemical aspects of food.
As a result of their work, they developed a number of techniques in the kitchen.
The movement initiated with these techniques is called molecular gastronomy
(Pedersen, Meyer, Nursten & Redzepi, 2006). Hervé defines molecular gastronomy as "a branch of science that studies the physico-chemical transformations
of edible materials during cooking and the sensory events associated with their
consumption" (Vega & Ubbink, 2008).

In the mid-20th century, the term "Molecular Gastronomy" was coined by
a group of chefs to describe a new style of food. A number of restaurant chefs
used scientific techniques to improve food quality, flavour and aesthetics. These
techniques have become increasingly popular in the gastronomy community
(Youssef, 2013).

Examples of New Culinary Trends from the World

When the researches on gastronomy and culinary movements are analysed, it
has been determined that the concept of "New Cuisine", which is accepted to
be born within the scope of French cuisine, has been accepted in Scandinavia,
Germany, Peru, Brazil, Italy, Spain, France and Turkey. Ferran Adrià played an
important role in bringing the new cuisine, which started from French cuisine, to a new dimension. Adrià transferred the techniques developed by two
Catalan scientists of Spain (Nicholas Kurti and Hervé This) on the chemical and
physical dimension of food from theory to practice. He called this movement
Techo Emotional (Gürsoy, 2014). Adrià later published the manifesto of this
movement.

New Scandinavian Cuisine (NSC)

In 2003, NSC founders Rene Redzepi and Claus Meyer organised the "Scandinavian Cuisine Symposium" shortly after opening the Noma restaurant. In 2004, one day before the second Scandinavian Cuisine Symposium (Meyers, 2024), chefs from Scandinavian countries came together in Copenhagen and created the manifesto of NSC (www.theworlds50best.com). This manifesto summarises the ten basic principles of NSC through values such as natural, ethical, seasonal, health, sustainable and quality (www.newnordicfood.org). Thanks to these Scandinavian culinary trends, NSC has demonstrated that chefs can also make exclusive dishes from organic, high quality products grown in their own geography. This innovative perspective has legitimised Scandinavian cuisine and made significant contributions to the revival and enrichment of culinary culture (Özkeşkek, 2019; Svejenova, Pedersen & Bykrjetflot, 2021).

In 2005, the Nordic Council of Ministers adopted the NSC manifesto as the ideology of the New Nordic food plan, supported by national development programmes (Meyers, 2024). When the NFM manifesto was published, a group of gastro experts took a cynical attitude towards it. One of the pioneers of NSC, Rene Redzepi, owner and head chef of Noma restaurant, ranked first in the World's 50 Best Restaurants list in 2010, 2011, 2012, 2014, 2021. This culinary trend has achieved success despite its short history (Ooi, 2017; www.theworlds50best.com). These achievements have made NSC more recognisable in the international gastronomy arena.

Before opening Noma restaurant in 2004, Redzepi worked at the French Laundry "French-style laundry" restaurant run by Thomas Keller in California, USA and Ferran Adria's restaurant in Spain. According to Redzepi, the experiences he gained in the kitchens of these businesses were a source of inspiration for him (www.spiegel.de). This culinary trend, which started in Noma restaurant, started to be adopted by other young chefs in Århus in Copenhagen and Stockholm. Other Northern European chefs, such as Redzepi, use local produce to produce contemporary dishes that are unique to this region (www.spiegel.de). Redzepi stated that he learnt while working at El Bulli restaurant that good quality food does not have to be from French cuisine or expensive foods (truffles, goose, etc.) (Heinzelmann, 2010).

New Anatolian Cuisine (NAC)

With the contribution of the modern cuisine trend initiated by Nouvelle cuisine, many cuisines in the world have been positively affected. In the new modern cuisine movements, the recipes of the local dishes that have been forgotten in the past have been revised thanks to today's modern technology. In Turkey, this trend is represented by NAC and local dishes reach a different dimension. NAC is fed with local products and the contents, presentations and tools and equipment used in Turkish cuisine allow innovative chefs to reinterpret the dishes in Turkish cuisine thanks to today's developing technology.

In 2009, Mehmet Gürs, the founder of NAC, and Tangör Tan, an anthropologist who graduated from the University of Gastronomic Sciences founded by Carlo Petrini, set out to discover local products grown in Anatolia. Since 2009, they have travelled around Anatolia and examined local products. On this journey, Tangör has tasted over 5000

different products from Bulgaria to Iran. Tangör, under the leadership of Mehmet Gürs, started to try the ingredients they received from the local people in the laboratory of Mikla restaurant. As a result of his researches, he laid the foundations of " NAC " with Gürs and his team's innovative approach to cuisine by using today's modern kitchen equipment (Cappelen, 2015). He is the person who started Istanbul's contemporary restaurant business and prepared the NAC manifesto (Foodinlife, 2022). NAC has published a manifesto. This manifesto seems to overlap with the basic principles of the "Nouvelle Cuisine" manifesto published by Gault in 1973.

Turkey's large surface area in terms of geographical and ethnic diversity, the coexistence of different religions, migration due to its geopolitical position has enabled the country to have a rich cultural accumulation. This accumulation also shows itself in the culinary culture. "NAC" is the approach that best adopts the slow food movement in Turkey, which adopts the principle of traditional cuisine, supporting local producers and healthy nutrition.

NAC has adopted the principle of taking local products produced by small-scale producers and bringing a different dimension to the dishes made in Anatolia by utilising today's technology. However, the rich Anatolian cuisine, which is about to be forgotten, has been influenced by the food cultures of many communities from the past to the present. NAC presents these interactions without making any distinction, food cultures together. In this context, New Anatolian cuisine leads the way in creating a bond with our past nutrition culture.

According to Gürs and his team, they have gained deep knowledge about the products grown in Anatolian lands, the specific methods and habits of the region. As a result of their research, they have contributed to the formation of a wide network between the real owners of the land and the chefs (Foodinlife, 2022). Gürs emphasises that the basis of NAC is "no farmer, no food, no food, no future" (Toprakoğlu, 2015). With this statement, it is understood how important the farmer or producer is for our future. We need to know the value of the farmer in order to transfer our culinary culture to future generations. The philosophy of NAC is to bring our rich cuisine, which is about to be forgotten, back to the surface instead of creating from nothing. Acting within the principle of sustainability, NAC builds the culinary culture of today and the future by feeding on our past culinary cultures. In addition, it contributes to the preservation of our culinary culture and gives our traditional customs and traditions a different perspective in today's conditions.

"World's 100 Best Restaurants" in 2015 with NAC Mikla, which entered the list in 96th place, jumped 40 places to 56th place in 2016 and continued its climb to 51st place in 2017. Mikla is the only Turkish restaurant to be included in the list for three consecutive years (www.turizmsurasi.kulturturizm.gov.tr). In 2018, the "World's 50 Best Restaurants" in the Michelin Guide (https://www.theworlds50b est.com). Furthermore, the Michelin Guide ranks Mikla as a 1 star high quality restaurant (Michelin, 2024).

Mehmet Gürs has achieved these successes as a result of his modernisation of local Anatolian dishes. Gürs expresses this success as follows: "This is an award received with the New Anatolian Cuisine. In other words, we received an award with tarhana and anchovies. We have neither truffle nor caviar from wherever! We try to make creative and delicious dishes with the raw materials we buy from producers and small farmers in Anatolia" (Kopuz, 2015). Again, in a programme attended by Gürs, he stated that noble and distinguished food can also occur in products such as tarhana, anchovy, wheat, etc. However, he stated that these products should be original products, in other words, natural and a real product grown in Anatolia (Bildiğiniz Gibi Değil, 2017).

The international slow food organisation argues that the protection and survival of local products in the face of industrial products is through creating demand by offering these products to consumers. Mehmet Gürs and the people who adopt this movement have taken an important step to keep the values of our country alive (Örs, 2015).

Gürs states that good ingredients are needed to make good food, and one of the methods of obtaining good ingredients is to obtain them from nearby sources, and that the products used in the kitchen should travel less than me (Arslan, 2011). By procuring organic products grown in the region from farmers instead of industrial products, NAC is both aware of where the products are grown and helps the development of the local people.

Gürs calls Anatolian cuisine instead of Turkish cuisine because many ethnic groups have lived here in the land where we are located, and the modern version of this cuisine is called NAC (Demiriz, 2016). In this context, the NAC manifesto emphasises "free from national, ethnic and religious borders or barriers".

He stated that this culinary trend includes the dishes of many ethnic groups. He stated that if we understand the culinary culture and the dishes cooked here, we can cook the food of tomorrow. He also stated that it is necessary to learn the chemical reaction while cooking. Gürs said, "For example, while cooking pumpkin dessert in lime, we tried to understand what happens chemically there. What kind of chemical reaction happens when you soak quicklime with water? When we don't understand why, we just keep copying" (Toprakoğlu, 2015). Thanks to this culinary trend, local flavours that have been forgotten or have lost their importance are brought to the surface again and offer new original flavours by bringing them to their modern structure. In this context, NAC contributes to the further enrichment of our culinary literature.

Since vegetables and fruits grown in the season are preferred, the menus of the businesses that have adopted the FC change seasonally. People who prefer NAC consume meals prepared from healthy, delicious and nutritious natural vegetables and fruits grown in season, instead of preferring dishes that are harmful to health in fixed menus like people who have adopted fast food culture.

It contributes to the increase in the pleasure of food as people who prefer NAC taste foods that appeal to both palate and eye taste. In this context, the artistic interaction of this trend is seen in the dishes served. Since the dishes in NAC do not have standardised recipes, original dishes emerge as a result of the food inspirations created by the chefs. This allows guests to discover new tastes and new flavours. NAC, which takes its place among today's contemporary kitchens, acts as a bridge in creating the cuisine of the future by bringing together components such as being unique, open to innovation and feeding from rich Anatolian cuisine.

The contributions of Didem Şenol, Maksut Aşkar, Şemsa Denizsel, Civan Er, Kemal Demirasal and Semi Hakim, the leading chefs of contemporary Turkish cuisine, to the NAC pioneered by Gürs may be effective in taking this trend to a higher level (Cappelen, 2015).

It is known that tourists coming to our country have generally positive opinions about Turkish cuisine. However, tourists complain that the food is too oily, overly spicy, too sugary, etc. according to their own palates. It is even known that some tourists have digestive, stomach etc. discomfort. We can overcome these negative situations thanks to NAC. The flavours in NAC are light, organic, good quality and without excessive ingredients. In this context, while introducing the modern structure of our culinary culture to foreign tourists, we can overcome some negative situations related to our culinary culture (too oily, excessive spices, etc.) thanks to this trend.

Dimensions of New Culinary Movements

It has been revealed that "New Culinary Movements" basically take the deep-rooted culinary cultures of the region where the innovative chefs are located and reinterpret the local cuisine with an innovative perspective with today's modern culinary technology. When the literature on "New Culinary Movements" is analysed, it is seen that they are based on basic values such as freshness, simplicity, naturalness, creativity and originality. When the dimensions of the culinary movements below are analysed, in the motivation section, "Classic Cuisine" emphasises the protection of cultural heritage and the transfer of culinary culture to future generations. In the "New Culinary Movement", it encourages creativity by leaving the chef free. It also adopts an aesthetic understanding of cuisine. "Slow Food" emphasises the preservation of regional identity and tradition and states that "Fast Food" culture degenerates traditional culinary culture. In "Molecular Gastronomy", it is seen that chefs are in search of new scientific ways and new techniques are developed in the kitchen thanks to these scientific ways. NSC and NAC, on the other hand, adopt modern approaches while adhering to the traditional culinary culture as the basic philosophy of both cuisines.

In the section of culinary innovations, standards are specified in "Classic Cuisine" and institutions are created. In a way, there are strict rules in "Classic Cuisine" and the freedom of the chef is limited. "Nouvelle Cuisine" opposes the established culinary order and emphasises that chefs should be free. "Slow Food" embraces traditional methods rather than an innovative perspective and emphasises ethical values. "Molecular Gastronomy", on the other hand, emphasises surprise elements in the kitchen and tries to reconstruct flavours in scientific ways. NSC and NAC, on the other hand, adhere to the culinary culture and rediscover and revise the cuisine. "Classic Cuisine" adheres to tradition in shaping the expression of identity, while "Nouvelle Cuisine" opposes the strict rules of "Classic Cuisine". "Slow Food" reacts against fast life and fast food culture. "Molecular Gastronomy" contributes to cuisine with a range of techniques. NSC and NAC reinterpret the culinary culture with a modern perspective by protecting the regional identity.

In the organisation dimension, "Classic Cuisine" has a dominant structure and the leadership feature is emphasised. "Classic Cuisine" has a closed structure and there is no clear structuring. "Nouvelle Cuisine" has an impressive leadership feature at the forefront. "Slow Food" has a strong structure besides its impressive leadership. "Slow Food Movement" aims to spread its philosophy by supporting activities. "Nouvelle Cuisine" and "Slow Food" movement emphasise democratisation. "Molecular Gastronomy" also has a leadership on a decisive structure. In addition, culinary technical information is shared by advocating democratisation. "NSC and NAC" have an impressive structure in terms of organisation and influence other culinary cultures. "NSC and NAC" encourages the preservation of the traditional culinary structure and collective research by feeding on local ingredients. "NSC and NAC" encourages the adoption of innovative culinary philosophy by sharing knowledge and experience through national or international events.

Table 5.1. Culinary Movements

Dimensions		Culinary Movements					
		Cuisine	Nouvelle Cuisine	Slow Food	Molecular Cuisine	New Nordic Cuisine	New Anatolian Cuisine
Motivation	What	Creating a new national cuisine based on regional traditions and identities	Strong emphasis on creative freedom and the autonomy of chef	Strong emphasis on preservation of regional identities and traditions	Strong emphasis on creative freedom and investigation Moderate emphasis on regional identities and traditions	Strong emphasis on preservation of regional identities and traditions Moderate emphasis creative freedom and the autonomy of the chef	Strong emphasis on preservation of regional identities and traditions Strong emphasis on creative freedom and the autonomy of the chef
	How	Limiting creative freedom Formation of strict culinary rules and standards	Deconstruction of Classical Cuisine	Creating ethical consumption patterns	Developing new techniques	Creating ethical consumption patterns	Creating ethical consumption patterns
Culinary innovation	What	Introducing new culinary standards	Creating signature dishes	Non-applicable	Strong emphasis on deconstruction Minor level of recreation and rediscovery	Strong emphasis on recreation and rediscovery Minor level of deconstruction	Strong emphasis on recreation and rediscovery deconstruction Minor level of deconstruction
	How	Creating institutions and discourse	Breaking established culinary rules	Non-applicable	Purification of culinary concepts and elements of surprise Workshop	Workshop Anthropological excursions	Workshop Anthropological excursions
Form of identity expressions	Definition	A new national cuisine based on regional traditions	Reaction against the rigidity of Classical Cuisine	Reaction against fast life/fast food	A set of techniques	A region	A region

	Manifesto	Non-applicable	Created by external actors	Internally created since initiation	Internally created after recognition	Internally created since initiation	Internally created since initiation
	Empty label	Applied subsequently	Empty label Provided by external actors Active use of empty label	Active use of self-defined empty label	Avoiding labelling	Active use of self-defined empty label	Active use of self-defined empty label
	Leadership& structure	Leader centric structure	Charismatic leadership Leader-centric structure	Charismatic Leadership Grassroots-driven Strong, global institutions	Charismatic leadership Leader-centric structure	Charismatic leadership Leader-centric structure	Charismatic leadership Leader-centric structure
Organization	Democratization	Creating a cuisine of the people Restaurants	Partial Democratization of ingredients	Through grassroots structure	Democratization of ingredient	Democratization of ingredients Through open participation Transferring ideas to new locations	Democratization of ingredients Through open participation Transferring ideas to new locations
	Network& Collaboration			Establishing field-configuring events: Terra Madre, Slow Cheese, Slow Fish, etc.	Participation in field-configuring events	Establishing field-configuring events: MAD Participation in field-configuring events	Establishing field-configuring events: MAD Participation in field-configuring events

Source: Cappelen, 2015, s. 78–79

Results

It is seen that "New Culinary Movements" have taken their place in today's gastronomy literature with the emergence of innovative approaches from different geographies by chefs. When the philosophy of these movements is analysed, it is determined that they are generally based on freshness, simplicity, naturalness, creativity and originality. An important element here is that the motto that good and high quality food should be from French cuisine or expensive foods (truffle, goose, etc.) has been destroyed thanks to these culinary movements. Thanks to this culinary trend, it has been proved that local good, high quality and natural products can now be used to make dishes that will appeal to the world cuisine. These movements, which are referred to in the literature as "New Culinary Movements", contribute to the world cuisine by reinterpreting the dishes with the help of today's modern culinary justifications by feeding on traditional culinary cultures (Heinzelmann, 2010; Myhrvold, 2011, Beaugé, 2012; Özkeşkek, 2019; Svejenova et al., 2021). It is determined that chefs build the cuisine of the future by feeding on the deep-rooted culinary roots of their geography. It is seen that the philosophy of sustainability has an impact on the development of chefs' innovative perspectives. Another contribution to this innovative perspective is that the innovation in the kitchen is reflected in the values of chefs such as creativity and originality. It inspires the cuisine of the future as innovative chefs begin to be recognised in the world culinary culture literature.

It is seen that "New Culinary Movements" have a deep-rooted history in the historical process. When this process is analysed, it is determined that the roots of "New Culinary Movements" are based on "Nouvelle Cuisine", which is called the Fernand Point period of French cuisine. In the following process, it was observed that the "Slow Food Movement" that started in Italy contributed to the development of the "New Cuisine Movement". The "Slow Food Movement" basically acts on the philosophy of sustainability and since it supports local products, it overlaps with the chefs' perspective on local products and this has contributed to the development of the "New Culinary Movement". Thanks to the innovative perspectives of the chefs, it has contributed to the emergence of original flavours. In the development of these original flavours, chefs have turned to scientific techniques in order to develop kitchen tools and equipment and to increase aesthetics. In this direction, a group of chefs turned to "Molecular Gastronomy" and contributed to the enrichment of gastronomy literature by looking at "New Culinary Trends" from a different perspective. In the following years, innovative chefs such as Ferran Adria, Thomas Keller, Rene Redzepi, Osteria Francescaa, Roca Brothers have built the cuisine of the future by bringing a different, innovative perspective to gastronomy. It is seen that innovative chefs create new flavours by reinterpreting the local flavours of their geography. While making these flavours, they build the cuisine of the future by feeding on the local culinary cultures of the chefs. Innovative chefs take their cuisine to an advanced dimension by feeding on their own geographical and cultural values. This inspires the cuisine of the future and contributes to the restructuring of deep-rooted culinary cultures that are worn out.

"New Culinary Movements" bring a new perspective in gastronomy and contribute to the protection of cultural culinary heritage and enrichment of cuisine by acting with the philosophy of sustainability. These trends provide support for local ingredients by feeding on traditional cuisine culture. This is seen to contribute to the support of local small-scale producers. In the gastronomy scene, the local cuisine culture has been reinterpreted with the modernist perspective of the chefs and has an important place in the gastronomy world. With this new approach, chefs not only create new flavours but also take responsibility for social problems by addressing issues such as the protection of regional identity, social responsibility and sustainability. The contributions of creativity and innovative approaches are shown in the emergence of "New Culinary Movements" by chefs. In addition, it can be shown that these critical points have an important share in the formation of the "New Culinary Philosophy" by adopting social responsibility movements, advocating the protection of culinary culture and identity, and including scientific kitchen tools and equipment in the kitchen. It is thought that "New Culinary Movements" will play an important role in gastronomy in the following process (Cappalen, 2015, Foodinlife, 2022; Özkeşkek, 2019; Meyers, 2024; Elbullifoundation, 2024).

It is seen in the literature that the chefs who adopt the "New Culinary Movements" include natural and high quality foods. Seasonality is reflected in the preparation of meals. The nutritional value of food is preserved by not using long-term cooking techniques. It is seen that presenting the dishes on the plates in a simpler way instead of complex prevents a complex food structure. It has been determined that the chefs are fed from the traditional structure by analysing the dishes in classic cuisine cultures well and bringing the dishes into a modern structure.

References

Beaugé, B. (2012). On the idea of novelty in cuisine: A brief historical insight. *International Journal of Gastronomy and Food Science*, 1(1), 5–14.

Cappalen, S. M. (2015). *New Anatolian cuisine: Legitimising a culinary movement*. Unpublished Master Thesis. Denmark: Copenhagen, 2015.

Clark, P. P. (1975). Thoughts for food, I: French cuisine and French culture. *American Association of Teachers of French*, 49 (1), 32–41.

Drouard, a. (2008). French cuisine in the 19th and 20th centuries. In:P. Freedman (Ed.) The History of Food Taste (pp. 263–299). İstanbul: Oğlak Publications.

Escoffier, A. (1979). The complete guide to the art of modern cookery. (Trans. H. L. Cracknell and R. J. Kaufmann). Amsterdam: Elsevier.

Ferguson, P. P. (2000). Is Paris France? *American Association of Teachers of French*. 73 (6), 1052–1064.

Ferguson, P. P. (2014). Food in time and place: The American historical association companion to food history. In P. Freedman, J. E. Chaplin, and K. Albala (Eds.). The French Invention of Modern Cuisine (pp. 233–252). Usa: University of California Press.

Gillespie, C. H. (1994). Gastrosophy and nouvelle cuisine: Entrepreneurial fashion and fiction. *British Food Journal*, 96 (10), 19–23.

Goldstein, J. (2013). Inside the California food revolution: Thirty years that changed our culinary consciousness. Berkeley: University of California Press.

Gönel, F. D. (2002). Globalleşen dünyada (nasıl bir) sürdürülebilir kalkınma. *Birikim Dergisi*, 158(1), 72–80.

Gürsoy, D. (2013). Yiyelim, içelim, tarih bilelim. Istanbul: Oğlak Publications.

Gürsoy, D. (2014). Deniz Gürsoy'un gastronomy history. Istanbul: Oğlak Publications.

Güven, E. (2011). Yavaş güzeldir: "Yavaş Yemek"ten "Yavaş Medya'ya hızlı tüketime dair bir çözüm önerisi. *Selçuk İletişim*, 7(1), 113–121.

Heinzelmann, U. (2010). "An interview with René Redzepi: Noma. Copenhagen." *Gastronomica*, 10 (3), 97–101.

Larousse Gastronomique (2005). Klasik Fransız Yemekleri. (Translator: U. Erzurumluoğlu).,Istanbul. Oğlak Publishing.

Le Cordon Blue (1998). Classic French food.. (Translated: Ü. Erzurumluoğlu). Ankara: Dost Bookstore.

Levy, P. (1984). The official foodie handbook, London: Ebury Press.

Mahiroğulları, A. (2005). The effect of globalisation on cultural values. *In Journal of Social Policy Conferences*, 50, 1275–1288, Istanbul University.

Mallory, H. A. (2011). The nouvelle cuisine revolution: Expressions of national anxieties and aspirations in french culinary discourse 1969–1996. Unpublished Doctoral Thesis.Usa: Duke University, 2011.

Maviş, F. (2003). Endüstriyel yiyecek üretimi. Ankara: Detay Yayıncılık.

Mussmann, K. D. & Pahalı, C. (1994). Konaklama tesislerinde mutfak hizmetleri. In: F. Akyürek (Ed.). Eskişehir: Anadolu Üniversitesi Açıköğretim Fakültesi Yayınları.

Myhrvold, N. et al. (2011). Modernist cuisine: The art science of cooking. Germany: Taschen, Cologne

Ooi, C. S. (2017). In search of Nordicity: How new Nordic cuisine shaped destination branding in Copenhagen. *Journal of Gastronomy and Tourism*, 2, 217–231.

Özdemir, B. (2001). *Otel işletmelerinde mutfak yönetimi ve herşey dahil (all-inclusive) Uygulamasının mutfak yönetimine etkileri üzerine sektörel bir araştırma*. Akdeniz Üniversitesi,Sosyal Bilimler Enstitüsü, Yüksek Lisans Tezi, Antalya, 2001.

Özkeşkek, M. (2019). Yeni Anadolu mutfağı bağlamında Türkiye'nin yöresel köfteleri. Anadolu Üniversitesi, Sosyal Bilimler Enstitüsü, Turizm İşletmeciliği AnaBilim Dalı, Yüksek Lisans Tezi, Eskişehir, 2019.

Pedersen, T., Meyer, C., Nursten, H., & Redzepi, R. (2006). Gastronomy: the ultimate flavour science?. In developments in food science, 43, 611–616.

Petrini, C. (2003). Slow food: The case for taste. Columbia University Press.

Petrini, Carlo; Gigi Padovani (2011). Slow Food Revolution from Arcigola to Terra Madre: A New Culture of Life and Food (Translator: Ç. Ekiz).Istanbul: Sinek Sekiz Publications, 2011

Rao, H., Monin, P. & Durand, R. (2003). Institutional change in toque ville: Nouvelle cuisine as an identity movement in French gastronomy, *American Journal of Sociology*, 108 (4), 795–843.

Ritzer, G. (2011). McDonaldisation of Society (Translator: Ş. Kaya). Ayrıntı Publishing House, Istanbul.

Samancı, Ö. (2016). Culinary culture in the Middle Ages and Renaissance periods, the development of French cuisine in the modern era. In: H. Yılmaz and A. Dündar (Eds). History of Gastronomy. Eskişehir: Anadolu University Open Education Faculty Publications.

Svejenova, S., Pedersen, J. S., & Byrkjeflot, H. (2021). From innovation to impact: Translating New Nordic Cuisine into a Nordic food model 1. In The Making and Circulation of Nordic Models, Ideas and Images (pp. 229–250). Routledge

Tez, Z. (2012). History of flavour. Istanbul: Hayy Book Tomkies, K. K. (2010). Food services. New York: Ferguson Pub.

Vega, C., & Ubbink, J. (2008). Molecular gastronomy: a food fad or science supporting innovative cuisine?. Trends in food science & technology, 19(7), 372–382.

Yalcin, A. Y. S., & Yalcin, S. (2013). Can Cittaslow Movement be a model for sustainable local development?. *Journal of Social and Human Sciences*, 5(1), 32–41.

Youssef, J. (2013). Molecular Gastronomy at Home: Taking Culinary Physics Out of the Lab and Into Your Kitchen. Firefly Books.

Yurtseven, R. H. (2006). Slow Food and Gökçeada: A Managerial Approach. Ankara: Detay Publishing

Internet References

Arslan, G. (2011). http://www.milliyet.com.tr/inegine-incirine-iyi-bakan- ureticiariyor/pazar/haberdetay/17.07.2011/1415274/default.htm (Accessed: 22.01.2018)

Demiriz, İ. (2016). http://www.tempomag.com.tr/detail/mehmet-gurs-yeme-icme-politikbir-mesele (Accessed: 27.01.2018)

Elbullifoundation (2024) https://elbullifoundation.com/en/synthesis-of-elbulli-cuisine/ (Accessed: 30.04.2024)

Bildiğiniz Gibi Değil (2017) (Presenter: Kahraman, H. B.) Television broadcast].İstanbul: Ntv (Accessed: 20.01.2018)

Kırım, A. (2005). https://www.hurriyet.com.tr/dunyanin-en-gozde-yemek-akimi-avangard-mutfak-322911#:~:text=Bug%C3%BCn%20d%C3%BCn yan%C4%B1n%20en%20%C3%A7ok%20ilgi,Amerika'da%20da%20 h%C4%B1zla%20geli%C5%9Fiyor (Accessed: 30.04.2024)

Kopuz, B. (2015). https://beefandfish.com/roportaj/miklanin-yaraticisi-meh met-gurs-bizdene-truf-var-ne-havyar-bu-odulu-hamsiyle-tarhanayla-aldik. html (Accessed: 22. 01. 2018)

Meyers (2024) https://meyers.dk/en/the-new-nordic-cuisine-movement/ (Accessed: 30.04.2024)

Michelin(2024)https://guide.michelin.com/tr/tr/istanbulprovince/istanbul/res taurant/mikla (Accessed: 30.04.2024)

Foodinlife (2022) https://foodinlife.com/mehmet-gursun-miklasi-bir-kez-da-ha-dunyanin-en-iyi-restoranlari-listesinde/ (Accessed: 25.10.2024).

Örs, A. (2015). https://www.sabah.com.tr/yazarlar/cumartesi/ors/2015/04/18/ yerel- urunlerkorunmali (Accessed: 22.01.2018)

Toprakoğlu, N. (2015) https://www.haberturk.com/yasam/haber/1026536-iyi-yemek-icinbiraz-kimyager-olmak-lazim (Accessed: 19.01.2018)

http://www.newnordicfood.org/ ((Accessed: 10.01.2018)

https://www.spiegel.de/international/zeitgeist/the-nordic-food-revolut ion-foraging-in-the-forest-with-the-world-s-best-chef-a-759277.html (Accessed: 30.04.2024)

https://www.theworlds50best.com/blog/News/rene-redzepi-noma-dare-to-fail. html (Accessed: 10.01.2018)

https://www.theworlds50best.com/The-List-2018/41-50/Mikla.html (Accessed: 17.01.2018)

https://www.theworlds50best.com/previous-list/2022 (Accessed: 30.04.2024)

https://turizmsurasi.ktb.gov.tr/TR-204439/mehmet-gurs. (Accessed: 30.04.2024)

https://www.ecpi.edu/blog/a-brief-history-of-french-cuisine Accessed: 01.04.2024

Zuhal Özdemir Yaman[1] and Büşra Yeşilyurt Sağdiç[2]

Chapter 6 Cultural Heritage in Gastronomy

Introduction

The concept of culture covers a complex process that includes abstract and concrete elements. Architectural works, various historical works, written, printed or visual resources owned by societies represent the concrete elements of cultures. Values, beliefs, ethical behaviours, etc. that emerged throughout the historical process. Facts constitute the abstract cultural elements of societies. Culinary culture, one of the sub-codes of culture, also covers a unique concept of culture that includes concrete and abstract elements. Food sources, various tools, recipes and many different items used in the preparation of meals are the tangible values of culinary cultures. Nutrition and various habits formed around it; beliefs, traditions, rituals, etc. facts constitute the abstract aspects of culinary cultures.

Every society has a culinary culture shaped by its geography and historical process. Events that have a social impact, such as wars, migrations, and natural disasters, are the factors that play a role in the shaping and change of these cultural elements. Therefore, culinary cultures; It contains unique values due to the heterogeneous history of societies. These unique values may arise from concrete culinary culture elements, but they may also be affected by the intangible cultural elements of the society. This gives culinary cultures a unique heritage quality.

Tangible cultural artifacts belonging to communities are often important resources used in the promotion of the region in question and destination marketing. The intangible values that societies have are generally discussed in terms of the protection and maintenance of certain cultural values. A global effort is being made to protect and sustain these values. For this reason, it is thought that it is important to detail the relationship between gastronomy and cultural heritage and understand the current situation. In this section, the relationship between gastronomy and culture, regions with prominent gastronomy cultural heritages and intangible gastronomy cultural heritages will be discussed.

---

1 Assistant Professor, Bolu Abant İzzet Baysal University, Faculty of Health Sciences, Department of Nutrition and Dietetics, ozdemir_z@ibu.edu.tr
2 Research Assistant, Bolu Abant İzzet Baysal University, Faculty of Health Sciences, Department of Nutrition and Dietetics, busrayesilyurt@ibu.edu.tr

Gastronomy and Cultural Heritage

The act of feeding, in its most general definition; It is the most basic physiological action that individuals perform to survive since birth. Since the early periods of humanity, individuals have obtained, processed and consumed foods in various ways. Food has always been of vital importance to humankind; Civilizations were established in regions close to food sources. Since food resources are of critical importance in the life of societies, migrations and wars have been carried out for food. In the process, the meanings attributed to food have gone beyond being a 'basic need' and have been adopted as an integral part of social cultures.

Food and beverages are expressed as parts that connect individuals to the history, cultural identities, ethnic origins, lifestyles, and preferences of their generations (Holtzman, 2006). This definition shows that gastronomy elements are intertwined with many elements of culture. The most comprehensive relationship between gastronomy and culture is related to the observation of food at all stages from its production to its service. Every society has preparation and consumption habits that it has developed in its own historical process. This paves the way for the formation of unique cultural identities of societies. For example, religious beliefs, which are one of the important codes of cultures, can be decisive in terms of issues such as the preparation and service of food and beverages. Situations such as Muslim, Jewish, or Hindu individuals not consuming certain foods and beverages and taking faith-based rules into consideration in their preparation are related to the connection between cultural codes and consumption habits. Another example can be given through the effects of the geography in which societies live.

Each geography has its own climate and soil structure. This situation is decisive for the agricultural and livestock products grown. In Germany, where long winters occur, local dishes are dominated by winter root vegetables, which again reveals the characteristic consumption of the culture. All these consumption habits have formed cultural identities over the centuries. As a matter of fact, it is stated that gastronomy elements are at the center of cultural identity (Fischler, 1988).

Cultural heritage is a concept that encompasses unique cultural practices, values, and various traditions transmitted and learned from previous generations (Britwum and Demont, 2022). The concept of cultural heritage; It includes many elements such as agricultural products, various tools and equipment, dining etiquette, and symbolic values attributed to food and beverages (Ramli et al., 2016). Every society has nutritional habits shaped by its geography and the historical process it has lived through. This situation allows nutrition and the behaviours shaped around it to differ from society to society and the formation of a hetero-geneous cultural structure. Cultural heritages are generally shaped over centu-ries; It covers a rich and accumulated history. Therefore, individuals within the society have a critical role as guardians and carriers of gastronomic heritage and related traditions (Del Soldato and Massari, 2024).

Many national and international institutions develop applications for gas-tronomy heritage and organize events regarding them. Among these organi-zations and institutions, UNESCO (United Nations Educational, Scientific and Cultural Organization) stands out in terms of its global impact. UNESCO carries out various practices to protect and promote the gastronomic values of societies. The establishment of the Creative Cities Network, which adopts policies such as sustainability, intercultural dialogue and social harmony, as well as regional promotion and development, can be given as an example of these practices (UNESCO, 2024a). In cities classified in this context, concrete marketing of gas-tronomy items is generally at the forefront. The Intangible Cultural Heritage list, where the cultural background of food is discussed and evaluated together with its traditional intangible values, represents an important application for the rela-tionship between gastronomy and culture.

Intangible Cultural Heritage

Intangible cultural heritage: It includes relevant objects and phenomena that individuals or communities consider as part of their culture. These objects and facts are expressed through process, expressions, historical knowledge, and prac-tices. These practices, passed down through generations and constantly recre-ated, provide individuals and societies with a sense of identity and sustainability. This provides various contributions to societies, such as collective consciousness and commitment to culture. Another dimension of intangible cultural heritage is related to their economic gains. These legacies can benefit societies in vari-ous aspects such as growth and development, foreign exchange output, infra-structure development, economic and social development (Petronela, 2016). The fact that intangible cultural heritage is considered an important issue by many societies is directly linked to the globalization process. Although many societies differ from each other in terms of their concrete elements, they are in constant interaction in terms of consumption elements. This situation brings the concept of food heritage to the agenda.

The concept of food heritage can generally be expressed as a 'contemporary identification attempt' to distinguish community identities in a world that is becoming increasingly homogeneous because of globalization (Brulotte and

Di Giovine, 2016). It seems that food heritage is generally defined under two different categories. These are classified as 'heritage food' and 'food heritage'. Although they seem to be concepts that encompass each other, they differ from each other in meaning. The heritage food category is defined as "traditional local dishes prepared daily, which are a mixture of various cultures, religious beliefs and values, inherited from the past" (Omar et al., 2015). The concept of food heritage is explained as "the combination of tangible and intangible elements of food cultures accepted as common heritage". These legacies generally include both abstract and concrete elements such as food raw materials, materials and ingredients, preparation methods, recipes, consumption traditions, table manners, rituals, kitchen tools and equipment (Bessière and Tibère, 2010).

UNESCO defines the concept of cultural heritage as "the legacy of concrete and intangible qualities inherited from a society from past generations, preserved today and to be passed on to future generations" (UNESCO, 2017a). However, UNESCO expands its definition of the concept of cultural heritage and emphasizes intangible elements as well as concrete elements. In this regard, the concept of cultural heritage does not only include objects and objects; It has been stated that oral traditions, visual arts, social practices, rituals, holiday events, knowledge and practices about nature and the universe, and knowledge and skills about traditional production are the elements that constitute cultural heritage. (UNESCO, 2003).

The convention for the protection of intangible cultural heritage was accepted and put into force by UNESCO in October 2023 (Benedetta, 2020). On the other hand, the contract principles adopted in 2003 excluded food and the practices shaped around it. Foods were accepted as intangible cultural heritage in 2010. In 2010, UNESCO included the Mediterranean diet, Mexican cuisine, and French gastronomy in its representative list of the "Intangible Cultural Heritage of Humanity" (Medina and Aguilar, 2018). Considering the advantages such as food heritage attracting more and more attention, the realization that it is an important experience channel for tourists when visiting a region, and its cultural sustainability effects, many societies' desires to participate in this network has come to the fore (Almansouri et al., 2022).

Worldwide Examples of Intangible Cultural Heritage

As of 2024, there are a total of 730 heritage sites covering 145 countries on the UNESCO Intangible Cultural Heritage List. In addition, various practices and traditions from many different countries are included in the list of 'intangible cultural heritages that need to be urgently protected'. According to the list announced in 2023, among the intangible cultural heritages that need to be urgently protected, it includes Turkey's heritage titled 'traditional knowledge, methods and practices regarding olive cultivation'. In 2022, Ukrainian Borscht cooking culture was listed as one of the heritages that need to be urgently protected (UNESCO, 2024b).

National heritage from many areas is protected in the UNESCO Intangible Cultural Heritage List. However, it has been determined that there are 46 cultural heritage sites in the representative list based on food (UNESCO, 2024b). When we look at the intangible heritage of gastronomy protected by UNESCO, it is seen that many nations have their own traditional knowledge, skills, and practices. However, it has been determined that countries such as Italy, Belgium, United Arab Emirates, Saudi Arabia, Azerbaijan, Tunisia, and Turkey have registered at least three different gastronomy cultures in this list. It is thought that this effort to protect intangible heritage is important in terms of the issues in the literature. Some of the traditions and practices of these countries, which stand out with their intangible cultural heritage, listed by UNESCO, are presented below as examples.

Neapolitan Art 'Pizzaiuolo'

The art of Naples 'Pizzaiuolo' encompasses a traditional culinary practice in Naples, Italy. According to this traditional practice, the dough is prepared and cooked over wood fire; It includes unique production stages such as the rotating movement of the pizza master (UNESCO, 2017b). Not using technological tools and equipment in making traditional Naple's pizza; Preparation only by hand is one of the qualities that show that it is an 'art' that requires traditional knowledge and will be passed on from generation to generation. It is stated that this traditional preparation process takes place in four stages. Accordingly, first the *staglio* step, in which the dough balls are shaped, is applied and the second step called *ammaccatura* is started. In this step, the dough is spread, and its edges are raised. Then, starting from the middle of the dough, the ingredients are filled, and these steps are carried out in a clockwise spiral motion. In the fourth and final stage, the pizza is sent to the wood-fired oven with a rotating movement (La Morella, 2017). Neapolitan pizza is referred to as 'artisan pizza' and the people who prepare these pizzas are called pizzaiolo. Unlike other types of pizza, its size does not exceed a dinner plate and a limited number of ingredients such as basil and mozzarella are used in the middle of the pizza (Stazio, 2021). Another feature of this pizza is that the ingredients used in its production are traditionally produced in the Campania countryside, where the city of Naples is located (Lush, 2024).

Beer Culture in Belgium

There are approximately 1,500 types of beer prepared using different fermentation techniques in many regions of Belgium. Beer, which is considered an important heritage of social culture in terms of preparation and service styles; It has an important place in both the daily life of the Belgian people and on special occasions such as festivals (UNESCO, 2016). Beer is an important means of recognition for Belgium; It is stated that it symbolizes a distinctive element of culinary culture in the process of globalization and functions as an 'ambassador' in the promotion of the country (Persyn et al., 2010). Although Belgium is a relatively small country, the fact that it has the largest beer diversity in the world (Poelmans and Taylor, 2019) allows it to stand out with its unique gastronomic heritage.

In Belgian culinary culture, beer is an important element of culinary culture, not only as a beverage consumed on its own, but also used in the preparation of meals and in the washing phase of some types of cheese. In Belgium, there are many practices in which beer plays a leading role in daily life as well as special occasions and celebrations. This enables food to have meanings such as 'celebration' and 'sharing' in collective events. This situation brings to the fore the intangible elements of culinary cultures. In addition, the prevalence of craft brewing, which is generally run as a family business, as well as the large-scale beer industry, brings up situations such as the transfer of traditional knowledge and cultural knowledge (Poelmans and Ostyn, 2020). Beer production in these micro-scale production areas is generally artisanal. There is a need to keep this craft alive and promote it so that it can be passed on to future generations.

Arabic Coffee the Symbol of Generosity

The countries that have Arabic Coffee registered on the cultural heritage list as a symbol of generosity are the United Arab Emirates, Saudi Arabia, Oman and Qatar. Coffee is an important agricultural product with a rich deep-rooted history for the Arabian Peninsula. This agricultural product, which is widely found in the mountainous regions of Yemen, was discovered by the Arabs in ancient times and has become a cultural heritage for this region throughout the historical process (Temir, 2022).

According to the traditional preparation process, coffee beans are roasted over low heat and ground in copper mortars. The ground coffee beans are cooked in copper coffee pots by adding water and cooking over low heat. The cooked coffee is first transferred to a small coffee pot and then served in small coffee cups. At the same time, this preparation process is like a ceremony performed in front of the guests. The ready-to-serve coffees are first offered to the oldest or most important guest in the room (UNESCO, 2015).

Usually, up to three cups are served to one guest. The first cup of coffee offered is like an assurance of 'trust' towards the guest. This coffee symbolically means that the guest is protected and honoured by the host. It is also an indication that the guest is accepted into the host's personal space. The third coffee, which is usually the last service, is called 'sword cup'. This coffee represents a strong bond between the host and the guest and an unspoken agreement that they will act together against a possible enemy (Shryock, 2004).

Harissa, Knowledge, Skills, Culinary and Social Applications

Harissa, a type of spice prepared with hot pepper paste, is one of the important symbols of Tunisian culinary culture. It is stated that this spice, prepared as a paste-like mixture, is an integral element in the domestic practices and food traditions of the Tunisian society. This is not just about the sensory qualities of Harissa. While preparing Harissa, women prepare it jointly in their family or neighbourhood environment and act collectively in a joyful environment. In addition, a certain calendar is followed during the planting and harvesting of hot peppers, considering the 'unlucky times' (UNESCO, 2022). These practices point to the cultural background of spices. Practices such as seeing its preparation as a collective activity and people helping each other in preparation represent the aspects of this food that inspire unity and solidarity. However, the existence of various beliefs about planting and harvest dates is also related to the intangible values of food.

The main ingredient in making Harissa spice is hot red peppers. Harissa-themed festivals are held every October in the Nabeul region, where these peppers are produced. These festivals allow the promotion of traditional cultural elements. In addition, tourist tours that include participation in the Harissa production process and tastings also represent important practices for the promotion of culinary heritage and generating economic income (Othmani, 2021).

The Tradition of Making and Sharing Dolma is an Indicator of Cultural Identity

Dolma is the general name of dishes prepared by wrapping various fillings (usually rice, bulgur, spices, and meat) in vegetable or fruit leaves or by filling the inside of vegetables. This dish is widely consumed in the culinary cultures of many geographies such as the Mediterranean, the Caucasus, and Central Asia. It is one of the most popular foods in many countries such as Bulgaria, Georgia, Greece, Iran, Moldova, Turkey, and Azerbaijan (Aykan, 2016). On the other hand, it appears that the country listed under protection as Intangible Cultural Heritage is Azerbaijan. It is reported that Azerbaijan's commitment to 'promoting national festivals and cooking competitions involving experienced dolma practitioners' is effective on this situation (Hafstein, 2020).

The name of the dish Dolma comes from the Turkish verb 'to fill'. There are locally and traditionally prepared stuffed varieties in almost every region of Azerbaijan. Knowledge about the preparation and serving process of stuffed vegetables has been transferred from generation to generation and has become an important indicator of the identity of culinary culture. Stuffed vegetables prepared with various ingredients are served as one of the indispensable dishes in special days, celebrations, festivals, and festivities of the Azerbaijani society. In addition, there are practices aimed at transferring the knowledge and skills regarding dolma within the framework of the master-apprentice understanding. This situation enables the viability and sustainability of the stuffed culture (UNESCO, 2017c).

Iftar/Eftari/Iftar/Iftor and Socio-cultural Traditions

The culinary heritage, including iftar and socio-cultural traditions, was added to the Intangible Cultural Heritage list by UNESCO in 2023 as the common cultural heritage of Azerbaijan, Iran, Uzbekistan, and Turkey. The iftar tradition, which is one of the religious belief-based cultural values of culinary culture, covers the food practices continued during the month of Ramadan in these countries.

The month of Ramadan covers a faith-based practice period in which Muslim individuals fast at certain times of the day. According to this practice, Muslims stop eating and drinking close to sunrise and end their fast with the evening call to prayer at sunset. The meal ceremony in which food and drinks begin to be consumed after the evening adhan is recited is called 'iftar'. Before the iftar meal begins, various activities such as praying at the table and listening to music are held. Individuals who do not consume food or drink throughout the day start this meal by being thankful and thank the creator they believe sent these meals. In addition, ceremonies and rituals related to iftar can also be performed by individuals who do not fast. Knowledge and skills about this tradition are transferred to future generations through oral education and participation within the family. Family members usually prepare iftar tables in cooperation (UNESCO, 2023).

Iftar tables usually consist of crowded tables where family or friends are hosted; Special dishes and desserts are served for the month of Ramadan. Apart from indoor activities, mass events and practices are also held outside. Ramadan festivals and Ramadan tents where free mass iftars are held can be given as examples of these practices. It is possible for anyone from the public to join these tents. This symbolizes the society's culture of cooperation through iftars.

Results

Culinary cultures have a critical importance in creating the collective consciousness of societies, adhering to original values, and in situations that provide social benefit such as economic development. Therefore, it is concluded that the intangible aspects of gastronomy elements are an integral part of culture. The transfer of cultural knowledge to future generations is directly related to sustainability and preservation. Intangible cultural values have a fragile structure because they are based on knowledge, skill and practice. Globally recognized organizations have an important place in protecting these values. In this way, the unique intangible values of the culture are clearly expressed and protected. This situation has a critical importance in the protection of intangible culinary culture elements as well as their promotion. The perception of culinary cultures as authentic and original by different cultures can create a motivation for experience. Thus, it is possible for these cultural values to provide economic and social development.

It is seen that there are gastronomy values from many different geographies of the world that are included in the UNESCO Intangible Cultural Heritage List. It has been determined that the promotion of these values on a global basis provides many social, cultural, and economic contributions. In addition, it has been concluded that it is possible to guarantee cultural elements that have a craft nature and spread based on the transfer of traditional knowledge.

References

Almansouri, M., Verkerk, R., Fogliano, V., & Luning, P. A. (2022). The heritage food concept and its authenticity risk factors-Validation by culinary professionals. *International Journal of Gastronomy and Food Science, 28*, 100523.

Aykan, B. (2016). The politics of intangible heritage and food fights in Western Asia. *International Journal of Heritage Studies, 22*(10), 799–810.

Benedetta, U. (2020). Safeguarding Intangible Cultural Heritage and the environment. *Правоведение, 64*(1), 124–137.

Bessière, J., & Tibère, L. (2010). Innovation et patrimonialisation alimentaire: quels rapports à la tradition?. *Le mangeur*, 1–10.

Britwum, K., & Demont, M. (2022). Food security and the cultural heritage missing link. *Global Food Security*, 35, 100660.

Brulotte, R. L., & Di Giovine, M. A. (Eds.). (2016). *Edible identities: Food as cultural heritage*. Routledge.

Del Soldato, E., & Massari, S. (2024). Creativity and digital strategies to support food cultural heritage in Mediterranean rural areas. *EuroMed Journal of Business*, 19(1), 113–137.

Fischler, C. (1988). Food, self and identity. *Social science information*, 27(2), 275–292.

Hafstein, V. T. Festival as heritage/heritage as festival. In: Ullrich, Kockel; Cristina, Clopot; Baiba, Tjarve and Mairead, N., Craith (ed.) *Heritage and Festivals in Europe* (pp. 205–210). Routledge.

Holtzman, J. D. (2006). Food and memory. *Annual Review Anthropology*, 35, 361–378.

La Morella (2017). Art of Neapolitan "Pizzaiuolo", an Intangible Cultural Heritage of Humanity. https://www.la-morella.it/en/pizza-makers-unesco-world-heritage/ (Accessed: 20.05.2024).

Lush, E. (2024). UNESCO Food Culture: 30 Amazing Culinary Traditions Around the World. https://wander-lush.org/food-culture-unesco/ (Accessed: 20.05.2024).

Medina, F. X., & Aguilar, A. (2018). *13 sustainable diets: Social and cultural perspectives*. In: Barbara, Burlingame and Sandro, Dernini, (ed.) Sustainable Diets: Linking Nutrition and Food Systems. CABI, USA, pp. 131–136.

Omar, S. R., Karim, S., & Omar, S. N. (2015). Exploring international tourists' attitudes and perceptions: In characterizing Malaysian Heritage Food (MHF) as a tourism attraction in Malaysia. *International Journal of Social Science and Humanity*, 5(3), 321–329.

Othmani, W. (2021). Intangible heritage as a social construction of authenticity: The example of Tunisian cuisine. *Via. Tourism Review*, (19): 1–27.

Persyn, D., Swinnen, J. F., & Vanormelingen, S. (2010). Belgian beers: Where history meets globalization. *LICOS Discussion Paper Series*, 1–39.

Petronela, T. (2016). The importance of the intangible cultural heritage in the economy. *Procedia Economics and Finance*, 39, 731–736.

Poelmans, E., & Ostyn, T. P. (2020). On the existence of Belgian craft breweries: Explorative research at the microlevel. *The Geography of Beer: Culture and Economics*, 179–200.

Poelmans, E., & Taylor, J. E. (2019). Belgium's historic beer diversity: should we raise a pint to institutions?. *Journal of Institutional Economics*, *15*(4), 695–713.

Ramli, A. M., Zahari, M. S. M., Suhaimi, M. Z., & Talib, S. A. (2016). Determinants of food heritage towards food identity. *Environment-Behaviour Proceedings Journal*, *1*(1), 207–216.

Shryock, A. (2004). The new Jordanian hospitality: house, host, and guest in the culture of public display. *Comparative Studies in Society and History*, *46*(1), 35–62.

Stazio, M. (2021). Verace Glocal Pizza. Localized globalism and globalized localism in the Neapolitan artisan pizza. *Food, Culture & Society*, *24*(3), 406–430.

Temir, H. (2022). Arabic Qahwa and Its Serving as an Element of Cultural Heritage. *Harran İlahiyat Dergisi*, (48), 1–18.

UNESCO, (2003). Intangible Cultural Heritage Expertise Committee. https://unesco.org.tr/Pages/653/296/Intangible-Cultural-Heritage-Expertise-Committee (Accessed: 18.05.2024).

UNESCO (2015). Arabic coffee, a symbol of generosity. https://ich.unesco.org/en/RL/arabic-coffee-a-symbol-of-generosity-01074 (Accessed: 23.05.2024).

UNESCO (2016). Beer culture in Belgium. https://ich.unesco.org/en/RL/beer-culture-in-belgium-01062. (Accessed: 20.05.2024).

UNESCO (2017a). Tangible cultural heritage. https://unesco.org.tr/Pages/654/295/Tangible-Cultural-Heritage-Expertise-Committee (Accessed: 18.05.2024).

UNESCO (2017b). Art of Neapolitan 'Pizzaiuolo'. https://ich.unesco.org/en/RL/art-of-neapolitan-pizzaiuolo-00722#:~:text=The%20art%20of%20the%20Neapolitan,rotatory%20movement%20by%20the%20baker. (Accessed: 20.05.2024).

UNESCO (2017c). Dolma making and sharing tradition, a marker of cultural identity. https://ich.unesco.org/en/RL/dolma-making-and-sharing-tradition-a-marker-of-cultural-identity-01188 (Accessed: 23.05.2024).

UNESCO (2022). Harissa, knowledge, skills and culinary and social practices. https://ich.unesco.org/en/RL/harissa-knowledge-skills-and-culinary-and-social-practices-01710. (Accessed: 23.05.2024).

UNESCO (2023). Iftar/Eftari/Iftar/Iftor and its socio-cultural traditions. https://ich.unesco.org/en/RL/iftar-eftari-iftar-iftor-and-its-socio-cultural-traditions-01984 (Accessed: 24.05.2024).

UNESCO (2024a). Creativity and Cities. https://www.unesco.org/en/creative-cities/creativity-and-cities?hub=80094 (Accessed: 16.05.2024).

UNESCO (2024b). Browse the Lists of Intangible Cultural Heritage and the Register of good safeguarding practices. https://ich.unesco.org/en/lists (Accessed: 19.05.2024).

Zocchi, D. M., Fontefrancesco, M. F., Corvo, P., & Pieroni, A. (2021). Recognising, safeguarding, and promoting food heritage: challenges and prospects for the future of sustainable food systems. *Sustainability, 13*(17), 9510.

Sena Ekinci[1] and Nevzat Emrah Özçelik[2]

Chapter 7 Journey to Chocolate

Introduction

Throughout human history, chocolate and cocoa have been used for different purposes such as treatment of medical problems, religious rituals, marriage ceremonies, and indicators of power, and have occupied an important position in many areas such as social, religion, and trade from past to present. Cocoa, whose Latin name means "Food of the Gods", began to be consumed by the nobility in the form of a bitter drink in Latin American civilizations, and with the introduction of Europe, it reached its current form and became a product that people enjoy and can easily access. Chocolate is basically theobroma It is obtained from the fruit of the tree named cacao " Linnaeus ". The raw materials used in chocolate production vary according to their types and generally consist of substances such as cocoa, cocoa mass, cocoa butter, sugar, lecithin, vanillin and milk powder. Today, chocolate is a product whose popularity continues to increase due to its variety of uses, taste and appeal to all age groups.

This section basically covers the entire journey of cocoa during its transformation into chocolate in different dimensions. First, the definition and historical development of chocolate was examined Today's chocolate market is mentioned, considering the historical development of cocoa and chocolate consumed as beverages, chocolate production facilities, and their spread in the world and in our country. Secondly, mentioning the cocoa fruit and tree, their varieties and properties were focused on, and the chocolate making stages were examined in detail. Finally, chocolate types, their nutritional values and the properties contain are discussed. This study aims to examine chocolate comprehensively and contribute to the field.

---

1   Lecturer, Bolu Abant Izzet Baysal University, Head of Hotel, Restaurant and Food Services Department, Pastry and Bakery Programme, sena.ekinci@ibu.edu.tr
2   Lecturer, Bolu Abant Izzet Baysal University, Head of Hotel, Restaurant and Food Services Department, Pastry and Bakery Programme, nevzatemrah.ozcelik@ibu.edu.tr

Historical Development of Chocolate

The emergence of chocolate It is thought that the Mesoamerican civilization dates back to the Olmecs. It is known that cocoa comes from the word "kakawa" in the Olmec language and that after the discovery of the kakawa tree, these trees were cultivated and later developed and consumed by the Mayans, Toltecs and Aztecs living in similar geographies. B.C. It is rumored that containers used for making chocolate were found in the Hondelas-Ulua Valley in Latin America in 2000 (Sencer, 2018, p. 132; Alpözen, 2010, p. 16). B.C. It is documented that it started to be consumed in the form of bitter and unsweetened beverages by the Olmecs in the 1500s (Tınmaz et al. 2022, p. 297) . The Aztecs took this word, which is a combination of the Mayan words "choco" meaning noise and "atl" meaning water/liquid, from the word "xocolatl", which they likened to the sound made when mixing liquid chocolate. For the first time in history, B.C. It is documented in writing that it was consumed as a beverage under the name "xocolatl" by the Aztecs in 1100 BC (Tokuşoğlu, 2015, p. 1). It is known that at that time, various spices were added to the fermented cocoa paste and drunk as a bitter drink (Uzun, 2019, p. 32). It is known that the cocoa tree grew in the plains of southern Yucatan in the 600s AD during the Mayan period, and they consumed the beans as a hot drink by mixing them with water (Hastaoğlu & Taşçı, 2021, p. 2204). In ancient times, cocoa was called theobrama (which means drink of the gods in Latin) with its sharp and bitter taste and its awakening and invigorating properties.

It is known that in ancient times, cocoa beans were roasted in earthenware pots and ground between stones. Cocoa Drink; After drying, roasting and crushing the seeds, they were flavored and mixed with spices such as sugar cane, cinnamon, anise, musk and black pepper and consumed in the form of a hot and bitter drink (Ünvay, A., 2019, p. 17). Chocolate was used for many purposes such as religious, commercial and social status indicators during the Aztec and Mayan periods. It is known that cocoa, which is considered sacred religiously, was presented to the god in some ceremonies and rituals, used as money in commercial life (Gürsoy, 2021, p. 167), and exchange money during wars, medicine in various treatments, and during the Aztec period, taxes were collected on cocoa beans (Samancı, 2012, p. 27; Özden, 2023, p. 1591). Throughout history, it has been among the documents in the traditional drug treatment method (scorpion and bee stings, bronchitis treatment) in the Mexican region (Seçuk, 2020, p. 16). While chocolate was a drink consumed by nobles during the Mayan period, it is known that as its use became widespread, it was consumed by administrators, high-ranking soldiers, priests and private traders during the Aztec period (Alpözen, 2010, p. 16).

Europe's encounter with chocolate (cocoa) dates back to the 16th century. Although Columbus took the cocoa that he discovered during his Central American trip in 1502 to the Spanish King Ferdinand and Queen Isabella, it did not receive the attention which he expected. Spanish explorer Hernan After the discovery of Mexico, Cortes brought cocoa beans to Spain and then the process of spreading to Europe began (Gürsoy, 2021, p.157; Uzun, 2019, p.32; Sencer et al., 2018, p.133). It is recorded that Columbus introduced cocoa drink to Spain in 1528 (Beckett, 2009, p. 4) and that cocoa seeds and fruits were found in Yucatan during his fourth trip to America (Bingöl, 2019, p. 3).

In 1606, Trader Antonio in Carletti brought cocoa beans to Italy, laying the foundation for its spread throughout Europe. The first chocolate business was opened in London in 1657 (Tokuşoğlu, 2015, p. 10). As access to chocolate became easier, cocoa spread to many parts of Europe by the 1700s. In 1728, the Fry family established the first chocolate factory (Polat, 2019, p. 3). Swedish Carl Von Linnaeus, named the cocoa tree ' Theobroma', meaning food of the gods in 1753. (Akçiçek, 2023 p. 359). Englishman Joseph Townsend turned roasted cocoa beans into powder using a hydraulic pump in 1779.

Dutch chemist C. Johannes Van Houten developed a machine to extract cocoa butter by the pressing method and enabling modern chocolate production by patented chocolate powder in 1828. (Ercik, 2023, p. 21). In 1842, the Cadbury brothers started selling block chocolate in England. JS Fry&Sons, a company founded by Fry in Bristol, England, in 1847, is the company that produced the first plain chocolate tablet (Seçuk, 2020;13). Some time after Henry Nestle opened the Nestle factory in 1867, Nestle became the first factory to produce milk chocolate with the discovery of milk chocolate mixture by Swiss Daniel Peter in 1875 (Tokuşoğlu, 2015, p. 13). Rudolphe in 1880 Lindt contributed to the production of better quality chocolate by inventing the conching machine.

The first book showing that chocolate entered the Ottoman lands was "The indian Nectar or, A Religion on Chocolate", entered the Ottoman Palace through European diplomats in 1720 (Tınmaz et al., 2022, p. 294). The Ottomans met with chocolate in 1693, when the Italian Gemelli Careri ended his trip to Izmir. While chocolate was a product consumed by the upper classes in the Ottoman Empire until 1849, access to chocolate became easier towards the end of the 19th century with the start of chocolate sales in patisseries. The first written source of chocolate in the world was included in a recipe book in 1786, and during the Ottoman period, a dessert called 'chocolate flakes' was included in the 'New Cookbook' written in 1880 (Tınmaz et al. 2022, p. 296). As of the 19th century, chocolate changed form and appeared in solid tablet form and dessert form. In the 20th century, a chocolate sales office was opened by Nestle in Turkey in

1909 (Küçükyılmaz, 2021, p. 9). The first chocolate production facility in Turkey started operating in Feriköy in 1927 (Tokuşoğlu, 2015, p. 16).

Cocoa in Today's Commercial World

Today, cocoa is an important export product for developing countries and provides a significant source of income for the country's economy. The development of technology and the increase in demand have also paved the way for an increase in the export rates of chocolate. When current data is examined, according to Trademap 2022 data, Germany ranks first in the export table of cocoa and cocoa preparations with 6,5 billion US dollars. Germany's share in world exports is around 12 %. The list is followed by the Netherlands, Ivory Coast, Belgium and Italy (trademap.org). Table 7.1 includes world chocolate export data.

Table 7.1. World Chocolate Export Data

Exporting Countries	Issued Value (thousand US dollars)	Amount Exported	Quantity Unit	Unit Value (USD/unit)	In World Exports (%)
Germany	5.440.67	992.264	ton	5.483	16.1
Belgium	3.326.62	668.333	ton	4.977	9.8
Italy	2.439.82	411.615	ton	5.927	7.2
Poland	2.356.91	456.089	ton	5.168	7
Holland	2.246.47	477.360	ton	4.706	6.6

Source: trademap.org

The trademap database, Germany ranks first among the countries that export the most chocolate worldwide, with 992.264 tons. In addition to the above list, Canada ranks 6th (1.971.752 thousand tons), USA ranks 7th (1.736.490 thousand tons), France ranks 8th (1.452.062 thousand tons), United Kingdom ranks 9th (1,010,634 thousand tons). and Switzerland comes in 10th place with 882.155 thousand tons. In 2023 data, it is seen that Germany maintains its first place with 6,2 billion US dollars exported (trademap, 2024). According to current data based on UN COMTRADE and ITC statistics, 2023 data is not included as data for all countries are not available. Among the top 5 selling confectionery and chocolate companies in 2023, Mars Wrigley, Mondelez International, Ferrero, Hershey and Nestle are in the top 5 respectively, while the Turkish company Şölen ranks 53rd among the top 100 companies (snackandbakery.com).

Transformation from Cocoa to Chocolate

Cocoa tree is a tree called "theobroma" in Latin, belonging to the Sterculiaceae family, which grows in tropical and humid regions. The cocoa tree grows in the equatorial region, in regions with a hot and humid climate, between 20 degrees north and south, and attracts attention with its sensitivity to growing conditions. The cocoa tree, which is one of the main growing regions in Ecuador, Mexico, Central and South America, produces twice a year. Although the average height of the tree is between 12–15 meters, fruits are usually collected when they reach 3–4 meters in length in order to collect them more easily (Beckett, 2009, p. 12; Bingöl, 2019, p. 3). Today, cocoa is grown in a wide area, especially in West Africa, Southeast Asia and South America, as well as Ivory Coast, Ghana, Indonesia, Nigeria, Cameroon and Brazil. A *healthy* and productive cocoa tree can produce approximately 30 fruits per year. The average size of cocoa fruits is 15–30 cm, oval almond-shaped, and 30–40 beans are obtained from its contents. The seeds are 2–3 cm long and have dark red-brown-purple color transitions and are located inside the white fleshy part of the fruit. Criollo, Trinitario of cocoa beans There are 4 types: Nacional and Forastero. Criollo beans are considered the most valuable type, with their light color, thin skin and slightly bitter and refined aroma (Polat, 2019, p. 4). Forastero seed fruits are thicker and more durable than criollo, have a sharp aroma, high oil aroma and fruits are dark in color. The basic ingredient of chocolate mixture and most of the cocoa production is obtained from this variety (Parlatır, 2019, p. 18). The Trinitario species is a hybrid of the Criollo and Forastero species and stands out with its sharp and refined aroma and being easier to cultivate. Although the Nacional type has a mild aroma and grows in the Amazon region of Ecuador, it is in danger of extinction today.

The fruits obtained from the cocoa tree go through many delicate stages while turning into chocolate in an industrial environment. First, cocoa fruits are collected from the tree with the help of a machete and scythe from the field, and then the seeds are separated by breaking them with a stick. After the fermentation process in tubs (45–55 °C) for 6–10 days, the beans are washed/or directly dried (Parlatır, 2019, p. 18). The fermentation process is important for the formation of the aroma intensity of cocoa (Baysal, A., 2015, p. 356). The seeds are dried under solar or sunlight until the moisture content is 5–7 % to prevent mold formation in the product (Küçükyılmaz, 2021, p. 6). Dried cocoa beans are added to jute sacks and made ready to be sent to factories.

The first step in the factory is, separate the beans from their shells and reveal the cocoa nibs. As a result of this process, cocoa beans are separated from unwanted materials and shells. The next stage is the roasting process. With the cocoa nib roasting process, the average moisture content is reduced to 3 %. After the roasted cocoa nibs are cut into small pieces, liquid cocoa liquor (chocolate liquor) is created by the friction of the rollers as a result of the crushing process. Cocoa liquor is kept between 90–100 °C. It is then subjected directly to chocolate production or to the crushing process to separate cocoa powder/cocoa butter. The products added to the chocolate liqueurs sent to the mixing machines vary depending on the type and characteristics of the chocolate. The mixing process is carried out for 10–15 minutes at approximately 50–60 °C. Crystalline sucrose and cocoa mass are increased by increasing the surface area of the mixture with chocolate thinning machine rollers and reducing particle sizes until they reach 25–30 μm (Parlatır, 2019, p. 22). With this process, the dispersed particles in the chocolate are reduced to the desired size and smoothed, and the refining process is carried out. After this stage, the conching stage is carried out, which includes kneading, beating and aeration, which takes between 8–24 hours depending on the properties of the chocolate. The conching process aims to minimize the moisture in the cocoa mass, form a caramelized structure, reduce the undesirable amount of thick consistency, reduce the undesirable acidic taste, and achieve the desired level of smoothness in the mixture by minimizing the particles (Hastaoğlu and Taşçı, 2021, p. 2204; Özkan, 2019, p. 12). Products that go through the conching process are taken to the tempering boilers. Chocolates heated to 45 °C are reduced to 27 °C and raised again to 31 °C. The temperatures applied in the tempering process vary depending on the type of chocolate. After this process, molding, coating and dipping process(es) are applied to the chocolates according to their properties. After the products are cooled, they are packaged under appropriate conditions and made ready for distribution.

Processes during artisan chocolate making include many different operations. In order to speed up and facilitate the process steps of handmade chocolate, processes are generally carried out with couverture chocolate. Chocolates purchased in the form of couverture are first subjected to the tempering process. During chocolate processing, the temperature of the working environment is important in order for the process steps to proceed healthily. The basic process steps of handmade chocolate are; The melting process is divided into hand tempering, mold painting and molding (Ercik, C., İlhan, İ. & Keskin S.N., 2023 p. 2621–2623).

Tempering: Chocolates contain an average of 500 stable and unstable crystal structures (Ercik, 2023, p. 20). The heat treatment applied to chocolate oil to have the desired quality, consistency and properties is called tempering. This process ensures homogeneous distribution of stable and unstable crystals. It is obtained by melting, cooling and reheating chocolate. The aim here is to reach the crystal structure required for cocoa butter and its equivalents to achieve the desired quality in chocolate. As a result of successful tempering, the chocolate solidifies faster and the chocolate is prepared for the shaping stage. Unstable crystals first melt and mix with other crystals and the desired structure is achieved. The degrees of processing applied during the tempering process vary depending on the type of chocolate. Table 7.2 lists the average temperature ranges that should be applied to chocolates.

Table 7.2. Chocolate Tempering Degrees

Action Taken	Dark Chocolate	Chocolate Milk	White (Ivory) Chocolate
Melting (Heating Process)	46°–49 °C	43°–46 °C	43°–46 °C
Tempering (Cooling) Process	27°–29 °C	26°–28 °C	26°–28 °C
Reheating Process	31°–32 °C	30°–31 °C	29°–30 °C

Source: Talbdot, 1999; Tarrab, 2014; Erçik, 2023

In tempering, first the chocolate mass is melted and the oil it contains becomes completely liquid. The melting process can be carried out by different methods using microwave, bain-marie method and oven. (Tarrab, 2014, p. 10). If there is a tempering machine, it can also be done that way. Correctly tempered chocolate appears with features such as smooth appearance, absence of bubbles, shine, desired hardness level, homogeneity and easy shapeability.

Chocolate Types and Properties

The proportions and types of products used in chocolate making vary between countries. All ratios, except the amount of base fat that reduced-fat cocoa powder should contain, included in the cocoa and chocolate products communiqué implemented in our country, are parallel to the ratios in the European Union. The amount of sugar to be added to the chocolate mixture during chocolate preparation varies depending on the flavor intensity and roasting degree of the cocoa (Savarin, 2018, p. 105).

Although the product groups and quantities used in chocolate making vary according to country and company policies, the only substance that must be used in the world is cocoa butter (Varol & Kara, 2021, p. 200). 95–98 % of the fat in chocolate consists of cocoa butter and milk fat (Alpözen, 2010, p. 16). Although the most common use of cocoa butter is chocolate production, it is also used in the pharmacy and cosmetic industry. As a result of the presence of saturated fatty acids such as palmitic, stearic, linoleic and oleic in its content, it is solid at room temperature, yellowish in color and contributes to the formation of the desired properties in chocolate such as hardness, brittleness and melting in the mouth (Cisse & Yemişçioğlu, 2019, p. 37; Duyan, 2023, p. 17). The fact that cocoa butter is solid at room temperature and melts in the mouth at an average of 37 °C is a distinguishing feature among vegetable oils (Akçiçek, 2023, p. 358).

It is possible to group and examine chocolates in many ways (Sökmen (2005, p. 3) divided chocolates into 5 groups: black, milk, white, praline and filled chocolates. In another study, 7 main types were examined: milky, bitter, white, flavored, filled, praline, and coating/couverture. Erçik (2023, p. 23–27) In his study, chocolate types were classified according to their components (couverture, black, milk couverture, sweet), their forms (flake, milk flake, filled, praline, ganache) and other chocolates (confiseri, white chocolate, gianduja)., gianduja milk, chocolate para mesa, basic chocolate para mesa) reviewed as.

Chocolate types are distinguished from each other by their names, such as having different amounts of milk fat, cocoa butter, cocoa liquor and dry matter. Although there are many types of chocolate, they can basically be divided into three types: dark, milk and white chocolate, depending on the cocoa content they contain. The minimum total cocoa solids that dark chocolate should contain is 35 %, milk chocolate should be 25 %, the minimum cocoa solids should contain cocoa butter is 18 % in dark chocolate, the minimum cocoa solids should contain fat-free cocoa solids is 14 % in dark chocolate, and milk chocolate should contain at least 18 % of total cocoa solids. 2.5 % the minimum milk solids it should contain is 3.5 % in milk chocolate, 3.5 % in white chocolate, the minimum total of milk fat and cocoa butter it should contain is 25 %, the percentage of cocoa butter in its composition should be around 20 % in white chocolate (Sökmen, 2005, p. 3; Tokuşoğlu, 2005, p. 63). White chocolate differs from the other two types of chocolate with its lack of cocoa mass and its pale yellow/ivory color. White Chocolate basically contains cocoa butter, sugar, milk solids, soy lecithin and vanilla (Duyan, 2023, p. 16). Milk chocolate appears as a soft sweet product with a high sugar content and contains condensed milk or milk powder. Solvents such as ethyl alcohol, glycerol, propylene glycol in chocolate making; acids such as citric and fumaric; glyceryl Emulsifiers such as monostearate, lecithin, Polyglycerol (PGPR), artificial sweeteners, antioxidants and finally flavoring substances such as almond, anise and laurel oil are used (Alpözen, 2010, p. 17–18). Chocolates stand out because they provide energy to people as a result of the fat and carbohydrates they contain and are high in calories. The table below shows the approximate nutritional value of 100 grams of chocolate.

Table 7.3. Average Content for 100 g of Chocolate

	Plain	Milk	White
Energy (kcal)	530	518	553
Protein (g)	5	7	9
Carbonhydrate (g)	55	57	58
Fat (g)	32	33	33
Calcium (mg)	32	224	272
Magnesium (mg)	90	59	27
Iron (mg)	3	2	0.2

Source: Beckett, 2008: 197

The composition of chocolate mainly contains minerals such as protein, carbohydrates, fat, calcium, magnesium, iron, sodium and phosphorus. The amounts of these substances vary depending on the type of chocolate. Cocoa, the raw material of chocolate, is known to have positive effects on human health as it contains alkaloids such as phenolic antioxidants and theobromine (Tokuşoğlu, 2015, p. 2). As the first evidence that cocoa is beneficial to human health, it has been determined that the risk of arterial hypertension and the increase in death due to cardiovascular diseases of the Kuna natives living in Panama are reduced as a result of the cocoa they consume (Küçükyılmaz, 2021, p. 9). Cocoa products are polyphenolic compounds with antioxidant properties. It stands out with its fractions (e.g. flavonoids) (Duyan, 2023, p. 16).

Conclusion

Cocoa (chocolate), which was drunk with its hot, bitter and spicy aroma in the past, reached its current form by becoming solid and sweet over time with the addition of sugar by Europeans. The chocolates that consumed today have been created by adding cocoa mass, cocoa butter, sugar, and other substitute products, and have been turned into a sweet and solid edible product. The definition of chocolate varies depending on the chocolate type and ingredients. Chocolate basically consists of substances such as cocoa beans, refined sugar, cocoa butter, milk and dairy products, butter and lecithin. Chocolates can be grouped in different ways according to their components and forms. The carbohydrate, fat and protein content of chocolates vary depending on their type. Chocolate making stages basically consist of harvesting and processing, cleaning and roasting, grinding and turning into cocoa, mixing, thinning, conching, tempering, molding and packaging.

Although chocolate, whose raw material is cocoa, has many uses, knowing the properties of chocolate, working in accordance with its variety and characteristics, and knowingly applying processing techniques will increase the quality of the product. Choosing the right chocolate according to the product to be made, tempering processes, and carrying out the correct production processes are among the important factors in the successful emergence of the final product.

Today, chocolate has become a product that everyone can easily consume on special occasions, holidays, celebrations and in their daily lives, regardless of status, gender, race or age. Chocolate continues to attract attention today as it is a versatile product, increasing its applicability in many recipes. Many studies have shown that consuming chocolate has relaxing, pleasurable and happy effects (Özden, 2023, p. 1590–1592). As a result of current situations such as increasing consumer demands, market conditions, competition between companies, special food requirements, cost, alternative products, growth requirements of the business, elimination of deficiencies in existing products, increasing palate tastes, chocolate production and diversity have accelerated, and quality chocolate continues to be produced by developing different production techniques.

References

Akçiçek, A. (2023). *Tatlı ve Pastacılık.* (H. Koç, Ed.). Akademisyen Yayıncılık.

Alpözen, E. (2010). Dünden Bugüne Çikolata, *Gıda Yem Analiz Dergisi,6* 16–18.

Beckett, S. T. (2009). *Industrial Chocolate Manafacture and Use.* (4st ed.). Blackwell Publishing.

Beckett, S. T. (2008). *The Science of Chocolate,* (2nd ed.). Royal Society of Chemistry. https://doi.org/10.1039/9781847558053

Bingöl, İ. (2019). *Konçlama İşleminde Bazı Fiziksel Özelliklerin Değişim Kinetiğinin Farklı Çikolata Çeşitleri İçin Belirlenmesi.* [Yüksek Lisans Tezi, Siirt Üniversitesi]. Sosyal Bilimler Enstitüsü.

Cısse, V. & Yemişçioğlu, F. (2019). Cacao Butter and Alternatives Production. *Çukurova J. Agric. Food. Science 34*(1), 37–50.

Duyan, B. C. (2023). *Fonksiyonel Beyaz Çikolata Üretiminde Kapsüllenmiş Zeytin Yaprağının Kullanımı.* [Yüksek Lisans Tezi, Ondokuz Mayıs Üniversitesi]. Lisansüstü Eğitim Enstitüsü.

Ercik, C., İlhan, I. Keskin, S. N. (2023). Yöresel Ürünlerle İşlenmiş Gıdalara Yönelik Lezzet Algısının Tüketici Tutumları Üzerine Etkisi: Yeni Ürün Geliştirmede Dolgulu Çikolata Örneği. *Turizm ve Gastronomi Çalışmaları Dergisi, 11*(3), 2618–2638.

Ercik, C. (2023). *Yöresel Ürünlerle İşlenmiş Gıdalara Yönelik Lezzet Algısının Tüketici Tutumları Üzerine Etkisi: Yeni Ürün Geliştirmede Dolgulu Çikolata Örneği.* [Doktora Tezi, Nevşehir Hacı Bektaş Veli Üniversitesi]. Sosyal Bilimler Enstitüsü.

Gürsoy, D. (2021). *Deniz Gürsoy'un Gastronomi Tarihi.* Oğlak Yayıncılık.

Hastaoğlu, E. & Taşçı, Ş. (2021). Farklı İçerikli Çikolatalarda Bulunan Bileşenlerin Duyusal Olarak Tespit Edilebilirliğinin Araştırılması, *Turizm ve Gastronomi Çalışmaları Dergisi, 9*(3), 2203–2215. https://doi.org/10.21325/jotags.2021.888

Küçükyılmaz, K. (2021). *Sağlıklı Bireylerde Bitter Çikolata Tüketiminin Kan Basıncı ve Kan Parametrelerine Etkisinin Değerlendirilmesi,* [Yüksek Lisans Tezi, Doğu Akdeniz Üniversitesi]. Lisansüstü Eğitim Öğretim ve Araştırma Enstitüsü.

Memiş, Ş. (2023). Türkiye'nin İlk Küresel 'Yerel' Markası Nestle Osmanlı/Türk Olmayı Nasıl Bir Stratejiyle Başardı?, *Dumlupınar Üniversitesi Sosyal Bilimler Dergisi, 78,* 288–310. https://doi.org/10.51290/dpusbe.1343759

Özden, A. T. (2023). Çikolata Tüketimi ve Nostalji Eğilimi, *Nevşehir Hacıbektaş Veli Üniversitesi SBE Dergisi 13*(3), 1590–1608. https://doi.org/10.30783/nevsosbilen.1278210

Özkan, S. (2019). *Farklı Çikolata Çeşitlerinde Şeker Miktarının Azaltılmasının Duyusal Özelliklere Etkisinin İncelenmesi,* [Yüksek Lisans Tezi, İstanbul Teknik Üniversitesi]. Fen Bilimleri Enstitüsü.

Parlatır, B. (2019). *Çikolata Üretiminde Kakao Yerine Keçiboynuzu Unu Kullanımı.* [Yüksek Lisans Tezi, Ondokuz Mayıs Üniversitesi]. Fen Bilimleri Enstitüsü.

Polat, S. (2019). *Sakaroz Partikül Boyutunun, Sütlü Çikolata ve Kokolinde, Tekstür Su Aktivitesi ve Duyusal Özellikler Üzerindeki Etkisinin İncelenmesi.* [Yüksek Lisans Tezi, Siirt Üniversitesi]. Fen Bilimleri Enstitüsü.

Samancı, Ö. (2012). Chocolate, The Food of the Gods, *TSE Standard Economic and Technical Journal, 51*(604), 26–31.

Seçuk, B. (2020). *Artizan Çikolata Üretiminde Acı Ganaj Dolgulu Çikolata Geliştirilmesi ve Bazı Özelliklerinin Belirlenmesi.* [Yüksek Lisans Tezi, Necmettin Erbakan Üniversitesi]. Sosyal Bilimler Enstitüsü.

Sencer, G. M., Dadalı, C., Kaya, M., Çakır, B. & Elmacı, Y. (2018). Çikolatada Tat-Koku Emisyonu: Şeker Miktarını En aza İndirmek Amacıyla Farklı Aroma Gruplarının Kullanılması. *İstanbul Bilim Üniversitesi Florence Nightingale Tıp Dergisi 4*(3), 132–138. doi: 10.5606/fng.btd.2018.021

Snack and Bakery. (2024, May 29). *2023 Global Top 100 Candy Companies.* https://www.snackandbakery.com/candy-industry/2023/global-top-100-candy-companies#entireList

Sökmen, A. (2005). *Bazı Sükroz İkamelerinin Çikolatanın Reolojik Özelliklerine Etkisi.* [Yüksek Lisans Tezi, İstanbul Teknik Üniversitesi]. Fen Bilimleri Enstitüsü.

Tarrab, E. (2014). *Chocolate, Chocolate and More Chocolate.* Penn Publishing.

Tınmaz, O., Altunbağ, E. & Yıldırım, Ö. (2022). 1880–1980 Yılları Arasında Osmanlı ve Türkiye'de Yayımlanan Tarih Kitaplarında Çikolata ve Kakaonun Kullanımı, *Journal of Gastronomy, Hospitality and Travel 5*(1), 288–299. 10.33083/joghat.2022.131

Trademap. (2024, May 17). *List of expoters for the selected product in 2022 Product: 18 cocoa and cocoa preparations.* https://www.trademap.org/Country_SelProduct.aspx?nvpm=1%7c%7c%7c%7c%7c18%7c%7c%7c2%7c1%7c1%7c7c2%7c1%7c1%7c2%7c1%7c1%7c1

Trademap. (2024, May 17). *List of expoters for the selected product in 2022 Product: 1806 Chocolate and Order Food Preparations Containing Cocoa* https://www.trademap.org/Country_SelProduct.aspx?nvpm=1%7c%7c%7c%7c%7c1806%7c%7c%7c4%7c1%7c1%7c2%7c1%7c1%7c2%7c1%7c1%7c1

Tokuşoğlu, Ö. (2015). *Kakao, Çikolata ve Çikolatalı Ürünler Bilimi ve Teknolojisi.* Sidas Yayınları.

Varol, E. & Kara, H., H. (2021). Kakao Yağının Artizan Çikolata Yapımındaki Rolü ve Çikolata Kalite Kriterleri, *Safran Kültür ve Turizm Araştırmaları Dergisi. 4*(2), 200–220.

Uzun, B. (2019). *Türkiye Çikolatalı ve Şekerli Mamuller Sektörünün Uluslararası Rekabet Gücünün İncelenmesi* [Yüksek Lisans Tezi, İstanbul Ticaret Üniversitesi]. Dış Ticaret Enstitüsü.

Ünvay, A., F. (2019). İspanya'dan Osmanlı'ya: Bazı Yeni Kaynaklar Işığında Çikolatanın Tarihi Serüvenine Katkı. *Ahi Evran Üniversitesi Sosyal Bilimler Enstitüsü Dergisi, 5*(1), 16–27.

Gökhan Şalli[1] and Sercan Kadam[2]

Chapter 8 General Characteristics and Historical Processes of Turkish Cuisine

Introduction

The concept of nutrition is a biological action. This type of approach to nutrition refers to the process of meeting the nutritional and energy needs of human metabolism. However, the process of supplying the nutrients necessary to provide the energy in question, making them suitable for human consumption, and consumption behavior turns nutrition from being a purely biological action into a cultural phenomenon (Beşirli, 2017). Culture is defined as all the material and spiritual elements possessed by individuals in society. When the origins of human behavior and values are examined, it is seen that most of these elements are acquired as a result of learning. In this respect, culture is the whole of "complex elements that include individuals' knowledge, learning, beliefs, moral rules, traditions, customs and values" (Odabaşı and Barış, 2007: 314). Culture found in every moment of daily life; it has a pure and autonomous structure that operates as a living process. When the food habits of nations are examined, it is seen that there is differentiation among them and that this differentiation stems from culture. When individuals living in different countries and societies meet, one of the first topics of conversation is undoubtedly food culture. Turkish culinary culture is important in terms of being influenced by other cultures with which we interact and eating and drinking habits shaped according to geographical conditions. Culinary culture, which bears the traces of the agricultural products grown in the region, the region's geography, climate and cultural structure, is the culture of the people living in that region. It is also closely related to people's lifestyles (Bayram and Saklı, 2021: 592).

Turkish cuisine is an important element of Turkish culture and one of the few cuisines of the universal cultural environment. Turkish culinary culture

---

1   Lecturer, Anadolu University, Eskisehir Vocational School, Department of Culinary, gsalli@anadolu.edu.tr
2   Lecturer, Bülent Ecevit University, Devrek Vocational School, Department of Culinary, sercan.kadam@beun.edu.tr

owes its richness to historical events, geographical conditions, cultural, ecological and economic structure, traditions and customs, and interaction with
other universal cultures throughout history. Turkish cuisine, foods and beverages used by people living in Turkey in their diet, their preparation, cooking
and preservation; It is defined as the tools, equipment and techniques required
for these processes, as well as eating habits and all practices and beliefs that
develop around the kitchen (Sürücüoğlu and Özçelik, 2008). During its
centuries-long development, Turkish cuisine has created a unique culinary
culture with its food diversity, cooking techniques, table settings, service methods and foods compiled for winter (Arman, 2011). Turkish Cuisine, which has
one of the richest culinary cultures in the world, generally includes stews prepared using grains, meat and various vegetables, soups, dishes made with olive
oil, dishes made with local herbs, and sweet and salty pastries. This cuisine
has also created unique healthy foods such as molasses, yoghurt, tarhana and
bulgur. This rich food and beverage culture, where each region produces its
own special tastes, stands out especially on important days, invitations and
ceremonies. Turkish Cuisine offers an example of a healthy and balanced diet
in terms of the variety of seasons, variety of products and ability to satisfy the
palate, as well as the dishes and various products it contains (Aydoğdu and
Mızrak, 2017).

In addition to having a deep-rooted history, the Turkish nation also has a rich
cultural structure. In Turkish cuisine, on the one hand, the influences of steppe
culture and, on the other hand, the favorable diversity of the Mediterranean
geography are included in the culinary culture. While one reason for the richness
of Turkish cuisine is the abundance and diversity of food and beverage items,
another reason can be said to be the fact that the Turks have an ancient history
(Durlu Özkaya and Cömert, 2017: 7).

The emergence of Turks on the stage of history begins in the Central Asian
region. Turks, who mostly adopted a nomadic lifestyle in this region, later
reached Anatolia, causing their culinary culture to enrich and their eating
and drinking habits to undergo some changes. The Central Asian Turks,
Seljuk and Ottoman Empire periods have a great influence on the formation
of Turkish Cuisine. In addition, the civilizations that lived in Turkey have
a great influence on the shaping and enrichment of today's Turkish cuisine
(Güler and Olgaç, 2010). At this stage, the structure of Turkish culinary culture can be examined in five periods. Firstly, the Central Asian Turkish cuisine before Islam and under the influence of Islam, Seljuk cuisine, Ottoman
cuisine, Republic Period cuisine and finally the Modern Period cuisine were
examined in this study.

Cuisine of the Pre-Islamic Central Asian Period

In the pre-Islamic period, Turks spread over a wide geography, starting from Central Asia, including the Caucasus, the northern regions of the Black Sea and the plains of Hungary. Agriculture and animal husbandry stand out among economic sources of income. The nomadic horse culture that was born and developed in these lands has become the way of life of the Turks. Turks, who had herds of horses and sheep, migrated to large pastures in the spring and descended to the arid valleys and especially river banks in the autumn. Since they built their own tents and lived there, they had no difficulty in moving places. In addition, they produced their own beds and necessary clothing (Göde et al., 2021). In this period, when horse-riding nomadic culture was dominant, the first foods of the Turks were products made from wheat and milk, such as flour and yoghurt, and the meat of animals such as horses and sheep, which they also used for riding, and their first drinks; It consisted of kumiss (a fermented drink prepared from mare's milk). In addition, vinegar, molasses and wine made from grapes were consumed by the Turks during this period (Kızıldemir et al., 2017). In Turkish cuisine, milk is also consumed with dairy products such as oil, cheese, yoghurt, ayran, cottage cheese, and by making dishes with milk yoghurt or using it in milk desserts (Güler, 2010). Livestock has been the most important economic resource that Turks have relied on throughout history. In Central Asia, A.D. VI. and VIII. According to the findings obtained from the graves dating back to the 19th century, it was concluded that sheep and horse meat were eaten the most, and in addition to these, beef and deer meat were also consumed. Gradually over time, the consumption of horse meat and venison completely disappeared. VIII. Finding bird and fish remains in graves built after the 11th century is an indication of a change in food culture (Ögel, 1982).

It is known that in addition to the meat of the slaughtered animal, its offal, especially the liver, head, spleen, heart, kidney, tripe, brain and large intestine, are also used. The meat and offal of the slaughtered animal were cooked in earthen wells called "tandoor" or by turning them over a fire. In addition, to preserve the meat, in the autumn and winter months, animals are slaughtered, the meat is cut into small pieces, then cooked with tail fat, and then stuffed into cubes and stored in roasting form. Foods such as roasting, pastrami and sausage, which are obtained by salting and seasoning meat and drying it on a hanger, are still made in villages today as preparations for winter (Sürücüoğlu and Özçelik, 2008). The second economic resource that the Turks relied on was wheat. Pastries made with wheat flour have always been at the forefront (Güler, 2010). In addition to wheat, barley, millet, vetch, sesame and rice are among the grains cultivated. It is also known that the Oghuz tribe of the Turks preferred a settled life and engaged in agriculture and fishing during this period. The existence of agriculture among the Turks dates back to B.C. It dates back to the mid-1st century. The tools called "Crushed Stones" that have emerged in kurgans since this date are an indication that Turks have been farming grain since ancient times (Sürücüoğlu and Özçelik, 2008). It is understood that the value Turks attach to kitchen tools and equipment is evident from the way they cook meat in religious ceremonies and feasts in special ceremonies since Central Asia. The discovery of flat-bottomed, wide-mouthed handleless vessels and drinking glasses found in excavations in Central Asia shows that the Turks had a developed culinary culture even at that time. Various other cups, small knives, spoons, handled casseroles and different types of kitchen utensils found in Central Asia are also an indication of this (Abalı, 2017).

Cuisine of the Islamic Period and Seljuk Principalities Period

As a result of nomadic life, the Seljuks came to Mesopotamia and Anatolia and were interested in agriculture due to the fertile soil structure. During this period, people who realized that their nutritional needs could be met more easily from these fertile lands settled in these regions. With the transition to settled life, Turkish culinary culture has developed more. Although there are many factors that affect the eating and drinking habits and culinary culture of a society, one of them is the agricultural products grown in the region (Bayram, 2021: 291). With the effect of settling down, agricultural products have been produced and consumed more frequently, especially when compared to nomadic life. This society, which has adopted Islam, prefers a simple life away from ostentation, which limits access to information about the food culture of the Seljuk period in this period we live in (Şahin, 2008). At that time, they built a section in their homes where meals were prepared, just like today, and they called this place aslık. They consumed the food in two meals and called these meals mid-morning and dinner. Since it was around noon in the morning, they consumed foods that made them full, such as pastries. The existence of a meal called Kuşluk in Turkish cuisine in the past led to the creation of such a meal in the coming years. Today, the mid-morning meal is universally used under the name brunch. (Demirgül, 2018: 111). As in Central Asian Turks, meat consumption is very high in this period. Sheep and goat meat are consumed very frequently. Biryan is also used in dishes made with meat. Büryan kebab is a dish from this period that has survived to this day. It is made very frequently especially in Siirt and Bitlis regions and has become identified with these regions. The richness of Turkish culinary culture and the fact that there are dishes from that period that have survived to the present day is proof of how deep-rooted and diverse the cuisine is. Another dish that was made during this period and is still made today is toyga soup, tattoo, etc. The products were also made at that time and are included in today's cuisine (Demirgül, 2018: 111). During the Seljuk period, they were not a society that consumed as much vegetables as in previous periods. Especially in the culinary culture of this period, offal consumption is very high. During this period, there are table manners rules that have survived to this day. In the culinary culture of this period, the table was laid out to prevent the pieces of bread from spilling on the floor while eating, and the meal was eaten from the top. Rules such as not sitting at the table before the adults sit down as it is today, and not starting the meal before the adults start, are the rules in the culinary culture of this period (Kızıldemir et al., 2014: 197).

Seljuk cuisine has become very enriched by passing through the selective sieve of the Islamic religion both the tradition it has and the advantages that Anatolia has brought to them, where it migrated. As a continuation of the nomadic tradition, meat, milk and dairy products, which have been widely consumed among the Turks for a long time, as well as grain and flour products, dishes made from different types of vegetables, a very rich fruit culture, desserts, sherbets and pickles, constituted the main ingredients of the cuisine of the period (Şahin, 2008; Közleme, 2012: 125). Sherbets made from various fruits, honey or sugar were among the most widely consumed beverages during the Anatolian Seljuk and Principality periods. These sherbets, consumed by all segments of the population, were flavored with various spices. Families with trees such as apricots, grapes and pomegranates in their gardens or with several beehives usually produced their own sherbet. In big cities, there were sherbet shops selling sherbet in glasses. In addition to sherbet, ayran was the most consumed beverage (Şahin, 2008).

Ottoman Era Cuisine

The Ottoman Empire is one of the empires that holds an important place in history, where a wide variety of cultures, languages and religions lived together for centuries. Although it hosted many cultures together, the culinary culture of the empire, the majority of which was created by the Turks, is still one of the richest cuisines that are discussed and researched today. Chinese cuisine, like the Ottoman cuisine, is one of the cuisines that has a very old history and is very attached to its traditions. However, the fact that the Chinese Empire was based on a monocultural society ensured that its cuisine remained loyal to traditions and the recipes were preserved until today (Şavkay, 2000). The Ottoman sultans made it possible for the ethnic groups living in their lands to practice their religion, language and culture freely. Thus, Ottoman cuisine became richer with this tolerance and the traditions brought by other cultures. Considering the vastness of its land, the diversity and richness of water and vegetation has taken its place in history as one of the richest cuisines in terms of gastro-geography. The foundations of Ottoman cuisine are based on Turkish culinary tradition and Islamic understanding. Turkish culinary understanding was created based on the "meat-milk-dairy products" triangle; With the influence of Islamic understanding, alcohol was kept away from this cuisine (Şavkay, 2000).

The development of the Ottoman Empire was also reflected in Turkish Culinary culture. 15th century the meals are few and simple in variety; It experienced its most glorious years in the 16th century. This glorious period continued in the 17th and 18th centuries, but the impoverishment of the Ottoman Empire in the 19th century also affected the Turkish Culinary culture. Another reason why Turkish Culinary culture developed during the Ottoman Empire was that the Ottoman Empire dominated a very wide geographical area and as a result, it was introduced to and influenced by many different cultures (Tuncel, 2000:50). Kitchen in the Ottoman Empire is an important part of Palace life. The Sultan, his officials, and the nobles saw gathering around a table as a social activity, so the Palace kitchen has always been a place seeking innovations and producing delicious and rich dishes. Chefs competed with each other to produce dishes that the sultan's officials liked and to make the banquets more spectacular, contributing to the enrichment of Turkish culinary culture (Ciğerim, 2001:56). During the Ottoman Empire, Turkish culinary culture was divided into two: Palace cuisine and Folk cuisine. The palace kitchen is the sumptuous tables prepared for the Sultan, the Valide Sultan and the people of the Divan. In order to feed the crowded palace circle, cooks invented new dishes. With a staff of up to 1200, they tried to meet not only the palace surroundings but also the food needs of the guests (Yılmaz, 2002:53). The development of the palace cuisine started when Mehmet the Conqueror built new kitchens in the Topkapı Palace in the second half of the 15th century (Mussmann and Pahalı, 1994:17). These kitchens, overlooking the Marmara Sea and attracting attention with their numerous domes and chimneys, were called "New Palace" (Gürkan, 2007:5). With the conquest of Istanbul by Mehmet the Conqueror in 1453, great changes took place in the Ottoman cuisine in the palace. Consumption of seafood increased significantly during this period. Also in this period, with the Fatih Code, eating rules began to be implemented for the first time in the Ottomans. During the reign of Sultan Mehmet the Conqueror, emphasis was placed on the simplicity and satisfyingness of the food rather than its variety. Among the dishes served to the officials in the palace were cabbage soup, baklava, biryani with yoghurt and spinach, yoghurt dessert with molasses, chard and ayran with yoghurt, and sherbet (Ünver, 1981). As the Ottomans improved their relations with the West in the 19th century, our culinary culture began to be influenced by Europe. First, innovations in table manners began, and later on, tables instead of trays, chairs instead of cushions, plates that everyone used instead of common pots, and forks, knives and water dishes began to be used in palaces. Although it was not as spectacular as the Palace cuisine during the Ottoman Empire, the folk cuisine was also very rich in terms of taste and variety. The people, who have a hospitable nature, have made great efforts to make their guests enjoy the prepared meals and have created special flavors for this purpose.

During the Ottoman period, cuisine developed on three pillars. These; palaces, mansions and chefs, resulting in the famous Turkish cuisine in Istanbul. The kitchen in the Ottoman Palace was an important part of palace life. The palace kitchen has always made innovations, created many dishes, and has become a place where delicious and rich varieties are served. The six-century history of the Ottoman Empire has an important place in the formation of Turkish culinary culture. In addition, the richness of the geography of the Empire, which spanned three continents and hosted different cultures and beliefs, made this culture original and unique (Samancı and Croxford, 2006). In local cuisines in Anatolia, meat and meat dishes interact with each other and create a new synthesis. Olive oil and fish from the Aegean islands and coasts, meat dishes, appetizers and sherbet desserts from the south all came together in these lands under the influence of Byzantine and Roman culinary culture. The Ottoman lands reaching the Middle East, Southern Mediterranean and Europe further expanded the scope of Anatolian Food culture (Gürsoy, 1995).

Republic Era Cuisine

To examine the cuisine of the Republican period, it is generally divided into two main categories: Istanbul cuisine and Anatolian cuisine. These two cuisines have played an important role in the development of Turkish cuisine since the first years of the Republic. Istanbul cuisine was featured more in written sources, especially in the first years of the Republic. This cuisine is nourished by the historical and cultural riches of Istanbul, the capital of the Ottoman Empire. Istanbul cuisine was influenced by the palace cuisine and incorporated traditional Ottoman dishes. At the same time, the multicultural structure of Istanbul has brought diversity to the city's cuisine (Akın et al., 2015; Solmaz and Altıner,

2018). The fact that Istanbul has been the capital of various great states throughout history has caused this unique city to have a multinational and multicultural structure. This richness was also reflected in Istanbul cuisine and shaped
the basic features of this culinary culture. Among the main characteristics of
Istanbul cuisine, it is important that the meals served are both satisfying and
light. This feature emerged as a result of Istanbul hosting immigrants from different cultures throughout history and influencing the cuisines of these cultures.
Istanbul cuisine is known for its healthy and delicious dishes and offers a visual
feast to the tables. In addition, the fact that Istanbul is a large trade center has
enabled the availability of a wide variety of food products in the city. Istanbul's
ports have allowed ingredients from all over the world to enter this cuisine. This
has enriched Istanbul cuisine and allowed various tastes to come together. While
Istanbul cuisine carries the legacy of the Ottoman Empire, it carries traces from
all over Anatolia along with migrations. For this reason, Istanbul cuisine is the
meeting point of many different cultures and tastes. It can be said that this rich
cuisine, which continues to influence the cuisines of Turkey and even neighboring countries, offers a perfect city model with the historical and cultural richness
of Istanbul. (Kızıldemir et al., 2014).

On the other hand, Anatolian cuisine was a major factor in the formation
of dishes during the Republic of Turkey period. This cuisine reflects the rich
agricultural products, local flavors and traditional dishes of Anatolia. During
the Republic of Turkey period, meals were formed as a result of the blending
and interaction of the culinary cultures of various communities and states that
lived in different regions of Anatolia. In Anatolian cuisine, at the beginning of
the Republican period, in a period when communication and technological
developments were limited, dishes specific to certain regions were preserved and
traditional flavors were widely consumed in limited geographical areas. Since
communication tools were limited in this period, recipes and cooking methods
were generally limited to oral traditions and information passed down from generation to generation within the family. However, the increasing prevalence of
communication and technological developments in the following years allowed
local dishes from different regions of Anatolia to be known and prepared in
other regions as well. With these developments, Anatolian cuisine has reached a
wider audience, and different local dishes have become popular in other regions
as well (Akın et al., 2015). Anatolian cuisine reflects a rich and diverse culinary
culture. Factors such as table setting, cooking methods and foods prepared for
winter emphasize the diversity and richness of this cuisine. For this reason, it is
not possible to talk about a homogeneous culinary culture; because Anatolian
cuisine has been shaped by the interaction of communities and cultures that

have lived in different geographical regions throughout history. The cornerstone of Anatolian cuisine is folk cuisine.

Folk cuisine may differ in rural and urban areas. In rural areas, traditional table manners still continue on the ground or on trays. This is a reflection of the traditional lifestyle. People engaged in agriculture and animal husbandry in rural areas generally cook with the ingredients they produce (Kızıldemir et al., 2014). The most consumed food by Turks is wheat, and bulgur and bulgur made from it are also present in the cuisine of this period. The second important agricultural product is rice. Corn is generally consumed in the Black Sea region. Wheat flour is generally used in bread making. In Turkish cuisine, meat was considered a prestige food even during the Republic period. The meat used in cuisine is mutton, but it is not as common as it used to be. The main reason for this is the deterioration of the economic situation of many Turks. During this period, meat is consumed only at banquets and special occasions. Even if meat is used, it is mostly used in small amounts and in combination with various vegetables and grains. Meat consumption is as low in rural areas as in urban areas (Merdol, 1997). Foreign migrations that started in the 1950s led to an increase in Turkey's proximity to western culture, and this change was also reflected in kitchen utensils and food culture. In the same period, the rapidly increasing urbanization phenomenon also significantly affected the culinary culture. The urbanization process has changed traditional food preparation and consumption habits. During this period, in the modernizing society, the time spent on cooking decreased and the profile of women producing food at home was replaced by working women. Additionally, families living in apartments had to prepare meals in narrow spaces. This has made the food preparation process more practical and faster (Dilsiz, 2010).

Modern Period Cuisine

The modernization process in Turkey accelerated especially during the Republican period, and this transformation caused a serious disconnection with traditional values. This disconnection has been felt in many areas of life, and the food and beverage culture has also been affected by this. However, tradesmen and craftsmen, like small businesses, have not completely lost their ties with tradition. In the 1960s, there were very few places such as steakhouses, kebab shops and ocakbaşı in Istanbul. However, with the arrival of Black Sea pita makers to Istanbul, restaurants that continue the Anatolian tradition also gained popularity in the city. Later, places selling kebab and lahmacun began to appear in almost every district. After 1983, the increase in the living standards of the Turkish people led to pub-type bars becoming widespread, as in England. In addition, influenced by world cuisine, Turkey witnessed the opening of ethnic restaurants serving Italian, French, Japanese and Chinese cuisine. During this period, five-star international chain hotels and restaurants began to operate in Turkey. This situation enabled the Turkish food and beverage industry to become more competitive internationally (Gürsoy, 2013). As a result, the modernization process in Turkey has caused major changes in the food and beverage culture. In addition to traditional Turkish cuisine, many new venues have opened that are influenced by world cuisine and offer international tastes. This contributed to the diversification of Turkey's food culture and its recognition in the international arena. However, local tastes such as traditional Turkish dishes and street foods are still of great importance.

On the other hand, the development of industry and the development of techniques during the republic period affected the nutritional habits in our country, as in the rest of the world (Sürücüoğlu and Özçelik, 2008). With the development of trade and mass media, methods of preserving and accessing foods out of season have also been developed (Merdol, 1998). The meals that were eaten for two meals during the nomadic period of the Turks increased to three meals during this period. In addition, the development of industry and technology and the increasing costs changed by living conditions have brought about the entry of women into working life. These conditions have led to the emergence of the need to eat in a short time and outside the home, such as fast food and restaurants. In addition, during the socio-cultural change process, the ready-made food industry also developed in our country due to the increase in people living alone in this period (Önçel, 2015).

During this period, the use of animal fats decreased for health reasons and the use of sunflower, olive oil and margarine increased. Developments in culinary culture have also occurred with the increase in ready-made foods such as canned food and food additives. Twentieth century the fact that the products of Genetically Modified Organisms have started to be used in foods in recent years has caused negativities in the preservation and transfer of both foods and traditional culinary culture to future generations. While the use of sauce in meals is low, the use of excessive sauce, the use of food additives and sweeteners, and the fact that the dishes are cooked in natural gas and electric ovens instead of tandoori or black ovens have caused the traditional Anatolian culinary culture to change and difficulties in preserving it and transferring it to the next generations (Akın et al., 2015: 45). Fast-paced living conditions and fast-paced eating habits were included in the culinary culture of the Republican period. This eating habit, which has an impact all over the world, is known as fast food. This eating habit, which has a lot of consumption in this period, is not preferred in terms of health and does not constitute a nutritional culture suitable for our culinary culture.

Although developments in industry seem to have overtaken traditional cuisine, the increase in the level of education in societies and the public's greater awareness of healthy living have led to changes in eating habits in the process. For example, butter or "clarified butter", which was preferred in the past, was replaced first by margarine and later by olive oil and other oils, the despised beef, lamb and mutton were replaced, and white bread, the indicator of wealth, was replaced by natural village breads. (Özçelik and Sürücüoğlu 2007). The establishment of metropolitan cities within the borders of the country and the rapidly increasing population in these cities due to migration every year have led to changes in consumption habits inside and outside the home. While the diet based on fast consumption, called fast food, has started to be preferred in metropolitan cities, it has also given a new identity to street food, which we define as fast food. Food products such as gevrek, simit, boyoz, boza or raw meatballs, which we are accustomed to being sold by mobile carts, can now be easily purchased from chain sales points. The concept of restaurant has also developed rapidly and gone beyond the presentation of home-style meals, which we call tradesmen restaurants, and has enabled the restaurant concept in Europe to be established in Turkish cuisine. These types of restaurants, which have made changes in the presentation style of Turkish cuisine, have managed to become among the examples that showcase Turkish cuisine to the world today. Recently, gastronomy-themed festivals and organizations have increased and started to contribute to the development of Turkish cuisine (Saklı and Bayram, 2021: 651).

General Features of Turkish Cuisine

Although Turkish cuisine has a rich structure, it also has some unique features. In this context, the general characteristics of Turkish cuisine can be listed as follows (Arlı, 1982; Doğdubay and Giritlioğlu, 2011:446):

1. Turkish cuisine is generally based on agricultural and animal products.
2. Our meals vary depending on the geographical regions where our people live.
3. Turkish food varies according to social structure throughout its historical development.
4. Turkish dishes vary according to special occasions and ceremonies.
5. Traditions, customs and religious beliefs have affected food types.

6. In Turkish cuisine, habits play an important role in food.
7. Bread has a very important place.
8. Butter, tallow, tail fat and olive oil are used in significant amounts, especially in the Aegean region.
9. Although there are many types of food, pastries come first.
10. The place of bulgur is important.
11. Yogurt is very important in Turkish cuisine.
12. Although there are various kebabs, there are juicy meat dishes called stew.
13. Onion is used both in the preparation of meals and as a salad ingredient.
14. Although there are many types of vegetables, it is common to cook them with onions, tomato paste or tomatoes along with meat.
15. The use of spices and herbs such as parsley, dill and mint is common in meals.
16. In Turkish cuisine, decoration is not given much importance. Care is taken to ensure that the food tastes more than it looks. However, recently the art of plate decoration and painting has just begun to develop.
17. The use of sauce is not included in Turkish cuisine. Instead of sauce, tomato paste and food juices are used.
18. In Turkish cuisine, dishes are flavored with fruits or dried fruits, and these fruits are often cooked in oil and consumed as food.
19. Molasses is used as a sweetener in desserts.

Factors Affecting the Formation of Turkish Culinary Culture

It is seen that the changes experienced in Turkish cuisine from past to present are due to various reasons and the changes continue. When examining the eating and drinking habits of Turks, it is seen that the following factors are effective (Güler, 2010:26).

• Effect of Agricultural Structure and Nomadic Culture
• Influence of Other Societies
• Differentiation According to Socio-Economic Level
• Behavior Patterns in Turks
• Dishes Difference by Region
• Tradition of Community Eating

In addition to these mentioned effects, factors such as geographical discoveries, the influence of today's mass media and the development of the food industry have also been effective in the change and development of Turkish culinary culture.

Results

It is seen that Turkish food culture has original and unique values thanks to the synthesis of physical and social identity differences of the civilizations living within it. As mentioned, Turkish culture contains a wide range of accumulations developed by the articulation of various civilizations. Turkish cuisine was influenced by many different culinary cultures in this geography during the Ottoman period, and as a result, it created a rich culinary culture. The ruins found in Çatalhöyük were created by the intersection of Turkish culinary culture with the Central Asian steppes and Anatolian civilizations. Central Asian Turks were mostly engaged in agriculture and animal husbandry. Among the dishes, pastries made from wheat flour came to the fore. Meat, flour and oil were the basic ingredients of meals in the Turkish culinary culture of the Seljuk period. During the Seljuk period, food varieties were developed by adding or mixing one food item to another, using various cooking methods. During the Ottoman period, the cuisine developed on the basis of three elements: palace/mansion and cooks, thus creating the famous Turkish cuisine in Istanbul. For Ottoman Turks, the kitchen was an important part of palace life. The Turks, who adopted a nomadic lifestyle like many civilizations, migrated during the periods of history known as Central Asia and settled in Mesopotamia and Anatolia, and the periods of the Principalities and Seljuks, the Ottoman Empire and the Republic of Turkey took place. In these different periods, Turks merged with many civilizations. It has been influenced by many different culinary cultures in this geography, and as a result, it has created a highly developed and evolved cultural heritage.

The fact that Anatolia was the first region where agricultural activities began, served as a bridge between three continents, and witnessed the interaction of different cultures throughout history played a major role in making Turkish cuisine one of the best cuisines in the world in terms of product variety and taste. Turkish culinary culture reflects the characteristics of the geography in which it develops. For the nomadic Old Turkish states, the need for food was met as a result of great sacrifices. Storing food as well as cooking it has been a problem for the Turks who have always lived as nomads. For the Ancient Turks who lived on horseback, the fastest meal was the meal cooked over a naked fire. With the transition to a settled lifestyle, the diversity of food products has increased and the way has been opened for growing healthy food. In this period when cattle breeding began, nutritional habits began to change gradually. Ottoman period palace cuisine was a turning point in Turkish culinary culture. Ottoman cuisine, an imperial cuisine, did not hesitate to open its doors to the cultures of groups belonging to different races and religions. Turkish culinary culture, which has evolved over hundreds of years and has survived to the present day, has created a rich mosaic with the cultures of three continents and has carried this diversity to the present day.

References

Abalı, I. (2017). "Kitchen Utensils in the Context of Their Functions". *Ulakbilge*, 5 (10): 383–392.

Akın, G., Özkoçak, V. & Gültekin, T. (2015). Development of Traditional Anatolian Culinary Culture from Past to Present. Ankara University Faculty of Languages, History and Geography Journal of Anthropology, 30, 33–51.

Anadolu Agency. (2022). From: https://www.aa.com.tr/tr/yasam/bursa-ovasin-da-hasadi-suren-santa-maria-armudu-dalinda-satiliyor/2659683 Accessed on: 26.05.2024.

Arlı, M. (1982). "Turkish Cuisine in a General Overview" Symposium Proceedings, 31 October-1 November, Ankara: Ankara University Press.

Arman, A. (2011). "Problem of Promotion of Turkish Culinary Culture: The Example of Mengen Cuisine". Master's Thesis, Düzce University Institute of Social Sciences, Düzce, 116.

Aydoğdu, A. & Mızrak, M. (2017). Historical Association of Azerbaijan and Türkiye Culinary Culture and Determination of Its Current Situation. *International Journal of Turkish World Tourism Research*, 2(1), 15– 25.

Bayram, F. (2021). Dessert, Cake and Pastry Concepts, Principles and Sample Applications, Alper KURNAZ, Serkan ŞENGÜL, Ed., Detay Publishing House, Ankara, 291–319.

Bayram, F. & Saklı, B. A. (2021). Türkiye Flavor Routes, İrfan YAZICIOĞLU, Ümit SORMAZ, Cihan CANBOLAT, Ed., Detay Publishing House, Ankara, ss. 592–602, 2021.

Beşirli, H. (2017). Sociology of Food Sociological Perspective on Food and Cuisine. Phoenix Publishing House.

Ciğerim, N. (2001). Research on Turkish Culinary Culture: A Look at the Development and Interaction of Western and Turkish Cuisine and the Place of Turkish Cuisine in Food and Beverage Services. Publication 28, Ankara.

Demirgül, F. (2018). Turkish Cuisine from Tent to Palace. *International Journal of Turkish World Tourism Research*, 3(1), 105–125.

Dilsiz, B. (2010). Gastronomy and Tourism in Turkey (Istanbul example) [Master's Thesis]. Istanbul University.

Doğdubay, M. & Giritlioğlu, İ. (2011), Culinary Tourism, (Editors: Necdet Hacıoğlu and Cevdet Avcıkurt), Touristic Product Diversification, 2nd Edition, Ankara: Nobel Publishing.

Durlu-Özkaya, F. & Cömert, M (2017). Journey to Turkish Cuisine. Ankara: Detay Publishing, 33–146.

Göde, G., Kayaardı, S., Uyarcan, M. & Söbeli, C. (2021). Change of Turkish Food Culture and Nutrition Habits in the Development Process of History. *Food and Health*, 7(3), 216–226.

Güler, S. (2010). "Turkish Culinary Culture and Eating Habits". *Dumlupınar University Journal of Social Sciences*, 26: 24–30.

Güler, S. & Olgaç, S. (2010), "Opinions of Undergraduate Students on the Promotion and Marketing of Turkish Cuisine" (Anadolu University School of Tourism and Hotel Management Example), *Dumlupınar University Journal of Social Sciences*, 28, 227–238.

Gürkan, O.T. (2007). Local Turkish Cuisine, Istanbul: Yaylim Publishing.

Gursoy, D. (1995). The Evolution of Food and Cooking. Istanbul: Sofra Yemek Production and Service Inc., Kurum Publishing.

Gürsoy, D. (2013). Let's Eat and Drink, Let's Know Its History Gastronomy from Past to Today. Istanbul: Oğlak Publishing.

Kızıldemir Ö., Öztürk, E. & Sarıışık, M. (2017). "Characteristics of Turkish Culinary Culture and Changes in the Republican Era". VI. National II: International Eastern Mediterranean Tourism Symposium, 14–15 April, 349–356, Gaziantep.

Kızıldemir, Ö., Öztürk, E. & Sarıışık, M. (2014). Changes in the Historical Development of Turkish Culinary Culture. *AIBU Social Sciences Institute Journal*. 14(3), 191–210.

Közleme, O. (2012). Turkish Culinary Culture and Religion [Doctoral Thesis]. Marmara University.

Merdol, T. K. (1997). Eating Habits of Turks in the Eyes of Foreigners. Among Researches on Turkish Culinary Culture (119–138) Takav Printing House.

Merdol, T.K. (1998). "Societies and Nutrition Habits from History to the Present", Research on Turkish Culinary Culture, Turkish Folk Culture Research and Promotion Foundation Publications Publication No: 22, p. 135–143.

Mussmann, K.D. & Pahalı, C. (1994). Culinary Services, Anadolu University Open Education Faculty Publications Publication No: 397, Eskişehir.

Odabaşı, Y. & Barış, G. (2007). Consumer Behavior. Istanbul: MediaCat.

Ögel, B. (1982). "Development of Turkish Cuisine and Turkish Historical Traditions", Turkish Cuisine Symposium Proceedings, Ministry of Culture and

Tourism, National Folklore Research Department Publications, Ankara, 15–18.

Önçel, S. (2015). "Evaluations on Turkish Cuisine and Its Future" *Journal of Tourism and Gastronomy Studies.* 3(4), 33–44.

Özçelik, A. & Sürücüoğlu, M. (2007). Historical Development of Turkish Cuisine and Nutrition Culture. http://www.ayk.gov.tr/ Access Date: 11 April 2024.

Saklı, B. A. & Bayram, F. (2021). Türkiye Flavor Routes, İrfan YAZICIOĞLU, Ümit SORMAZ, Cihan CANBOLAT, Ed., Detay Publishing House, Ankara, ss. 648–659.

Samancı, Ö. & Croxford, S. (2006). XIX. Century Istanbul Cuisine. Medyatik Publications, Istanbul.

Solmaz, Y. & Altıner, D. D. (2018). An Evaluation on Turkish Culinary Culture and Nutrition Habits. *Safran Journal of Culture and Tourism Research,* 1(3), 108–124.

Sürücüoğlu, M. S. & Özçelik, A. Ö. (2008). Historical development of Turkish cuisine and nutrition culture. ICANAS Congress: Proceedings (1289–1310) Material Culture III. Skin. Ataturk Culture, Language and History Higher Institution Publications.

Şahin, H. (2008). Turkish Seljuk and Principality period cuisine. In Turkish cuisine (39–55) Ministry of Culture and Tourism Publications.

Şavkay, T. (2000). Ottoman Kitchen. Istanbul: Detay Publishing House.

Tuncel, M. (2000). "Adaptation of FastFood System to Turkish Cuisine and an Practices", Unpublished Master's Thesis, Anadolu University Social Sciences Institute Tourism and Hotel Management Department, Eskişehir.

Ünver, A. S. (1981). Meal Procedures and Times in the Seljuks, Principalities and Ottomans. Turkish Cuisine Symposium Proceedings. Ankara: Culture and Tourism.

Yilmaz, A. (2002). Our Workplace is Kitchen Our Profession is Cooking Our Art, Istanbul.

Betül Öztürk[1], Didem Tiraş[2], and Karahan Kara[3]

Chapter 9 Phygitalization in Gastronomy

Introduction

The advent of rapidly developing and changing technology and digital transformation has brought humanity to the threshold of the fourth industrial revolution, which began with the invention of the steam engine in 1760. The initial phase, which was particularly evident in the textile and steel industries, marked the shift from an agrarian and feudal social order to the advent of the factory as the dominant mode of production, accompanied by the emergence of the railroad as the primary mode of transportation. This period, which commenced in 1900, marked the beginning of the second industrial revolution. The advent of internal combustion engines that utilised petroleum and electricity as power sources signified the start of a new era of rapid industrialisation. It is notable that the third industrial revolution commenced in 1960, marking a transition to the integration of information technology and the use of electric power for mass production. The fourth industrial revolution is currently in progress, encompassing computer-generated product designs and internal dimensional printing (Prisecaru, 2016).

These developments have had a profound impact on the industries concerned, as well as on tourism and gastronomy. This has not only led to a digital transformation with the help of the smart technology but also a new term: phygital gastronomy. The digital transformation has not only been integrated into the kitchen or food-beverage business, but consumers have also started to be interested in experiencing the technological innovation in the gastronomy field just like they did in the other industries (Verhoef et al., 2021). In order to optimise the satisfaction of the senses, which are crucial for the food and beverage industry, various innovations have been conducted in the field of phygitalization, utilising creative services or experiences for the consumers. This chapter presents a

---

1 Assistant Professor, Izmir University of Economics, School of Applied Management Sciences, Department of Gastronomy and Culinary Arts, betul.ozturk@ieu.edu.tr
2 Research Assistant, Izmir University of Economics, School of Applied Management Sciences, Department of Gastronomy and Culinary Arts, didem.tıras@ieu.edu.tr
3 Research Assistant, Izmir University of Economics, School of Applied Management Sciences, Department of Gastronomy and Culinary Arts, karahan.kara@ieu.edu.tr

definition of phygital gastronomy and an analysis of the progression of digital transformation, with an analogy to phygital transformation. It also presents the most effective global practices in this field. In order to observe the visuality and the experiences of the gastronomy industry applications, the web addresses were provided for the readers.

The Phygital Concept

The term "phygital" was first proposed by the Australian marketing agency, Momentum, in 2013 (Belghiti et al., 2017, Mele & Russo Spena, 2022) to describe a strategy that transcends the boundaries of digital marketing and as being a new form of a hybrid consumption experience (Klaus, 2021). Information technology is employed to create satisfied and profitable customer experiences that direct customers to navigate between online and offline offerings (Batat, 2022). Furthermore, it is employed to create a digital environment that becomes a physical reality, thus providing a tool for more enriched and enjoyable communication for the users (Nofal et al., 2017).

Augmented reality (AR), virtual reality (VR), mixed reality (MR), Internet of Thing (IoT), artificial intelligence (AI) are some of the digital applications classified as immersive technologies which facilitates the transformation of digital to phygital (Andrade & Dias, 2020; Mele et al., 2023). The convergence of the physical and digital environments has given rise to two additional terms within the field of phygital terminology: phygitization, which denotes the combination of digital tools with physical devices to create a novel phygital iteration, and phygital transformation, whereby traditional or existing physical objects are incorporated into a digital product. For service-based businesses seeking to create phygital versions that generate new business value, this process may be considered analogous to the digital terms outlined by Gembali (2023), specifically digitalisation to phygitalization or digital transformation to phygital transformation.

AR technology enables users to experience the tangible environment in a natural way, with the enhancement of an overlaid digital environment (Tom Dieck & Jung, 2017). VR enables users to interact with a computer-generated new world in real time, resulting in a multisensorial approach that does not change the physical location, which is defined as a virtual environment (VE) (Zheng et al., 2018; Fan et al., 2022). Furthermore, VR engages all five senses (Guttentag, 2010; Wohlgenannt et al., 2020). In addition to the aforementioned immersive technologies, MR enables the convergence of the virtual and the actual worlds, creating a space wherein both digital and physical objects are present and interact simultaneously. This allows for seamless navigation

between the two realms, enabling users to interact with both digital and physical objects (Sala, 2021). In contrast to VR and AR, there is no single definition for MR (Speicher et al., 2019). A number of interactive equipment and
tools are available to assist individuals in becoming more immersed in the virtual environment, including gloves, headsets, and helmets (Desai et al., 2014).
Given that VR was initially developed in conjunction with flight simulators
(Pantelidis, 2009), it is perhaps unsurprising that education has been one of the
earliest areas to benefit from this technology. The application of VR technology
has the potential to impact a number of academic disciplines, including medical and science education, engineering, social sciences, foreign languages, and
distance learning (Boyles, 2017). AR allows computer-generated and real-world
content to be combined in real time and is already being used in fields as diverse
as medicine and manufacturing (Soete, et al., 2015). With the proliferation of
phones and other technological devices, the use of augmented reality in various fields is becoming more widespread such as medicine, (Eckert et al., 2019),
architecure, engineering (Chi et al., 2013), education(Wu et al., 2013), tourism
(Yung & Khoo-Lattimore, 2019) and gastronomic (Chai et al., 2022). In this
context, there are also several platforms that implement the digital transformation in different aspects, such as Google Arts and Culture, provided by the
Alphabet company since 2011, which facilitates the heritage. Other examples
such as the Metaverse Studio augmented reality platform or the 3D publishing
platform Sketchfab also implement virtual heritage with the help of virtuality
(Debattista, 2023).

Phygital Practices in Gastronomy

In light of the technological advancements that have occurred in recent times,
food and beverage businesses have begun to utilise technological innovations in
order to convey the desired message to their customers regarding the theme or
atmosphere of the business (Keskin & Hacı Bektaş, 2021). VR and AR technologies have begun to be utilized in gastronomy with the objective of enhancing the
dining experience (Çöl, et al., 2023). The advent of AR has the potential to enable
restaurants to virtually display menus, food products, and their customisation.
This has the potential to enhance the dining experience for customers by allowing
them to visualize the food before ordering (Batat, 2021). A study was conducted
to determine the effects of ambient lighting and three-dimensional shapes on
taste perception. The findings demonstrated that round-shaped products were
perceived as sweeter than spiky ones. This was attributed to the tactile receptors
in the mouth. Moreover, it has been demonstrated that when the environmental

lighting is of a high intensity, the perceived sweetness of the tasted product is reduced (Cornelio et al., 2022).

To enhance the dining experience, Amin et al. (2022) developed an app to enhance the visual appeal of menus. This application allowed customers to view the dishes they would be ordering in three dimensions (3D) using a Quick Response (QR) code, along with detailed information such as the price of the dish, the ingredients used, the nutritional content, and the calories. Evaluation of the application by volunteer participants concluded that it can help customers in make food choices, which in turn can increase satisfaction, restaurant sales, and the creation of a loyal customer profile. In a similar study, a projection was used to illustrate the menu options and deep learning and emotion reading technologies were used to assess customers' reactions to the menu options. The results of the study showed that most participants expressed satisfaction with the new technological concept and a willingness to visit the restaurant again (Dampage et al., 2021). QR codes and AR have also been used to preserve and archive traditional dishes. The Augmented Reality application aims to preserve and promote traditional Indonesian dishes in a digital environment. The application uses a QR code to facilitate the viewing of three traditional Indonesian dishes in 3D, accompanied by their names, ingredients, and recipes (Weking & Albertus, 2020). In a similar study conducted by Solmaz and Pekerşen (2022), the local dishes of Konya, including Etli Ekmek, Düğün Pilaf, Sac Arası, Fırın Kebab, and Bamya Soup, were selected for analysis. Images of the selected dishes were included in the KonyAR mobile application, and QR codes were placed at selected traditional restaurants. Participants in the study were selected based on their consumption of the dishes in question in traditional restaurants in Konya. The results of the study showed that the majority of participants found the application both enjoyable and useful.

In addition to restaurant applications, AR is also employed in the field of gastronomy tourism. The tourism industry has been one of the most severely impacted sectors during the Covid-19 pandemic. The closure of restaurants, bars, and cafés has also affected gastronomy tourism in destinations. Consequently, research has commenced on activities that people can engage in from home while maintaining social distance. Vitique's restaurant in Greti, Italy, has developed the digital dining concept "Chef Tabl-e." The concept enabled customers to communicate with the chef online, cook their own meals at home using the chef's recipes, and participate in digital wine tastings (Garibaldi & Pozzi, 2020).

AR technology strives to enhance the dining experience by affecting multiple senses. One of the most illustrative examples of this phenomenon is the establishment known as "Le Petit Chef". In this concept, animations projected onto plates are designed to entertain guests during the meal. A study on the "Le Petit Chef" concluded that the use of AR can influence customers' perceptions of the restaurant. The participants indicated that the experience was satisfactory in terms of visual and auditory stimulation, and the interactivity was consistent with their expectations. The experience was reported to be socially satisfying, as it facilitated communication with other customers in the restaurant. The animated shows prompted the participants to consume their meals at a slower pace and to derive greater enjoyment from them (Batat, 2021). Examples of restaurants with a similar concept include Dinner Tales (https://www.dinnertales.com) and Krasota (https://krasota.art/en) in Dubai. Dinner Tales comprises three distinct menus: Seven Paintings, Banquet of Hoshena, and Message in a Bottle. Each menu is unique, with varying course offerings. For instance, Seven Paintings is a seven-course menu that focuses on renowned painters, while Message in a Bottle is a five-course menu that explores the concept of the sea ("Dinner Tales," 2024). Krasota is a restaurant that combines visual art with gastronomy, featuring two distinct gastronomic shows which are Imaginary Art and Imaginary Future. The "Imaginary Art" is centred on the works of renowned artists and "Imaginary Future" is a futuristic exploration of the potential evolution of humanity ("Krasota," n.d.). Inamo (https://www.inamo-restaurant.com), a restaurant in London, employs AR technology to enhance the dining experience. Interactive smart dining tables enable customers to access a touchscreen e-menu, which offers a range of options. These include learning about smart meals, playing games, accessing environmental information, and decorating the tables with pictures and graffiti according to individual preferences. Another noteworthy aspect of the restaurant is the realistic representation of dishes selected from the e-menu on the plates of customers (Aksoy, 2016).

A number of innovative restaurants around the world are utilising virtual reality technology to enhance the dining experience. In 2014, the restaurant Sublimotion (www.sublimtoinibiza.com), situated on the Spanish island of Ibiza, was established. It was founded by two Michelin-starred chefs, Paco Roncero, who devised a three-hour experience involving more than 28 waiters. During the course of this experience, consumers were served a 20-course haute cuisine menu that incorporates virtual reality (VR) technology with the help of Samsung Gear VR headsets. This technology enabled consumers to be immersed in a fantasy world during the dinner (Batat & Batat, 2019, Talukdar, 2022). The Fat Duck restaurant (https://thefatduck.co.uk/) in the United Kingdom is one of the first restaurants to digitally enhance its service with background soundscapes. A seafood dish, designated the Sound of the Sea, was served to guests. This dish consisted of a conch shell with an MP3 player wired in. As the diners put on the earbuds, they begin to hear the sound of crashing waves and seagulls overhead before the dining experience commences (Spence, 2023).

Another restaurant that employs various multi-sensory technological devices to create a context as the dish arrives is Ultraviolet, created by chef Paul Pairet (https://uvbypp.cc/). Over the course of three hours, 19 to 21 courses are served, accompanied by a change in the surrounding atmosphere as a result of the various technological devices. The restaurant can accommodate up to 12 guests at a time, seated at one table in a single room. The dining experience is enhanced by a variety of technological devices integrated into the design, including 360-degree wall projection, table projectors, dry scent projectors, ultraviolet lighting, stage lighting, beam light speakers, and a speaker system. Ultraviolet shares the concept of "food for thought" with the restaurant known as "The Alchemist" (Yemsi-Paillissé, 2024). The Alchemist (https://alchemist.dk/) was established by the chef Rasmus Munk in 2015 (Brønnum and Munk, 2019). The restaurant places a particular emphasis on the sounds, music and theatre. Over the course of approximately five to six hours, patrons will be served 40 dishes in five distinct rooms: the Installation Room, the Lounge, the Dome Room, the Playground, and the Balcony. Each room is imbued with a distinctive ambience that collectively constitutes a comprehensive dining experience (Yemsi-Paillissé, 2024).

In addition, the utilisation of technological tools for the design of cultural itineraries has the potential to facilitate the implementation of dynamic approaches to cultural experiences (Sfodera et al., 2020). Furthermore, the development of a digital ecosystem represents a crucial step in the delivery of an optimal customer experience in the sector (Clemente et al., 2024). The Food Democracy Museum (FDM) is a non-formal and digital museum created with the aim of promoting food and wine traditions and supporting the local cultural heritage of the city of Verona (Italy) as a phygital project that creates an experience for visitors. A web-based application serves as the guide for this initiative, illuminating the interconnections between food and beverage traditions and the historical, architectural, and cultural aspects of Verona, thereby offering visitors the chance to gain deeper insights into lesser-known aspects of the city's culture, beyond the traditional highlights (Baratta et al., 2022).

Additionally, phygital gastronomy experiences have been developed with the objective of enhancing the quality of home cooking in the home kitchen. A number of applications have been developed that utilise the Internet of Things (IoT) in conjunction with smart and augmented reality (AR) technologies. Examples of developments related to phygital gastronomy at home include counter intelligence (Bonanni et al., 2005), user-centric smart kitchen (Hashimoto et al., 2008), AREasycooking (Iftene et al., 2020), Interactive MRcooking assistant (Zhai et al.,

2020), Magic Leap One (Majil et al., 2022), and AR kitchen machine (Ricci et al., 2022). Furthermore, augmented reality games such as "Let's Cook" have been proposed, which utilise tangible objects on the tabletop in conjunction with multimodal interaction of multimedia output. This enables children with cognitive disabilities to learn to prepare simple dishes in a fun and engaging manner (Papadaki et al., 2018).

Conclusion

The term 'phygital' is used to describe the integration of physical and virtual space, offering users and consumers a novel experience through a hybrid perception of space and its interaction in the same location at the same time. While this interaction develops in the restaurant sector with tools such as innovative service, presentation, or expression in the field of gastronomy, as in every sector, it may also offer new opportunities to everyone who wants to experience the digital creativity that comes with digital change in museums to ensure continuity in the field of cultural heritage. Although it is mainly used by practitioners, research on its theoretical development is sparse because the concept of phygital is very new.

This chapter presents a summary of the most effective practices for integrating physical and digital objects or applications, such as context, space, customer, applications, and consumption experience, in a phygital context within the field of gastronomy. It also outlines the customer or user experiences that facilitate the development of new phygital forms.

Although the phygital phenomenon is a concept that enables the creation of an interaction network between people using digital tools, guided by smart technologies, it should not be forgotten that the phygital transformation process leads to a change in social relations, with an increase in the individualisation of people and the interactions of communities with each other on a global scale.

References

Aksoy, M. (2016). Restoranlardaki Teknolojik Yeniliklerin Deneyim Pazarlaması Açısından Değerlendirilmesi Assessment of the Technological Innovations in Restaurants in terms of Experience Marketing. Retrieved from https://www.researchgate.net/publication/310994877

Amin, S. N., Shivakumara, P., Jun, T. X., Chong, K. Y., Zan, D. L. L., & Rahavendra, R. (2022). An Augmented Reality-Based Approach for Designing Interactive Food Menu of Restaurant Using Android. Artificial Intelligence and Applications, 1(1), 26–34. https://doi.org/10.47852/bonviewaia2202354

Andrade, J. G., & Dias, P. (2020). A phygital approach to cultural heritage: *Augmented reality at regaleira. Virtual Archaeology Review, 11(22)*, 15–25. http://hdl.handle.net/10400.14/32270

Baratta, R., Bonfanti, A., Cucci, M. G., & Simeoni, F. (2022). Enhancing cultural tourism through the development of memorable experiences: the "Food Democracy Museum" as a phygital project. *Sinergie Italian Journal of Management, 40*(1), 153–176.

Batat, W. (2021). How augmented reality (AR) is transforming the restaurant sector: Investigating the impact of "Le Petit Chef" on customers' dining experiences. Technological Forecasting and Social Change, 172. https://doi.org/10.1016/j.techfore.2021.121013

Batat, W. (2022). *Strategies for the digital customer experience: Connecting customers with brands in the phygital age*. Edward Elgar Publishing.

Batat, W., & Batat, W. (2019). Experiential setting design. The New Luxury Experience: Creating the Ultimate Customer Experience, 113–139.

Belghiti, S., Ochs, A., Lemoine, JF., Badot, O. (2018). The Phygital Shopping Experience: An Attempt at Conceptualization and Empirical Investigation. In: Rossi, P., Krey, N. (eds) Marketing Transformation: Marketing Practice in an Ever-Changing World. AMSWMC 2017. Developments in Marketing Science: Proceedings of the Academy of Marketing Science. Springer, Cham. doi.org/10.1007/978-3-319-68750-6_18

Bonanni, L., Lee, C. H., & Selker, T. (2005). CounterIntelligence: Augmented reality kitchen. In *Proc. CHI* (Vol. 2239, p. 45).

Boyles, B. (2017). Virtual reality and augmented reality in education. *Center For Teaching Excellence, United States Military Academy, West Point, Ny, 67*.

Brønnum, L. B., & Munk, R. (2019). Holistic Cuisine–A focus beyond the plate. International journal of gastronomy and food science, 15, 32–35.

Chai, J. J. K., O'Sullivan, C., Gowen, A. A., Rooney, B., & Xu, J. L. (2022, June 1). Augmented/mixed reality technologies for food: A review. Trends in Food Science and Technology, Vol. 124, pp. 182–194. Elsevier Ltd. https://doi.org/10.1016/j.tifs.2022.04.021

Chi, H. L., Kang, S. C., & Wang, X. (2013). Research trends and opportunities of augmented reality applications in architecture, engineering, and construction. Automation in Construction, 33, 116–122. https://doi.org/10.1016/j.autcon.2012.12.017

Clemente, L., Iodice, G., Carignani, F., Greco, F., & Bifulco, F. (2024). Phygital approach to value co-creation in international museums. *Measuring Business Excellence*.

Cornelio, P., Dawes, C., Maggioni, E., Bernardo, F., Schwalk, M., Mai, M., & Obrist, M. (2022). Virtually tasty: An investigation of the effect of ambient lighting and 3D-shaped taste stimuli on taste perception in virtual reality. *International Journal of Gastronomy and Food Science, 30*, 100626.

Çöl, B. G., İmre, M., & Yıkmış, S. (2023). Virtual reality and augmented reality technologies in gastronomy: A review. E Food, 4(3). https://doi.org/10.1002/efd2.84

Dampage, U., Egodagamage, D. A., Waidyaratne, A. U., DIssanayaka, D. A. W., & Senarathne, A. G. N. M. (2021). Spatial Augmented Reality Based Customer Satisfaction Enhancement and Monitoring System. IEEE Access, 9, 97990–98004. https://doi.org/10.1109/ACCESS.2021.3093829

Debattista, M. G. (2023). Physical, digital or phygital? Assessing the educational potential of virtual reality in heritage interpretation. Malta Review of Educational Research, 17(1), 51–72.

Desai, P. R., Desai, P. N., Ajmera, K. D., & Mehta, K. (2014). A review paper on oculus rift-a virtual reality headset. *arXiv preprint arXiv:1408.1173.*

Dinner Tales. (2024). Retrieved May 29, 2024, from https://www.dinnertales.com/dineamation

Eckert, M., Volmerg, J. S., & Friedrich, C. M. (2019). Augmented reality in medicine: Systematic and bibliographic review. JMIR MHealth and UHealth, Vol. 7. JMIR Publications Inc. https://doi.org/10.2196/10967

Fan, X., Jiang, X., & Deng, N. (2022). Immersive technology: A meta-analysis of augmented/virtual reality applications and their impact on tourism experience. Tourism Management, 91, 104534 doi.org/10.1016/j.tourman.2022.104534.

Garibaldi, R., & Pozzi, A. (2020). Gastronomy tourism and Covid-19: technologies for overcoming current and future restrictions. In F. Burini (Ed.), Tourism Facing a Pandemic: From Crisis To Recovery (pp. 45–50). Università degli Studi di Bergamo.

Gembali, S. (2023). *Phygital Transformation: Adding Physical Devices to Digital Products to Improve the User Experience* [Master's Thesis, Massachusetts Institute of Technology]. https://hdl.handle.net/1721.1/151254

Guttentag, D. A. (2010). Virtual reality: Applications and implications for tourism. Tourism management, 31(5), 637–651 doi.org/10.1016/j.tourman.2009.07.003

Hashimoto, A., Mori, N., Funatomi, T., Yamakata, Y., Kakusho, K., & Minoh, M. (2008). Smart kitchen: A user centric cooking support system. In *Proceedings of IPMU* (Vol. 8, pp. 848–854).

Iftene, A., Trandabăţ, D., & Rădulescu, V. (2020). Eye and voice control for an augmented reality cooking experience. *Procedia Computer Science, 176,* 1469–1478.

Keskin, E., & Hacı Bektaş, N. (2021). Gastronomi 4.0 Üzerine Kavramsal Bir Araştırma Gastroia Journal of Gastronomy And Travel Research. Retrieved from https://www.researchgate.net/publication/353935232

Klaus, P. 'Phil.' (2021). Viewpoint: phygital – the emperor's new clothes? Journal of Strategic Marketing, 1–8. https://doi.org/10.1080/0965254X.2021.1976252

Krasota. (n.d.). Retrieved May 29, 2024, from https://krasota.art/en/about

Majil, I., Yang, M. T., & Yang, S. (2022). Augmented reality based interactive cooking guide. Sensors, 22(21), 8290.

Mele, C. and Russo-Spena, T. (2022), "The architecture of the phygital customer journey: a dynamic interplay between systems of insights and systems of engagement", European Journal of Marketing, Vol. 56 No. 1, pp. 72–91. https://doi.org/10.1108/EJM-04-2019-0308

Mele, C., Spena, T. R., Marzullo, M., & Di Bernardo, I. (2023). The phygital transformation: a systematic review and a research agenda. Italian Journal of Marketing, 2023(3), 323–349.https://doi.org/10.1007/s43039-023-00070-7

Nofal, E., Reffat, R. and Vande Moere, A. (2017), "Phygital heritage: an approach for heritage communication", Proceedings of the 3rd Immersive Learning Research Network Conference, Coimbra, pp. 26–9.

Pantelidis, V. S. (2009). Reasons to use virtual reality in education and training courses and a model to determine when to use virtual reality. *Themes in science and technology education, 2,* 59–70.

Papadaki, E., Ntoa, S., Adami, I., & Stephanidis, C. (2018). Let's cook: An augmented reality system towards developing cooking skills for children with cognitive impairments. In *Smart Objects and Technologies for Social Good: Third International Conference, GOODTECHS 2017, Pisa, Italy, November 29–30, 2017, Proceedings 3* (pp. 237–247). Springer International Publishing.

Prisecaru, P. (2016). Challenges of the fourth industrial revolution. *Knowledge Horizons. Economics, 8*(1), 57.

Ricci, M., Scarcelli, A., D'Introno, A., Strippoli, V., Cariati, S., & Fiorentino, M. (2022, June). A human-centred design approach for designing augmented reality enabled interactive systems: a kitchen machine case study. In *International Joint Conference on Mechanics, Design Engineering & Advanced Manufacturing* (pp. 1413–1425). Cham: Springer International Publishing.

Sala, N. (2021). Virtual reality, augmented reality, and mixed reality in education: A brief overview. Current and prospective applications of virtual reality in higher education, 48–73 doi: 10.4018/978-1-7998-4960-5.ch003

Soete, N., Claeys, A., Hoedt, S., Mahy, B., & Cottyn, J. (2015). Towards mixed reality in SCADA applications. IFAC-PapersOnLine, 28(3), 2417–2422. https://doi.org/10.1016/j.ifacol.2015.06.450

Solmaz, R., & Pekerşen, Y. (2022). Evaluation of Augmented Reality and Consumer Perceptions in Traditional Dishes. Journal of Culinary Science and Technology. https://doi.org/10.1080/15428052.2022.2060889

Speicher, M., Hall, B. D., & Nebeling, M. (2019). What is mixed reality? In Proceedings of the 2019 CHI conference on human factors in computing systems (pp. 1–15).

Spence, C. (2023). Digitally enhancing tasting experiences. *International Journal of Gastronomy and Food Science, 32*, 100695

Sfodera, F., Mingo, I., Mattiacci, A. and Colurcio, M. (2020), "Night at the museum: technology enables visitor experiences", Sinergie Italian Journal of Management, Vol. 38 No. 1, pp. 231–250.

Talukdar, N. (2022). Luxury food experiences: A proposition of a conceptual framework for food innovation and well-being. In *The rise of positive luxury* (pp. 192–213). Routledge.

Tom Dieck, M. C., & Jung, T. H. (2017). Value of augmented reality at cultural heritage sites: A stakeholder approach. Journal of destination marketing & management, 6(2), 110–117. doi.org/10.1016/j.jdmm.2017.03.002

Weking, A. N., & Albertus, J. S. (2020). A Development of Augmented Reality Mobile Application to Promote the Traditional Indonesian Food. IJIM International Journal: Interactive Mobile Technologies, 14(9), 248–257. Retrieved from https://online-journals.org/index.php/i-jim/about/editorialTeam

Wohlgenannt, I., Simons, A., & Stieglitz, S. (2020). Virtual reality. *Business & Information Systems Engineering, 62*, 455–461.

Wu, H. K., Lee, S. W. Y., Chang, H. Y., & Liang, J. C. (2013). Current status, opportunities and challenges of augmented reality in education. Computers and Education, 62, 41–49. https://doi.org/10.1016/j.compedu.2012.10.024

Verhoef, P. C., Broekhuizen, T., Bart, Y., Bhattacharya, A., Dong, J. Q., Fabian, N., & Haenlein, M. (2021). Digital transformation: A multidisciplinary reflection and research agenda. Journal of business research, 122, 889–901 doi.org/10.1016/j.jbusres.2019.09.022

Yemsi-Paillissé, A. C. (2024). Fine dining multisensory restaurants and intermediality: an exploratory case study on Ultraviolet and The Alchemist. *International Journal of Gastronomy and Food Science, 35*, 100882.

Yung, R., & Khoo-Lattimore, C. (2019). New realities: a systematic literature review on virtual reality and augmented reality in tourism research. Current

Issues in Tourism, Vol. 22, pp. 2056–2081. Routledge. https://doi.org/10.1080/
13683500.2017.1417359

Zhai, K. Y., Cao, Y. M., Hou, W. J., & Li, X. M. (2020). Interactive Mixed
Reality Cooking Assistant for Unskilled Operating Scenario. In Virtual,
Augmented and Mixed Reality. Industrial and Everyday Life Applications:
12th International Conference, VAMR 2020, Held as Part of the 22nd HCI
International Conference, HCII 2020, Copenhagen, Denmark, July 19–24,
2020, Proceedings, Part II 22 (pp. 178–195). Springer International
Publishing.

Zheng, J. M., Chan, K. W., & Gibson, I. (1998). Virtual reality. *Ieee Potentials*, *17*(2), 20–23.

Erdi Eren[1] and Aybuke Ceyhun Sezgin[2]

Chapter 10 Reintroduction of Sprouts and Microgreens to the Gastronomy World

Introduction

The world of gastronomy consists of a structure that starts from the field and continues until the table. It even includes sustainability practices with the proper utilisation of waste afterwards. This complex structure is intertwined with agricultural practices at the beginning, marketing in purchasing/preference periods, food sciences in the preparation stages of products, artistic practices in food presentation and design, nutritional sciences in consumption and post-consumption processes, environmental sciences and sustainability concepts in waste management stages. Progressing by considering the best possible practices at all stages paves the way for a consumption cycle that supports sustainability without harming nature and consumers who are fed with properly produced healthy foods and are satisfied with their choices.

Modern nutrition trends have led to the introduction of new foods that were previously more limited in consumption and paved the way for some foods that have been consumed for thousands of years to be rediscovered and integrated into human life. At this point, sprouts and microgreens represent a significant product group. Even though they are different products, these concepts are often confused. Sprouts are usually harvested 3–5 days after the seed is moistened. The whole plant is consumed, and they are smaller than microgreens. Microgreens (or shoots) are basically immature plants produced from vegetable, grain, or wild plant seeds. Their maturation period is 7–21 days, depending on the genus. They are consumed without roots and seed pods (Galieni et al., 2020). It is estimated that sprouts were consumed by germinating seeds in 3000 BC. The production of microgreens started in California in the 1980s. Although both product groups are consumed as immature greens, they have major differences. Sprouts are usually grown in dark and high-humidity environments. Microgreens are much

---

1 Instructor., Alanya University, Faculty of Art and Design, Department of Gastronomy and Culinary Arts, erdi.eren@alanyauniversity.edu.tr
2 Assoc. Prof. Dr., Ankara Hacı Bayram Veli University, Faculty of Tourism, Department of Gastronomy and Culinary Arts, aybuke.ceyhun@hbv.edu.tr

more aromatic than sprouts and have a broader spectrum of colours (green for radish and celery, red for amaranth, yellow for etiolated corn, and multicolour for beet and mustard) and varieties. In addition, their yield and shelf life are lower (Di Gioia et al., 2017; Ebert, 2022).

In any case, despite their small size, sprouts and microgreens have an essential place in the world of gastronomy with their great contributions to nutritional value, taste, and visual appeal. Although studies on these plants have increased in recent years, it is seen that researches have focused on issues such as nutritional values, health effects, and microbial safety of the products. There are also many sources that describe in detail the process of growing sprouts and microgreens. This chapter will evaluate microgreens and sprouts from a gastronomy perspective. In particular, their place and creative uses in the kitchen will be discussed, and a situation assessment will be conducted. In general terms, this chapter is intended to be a resource for the use of sprouts and microgreens in the gastronomy world.

Sprouts

When the history of humanity is evaluated in terms of nutritional anthropology, it is thought that the first consumptions consisted of edible flowers, wild herbs, raw seeds, and sprouts found in the environment, focusing on survival by filling the stomach. The fact that such products could be consumed without any processing ensured the survival of the modern ancestors of humanity, who were still quite alien to the world. During these times, the first wild versions of the sprouts that are now back on our plates were consumed.

Records of sprouts date back hundreds of years after the first conscious possible germination processes. Soy sprouts are mentioned in Chinese texts as early as 200 AD. At the end of the 16th century, a famous Chinese doctor wrote in his medical treatise that sprouts could reduce inflammation, be used as a laxative, relieve rheumatism and improve the body. Many documents show that sprouts were sold in Chinese markets from the early 1900s. In winter, especially in the northern regions of China, sprouts were a vital food source when few other vegetables were available (Shurtleff and Aoyagi, 2013; Wallentinson et al., 2018).

Sprouts have many benefits for producers and consumers. Especially the fact that they only need water during their development makes their high-volume production possible and budget-friendly. In sprout cultivation, seeds undergo soaking in water, with the duration and temperature tailored to their variety and dimensions. This step elevates the seeds' moisture levels, facilitating germination within the designated timeframe. (Mir et al., 2017). After the sprouts grow into shoots and are placed in the light, a new process begins. The sun's rays help the shoots to convert water and carbon dioxide from the air into energy-rich carbohydrates and oxygen. The stem and tiny leaves start to turn green. During this process, chlorophyll is formed, and chlorophyll cells are needed to create new energy (Wallentinson et al., 2018).

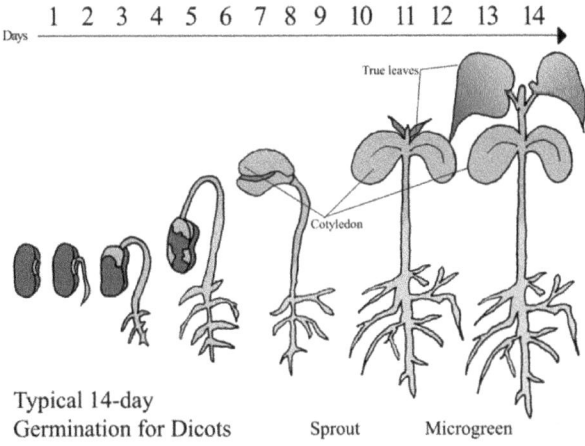

Figure 10.1. Growth and Development of Bean Sprouts & Microgreens (Riggio et al., 2019)

Figure 10.1 shows the typical 14-day germination period for beans to develop from seed into a dicot. Germination time for sprouts and microgreens varies according to the plant variety. To maintain high humidity levels and support the sprouting process, the seeds should be rinsed or sprinkled multiple times a day. During germination, significant changes occur in the composition and concentrations of the plant. Studies show that germinating seeds can contain 2 to 10 times more phytochemicals than commercial adult plants. Furthermore, sprouts and microgreens are characterised by low calories and glycaemic index. In today's society, which is more conscious and concerned about healthy lifestyles and disease prevention, these products seem to be highly desirable products (Wojdyło, 2020).

POPULARITY (%)

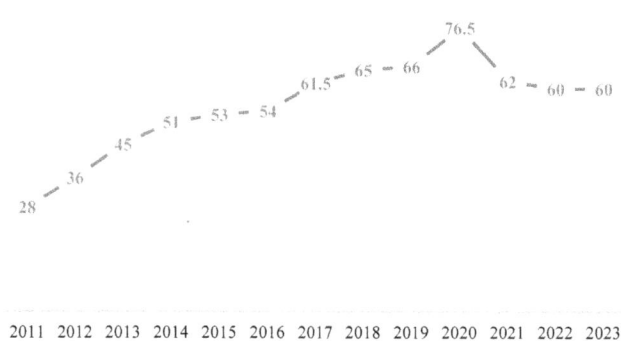

2011 2012 2013 2014 2015 2016 2017 2018 2019 2020 2021 2022 2023

Figure 10.2. "Sprouts" Popularity on the Internet (Google Trends, 2024)

Figure 10.2 shows internet searches for 'sprouts' between 2011 and 2023. The increasing interest of consumers in recent years is noteworthy. It is thought that the increase, especially in 2020, is due to the tendency towards sprouting practices at home in parallel with consumers' increasing interest in artisanal products during COVID-19-induced quarantine processes. With the end of the pandemic, it is seen that the decrease in artisanal practices has started to be replaced by industrially produced foods again. However, the habits gained in this period accelerated the integration of niche products into the kitchen, primarily through practices such as growing sprouts and incorporating them into recipes. Sprouting methods known and applied for centuries have become very popular, especially in recent years, via the return to traditional unprocessed foods due to technological developments in nutritional science.

Microgreens

Microgreens, the immature shoots of crops such as sunflowers, peas, chard, beetroot, spinach, kale and coriander, are an emerging crop group relative to sprouts. Microgreens have recently become very popular in developed countries due to the growing interest in gourmet food, healthy eating and indoor plant cultivation. Their shelf life is quite short, and they are commonly utilized as a sauce, seasoning, or garnish for dishes (Bhaswant et al., 2023). Microgreens can be easily confused with fresh herbs such as basil, oregano, and coriander, baby greens such as baby spinach or sprouted seeds (Riggio et al., 2019; Rouphael et al., 2021).

The worldwide microgreens industry, which was worth a substantial USD 1.8 billion in 2022, is on a positive trajectory and is expected to reach an impressive USD 2.6 billion by 2031. This growth, with a compound annual growth rate of 11 %, showcases the increasing demand for these nutrient-rich greens (straits-research.com, 2023). The COVID-19 pandemic initially posed challenges for the microgreens market, leading to a decline in sales due to disruptions in the supply chain and the closure of important outlets like restaurants and grocery stores. However, this period also sparked greater consumer interest in fresh, healthy products and home gardening, which helped the market bounce back and expand. The resilience of the microgreens industry is evident in its recovery after the pandemic and its ongoing growth (microgreensworld.com).

Microgreens are an exotic type of edible greens seen in luxury grocery stores and restaurants and have gained popularity as a new culinary trend, especially in recent years. Soft in texture and colour, microgreens contribute a range of excellent attributes that elevate the sensory characteristics of main courses. They are gathered just above the roots and enjoyed fresh. In contrast to sprouts, they need sunlight for optimal growth and are cultivated in soil or other mediums like peat moss, vermiculite, and perlite. Microgreens represent a group between sprouts and baby greens/vegetables in size. Especially in the 1990s, they gained recognition with their use in the presentations of high-end restaurants (Mir et al., 2017).

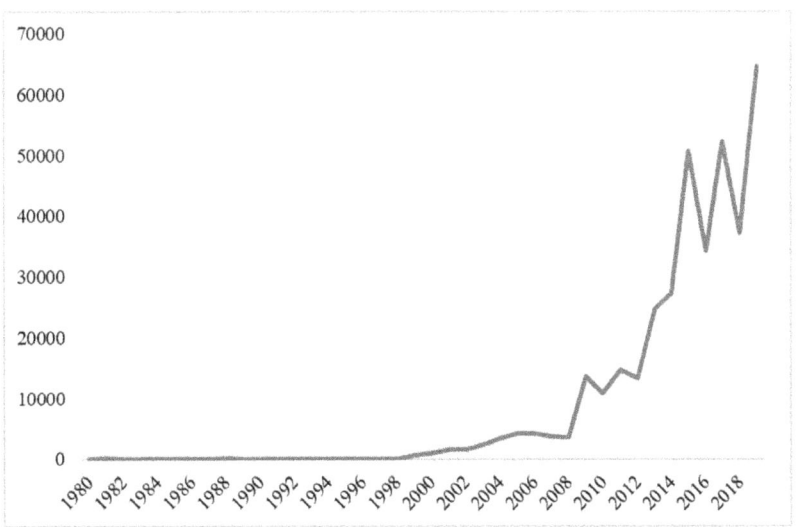

Figure 10.3. Occurrence of "microgreens" in Books between 1980 and 2019 (Ngram Viewer, 2024)

Figure 10.3 shows the frequency of use of "microgreens" in books between 1980 and 2019. Since the late 1980s, when microgreens were introduced into our lives, research and attention to these plants have increased and intensified. Especially considering the rate of increase after 2000, it is seen that the nutritional properties and gastronomic contributions of the products have become more popular with a clearer understanding. The consumer response to microgreens, high price levels and short production times have attracted many urban farms and greenhouse growers to invest in this area. Still considered a relatively new product group, microgreens are considered a "superfood" due to their great potential (Kyriacou et al., 2016).

Nutritional Values, Health Effects, and Safety

Globally developing technology and increasing levels of awareness have made consumers more conscious of their food choices. The effects of many more foods and food components on human metabolism are now known. In light of these developments, interest in foods with high nutritional values is increasing. For the growing number of people who want to produce their own food, the 'micro-garden' represents a real opportunity to produce low-cost fresh vegetables at home that are beneficial to human health all year round (Renna et al., 2016).

Sprouts are produced by soaking the seeds and then germinating them in a moist environment. However, microgreens are soaked very briefly and harvested over the growth medium between the opening of the cotyledon and the appearance of the first set of true leaves (Riggio, 2019). If microgreens are allowed to continue to grow, they put on their next set of true leaves. True leaves are the leaves of a plant that distinguish it from another plant. Since seeds are genetically coded to grow and develop into a mature crop, their nutrients are bound up thoroughly. By soaking and sprouting, the seed opens and begins to grow. Its nutrient levels rise and become more available. Substances within the seed start to break down (Wallentinson et al., 2018).

Compared to grown vegetables, sprouts contain more dominant antioxidant compounds and are concentrated in taste and odour. Therefore, sprouts can be a rich source of nutrients for consumer categories with special dietary preferences, such as vegetarians and vegans. However, there are significant differences between species. The lack of a generally accepted sprouting procedure, regulatory-based appropriate food labelling, and the scarcity of clinical studies and data constitute the problems related to the subject (Lemmens et al., 2019).

The sprouts are typically consumed a few days after they begin to grow, ensuring that their nutrient levels remain very high. For instance, soybean sprouts contain twice the protein of eggs but only a tenth of the fat, making them valuable as dietary supplements that can enhance health and wellness. Some sprouts, like mung beans, are rich sources of ascorbic acid, with over 50 mg/100 g in fresh weight. The B group vitamins can increase up to three times during germination, making sprouts a good source of vitamin B12. Soybean sprouts have relatively high concentrations of isoflavonoids, which can help protect against cancer, cardiovascular disease, and osteoporosis, although their levels are much lower in other legumes (Di Gioia et al., 2017).

Gupta and Brar (2015) reported a significant increase in protein and crude fibre contents and a decrease in crude fat and carbohydrate values in all wheat, barley, oats, mung bean, soybean and cowpea products as a result of the germination process. Erba et al. (2019), examined the nutrient concentration of sprouted chickpeas and green peas and reported an increase of about 10 % in protein values due to sprouting. They reported a slight decrease in the antioxidant capacity of these two products due to sprouting. In their review, Ikram et al. (2021) reported the mineral changes in amaranth, buckwheat, millet, quinoa and sorghum after sprouting. A significant increase in mineral levels was observed in all sprouted products. A similar situation was reported for antioxidant capacity and total phenolic compound content.

Sprouts are commonly known for their health benefits and are more often associated with promoting wellness then microgreens. They are known to have high levels of nutrients and bioactive compounds including flavonoids, hydroxycinnamic acids, vitamins, and glucosinolates, as well as minerals and carotenoids. These phytochemicals appear to have a crucial role in safeguarding the human body against chronic conditions such as cardiovascular diseases, diabetes, and cancer (Wojdyło et al., 2020). When seeds sprout, polysaccharides break down into oligo- and monosaccharides, fats into free fatty acids, and proteins into oligopeptides and free amino acids. These processes support the biochemical mechanisms in our body and enhance the efficiency of enzymes that break down proteins, carbohydrates, and fatty acids. Therefore, germination can be seen as a form of pre-digestion that aids in breaking down complex materials into basic building blocks. Throughout germination, antinutrients (such as trypsin inhibitor, phytic acid, pentosan, and tannins) decrease, while compounds with health-protective effects and phytochemical properties are also produced (Márton et al., 2010).

Significant differences in a number of micronutrients can be observed in species and cultivars of many microgreens. Exposure of microgreens to various amounts and qualities of light and media treatments can positively affect the levels of bioactive compounds. It is also worth noting that compared to conventional vegetables, which are usually used cooked, the consumption of raw microgreens has the advantage of preventing the loss of nutrients or the degradation of vitamins (Di Gioia et al., 2017). A study by Xiao et al. (2012), analysing the concentration of vitamins and carotenoids in 25 varieties of microgreens, showed that microgreens had a tenfold higher content of antioxidant compounds than everyday vegetables harvested at the ripening stage. Additionally, the number of vitamins in red cabbage microgreens showed much higher vitamin C, E and K content for the same species harvested at the ripening stage. Considering that total phenolic content is strongly characterised by flavour characteristics such as sourness, astringency and bitterness, it can be predicted that the overall TPC values of microgreens are also exceptionally high.

Sprouts and microgreens grow best at moist and room temperature. Unfortunately, microorganisms also thrive under these conditions. Therefore, they can be exposed to optimal temperature and humidity levels for the growth of mesophilic bacteria, including many human pathogens. This raises food safety concerns, one of the most significant issues in using sprouts and microgreens, which are usually consumed without heat treatment. Sprouts and microgreens are usually harvested by hand, which poses a microbiological risk. Many foodborne illnesses have been associated with sprouts and microgreens. However, studies have shown that the seeds are more suitable for microorganism growth than the true leaves. This suggests that microgreens may be safer than sprouts (Reed et al., 2018; Verlinden, 2019). Sources of microbiological contamination of microgreens include numerous factors such as contaminated seed or fertiliser, irrigation water, soil, livestock/wildlife. If seeds are contaminated, pathogens can be internalised from the beginning of the growth process and once introduced, are very difficult to remove. Sprouts and microgreens can be easily grown at home, making regular control and analysis impossible.

Like any other food product, sprouts and microgreens must be handled safely. Low temperatures, light, and modified atmosphere packaging are effective and can sometimes extend microgreens' shelf life. Braunstein (2013), stated that the best way to store clipped sprouts or microgreens is in a glass or food-safe plastic container with a lid. If necessary, it is okay to store microgreens in a bag and handle the greens and bag gently. The refrigerator's thermostat should be set close to the freezing point (except for amaranth and basil), and they can be stored fresh for two weeks or longer.

Culinary Use

The culinary use of sprouts and microgreens in the kitchen, especially in product development-focused studies, has recently increased. With the promotion of perceptions that sprouts and microgreens are safe, can improve flavour, add colour, and improve the visual appearance of dishes, the products have become the focus of chefs and consumers in modern gastronomy. The contribution of microgreens in the creative designs and concentrated flavours of the dishes served today is relatively high (Örnek, 2021). The main important features of sprouts and microgreens that make them interesting and attractive from a gastronomic perspective are that the first leaves emerging from the seed are characterised by a wide variety of colours (green, yellow, red, purple), textures (soft, crisp, juicy) and flavours. Microgreens can be used as a garnish or decorative element in new recipes and current plate presentations. All products used in the art of plate decoration must be of food quality, i.e., suitable for human consumption. In addition to enriching the visual appearance, chefs also use them as a supportive element of flavour and aroma (Renna et al., 2016).

Similar to other foods, the overall acceptability of microgreens is highly dependent on sensory attributes (e.g. flavour, bitterness, astringency, grassiness, warmth and sourness). A strong correlation was noted between the flavour of the sprouts and the panellists' overall preference for the sample. Respondents who were more familiar with microgreens and had a higher level of education were more likely to purchase microgreens. Microgreens rich in allyl isothiocyanate have solid and spicy flavours similar to mustard and wasabi. While these microgreens are preferred by those who enjoy spicy foods, they are less acceptable to individuals who dislike spicy flavours. People who favour sweet and mild tastes may not appreciate the pungent microgreens, even though they are high in glucosinolates and isothiocyanates, which are beneficial for health. With these flavours, microgreens offer the possibility of different taste combinations (Michell et al., 2020; Zhang et al., 2021).

As living plants, microgreens require adequate light to maintain photosynthesis; otherwise, they may turn yellow and wilt. While initially appear fresh and vibrant when taken from optimal greenhouse conditions, their quality and flavour can rapidly deteriorate once moved to a restaurant kitchen or cooler (Renna et al., 2016). In general, problems integrating these products into culinary practices are associated with their short shelf life. The products should be consumed within a short time after harvesting. Especially in the packages to be used for storage after harvesting, there must be channels that can take air to prevent condensation or evaporation on the inner surface of the products.

Gilbertie and Sheehan (2015), in their book "Cooking with Microgreens", provide information on growing sprouts and microgreens and give some examples of recipes where these products can be used. The recipes, which consist of ten different topics, including appetisers, soups, salads, entrees, side dishes, sauces, dressings, sandwiches and smoothies, include creative techniques and applications. In this chapter, five different courses containing sprouts and microgreens were given, including a starter, soup, salad, main dish and dessert. All the images presented in this study were generated by artificial intelligence (Canva). In this context, the relevance of support from artificial intelligence, especially in the use of innovative products in gastronomy, is also seen. Issues such as how a food to be prepared could possibly look like or the harmony of a product to be integrated into a recipe can be concretised with AI-supported tools.

Salmon carpaccio with sprouts/microgreens

Preparation

✓ Cut the salmon into very thin slices and put on a serving plate.
✓ Drizzle the lemon juice and olive oil over the salmon slices.
✓ Season with salt and pepper.
✓ Sprinkle the sprouts/microgreens over the salmon slices.
✓ Optionally, garnish with capers and red onion rings.

Vegetable soup with sprouts/microgreens

Preparation

✓ Add the olive oil to a large saucepan and heat. Add the chopped onion and garlic and fry until soft.
✓ Add the diced carrot, celery, potato and zucchini. Saute for a few more minutes.
✓ Add the vegetable stock and bring the soup to a boil.
✓ Once boiling, reduce the heat and simmer for about 20 minutes until the vegetables are tender.
✓ Add the salt, pepper, oregano and basil.
✓ Remove the soup from the heat and let it cool slightly.
✓ Ladle the soup into bowls and serve with optional lemon wedges and grated parmesan cheese.
✓ Sprinkle the sprouts/microgreens and serve.

Quinoa salad with sprouts/microgreens

Preparation

✓ Boil the quinoa in water or vegetable broth and leave to cool.
✓ Put the cooled quinoa in a large bowl.
✓ Add the chopped cucumber, cherry tomatoes, red pepper, red onion, mint, and parsley.
✓ Season with olive oil and lemon juice, salt, and pepper.
✓ Sprinkle the sprouts/microgreens on top and serve.

Burger with sprouts/microgreens

Preparation

✓ Heat a skillet or grill over medium high heat.

✓ Place the patty and cook for about 5–7 minutes on each side, until brown and cooked through.

✓ While cooking, place the cheddar cheese slices, if using, on top of the meatballs to melt the cheese.

✓ Cut the burger buns in half and lightly toast the insides on the grill or in a skillet.

✓ Place the cooked patty over bun.

✓ Add the sliced tomatoes on top of the meatballs.

✓ Place the sprouts/microgreens to give the burger a fresh and crispy touch.

✓ Place the top bun slice.

✓ Serve with fries or salad on the side.

Chocolate mousse with sprouts/microgreens

Preparation
✓ Melt the chocolate with a bain-marie and let it cool a little. ✓ Beat the egg yolks and granulated sugar with a mixer, add the melted chocolate and mix. ✓ In a separate bowl, whip the cream and add it to the chocolate mixture. ✓ In a clean bowl, whisk the egg whites until stiff peaks form and gently fold into the chocolate mixture. ✓ Divide the mousse into serving bowls and refrigerate for at least 2 hours. ✓ Garnish with the sprouts/microgreens and serve.

Conclusion

When all the information in this chapter is considered, sprouts and microgreens can be considered among the foods with the highest nutritional value and health benefits that can be grown under such easy conditions. These superfoods, which can be grown in such a short period of time using only seeds, the right temperature and a small amount of water, are becoming the focus of more consumers every day. Additionally, one of the best things about growing these crops is that consumers can harvest them whenever they want to eat them. Their health benefits, high economic value, environmental friendliness and ease of integration into the kitchen make these increasingly popular products necessary. Especially, as seen in this chapter, considering the fact that they can be used in every course from starter to main course and dessert, the visual aesthetics and the contribution they provide to nutritional values, the place of these products in gastronomy is getting stronger and stronger.

To increase the contribution of sprouts and microgreens to the gastronomy world and to benefit more from these products, education and awareness of these products should be increased. Workshops and seminars to be organised will increase interest and awareness in this product group in general. It is also of great importance to develop new species through R&D studies or to deepen research on existing varieties. Supporting local production and developing distribution channels will also encourage the cultivation of sprouts and microgreens and facilitate access to quality products. In this regard, online sales support the market quite well. Training chefs and culinary professionals on how to grow sprouts and microgreens will make these products more accessible and easier to integrate into meals. Recipes and usage suggestions to be shared with consumers during the marketing and promotion stages will strengthen communication and increase the gastronomic value of the products. It is recommended to increase the popularity of these products, primarily through collaborations and networking, for example, by organising gastronomy festivals and events.

References

Bhaswant, M., Shanmugam, D. K., Miyazawa, T., Abe, C., & Miyazawa, T. (2023). Microgreens—A comprehensive review of bioactive molecules and health benefits. *Molecules*, 28(2), 867.

Braunstein, M. M. (2013). Microgreen garden: Indoor grower's guide to gourmet greens. Book Publishing Company.

Canva. From: https://www.canva.com/magic-home Accessed on: 20.05.2024.

Di Gioia, F., Renna, M., & Santamaria, P. (2017). Sprouts, Microgreens and "Baby Leaf" Vegetables. Minimally Processed Refrigerated Fruits and Vegetables, 403–432.

Ebert, A. W. (2022). Sprouts and microgreens—novel food sources for healthy diets. *Plants*, 11(4), 571.

Erba, D., Angelino, D., Marti, A., Manini, F., Faoro, F., Morreale, F., … Casiraghi, M. C. (2019). Effect of sprouting on nutritional quality of pulses. *International Journal of Food Sciences and Nutrition*, 70(1), 30–40.

Galieni, A., Falcinelli, B., Stagnari, F., Datti, A., & Benincasa, P. (2020). Sprouts and microgreens: Trends, opportunities, and horizons for novel research. *Agronomy*, 10(9), 1424.

Gilbertie, S. And Sheehan, L. (2015). Cooking with Microgreens: The Grow-Your-Own Superfood. Countryman Press; 1st edition.

Google Trends (2024). From: https://trends.google.com/trends/ Accessed on: 10.05.2024.

Gupta, S., & Brar, J. (2015). Formulation and evaluation of malted ingredient mixes. *International J. Food & Nutri. Sci*, 5(3), 182–190.

Ikram, A., Saeed, F., Afzaal, M., Imran, A., Niaz, B., Tufail, T., … & Anjum, F. M. (2021). Nutritional and end-use perspectives of sprouted grains: A comprehensive review. *Food science & Nutrition*, 9(8), 4617–4628.

Kyriacou, M. C., Rouphael, Y., Di Gioia, F., Kyratzis, A., Serio, F., Renna, M., … & Santamaria, P. (2016). Micro-scale vegetable production and the rise of microgreens. *Trends in Food Science & Technology*, 57, 103–115.

Lemmens E., Moroni A.V., Pagand J., Heirbaut P., Ritala A., Karlen Y., Lê K.A., Van den Broeck H.C., Brouns F.J., De Brier N., et al. (2019). Impact of cereal seed sprouting on its nutritional and technological properties: A critical review. *Comprehensive Reviews in Food Science and Food Safety*, 18(1), 305–328.

Márton, M., Mándoki, Z., Csapo-Kiss, Z. S., & Csapó, J. (2010). The role of sprouts in human nutrition. A review. *Acta Univ. Sapientiae*, Alimentaria, 3. 81–117

Michell, K. A., Isweiri, H., Newman, S.E., Bunning, M., Bellows, L.L., Dinges, M. M., … & Johnson, S.A. (2020). Microgreens: Consumer sensory perception and acceptance of an emerging functional food crop. *Journal of Food Science*, 85(4), 926–935.

Microgreensworld.com. From: https://microgreensworld.com/knowledgebase/microgreens-economics Accessed on: 20.05.2024.

Mir, S. A., Shah, M. A. & Mir, M. M. (2017). Microgreens: Production, shelf life and bioactive components. *Critical Reviews in Food Science and Nutrition*, 57(12), 2730–2736.

Ngram Viewer (2024). From: https://books.google.com/ngrams/ Accessed on: 10.05.2024.

Örnek, A. (2021). Yiyecek içecek sektöründe yenilebilir çiçekler ve mikro filizler. Gastronomi Araştırmaları. pp. 103–109. Çizgi Kitabevi.

Reed, E., Ferreira, C.M., Bell, R., Brown, E.W., & Zheng, J. (2018). Plant-microbe and abiotic factors influencing Salmonella survival and growth on alfalfa sprouts and Swiss chard microgreens. *Applied and Environmental Microbiology*, 84(9), e02814–17.

Renna, M., Di Gioia, F., Leoni, B., Mininni, C. & Santamaria, P. (2016). Culinary assessment of self-produced microgreens as basic ingredients in sweet and savory disches. *Journal of Culinary Science & Technology*, 1–17.

Riggio, G. M., Wang, Q., Kniel, K. E., & Gibson, K. E. (2019). Microgreens—A review of food safety considerations along the farm to fork continuum. *International journal of food microbiology*, 290, 76–85.

Rouphael, Y., Colla, G., & De Pascale, S. (2021). Sprouts, microgreens and edible flowers as novel functional foods. *Agronomy*, 11(12), 2568.

Shurtleff, W., & Aoyagi, A. (2013). History of Soy Sprouts (100 CE To 2013): Extensively Annotated Bibliography and Sourcebook. Soyinfo Center.

Straitsresearch.com (2023). From: https://straitsresearch.com/report/microgreens-market Accessed on: 20.05.2024.

Verlinden, S. (2019). Microgreens. *Horticultural Reviews*, 85–124.

Wallentinson, L., Weibull, L., & Nevermann-Ballandis, I. (2018). Sprouts, shoots, and microgreens: Tiny plants to grow and eat in your kitchen. Skyhorse Publishing.

Wojdyło, A., Nowicka, P., Tkacz, K., & Turkiewicz, I. P. (2020). Sprouts vs. microgreens as novel functional foods: Variation of nutritional and phytochemical profiles and their in vitro bioactive properties. *Molecules*, 25(20), 4648.

Xiao, Z., Lester, G. E., Luo, Y., & Wang, Q. (2012). Assessment of vitamin and carotenoid concentrations of emerging food products: edible microgreens. *Journal of agricultural and Food Chemistry*, 60(31), 7644–7651.

Zhang, Y., Xiao, Z., Ager, E., Kong, L., & Tan, L. (2021). Nutritional quality and health benefits of microgreens, a crop of modern agriculture. *Journal of Future Foods*, 1(1), 58–66.

Seda Yilmaz[1]

Chapter 11 Tourist Typology and Memorable Gastronomic Experience

Introduction

In recent years, it has been found that tourists, who shape tourism activities and are the determinants of tourism activities, are looking for an experience related to the product they purchase beyond the purchase of a tourism product (Morgan et al., 2010; Eryılmaz & Zengin, 2014). Moreover, tourists seek vacations to have fun, gain new knowledge, and remember positive emotions (Holbrook & Hirschman, 1982; Pine & Gilmore, 1999). This situation brings with it the need to offer memorable and attractive gastronomic experiences to tourists and gastronomic tourism products in the gastronomic tourism market. The gastronomic experience can offer the opportunity to have an experience that adds value to the visit to a destination, including all travel motivations whose primary motivation is other than food and drink, and attracts tourists to the region (Ruschmann, 1997). In this context, destinations have become an attraction factor for tourists participating in gastronomic tourism.

The travel motivations of tourists participating in gastronomy tourism activities and their expectations about destinations shape the services offered by food and beverage establishments that provide gastronomic experiences. In this case, it can be said that the gastronomic experiences tourists expect are parallel to their tourist typologies.

This study examines the concepts of tourist typology in studies conducted in the field of gastronomy and the types of tourists identified in the studies. The concept of memorable gastronomic experiences, factors that make gastronomic experiences memorable, and the effect of tourist typologies on the memorability of gastronomic experiences are discussed, and a general framework is drawn.

---

1   PhD Student, Akdeniz University, Tourism Faculty, Department of Gastronomy and Culinary Arts sedaipek48@gmail.com

The Concept of Tourist Typology

The concept of a tourist typology can be elucidated by first addressing why people travel. In a study on the motivations of backpacking tourists, Dann posited that these tourists travel for social and psychological reasons such as escape, prestige, self-actualization, or adventure. In other words, they are driven to travel to destinations that align with their interests. In this context, the push-and-pull framework posits that individuals are driven by intrinsic motivations to travel and influenced by external factors in the destinations they intend to visit (Dann, 1977, 1981). Similarly, Crompton (1979) conducted a study of tourists on vacation for pleasure and concluded that they travel for motivations such as getting away from routine and mediocrity, relaxation, gaining prestige, improving kinship and friendship relations, strengthening social interaction, and self-knowledge. From this perspective, it can be seen that the underlying basis of the formation of tourist typologies is tourists' travel motivations. These motivations have been identified as the search for information in some studies, participation in activities in some studies, and the search for authenticity in others (Boyne, 2003; Chang et al., 2010; Hjalager, 2004; Ignatov & Smith, 2006; Witschge et al., 2016; Özdemir & Seyioğlu, 2017). Furthermore, in a study conducted by Boyne in 2003 to ascertain the motives behind tourist travel, it was determined that tourists embark on journeys in pursuit of novel, distinctive, and intellectual information (Boyne, 2003).

A review of the literature on tourist typologies reveals considerable diversity of typologies. In their study on determining tourist typology, Şimşek and Selçuk (2018) employed a questionnaire to survey tourists and subsequently identified five distinct groups through cluster analysis, aligning their findings with the data obtained. These include the following typologies: organicist, innovative, aiming and loving to learn, food-oriented, and localist (Şimşek & Selçuk, 2018). Conversely, in his 1972 study, Cohen identified four distinct types of tourists. The first was organized mass travel for a specific purpose within a planned and specific program. The second was the participation of an individualist mass in tourist trips. Third, the explorer was mass-oriented towards different experiences. The fourth was rambling tourists in an utterly spontaneous flow (Cohen, 1972).

Upon examination of studies classifying the typologies of tourists participating in gastronomy tourism activities, it becomes evident that in the study conducted by Ignatov and Smith (2006), tourists were classified according to their preferences for participation in gastronomy activities. Accordingly, three different typologies have been proposed: wine tourists, food and wine tourists, and food tourists (Ignatov & Smith, 2006).

Özdemir and Seyioğlu defined three different tourist typologies as authenticity seekers, moderates, and comfort seekers in a study conducted in 2017. This study aimed to examine tourist behavior from the perspective of authenticity seeking in gastronomic experiences. It is noteworthy that the travel motivation of tourists is the search for authenticity (Özdemir & Seyioğlu, 2017).

In a study conducted in 2004 on tourist groups participating in tourist activities in Randers Fjord, a relatively underdeveloped region of rural Denmark, Hjalager identified four different tourist typologies: experimentalist, recreationalist, imitative, and existentialist (Hjalager, 2004). In this study, it was found that while for recreational and imitative tourists, food and beverage products are not a primary consideration in touristic destinations, for experimentalist and existentialist tourists, food and beverage products are as important as the reason for choosing the destination.

Tikkanen (2007), identified tourists engaged in gastronomic tourism as "culinary tourists" and posited that these tourists exhibit five distinct travel motivations. These include the appreciation of food as a complete attraction, the purchase and consumption of culinary products by tourists, the valuation of food as a valuable and sought-after commodity, the examination of food as a cultural phenomenon, and the pursuit of a connection between tourism and food production (Tikkanen, 2007).

In a subsequent study, it was observed that tourists engaged in gastronomic tourism were depicted as "foodies" within the context of the typology of tourists. This study posits that the fundamental motivation underlying tourists' participation in gastronomic tourism activities is their inclination to engage in such activities (Lawrence & Robinson, 2014). Similarly, in Chang's study, in which tourists' participation in gastronomy tourism trips constituted travel motivation, tourists were categorized as observers, participants, and browsers (Chang et al., 2010).

In the research conducted by Crespi, Volbona, and Dimitri in 2016 to determine the types of tourists, several typology suggestions were presented. Two distinct categories of tourists were identified in the food markets: those disinterested in the market and those passionate about food markets.

When studies on tourist typologies in the literature are evaluated, the main variables that many studies focus on are as follows:

- Travel motivations,
- Food and beverage preferences when traveling,
- Food shopping preferences in destinations,
- It was observed that they have attitudes toward restaurant preferences.

Furthermore, empirical and conceptual studies of tourist typology indicate that the determinants of tourist typology are social and demographic factors, participation, interest, and travel motivations. In contrast, the influencing factors were destination preference, travel behavior, and food preference.

Concept of Memorable Gastronomic Experience

One of the components of this study was a memorable food experience. When we talk about memorable gastronomic experiences, we think about experiences that are perceived as positive, excellent, and memorable in the minds of tourists. One way to better understand the definition of positive experiences is to focus on memorability (Ritchie & Crouch, 2003; Tung & Ritchie, 2011).

Memorable gastronomic experiences are a phenomenon that has received much attention in recent years. A review of studies on memorable gastronomic experiences shows that they focus on how tourists choose one trip or activity over another and the reasons behind these choices. In these studies, a memorable gastronomic experience is defined as memorizing a pleasant gastronomic experience with its positive characteristics (Antón et al., 2019).

In a study by Oğan and Durlu Özkaya, in which they examined the gastronomy and gastronomic experiences of tourists visiting Artvin, it was concluded that food has an essential place in tourists' visit to the region; they liked the local food, were satisfied with the food and beverage service they purchased in the region, and had memorable positive impressions in the region (Oğan & Durlu Özkaya, 2021). From this perspective, it is understood that not only the eating and drinking behavior of tourists, but also the products and services they purchase and the positive emotions they feel are part of the gastronomic experience.

Studies have been carried out to understand the variables ensuring the memorability of memorable gastronomic experiences. In a study conducted by Badu-Baiden et al. on US tourists visiting Europe and Asia in 2022, it was found that the dimensions of memorable local gastronomic experiences and their impact on destination loyalty differed according to tourists' personal gastronomic characteristics. It was also found that the factors that ensure the memorability of tourists' gastronomic experiences are hospitality, social interaction, and neophilia (Badu-Baiden et al., 2022).

On the other hand, Stone et al. carried out a comprehensive study of about one thousand tourists from four different countries to determine the memorable gastronomic experiences of tourists and the elements that make these experiences memorable. Accordingly, it was found that the five main elements that make tourist experiences memorable are food and drink consumed, location/

environment, friends, opportunity, and tourism elements, such as innovation and authenticity (Stone et al., 2018). In a similar study, Williams et al. identified seven primary outcomes that ensured memorability of gastronomic experiences. These include intentional and accidental gastro-tourists, trip stages, food-related risk-taking, interdependent co-created tourist-host relationships, authenticity, sociability, and emotions (Williams & Williams, 2019).

Another study on the memorability of gastronomic experiences was conducted among a group of tourists visiting Rovaniemi, Finland. It was found that the element that makes the gastronomic experiences of tourists memorable is the taste, which is familiar to all tourists. It was found that the mentioned taste element also gained importance in pleasant and happy moments (Sthapit, 2019).

In a study conducted in 2018, Goolaup introduced a different perspective on the factors that influence the phenomenon of memorable gastronomic experiences. They found that gastronomic tourists perceive surprise and extraordinary gastronomic experiences differently, depending on their food cultural capital. Accordingly, it was concluded that tourists with high cultural capital were surprised by the simplicity or complexity of their surprise or extraordinary experience. In contrast, those with low cultural capital are surprised by the originality of the experience (Goolaup et al., 2018). In an empirical study conducted by Goolaup and Mossberg, they interviewed a group of tourists about factors that influence the memorability of their gastronomic experiences. It was concluded that the factors that most influence tourists' memorable experiences are the uniqueness of gastronomic experiences, sense of togetherness, understanding, hospitality, luxury, and gastronomic destinations' natural and environmental characteristics (Goolaup & Mossberg, 2017). Accordingly, as in other studies, the fact that tourists are together and have a good time is an essential factor in the memorability of their gastronomic experiences.

Some studies of memorable gastronomic experiences have highlighted that gastronomic experience is a dynamic phenomenon. These studies have found that the most important factors influencing the memorability of gastronomic experiences are the souvenirs received in the destinations and what is told and shared about the destination (Björk & Kauppinen-Raisanen, 2016; Sthapit, 2017; Sthapit et al., 2019; DiClement et al., 2020).

The Relationship between Tourist Typology and Unforgettable Gastronomic Experience

When the concepts of memorable gastronomic experience and tourist typology are evaluated together, it can be concluded that the concept of tourist typology is a cue for understanding why and how tourists react to local gastronomic experiences. One of the tourists' reactions to the gastronomic experience is a memorable gastronomic experience. Therefore, it is assumed that gastronomic experiences that remain in the memory of tourists participating in gastronomic tourism due to local food experiences are related to the concept of tourist typology. This relationship suggests that tourist typology is a variable that influences the level of memorability of gastronomic experiences.

According to Gupta et al. (2020), perceptions felt during food experiences in tourist destinations effectively form memorable experiences.

On the other hand, a study conducted by Ryu et al. in 2012 also supports this idea with the view that food that reflects the restaurant's image directly affects the value that customers perceive about the restaurant. In this context, it is understood that essential criteria such as the ambience of the environment, the attractiveness of the atmosphere, the taste-smell-color harmony of the gastronomic product, taste, and other elements directly affect the value perceived by tourists about the gastronomic experience during the gastronomic experience, which is the basis of the travel motivation of tourists participating in gastronomic tourism. In this case, perceived value is believed to be vital for determining memorability. The relationship between tourist typology, perceived value, and recall can be explained using a simple conceptual model as follows:

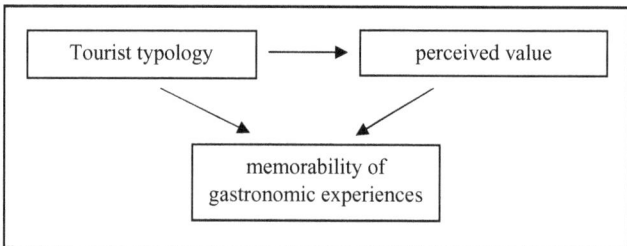

Figure 11.1. The Impact of Tourist Typology on the Memorability of Gastronomic Experiences

In the above model, the tourist typology directly affects the perceived value and memorability of gastronomic experiences. Based on this model, it is assumed that the memorability of the gastronomic experience is in effect with the tourist type, and the value perceived by tourists after their gastronomic experiences may affect whether or not the gastronomic experiences will be memorable.

Results

Examining the studies on tourist typology in the field of gastronomy, it can be seen that there are tourist typologies in the field of gastronomy, and these typologies are determined conceptually or empirically through determinant variables. Based on the theoretical basis of these studies, there are general studies on tourist typologies in the tourism field (Boyne et al., 2003; Hjalager, 2004; Özdemir & Seyioğlu, 2017).

When examining the effect of tourist typologies on memorable gastronomic experiences, it was concluded that some empirical studies directly impact the memorability of gastronomic experiences. In these studies, the variables that influenced memorability were place attachment and behavioral intention (Sthapit et al., 2017; Anton et al., 2019). However, other factors that memorable gastronomic experiences are togetherness and social interaction, hospitality, atmosphere, location/environment, emotions, shared stories about gastronomic destinations, souvenirs, information seeking, participation, local culture and local food, and unusualness and surprise (Sthapit, 2017; Williams & Williams, 2018; Goolaup & Mossberg, 2017; Stone et al., 2017; Goolaup, 2018; Anton et al., 2019; Badu-Baiden et al., 2022).

On the other hand, studies that concluded that memorable gastronomic experiences have a dynamic rather than a static structure stated that the elements that make gastronomic experiences unforgettable are souvenirs, stories about the destination, and what is shared (Björk & Kauppinen-Raisanen, 2016; Sthapit, 2017; Sthapit et al., 2019; DiClement et al., 2020).

As a result, why gastronomic experiences may be memorable is directly related to the stimuli, components, and interactions of these experiences. However, the fact that gastronomy has a diverse, aesthetic, dynamic, and exciting nature makes this situation inevitable. Whether positive or negative, it is thought that the moments, emotions, or objects that all individuals with sufficient cognitive skills consider worth remembering leave a trace in their memories and bring together the components of the gastronomy experience. Tourists' travel motivations and their tourist typologies are the antecedents of the gastronomic experience.

References

Antón, C., Camarero, C., Laguna, M., & Buhalis, D. (2019). Impact of authenticity, degree of adaptation, and cultural contrast on travelers' memorable gastronomy experiences. Journal of Hospitality Marketing & Management, 28(7), 743–764.

Badu-Baiden, F., Correia, A., & Kim, S. (2022). How do tourists' memorable local gastronomy experiences and personal gastronomic traits influence destination loyalty? A fuzzy set approach. Journal of Travel & Tourism Marketing, 39(5), 501–515.

Björk, P., & Kauppinen-Räisänen, H. (2016). Local food: source of destination attraction. International Journal of Contemporary Hospitality Management, 28(1), 177–194.

Boyne, S., Williams, F., & Hall, D. (2003). On the trail of regional success: Tourism, food production, and the Isle of the Arran Taste Trail. In Tourism and gastronomy (pp. 105–128). Routledge.

Chang, R. C., Kivela, J., & Mak, A. H. (2010). Food preferences of Chinese tourists. Annals of tourism research, 37(4), 989–1011.

Cohen, E. (1972). Toward a sociology of international tourism. Social Research, 39, 164–82

Crespi-Vallbona, M. & Dimitrovski, D. (2016). "Food Markets Visitors: A Typology Proposal". British Food Journal, 118(4), 840–857.

Crompton J.L. (1979). Motivations for pleasure vacation. Annals of Tourism Research 6(4): 408–424. Crossref.

Dann, G. M. (1977). Anomie, ego-enhancement, and tourism. Annals of Tourism Research 4(4): 184–194.

Dann, G. M. (1981). Tourist motivation an appraisal. Annals of Tourism Research 8(2): 187–219.

Di-Clemente E, Hernández-Mogollón JM, Campón-Cerro AM (2020) Tourists' involvement and memorable food-based experiences as new determinants of behavioural intentions towards typical products. Current Issues in Tourism 23(18): 2319–2332.

Eryilmaz, B. ve Zengin, B. (2014). Sosyal Medyada Konaklama İşletmelerine Yönelik Tüketici Yaklaşımları Üzerine Bir Araştırma. İşletme Bilimi Dergisi, 2 (1), 147–167.

Goolaup, S., Solér, C., & Nunkoo, R. (2018). Developing a theory of surprise from travelers' extraordinary food experiences. Journal of Travel Research, 57(2), 218–231.

Goolaup, S., & Mossberg, L. (2017). Exploring the concept of extraordinary related to food tourists' nature-based experience. Scandinavian Journal of Hospitality and Tourism, 17(1), 27–43.

Gupta, V. Sajnani. M. S-Dixit & Khanna, K. (2020): Foreign tourist's tea preferences and relevance to destination attraction in India. Tourism Recreation Research, 181662.

Hjalager, A. M. (2004). Sustainable leisure life modes and rural welfare economy. The case of the Randers Fjord area, Denmark. International Journal of Tourism Research, 6(3), 177–188.

Holbrook MB, Hirschman E (1982). The experiential aspects of consumption: Consumer fantasies, feelings and fun. Journal Of Consumer Research 9(9): 132–140.

Ignatov, E., & Smith, S. (2006). Segmenting Canadian culinary tourists. Current issues in tourism, 9(3), 235–255.

Lawrence, M. S., Stojanov, P., Mermel, C. H., Robinson, J. T., Garraway, L. A., Golub, T. R., … & Getz, G. (2014). Discovery and saturation analysis of cancer genes across 21 tumour types. Nature, 505(7484), 495–501.

Morgan M., Lugosi P. ve Ritchie, J. R. B. (2010). The Tourism And Leisure Experience: Consumer and Managerial Perspectives. Channel View, Bristol

Oğan, Y., & Durlu-özkaya, F. (2021). Artvin'i ziyaret eden turistlerin gastronomi deneyimleri üzerine bir inceleme. Güncel Turizm Araştırmaları Dergisi, 5(2), 211–227.

Özdemir, B., & Seyioğlu, F. (2017). A conceptual study of gastronomical quests of tourists: Authenticity or safety and comfort?. Tourism management perspectives, 23, 1–7.

Pine BJ, Gilmore JH (1999). The Experience Economy: Work is Theatre & Every Business a Stage (Harvard Business Press, England).

Ritchie J. R., Crouch G. (2003). The competitive destination: A sustainable tourism perspective. Cambridge, MA: CABI. Crossref.

Ruschmann, D (1997) Turismo e planejamento sustentável: a proteção do meio ambiente (Campinas: Papirus).

Ryu, K. Lee, H. & Gon Kim, W. (2012). The influence of the quality of the physical environment, food, and service on restaurant image, customer perceived value, customer satisfaction, and behavioral intentions. International Journal of Contemporary Hospitality Management, 24(2), 200–223.

Sthapit, E., Björk, P., & Coudounaris, D. N. (2017). Emotions elicited by local food consumption, memories, place attachment and behavioural intentions. Anatolia, 28(3), 363–380.

Sthapit, E. (2019). Memories of gastronomic experiences, savoured positive emotions and savouring processes. Scandinavian Journal of Hospitality and Tourism, 19(2), 115–139.

Sthapit, E., Coudounaris, D. N., & Björk, P. (2019). Extending the memorable tourism experience construct: an investigation of memories of local food experiences. Scandinavian Journal of Hospitality and Tourism, 19(4–5), 333–353.

Stone et al, M. J., Soulard, J., Migacz, S., & Wolf, E. (2018). Elements of memorable food, drink, and culinary tourism experiences. Journal of Travel Research, 57(8), 1121–1132.

Şimşek, A., & Selçuk, G. N. (2018). Gastro Turistlerin Tipolojisinin Belirlenmesi: Gaziantep Ölçeğinde Bir Uygulama. Uluslararası Türk Dünyası Turizm Araştırmaları Dergisi, 3(1), 28–43.

Tikkanen, I. (2007). Maslow's Hierarchy and Food Tourism in Finland: Five Cases. British Food Journal, 109(9), 721–734.

Tung V., Ritchie J. R. (2011). Exploring the essence of memorable tourism experiences. Annals of Tourism Research, 38, 1367–1386. Crossref. ISI.

Williams, H. A., Yuan, J. J., & Williams, R. L. (2018). Characteristics and practices of gastro-tourists: Application for a 6+ gastro-cluster destination development model. Gastronomy and Tourism, 3(3), 177–190.

Witschge, T., Hermida, A., Domingo, D., & Anderson, C. W. (2016). The SAGE handbook of digital journalism. The SAGE Handbook of Digital Journalism, 1–624.

Hilal Kul[1]

Chapter 12 The Effect of Gastronomy Trends on Accommodation Preferences; Therapeutic Nutrition Tendency in Tourism Behavior

Introduction

Tourism is one of the main multidisciplinary fields that affects many disciplines (Cohen, 1984; Gulcan, 2010). These fields include disciplines that are shaped by life and shape life, such as geography, sociology, anthropology, history, philosophy, chemistry, medicine, art, aesthetics, archaeology, psychology, ethnography, pale-ography, and economics (Goksan, 1978; Gulcan, 2009; Yuksel, 2010). Tourism, in terms of the areas it is affected by developed serves as an important bridge that transfers culture between yesterday, today and tomorrow (Izgi, Istanbullu-Dincer, Cetin, Demiroglu and Aslan, 2007; Sert and Ikiz, 2012). When tourism and tourist orientations, factors affecting tourism motivation, satisfaction rates of tourist expectations before and after tourism activity are examined on a yearly basis, the effect of classical tourism and innovative tourism approaches on tourism mobility has emerged as a determining factor (Zogal ve Emekli, 2017). Since economic, political and social change is intertwined with the individual, and individual changes are intertwined with the society, reading the change process of tourism and making process analyzes are based on the analysis of the economic and political change processes of societies (Kongar, 2010). The characteristics of the classical tourism model included in the literature with the definition of classical tourism or traditional tourism, covering the period until the 1980s; It is similar to the economic and psychological characteristics exhibited by countries after the end of the Second World War (Evcin, 2016; Ozen, 2017). With the great changes that took place in the world political arena after the Second World War (1939–1945), the effect of the war on economic factors, and the differentiation of countries' economic and tourism approaches, the economic potential of tourism was realized and studies on tourism were increased (Ates, Akmese and Karabiyik, 2020; Lane, 2009; Unluonen, Tayfun and Kiliclar, 2007). Tourism activity, which gained momentum with the classical tourism approach in the

---

1   Kilis 7 Aralik University, Vocational School of Tourism and Hotel Management, Department of Culinary, hilal.kkul@gmail.com

1950's and 1960's, went through a period of stagnation as a result of the great economic crisis experienced worldwide in 1973 (Smith, 1995; Soyak, 2009). The Fordist economic model, which was shaped within the framework of the policies developed by Taylor, was the dominant economic understanding in the world until 1973 and appeared in the literature as "Fordism" as Gramsci (1971) stated; "It has re-planned the individual by designing the way the individual and society live and feel" (Alien, 1992). The Fordist economy model is the period that glorifies fabrication production, focuses on the production capacity of goods with cheap labor, and attaches importance to standardization, speed and maximum efficiency (Harvey, 1997). It has been supported by academic studies that people living in this model, where the importance of doing the job in a standard way with maximum efficiency rather than individual characteristics, exhibit behaviors of choosing among the offered ones without questioning their own preferences in tourism mobility (Roney, 2002). Tourism model based on the Fordist model; It can be explained as the period in which tour operators play the decisive role in tourism mobility, offered to tourists with packages determined by tour operators (Gartner and Holecek, 1983; Murray, 1989). In the classical tourism model, the structure, geographical conditions, history, cultural assets and products of the destination are very important; coastal tourism and cultural tourism titles have been the destination features highlighted by tour operators in the tourism market (Kozak, Evren and Cakir, 2013). With the changing dominant economic model as of the 1980s, job and working definitions were made based on the characteristics and preferences of the individual, changes in the political structures of the states and the implementation of the global economic model.

Its use has formed the basis of the experiential-innovative model by reflecting on tourist behavior (Cutler and Carmichael, 2020; Hjalager, 2015; Sugiyarto, Blake and Sinclair, 2003). The main determining factors of the innovative tourism model are tourists' expectations of having active experiences by taking a participatory role in tourism activities and tourist psychology (Altunel, 2015). The problem of people, structures and lives becoming similar, which are among the negative consequences of globalization, whose impact intensified in the 1990s. The feeling of repeating the same thing that occurs in the individual as a result of similarity, are among the driving forces of experiential tourism motivation (Harlak, 1995). With digitalization and accessibility becoming a part of the daily flow of life, the use of social media, smartphones, the internet and digital applications have become a part of the daily flow of life, and the transformation of the use of social media, smartphones, the internet and digital applications into the motivation to obtain and share experience in tourism mobility brings the emphasis on having different experiences to the fore day by day (Kellner, 1995;

Pabel and Prideaux, 2016). In the 21st century innovative-creative-experiential tourism mobility, the acommodation structures of the destinations "different" atmospheres, different consepts, different gastronomy trends of the acommodation structures alive are the main convincing reasons for tourists motivated by experience to participate in tourism activities (Larsen, 2014). The need for experience, which is one of the main reasons guiding 21st century tourism activities, brings "trends" to the fore with the intense use of social media language.

Accommodation establishments were seen only as economic business models in the classical tourism period. The changing and developing conjuncture has also changed the planning and management methods of accommodation establishments concepts and trends have become the main marketing elements of accommodation structures. Gastronomy trends, one of the attractive elements of the last quarter of the century, have begun to be used as one of the themes of accommodation establishments. Gastronomy trends are an important marketing element of the 2000's. Accommodation establishments that organize nutrition programs for the treatment of certain ailments are particularly noteworthy. This gastronomy theme is called therapeutic theme.

The trend means in the English the popular. It is one of the English words frequently used to describe popular preferences in the literature. The word therapeutic is a word of French origin. It is used to describe therapeutic foods and foods used in physiological and psychological diseases. One of the rising trends in gastronomy in the 21st century has been the therapeutic nutrition trend. These trends may be trends covering a style of behavior that concerns the whole of life, such as Ancient Greece/Classical Anatolia, Prophetic Medicine, Hilts and Temperaments, Ayurveda, Phytotherapy, Qi examples. There may also be trends involving nutritional techniques used in the treatment of specific physiological-psychological disorders such as Autism, Celiac, MS, Alzheimer's, Obesity, and Diabetes. The therapeutic nutrition trends covers all of the examples above. It may also be a dietary choice based on a philosophy such as vegetarian diet, vegan diet, green diet, Mediterranean diet, ketogenic diet, high protein diet, gluten-free diet, diet according to colors, diet according to blood type. Apart from these, accommodation facilities where healthy life "camps" are implemented, yoga-themed accommodation facilities, detox facilities, facilities combining spa and healthy gastronomy stand out as attractive features in the market. However, if these nutritional choices are not a treatment-oriented diet, they should not be called therapeutic nutrition. They can be considered as gastronomy trend or popular currents in gastronomy. The first of the important elements of therapeutic gastronomy trends is traditional gastronomic experiences (Chang and Mak, 2018). Stages of obtaining raw materials - crop planting, milking, egg collection, harvest times, olive oil, soap, tomato paste, canning, drying, molasses, tarhana, fragrance, food and beverage, etc. process - such as cooking, presentation of products. Traditional gastronomy experiences, which can be included in the tourism process of destinations, every stage of which is planned until the moment of consumption, offer tourists a wide range of experience options (Ercik, Yetim, Akdag, & Celik, 2018). The use of traditional dishes, which are examples of product and culture combination, in therapeutic gastronomy has an important role in meeting the experience needs and expectations of tourists participating in tourism and in their behavior of revisiting the destination (Basat, Sandikci and Celik, 2017; Horng and Tsai, 2012; Nebioglu, 2016). In recent years, the increasing rate of gastronomy routes and gastro tours and tours preferred by tourists who are prone to experiential tourism are important indicators showing the place of traditional dishes in tourism activities (Bessiere, 2013; Björk and Kauppinen-Räisänen, 2014). The difference in experience provided by traditional dishes; when the taste, aroma, appearance and smell advantages of food are combined and marketed with other material and spiritual heritages of the destination and the authentic elements of the destination, an increase in tourism activities occurs due to the increase in satisfaction obtained from tourism activities. This increase is one of the expected and normal results. Marketing of accommodation establishments combines traditional products with the therapeutic gastronomy trend increases profitability (Andersson, 2017; Aslimoski and Gerasimoski, 2012; Monica Hu, Chen and Ou, 2009; Pine and Gilmore, 1998).

Therapeutic nutrition trend in tourist behavior highlights accommodation establishments as a destination. Establishments that provide therapeutic services and support this service with therapeutic gastronomy also increase the multiplier effect in the tourism market. These establishments which are generally established in blue and green areas, natural areas such as forests, seas, rivers and lakes, away from city life and stress, expand their markets with slogans such as nutrition for health. They also combine nutrition concepts for health with a theme. These concepts are turning into a trend in tourist preferences. Accommodation establishments that serve within the concept of therapeutic nutrition offer services that include one or more of the chefs, dietitians, sports trainers, doctors and other supporting professions who are knowledgeable in the field. Accommodation establishments that provide services in this way create an attractive trend in tourism behavior. The trend enables the company to increase its market share. The primary goals of establishments are making profits and maintaining the business, and with the increase in options, the experience aspects of accommodation establisments also come to the fore.

Conclusion

According to the discipline of psychology; "Experience, it refers to the totality of knowledge, skills and attitudes that a person acquires through direct perception and activities." Experience has become one of the important reasons for tourist needs, expectations and preferences. This need is an important driving force that directs tourism movements. It is effective in the destination preferences of the 21st century. Experience combines gastronomy and accommodation tourism. As a result of changing country conjunctures and developing technology after 1980's, the existence activities of accommodation establishments have changed direction and mobility with the widespread use of the Internet, smart phones and social media. Innovative-experiential tourism has become an important part of tourism in our country as well. By the 2000's, experience in tourism mobility, with the influence of visual transmissions due to its easy accessibility and recognition, has become one of the factors that increase the need for tourism. The touristic products, assets and accommodation facilities of destinations, which are one of the most important determinants of tourist orientation, are in line with changing needs and demands. It started to be planned and marketed by highlighting its attractive elements and enriching it with multiple experiences. Planning without focusing on the distinctive features of tourist enterprises and destinations planned with the traditional tourism approach causes problems such as the homogeneity problem brought by globalization, the decrease in the pleasure of tourism activities, and the failure to meet the expectations of tourists. As a result of the perception of mediocrity, the desire to revisit the destination, which is one of the main purposes of destination planning, is becoming one of the rare touristic behaviors. Especially the fact that accommodation establishments are not preferred among many options has become a problem in the tourism market. In solving this problem, gastronomy and new gastronomy trends are important attractive features for tourists. Especially businesses that provide services for a specific ailment are preferred. In businesses where the therapeutic gastronomy movement dominates, the local product market has become one of the marketing tools of businesses. The use of natural and local products in the kitchens of accommodation establishments, gastronomy trends applied for disease treatments such as healthy kitchen, green kitchen, gluten-free kitchen, waste-free kitchen, alkaline kitchen, chemical-free kitchen contribute to sustainable tourism establishments. Tourist programs, therapeutic gastronomy and health activities supported by routes significantly increase the tourism income of accommodation establishments and the destination.

References

Alien. J. (1992). Post-industrialism and post-fordism. Hall, S. D. ve McGrew, T. (ed.) Modernity and ItsFutures Inside, Polity Oxford: Press: (1), 70–204.

Altunel, M. C. (2013). Turistlerin beklenti ve deneyimleme kalitesinin tavsiye etme kararina etkisi: Muze ziyaretcileri uzerine bir arastirma (Doctoral dissertation, DEU Sosyal Bilimleri Enstitusu).

Andersson, T. D. (2007). The tourist in the experience economy. Scandinavian Journal of Hospitality and Tourism, 7(1), 46–58.

Aslimoski, P. ve Gerasimoski, S. (2012). Food and nutrition as tourist phenomenon. Procedia- Socialand Behavioral Sciences, 44, 357–362.

Ates, A., Akmese, H. ve Karabiyik, G. H. (2020). Gastronomi ve Turizm Iliskisi, Adiyaman: Iksad Yayinevi.

Basat, H.T., Sandikci, M. ve Celik, S. (2017). Gastronomik Kimlik Olusturmada Yoresel Urunlerin Rolu: Urunlerin Satis ve Pazarlanmasina Yonelik Bir Ornek Olay İncelemesi, Journal of Tourism and Gastronomy Studies, 5(2): 64–76.

Bessiere, J. and Tibere, L. (2013). Traditional food and tourism: French tourist experience and foodheritage in rural spaces. Journal of the Science of Food and Agriculture, 93(14), 3420–3425.

Björk, P. and Kauppinen-Räisänen, H. (2014). Culinary-gastronomic tourism–a search for local food experiences. Nutrition ve Food Science, 44(4), 294–309.

Chang, R.C.Y. and Mak, A.H.N. (2018). Understanding gastronomic image from tourists' perspective: Are pertory grid approach. Tourism Management. 68: 89–100.

Cohen, E. (1984). The Sociology of Tourism: Approaches, Issues, and Findings, Annual Review of Sociology, Vol.10, 373–392.

Cutler, S. Q., and Carmichael, A. B. (2010). The Dimensions of Tourist Experiences. M. Morgan, P. Lugosive J.R.B, Ritchie, (Ed), The Toruism and Leisure Experiences-Consumer and Managerial Perspectives. Great Britain: Channel View Publications. S.3–27.

Evcin, E. (2016). Ikinci Dunya Savasi'nin Turkiye Turizminde Yarattigi Firsatlar. Tarihin Pesinde Uluslararasi Tarih ve Sosyal Arastirmalar Dergisi, (15), 129–153.

Ercik, C., Yetim A., Akdag G. ve Celik, R. (2018). Agro-Turizm ve Gastronomi İliskisi: Yenilikci Bir Turizm Yaklasimi, Uluslararasi Avrasya Dogal Beslenme ve Saglikli Yasam Zirvesi Kongre ve Sergi, 12–15 Temmuz 2018, Ankara, s. 1086.

Gartner, W., and Holecek, D. (1983). Economic Impact of Annual Tourism Industry Exposition. Annals of Tourism Research 10: 199–212.

Goksan, E. (1978). Turizmoloji. Izmir: Ugur Ofset.

Gramsci, A. (1971). Americanism and Fordism. Hoare. Q. ve Noweli-Smith G. (ed.) Selections from the Prison Notebooks of Antonio Gramsci Inside, Londra: Lawrence and Wishari. 277–318.

Gulcan, B. (2009). Turizmin Disipliner Evrimi, Ticaret ve Turizm Eğitim Fakültesi Dergisi, (1), 186–206.

Gulcan, B. (2010). Turizmin Disipliner Gelişimini Tamamlaması Yolunda Disiplinlerarası Çalışmaların Önemi, I. Disiplinlerarası Turizm Araştırmaları Kongresi, 129–141.

Harlak, H. (1995). Psikoloji ve Turizmin Kesisme Noktasi. Turizm Psikolojisi, Prof. Dr. Hasan Zafer Doğan Ani Kitabi, M. Korzay ve B. Himmetoglu (drl). Bogazici Universitesi s. 111–117.

Harvey. D. (1997). Postmodernligin Durumu. (Cev: S. Savran). Istanbul: Metis Yayinlari.

Horng J.S and Tsai C.T. (2012). Culinary Tourism Strategic Development: An Asian-Pacific Perspective. International Journal of Tourism Research 14: 40–55.

Hjalager, A. M. (2015). Turizmi Degistiren 100 Yenilik. (Cev. Guler, O., Akdag, G., A., Cakıcı, A. C. and Benli, S.), Anatolia: Turizm Arastirmalari Dergisi, 290–317.

Izgi, M. T., Istanbullu-Dincer, F., Cetin, G., Demiroglu, O. C. ve Aslan, E., (2007). Turizmoloji Nedir? Turizmbilim Uzerine Yapilan Teorik Calismalarin Bir Analiz Calismasi. Cesme Ulusal Turizm Sempozyumu (pp. 490–502). Izmir, Turkiye.

Kellner, D. (1995). Cultural Studies, Identity and Politics Between The Modern and Postmodern Media Culture, Simultaneously Published in USA and Canada by Routledge.

Kongar, E. (2010). Toplumsal Degisme Kuramlari ve Turkiye Gerçegi. Istanbul: Remzi Kitabevi.

Kozak, M. A., Evren, S. ve Cakir, O. (2013). Tarihsel süreç icinde turizm paradigmasi. Anatolia: Turizm Arastirmalari Dergisi, 24(1), 7–22.

Lane, B. (2009). Thirty Years of Sustainable Tourism: Drivers, Progress, Problems and the Future, NewYork UK: Routledge, 19–22.

Larsen, J. (2014). The Tourist Gaze 1. 0, 2. 0, and 3. 0. In A. A. Lew, C. M. Hall, and A. M. Williams (Eds.) The Wiley Blackwell Companion to Tourism, Oxford: John Wiley ve Sons.

Monica Hu, M. L., Chen, T. K. and Ou, T. L. (2009). An importance–performance model of restaurant dining experience. In Advances in Hospitality and Leisure. Bingley: Emerald Group Publishing Limited.

Murray, R. (1989). Fordism and Post-Fordism, Hall, S. ve Jacques, M. (ed.). New Times. Lawrence and Wishart, London, 38–47.

Nebioglu, O. (2016). Yerel Gastronomik Urunlerin Turizmde Kullanilmasini Etkileyen Unsurlar (Yayinlanmamis Doktora Tezi). Akdeniz Universitesi, Sosyal Bilimler Enstitüsü, Turizm İsletmeciligi ve Otelcilik Ana Bilim Dali, Antalya.

Ozen, Y. (2017). Psikolojik Travmanin Insanlik Kadar Eski Tarihi. The Journal of Social Science, 1(2),104–117.

Pabel, A., and Prideaux, B. (2016). "Social Media Use in Pre-Trip Planning By Tourists Visiting A Small Regional Leisure Destination". Journal of Vacation Marketing, 22(4).

Pine, B.J. and Gilmore, J.H. (1998). Welcome to the experience economy, Harvard Business Review,76(4), 97–105.

Roney, S. A. (2002). Fordizmden Post Fordizme Gecis Surecinin Turizme Yansimalari: Kitle Turizmi ve Alternatif Turizm. Anatolia: Turizm Arastirmalari Dergisi, 13(1), 9–14.

Sert, S., and A. Nalcaci Ikiz. (2012). Turizmin bilimsel konumuna iliskin akademisyenlerin tutumlari uzerine bir arastirma." VI. Lisansustu Turizm Ögrencileri Arastirma Kongresi, Ankara: 523–535.

Smith, S. L. J., (1995). Tourism Analysis, England: Longman Harlow.

Soyak, A., (2009). Turkiye'ye Yonelik Yabanci Turizmin İktisadi Etkileri: Akdeniz ve Ege Bolgeleri Uzerine Bir Arastirma, Istanbul: Derin Yayinlari.

Sugiyarto, G., Blake, A. and Sinclair, M. T. (2003), "Tourism and globalization: Economic impact İn Indonesia", Annals of Tourism Research, Vol. 30 No. 3, pp. 683–701.

Unluonen, K., Tayfun, A. ve Kiliclar, A. (2007). Turizm Ekonomisi. Ankara: Nobel Yayin Dagitim.

Yuksel, A. (2010). Turizm Belirsizin Bilimi, Seyahat ve Otel İşletmeciliği Dergisi, 7(2).

Zogal, V. ve Emekli, G. (2017). Yaratici Turizme Kavramsal ve Cografi Bir Yaklasim. Ege Cografya Dergisi,26(1), 21–34.

Nazanin Nikeghbal[1] and Hilmi Rafet Yüncü[2]

Chapter 13 Comparison of Turkish-Iranian Dishes in the 15th Century

Introduction

The common food culture that exists between countries today has emerged because of the interaction with historical, political, economic and cultural developments that have been experienced since ancient times. This partnership is very common in countries that are geographically close to each other. For example, Türkiye and Iran, two neighboring countries, have interacted from different perspectives throughout history. Both countries have very rich cultures due to their geographical location and cosmopolitan ethnic structure. This cultural richness is also reflected in their cuisine. As a result of the intense relationship between the two countries dating back to pre-Islamic times, there are many similarities in their culinary cultures today. Food and beverage names, ingredients used, recipes, eating and drinking habits and beliefs are among the issues that can be considered. The Islamization of the two countries has affected their cuisines as well as in every field, making the similarities even more evident. Nowadays, food has great importance in both countries. In fact, for Turks and Iranians, food is not only a means of satiation, but also a tool they use to express their identity, togetherness, values, status and creativity.

Of course, in order to examine the common culinary aspects of these two bordering countries, whose roots go back to ancient times and sources of wealth come from their spread over a wide geography, it is necessary to research the food consumption patterns of centuries ago. In fact, the elements of eating and drinking, which are indispensable parts of life, have also found a large part in the literary works. When we look at these literary works from the perspective of food, the works of the 15th century are very impressive. Actually, the "Et'ime-süralık" movement became widespread in literature in the 15th century. The word "Et'ime" is the plural form of the Arabic word "taam", meaning

1   Anadolu University, Tourism Faculty, Department of Gastronomy and Culinary Arts, nazanin_nikeghbal@anadolu.edu.tr, https://orcid.org/0000-0002-1271-3177
2   Anadolu University, Tourism Faculty, Department of Gastronomy and Culinary Arts, hryuncu@anadolu.edu.tr, https://orcid.org/0000-0002-2876-004X

"food", meaning "food or things to eat" (Kanar, 2005). Et'ime-süralık means singing food and drink themed poems. In fact, if the lexical-semantic difficulties are overcome, the food and drink names mentioned in the literary "Eti'me" works can give us valuable information about dishes that have been forgotten or have changed (Algar, 1989). Mevlânâ Ebû İshak Hallâc-ı Şîrâzî, the pioneer of the Et'ime-süralık movement in the 15th century, left his mark with his work "Divan-i Et'ime" Thanks to the information about food and dishes in this work, important information was conveyed about the food consumption style of the period (İsfahani, 1923). Therefore, in this study, this work from Iranian literature will be discussed to examine food consumption in the 15th century, and the cookbook written by Muhammed bin Mahmud Şirvanî in the 15th century and other works containing food and beverage from Ottoman manuscripts[3] will be compared.

Divan-i Et'ime Work

Bushak's works in verse and prose were brought together under the name 'Dîvân-i Et'ime-i Mevlânâ Ebû İshâk Hallâc-i Şîrâzî (Macidi, 2005)'. Divan Etime was written in the Fars province of Iran at the end of the 9th Hijri century in order to whet the appetite of Bushak's lover (Gökyay, 1986). This work is a poetry divan containing a total of ten separate sections consisting of expressions about food. It was created by bringing together a few Persian odes, one Kurdish and one Lurk ode, the Esrâr-ı Çengâl[4] poem, as well as one hundred ghazals and his poems and prose writings arranged in many different patterns (Kaska, 2019).

The section that is of great importance to our study is the Sofre-i Kenzü'l-İştihâ section. Abdulganî Mirzayev, in his work *"Abu Ishaq and His Literary Activities"*, written in 1971, classifies the sections of Kenzü'l-iştiha based on foods as follows.

* First part: *Flour doughs*
* Second part: *Watery dishes such as soup and broth*
* Third part: *Food prepared on the street or in the market*
* Chapter four: *Pickles and Pickles*
* Fifth section: *Shah-taams (shah-foods) such as pilaf, Herise (Keşkek), tenük (thin) bread.*

---

3   The authenticity of the presence of these dishes in the Ottoman era has been approved by looking on scientific researches on Ottoman cuisine like works of Yerasimos (2002; 2014), Işın (2010), etc.
4   Secrets of the fork.

- Chapter six: *Fruits*
- Chapter seven: *Molasses and sherbets*
- Chapter eight: *Halvas*
- Ninth section: *Grocery store (containing food items)*
- Chapter ten: *Dishes for the poor* (Mirzayev, 1971).

The Cookbook of Muhammad Bin Mahmud Shirvani

Shirvani, a famous physician who made a name for himself in various subjects such as medicine, religion, herbals, nutritious, precious stones and food in the Anatolian geography in the first half of the 15th century, quoted Baghdadi's "Kitabü't-tabîh Mine'i-et'ime" while writing his cookbook. It is based on the Arabic work named "Fi Kable't-Tıbb (Argunşah, 1990)". But unfortunately, the name of the cookbook is unknown. Because the cover and the first page are torn. The only known copy of the Arabic work is registered in Sulaymaniyah Library, Hagia Sophia Section, number 3710. Since Shirvani wrote his book before the conquest of Istanbul, he must have seen and used this original copy or other copies that we have not yet identified in Bursa or Edirne (Perry, 2005).

In his Turkish book, Shirvani used the dishes in Baghdadi's book, but on the one hand, he researched and emphasized the health benefits of these dishes, and on the other hand, he added dozens of dishes. It is possible to find the herise (porridge) kabuniye, tuffahiye, köfte (meatballs), muhallebi (pudding), turşu (pickle) recipes, paluze (custards) recipes and pilaf (rice) varieties that Shirvani selected from the Ottoman cuisine and added in Baghdadi's book. This means that some of the dishes in the book Baghdadi wrote in the 13th century were known and prepared in the 15th century Ottoman cuisine. We learn from the records that dishes such as buğdayı aşı (wheat stew), dane birinç (rice seed meal), kadayıf (shredded wheat dessert), borani, halvas, kavurmalar (roastings), boza (thick), tırşular (pickles), muhallebi (pudding), paça aşı (trotter rebel), tutmaç (Tortilla Soup), etc., included in Baghdadi's book, were cooked in the palace kitchen during the reign of Fatih. Again, the food names we know from Shirvani's work, such as mutanca, kabuni, borani, chicken kalyesi, mantı, salma, zülbiye and memuniye, are on the menu of Fatih Sultan Mehmet. Considering that the Turkish capital is Bursa or Edirne, some of the dishes in Baghdadı's book are included in the Turkish food culture. It turns out that they were known in Anatolia before the time of Mehmed the Conqueror.

Also, since Shirvani's cookbook is a translation, to make sure that found foods definitely belong to the Turkic nation; other sources like banquet notebooks, wedding scenes, notebooks describing foods, documents listing palace meals, price notebooks, Dede Korkut stories, Mevlevi kitchen resources, Hacivat-Karagöz Plays, Camasbnâme-i Mûsa Abdî, etc. written in the same century were also checked.

Common Food Names Found in 15th Century Works

As a result of the document analysis of Turkish-Persian sources of 15th cen- tury, a total of 44 common dishes were obtained which has been categorized accord- ing to the titles of Shirvani's book. These dishes are listed in the Table 13.1.[5] At the same time, names of these dishes in today's Iranian and Turkish cuisine are added in separate columns, which have been extracted from cookery books, food encyclopedias and municipality culture portals. If the food is not consumed today, lines are left in the cell in the table.

Table 13.1. Comparison of Dishes Resulting from Document Analysis

	REBELS & SOUPS		
No	Dish Names of "Dîvân-i Et'ime"	Equivalents in the Ottoman Period	Dish's Version in Today's Iranian Cuisine	Dish's Version in Today's Turkish Cuisine
1	ناربا /Narbaa/ (Pomegranate Rebel)	Rummaniye (Pomegranate Rebel)	آش انار /Aash-e Anaar/	Nardan Aşı/ Narlı Pirinç Çorbası (Pomegranate Rebel / Pomegranate & Rice Rebel)
2	آش سماق /Aash-e somaagh/ (Sumac Rebel)	Sumakiye (Sumac Rebel)	آش سماق /Aash-e somaagh/	Ekşili Çorba (Minus Rebel)
3	سكبا /Sek-Baa/ (Vinegar Rebel)	Sikbac (Vinegar Rebel)	آش سركه /Aash-e Serke/	Sirkeli Patlıcan Çorbası (Eggplant Soup with Vinegar)
4	حبشی /Habashi/	Narlı Şirke Aşı (Pomegranate Vinegar Rebel)	حبشی /Habashi/	---

---

5   Phonetic of Persian words in this table has been written according to the Dehkhoda (1998).

Table 13.1. Continued

36	شکر بادام /Shekar-badam/ (Almond Cookie)	Şeker Badem (Almond Cookie)	سوهان عسلی بادام /Sōhaan -e Aseli Baadaam/(Almond Honey Suhan) بادام سوخته /Baadaam-e Sookhte/ (Burnt Almond)	Badem Kıtır (Crisp Almond)
37	زولبیا، حلقه چی /Zoolbiyaa/, / Halghechi/ (Kind of cookie)	Zülbiye/ Halkaçını Helvası (Kind of cookie)	زولبیا /Zoolbiyaa/ (Kind of cookie)	Zülbiye Tatlısı /Dessert of Zulbi/ Soğanlı Et (Zülbiye) (Zulbi is a name of the food which is kind of a meat with onion)
38	فالوده - پالوده /Faaloode/, / Paaloode/ (Sweet beverage containing starch jelly in the form of thin fibres)	Paluze (Kind of pudding or custards)	پالوده، فالوده /Paaloode/,/Faaloode/ (Sweet beverage containing starch jelly in the form of thin fibres)	Paluze (Kind of pudding or custards)
39	کلاج، لابرلا /Kolaaj/, /Laberla/ (kind of spongy cake)	Güllaç (Kind of rose pudding)	کلاچ میان پر /Kolaach-e Miyanpor/ (kind of spongy cake)	Güllaç (Kind of rose pudding)

YEASTS, BREADS ETC.

No	Dish Names of "Dîvân-i Et'ime"	Equivalents in the Ottoman Period	Dish's Version in Today's Iranian Cuisine	Dish's Version in Today's Turkish Cuisine
40	فطیر /Fatir/ (Unleavened bread)	Fetayir (Unleavened bread)	نان فطیر /Nan-e Fatir/ (Unleavened bread)	---
41	آبکامه /Abkaame/ (Bread for stew)	Abkâme (powdered bread)	---	---
42	کاک ـ نان خشک ـ نان بکسیملت /Kak/ Nan-e Khoshk/ Beksimat (Crust)	Huşknan (Crust)	نان کاک، نان یوخه Nan-e Kak/ Nan-ı Yukha (Crust)	Peksimet (Crust)

(continued on next page)

Table 13.1.   Continued

43	كماج /Komaaj/ (Kind of Spongy Cake)	Kömeç (Kind of Spongy Cake)	كماج /Komaach/ (Kind of Spongy Cake)	Kömeç (Kind of Spongy Cake)
		DRINKS		
No	Dish Names of "Dîvân-i Et'ime"	Equivalents in the Ottoman Period	Dish's Version in Today's Iranian Cuisine	Dish's Version in Today's Turkish Cuisine
44	افشره /Afshore/ (Expressed Juice)	Efşüre/ Şurup/ Cülab/ Efşüre- i Engür (Compote)	افشره، افشره انگور، شربت جُلاب (گلاب)، خوشاب Efşüre/ Efşüre-i Engür/ Şerbet-i Cülab (Gülab)/ Hoşab (Compote/ Expressed Juice)	Hoşaf (Compote)

Results

This study aims to determine the similarities in cuisines, the change processes of dishes and their place in cultures. In the method section, the food names in Divan-i Et'ime, their equivalents in the Ottoman period, and their versions in today's Iranian and Turkish cuisines are determined as four different periods, as seen in diagram 1. In this context, descriptions of the dishes, recipes, if any, and other information were researched. According to the findings, many common food names or recipe similarities found in these two culinary cultures today date back to ancient centuries. The 44 similar food, dessert and beverage names found as a result of document analysis show that these two culinary cultures are in constant interaction. Of course, this is an important part of the interaction, we should not forget that the two countries are under the influence of the Arab world. That's why the names of many dishes made in two cuisines are Arabic. When we look at today's cuisines, out of 44 similar dishes identified in the research, 38 dishes in today's Iranian cuisine and 38 dishes in Turkish cuisine still maintain their place in culinary culture. Of course, how common these dishes are or not varies. Although many of these dishes are only made in some regions today, the fact that these dishes are still cooked and not forgotten even after six centuries is an indication that efforts are made to value the old dishes of the two cultures and to survive. Of course, the reasons why the dishes are not very common in society and not consumed intensively can be discussed. Some of these reasons are the change in taste, the food not being passed on from the previous generation to the next, the development of kitchen equipment and naturally making the cooking process easier, the invention of new dishes as new products enter the kitchen due to geographical conditions, etc. reasons can be considered. For example, when analyzing documents in sources from the 15th century, we see that corn, beans and tomatoes are not mentioned at all in the ingredients. Because these products were only discovered in the 16th–18th centuries with the discovery of America. They have spread around the world over the centuries. In this context, when the dishes of the 15th century are compared with today's recipes, it is seen that the dishes with the same name are made with tomatoes, tomato paste, sauce, corn or beans in the new recipes. Similar developments have caused kitchens to change.

References

Algar, A. (1989). Bushaq of Shiraz. Poet, Parasite and Gastronome, *Petits Propos Culinaire, Londra: Prospect Books Ltd. 31.*

Argunşah, M. (1990). II. Murad Devrinin (1421–1451) Ünlü Hekimi Muhammed bin Mahmûd Şirvânî ve Türkçe Eserleri. E.Ü. *Sosyal Bilimler Enstitüsü Dergisi.* 4. 483–498.

Dehkhoda, A. (1998). Loghatnaame-ye Dehkhoda, *Tehran University Publications.*

Gökyay, O.S. (1986). Divan-ı Et'ime. III. Milletlerarası Türk Folklor Kongresi Bildirileri, *Maddi Kültür, Kültür ve Turizm Bakanlığı, Ankara. 5, 121–137.*

Işın. M. P. (2010), Osmanlı Mutfak Sözlüğü. *Kitap Yayınevi. s. 324.*

Isfahani. M. H. (1302/1923). Hallâc-ı Şîrâzî, Mevlânâ Ebû İshâk. Dîvân-i Et'ime: *Ebûzziyâ Matbaası. İstanbul.*

Kanar, M. (2005). Farsça-Türkçe Sözlük, Deniz Kitabevi, İstanbul, 2000. *Etimolojik Osmanlı Türkçesi Sözlüğü, Derin Yay., İstanbul.*

Kaska, C. (2019). Bushak ve Divân-ı Et'ime. *Turkish Academic Research Journal. 317–335.*

Macidi, M. (2005). Bushâk Et'ime. *Markaz-e Daayeratolmaaaref-e Bozorg-e İslamî. Tehran.*

Mirzayev, A (1971). "Abu Ishaq and His Literary Activities". *Danesh Publications. Tajikistan.*

Perry, C (2005). "A Baghdad Cookery Book By Muhammad bin Hasan al-Baghdadi". *Prospects Books.*

Yerasimos, S. (2002). Sultan Sofraları: 15. ve 16. Yüzyılda Osmanlı Saray Mutfağı, *Yapı Kredi Yayınları. İstanbul.*

Yerasimos, S. (2014). 500 Yıllık Osmanlı Mutfağı, *İstanbul: Boyut Yayıncılık.*

Esra Dogu Baykut[1]

Chapter 14 Plant-based Menus:
A New Trend for Restaurants

Introduction

A plant-based diet is one that emphasizes on foods derived from plant sources and excludes or minimizes animal products and processed products. Plant-based diets have attracted a lot of attention in recent years for reasons such as health, environmental sustainability, and ethical concern about animal welfare. The most important reasons why many people adopt a plant-based diet as a lifestyle is that people think that this lifestyle protects them from many chronic diseases, improves their general health and provides better weight control (Banks, 2018). For these reasons, people are now following innovations in plant-based foods in markets or restaurants.

Owing to the rising popularity of plant-based nutrition, the demand for plant-based options in restaurants is also increasing. More importantly, restaurants are also taking this into consideration and choosing to include such plant-based food options in the menu. Using plant-based menus in restaurants brings many benefits and challenges. Benefits of incorporating plant-based menus into restaurants include healthfulness, environmental sustainability, ethical considerations, culinary innovation/creativity, and increased customer appeal. The limitations that restaurants may face include maintaining nutritional balance, cost, limited menu options, difficulty in providing familiar tastes and textures, and low customer awareness.

This chapter aims to explain the basics of plant-based nutrition and provide an overview of the benefits and limitations of incorporating plant-based menus in restaurants. In addition, the factors that should be taken into consideration when creating a plant-based menu in a restaurant are also mentioned and what can be done to make the business stand out from the competition is explained.

---

1   Ph.D., Istanbul Medeniyet University, Tourism Faculty, Department of Gastronomy and Culinary Arts, esra.dogubaykut@medeniyet.edu.tr

The Basics of Plant-Based Nutrition

The primary goal of humans is to provide sufficient energy required for body functions to sustain life. However, nowadays, we consume much more food than we need because many foods are easily available throughout the year. Moreover, most of the foods we consume are full of sugar, salt, and trans fats. Because significant amounts of salt, nitrate, sugar, trans fats, and some chemicals are added to preserve and improve the taste of processed foods (Banks, 2018).

Plant-based diets focus primarily on plant products, limit saturated fat and sugar intake, and exclude heavily processed foods (Radd & Marsh, 2012; Wenz, 2020). The word "plant-based" refers to a broader range of foods, mainly derived from plants (vegetables, fruits, grains, legumes, seeds, oil, and nuts), while it can also refer to limited amounts of eggs, dairy, meat, and seafood (Alcorta, Porta, Tárrega, Alvarez, & Vaquero, 2021). The types of the plant-based diets can be seen in Figure 14.1. Among vegetarian diets, lacto-ovo-vegetarian is the most popular. In addition to the foods listed in Figure 14.1, the majority of vegans also avoid using honey and other animal products (Radd & Marsh, 2012).

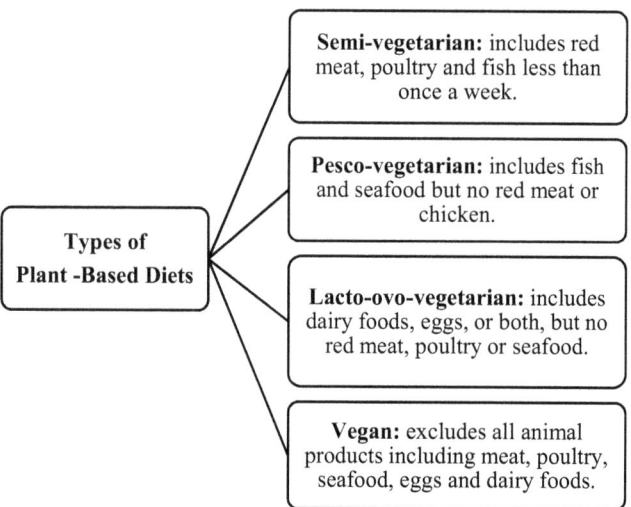

Figure 14.1. Types of Plant-based Diets (Radd & Marsh, 2012)

The key nutrients that may be deficient in a plant-based diet are protein, calcium, zinc, iron, omega-3 fats, vitamin B12, and vitamin D (Radd & Marsh, 2012; Pointke & Pawelzik, 2022). Therefore, it is often necessary to fortify plant-based diets with micronutrients, especially calcium, zinc, iron, vitamin B12, and vitamin D (McClements & Grossmann, 2021).

Additionally, plant-based foods also include a variety of products developed to replace products produced from animals, including dairy, eggs, fish, meat, and products using these as ingredients. The production of plant-based foods aims to bring plant-based foods closer to animal-derived foods by providing similar taste, texture, and nutritional composition (Maciel et al., 2022). Over time, plant-based alternatives for meat, milk, and eggs have been successfully developed. Nevertheless, further investigation is required to comprehend the correlation between the composition and characteristics of plant-based components and their capacity to produce meat, fish, egg, or dairy alternatives that people desire to eat (McClements & Grossmann, 2021).

Meat alternatives are produced based on proteins from plants such as legumes, cereals, pseudocereals, oil seeds, and algae. Legumes and cereals are used to produce meat alternatives of a desired texture and mouthfeel, because they contain proteins that are able to affect the structure of meat alternatives. Algae are used mainly as excellent sources of amino acids and bioactive peptides. Additionally, seeds can provide the fats needed for ideal texture, flavor, mouthfeel, and juiciness (Benković et al., 2023).

Legumes, nuts, seeds, cereals, and pseudocereals are used as raw materials for plant-based milk alternatives, also known as vegetable milk. Vegetable milks are water-soluble extracts with a visual similarity to bovine milk. Plant-based milks are made by firstly downsizing the raw material, then extracting it in water and homogenizing it, separating the liquid and solid phases, and finally formulating the finished product. As additional components, fats (to enhance sensory properties), gums (to improve plant milk stability), sugar, salt, minerals, and vitamins are added (Plamada et al., 2023).

Many studies have shown that plant-based animal product alternatives, including meat, yoghurt, milk, and cheese, offer various advantages in terms of nutritional qualities compared to traditional animal products (Pointke & Pawelzik, 2022). However, since each traditional animal product has unique nutritional benefits, it is crucial to remember that nutrient difference depend on the product category being compared.

Creating a Plant-Based Menu for a Restaurant

The increasing demand for plant-based foods every year is also seen as an opportunity for restaurants, and in recent years, many restaurants have been investigating how they should act to meet consumer demand without affecting their brand identity and profits (Jones, 2022). Innovative solutions and structural changes are needed for this transformation.

Restaurants can reduce the meat content of their menus by reducing the amount of meat in their menu items and increasing the amount of plant-based ingredients, or by using meat alternatives (tofu instead of chicken or beef, vegetable or quinoa patties instead of beef patties, etc.) (Reinders et al., 2017). This conversion is the easiest, quickest, and most convenient way to effortlessly accommodate flexitarian (semi-vegetarian) and even vegetarian consumers.

Nutrition education and labelling have been the most popular approaches to changing eating habits, with varying degrees of effectiveness. While eating plant-based foods can be beneficial, some consumers may feel that there are obstacles (such as insufficient protein and nutrient intake) that keep them from doing so. Providing information about the health benefits of a plant-based dishes influences consumers' food choices (Zhang, Jeong, Shao, & Jang, 2023). In restaurants, the dish of the day or chef's recommendation is considered to make it easier for consumers to choose plant-based foods (Bacon & Krpan, 2018; Perez-Cueto, 2021).

Plant-based food consumption can also be influenced by menu design and layout, which has a significant impact on consumer preferences. Simple menu design strategies can make significant differences. It is possible to influence customers' choices at restaurants without them recognizing it by using interventions known as 'nudge' or 'choice architecture' (Kurz, 2018; Taufik, Bouwman, Reinders, & Dagevos, 2022). These complimentary tactics recognized for successful behavior modification, to promote plant-based foods. Some examples of these interventions are redesigning menus, highlighting certain dishes using boxed or framed sections, marking products with signs or symbols, changing the default food offering and restricting access to the sale of specific food items (Parkin & Attwood, 2022).

Another important consideration in consumers' decision-making process is the names and descriptions of the food. Studies emphasize that focusing on what the dish contains (e.g. %100 plant-based, plant protein, rich in plant protein, veggie) rather than what it does not contain (e.g. meat-free, reduced meat, beef-less) will have a more positive effect (Attwood et al., 2020). Likewise, it is better to highlight the positive nutritional content (high protein, high fiber) than addressing the low levels of negative contents (low sugar, low fat).

The increasing number of plant-based dishes relative to meat dishes is also altering consumer preferences. Parkin and Attwood (2022) studied the effect of availability of vegetarian options on selection. Participants were assigned to

consumers, and the challenges and opportunities in the future. *Critical Reviews in Food Science and* Nutrition, 61(18), 3119–3128. https://doi.org/ 10.1080/10408398.2020.1793730

Attwood, S., Voorheis, P., Mercer, C., Davies, K., & Vennard, D., 2020. *Playbook for guiding diners toward plant-Rich dishes in food service.* World Resources Institute, Washington, DC, USA.

Bacon, L., & Krpan, D., 2018. (Not) Eating for the environment: the impact of restaurant menu design on vegetarian food choice. *Appetite*, 125, 190–200. https://doi.org/10.1016/j.appet.2018.02.006

Banks, O. (2018). *Plant-based diet: The plant-based diet for beginners.* CAC Publishing, Albuquerque. ISBN: 9781948489652

Benković, M., Jurinjak Tušek, A., Sokač Cvetnić, T., Jurina, T., Valinger, D., & Gajdoš Kljusurić, J. (2023). An overview of ingredients used for plant-based meat analogue production and their influence on structural and textural properties of the final product. *Gels*, 9(12), 921. https://doi.org/10.3390/gels 9120921

Clem, J., & Barthel, B. (2021). A look at plant-based diets. *Missouri Medicine*, 118(3), 233.

Fehér, A., Gazdecki, M., Véha, M., Szakály, M., & Szakály, Z. A (2020). Comprehensive review of the benefits of and the barriers to the switch to a plant-based diet. *Sustainability*, 12(10), 4136. https://doi.org/10.3390/su12104136

Grundy, E. A., Slattery, P., Saeri, A. K., Watkins, K., Houlden, T., Farr, N., … & Zorker, M. (2022). Interventions that influence animal-product consumption: A meta-review. *Future Foods*, 5, 100111. https://doi.org/10.1016/ j.fufo.2021.100111

Hemler, E. C., & Hu, F. B. (2019). Plant-based diets for personal, population, and planetary health. *Advances in Nutrition*, 10, S275–S283. https://doi.org/ 10.1093/advances/nmy117

Jones, P. (2022). Plant-based food in the hospitality industry: An exploratory case study of leading fast food outlets. *Athens Journal of Tourism*, 9. https:// doi.org/10.30958/ajt.9-2-1

Kahleova, H., Levin, S. & Barnard, N. (2017). Cardio-metabolic benefits of plant-based diets. *Nutrients*, 9(8), 848. https://doi.org/10.3390/nu9080848

Kurz, V. (2018). Nudging to reduce meat consumption: Immediate and persistent effects of an intervention at a university restaurant. *Journal of Environmental Economics and Management*, 90, 317–341. https://doi.org/10.1016/ j.jeem.2018.06.005

Macdiarmid, J. I. (2022). The food system and climate change: are plant-based diets becoming unhealthy and less environmentally sustainable?. *Proceedings of the Nutrition Society*, 81(2), 162–167. https://doi.org/10.1017/S002966512 1003712

Maciel, J. B., de Oliveira Silva, Y., Santos, S. S., Dionísio, A. P., de Sousa, P. H. M., & dos Santos Garruti, D. (2022). Plant-based gastronomic products based on freeze-dried cashew fiber. *International Journal of Gastronomy and Food Science*, 30, 100603. https://doi.org/10.1016/j.ijgfs.2022.100603

McClements, D. J., & Grossmann, L. (2021). A brief review of the science behind the design of healthy and sustainable plant-based foods. *NPJ Science of Food*, 5(1), 17. https://doi.org/10.1038/s41538-021-00099-y

Nolden, A. A., & Forde, C. G. (2023). The nutritional quality of plant-based foods. *Sustainability*, 15(4), 3324. https://doi.org/10.3390/su15043324

Parkin, B. L., & Attwood, S. (2022). Menu design approaches to promote sustainable vegetarian food choices when dining out. *Journal of Environmental Psychology*, 79, 101721. https://doi.org/10.1016/j.jenvp.2021.101721

Perez-Cueto, F. J. (2021). Nudging plant-based meals through the menu. *International Journal of Gastronomy and Food Science*, 24, 100346. https://doi.org/10.1016/j.ijgfs.2021.100346

Plamada, D., Teleky, B. E., Nemes, S. A., Mitrea, L., Szabo, K., Călinoiu, L. F., … & Nitescu, M. (2023). Plant-based dairy alternatives—A future direction to the milky way. *Foods*, 12(9), 1883. https://doi.org/10.3390/foods12091883

Pointke, M., & Pawelzik, E. (2022). Plant-based alternative products: Are they healthy alternatives? Micro-and macronutrients and nutritional scoring. *Nutrients*, 14, 601. https://doi.org/10.3390/nu14030601

Pope, L., Roche, E., Morgan, C. B., & Kolodinsky, J. (2018). Sampling tomorrow's lunch today: Examining the effect of sampling a vegetable-focused entrée on school lunch participation, a pilot study. *Preventive Medicine Reports*, 12, 152–157. https://doi.org/10.1016/j.pmedr.2018.09.010

Radd, S., & Marsh, K. A. (2012). Practical tips for preparing healthy and delicious plant-based meals. *MJAOpen*, 1, 41–48. https://doi.org/10.5694/mja11.11511

Reinders, M.J., M. Huitink, S.C. Dijkstra, A.J. Maaskant, & Heijnen, J. (2017). Menu-engineering in restaurants—Adapting portion sizes on plates to enhance vegetable consumption: A real-life experiment. *International Journal of Behavioral Nutrition and Physical Activity*, 14(1), 41. https://doi.org/10.1186/s12966-017-0496-9

Sabaté, J., & Soret, S. (2014). Sustainability of plant-based diets: back to the future. *The American Journal of Clinical Nutrition*, 100, 476S-482S. https://doi.org/10.3945/ajcn.113.071522.

Salehin, S., Rasmussen, P., Mai, S., Mushtaq, M., Agarwal, M., Hasan, S. M., Salehin, S., Raja, M., Gilani, S., & Khalife, W. I. (2023). Plant based diet and its effect on cardiovascular disease. *International Journal of Environmental Research and Public Health*, 20(4), 3337. https://doi.org/10.3390/ijerph2 0043337

Satija, A., & Hu, F. B. (2018). Plant-based diets and cardiovascular health. *Trends in Cardiovascular Medicine*, 28(7), 437–441. https://doi.org/10.1016/j.tcm.2018.02.004

Šmugović, S., Kalenjuk, P. B., Grubor, B., & Knežević, N. (2021). Vegetarian diet: perceptions and attitudes of hospitality management. *Researches Review DGTH*, 50(1), 70–77. https://doi.org/10.5937/ZbDght2101070S

Soto-Aguilar, F., Webar, J., & Palacios, I. (2022). Whole food plant based diet: its mechanisms for the prevention and treatment of obesity. *Revista de La Facultad de Medicina Humana*, 22(1), 22. https://doi.org/10.25176/RFMH. v22i1.3616

Taufik, D., Bouwman, E. P., Reinders, M. J., & Dagevos, H. (2022). A reversal of defaults: Implementing a menu-based default nudge to promote out-of-home consumer adoption of plant-based meat alternatives. *Appetite*, 175, 106049.

Wenz, G. (2020). *Plant-based diet cookbook for beginners: The complete guide to plant-based diet to heal your body*. Independently Published. ISBN: 9798635083154

Ye, T., & Mattila, A. S. (2021). The effect of ad appeals and message framing on consumer responses to plant-based menu items. *International Journal of Hospitality Management*, 95, 102917. https://doi.org/10.1016/j.ijhm.2021.102917

Yepes, M. F. (2015). Vegetarianism for public health and for the environment. In P. Sloan, W. Legrand, & C. Hindley (Eds.), The Routledge Handbook of Sustainable Food and Gastronomy. Routledge, Oxford, pp. 113–119. ISBN: 9780203795699

Zhang, X., Jeong, E., Shao, X., & Jang, S. (2023). Plant-based food is unhealthy— that's not true! How can corrective messages help promote plant-based menus in quick-service restaurants?. *International Journal of Contemporary Hospitality* Management, 35(9), 3216–3234. https://doi.org/10.1108/IJCHM-07-2022-0833

Önder Yayla[1] and Şeyda Yayla[2]

Chapter 15 Digital Nomads as Culinary Ambassadors

Introduction

The term "digital nomad" is described a new group of travelers who combine the freedom of travel with work opportunities made possible by modern technology (Makimoto and Manners, 1997). The advent of the Internet and mobile technologies has enabled individuals to work remotely, negating the need to be physically present in an office (Özgen Çiğdemli et al., 2024). It has led to the rapid proliferation of the digital nomad concept. This novel lifestyle, driven by the aspiration to explore diverse countries and cultures, has become an indispensable aspect of the lives of digital nomads.

Digital nomads do not merely engage in tourist activities in the places they visit; they also seek to immerse themselves in and understand local cultures (Liu and Lin, 2017; Richards, 2015; Setlak, 2018). In this process, local gastronomy and culinary culture become important areas of exploration for digital nomads. One way in which digital nomads contribute to cultural exchange is by experiencing different cuisines and sharing these experiences on digital platforms. Gastronomic tourism is defined as travel undertaken with the objective of discovering the culinary culture of a destination (Richards, 2002). Digital nomads play a significant role in gastronomic tourism by disseminating information about the cuisines of the destinations they visit. The dissemination of local foods and culinary culture via social media and other digital platforms enables a vast audience to gain access to these experiences, thereby facilitating cultural understanding and exchange.

This chapter examines the manner in which digital nomads facilitate cultural exchange through their culinary experiences, emphasizing their pivotal role as cultural ambassadors. The role of digital platforms and social media in this

---

1 Associated Professor, Osmaniye Korkut Ata University, Kadirli Faculty of Applied Sciences, Department of Gastronomy and Culinary Arts, onderyayla@osmaniye.edu.tr
2 Lecturer, Osmaniye Korkut Ata University, Kadirli Faculty of Applied Sciences, Department of Gastronomy and Culinary Arts, seydayayla@osmaniye.edu.tr

process will be evaluated. The influence of digital nomads on culinary culture is becoming increasingly evident, underscoring the significance of this novel travel and work style in facilitating cultural exchange. In this context, the role of digital nomads as culinary ambassadors not only contributes to the promotion of local gastronomy, but also builds bridges between different cultures and promotes global understanding and tolerance. This chapter seeks to examine the impact of digital nomads on food tourism and to propose potential future developments within a conceptual framework.

The Concept of Digital Nomadism

Definition and Characteristics

Digital nomads are individuals who work without being tied to a physical office thanks to the Internet and mobile technologies. This lifestyle consists of people who can work remotely and therefore travel continuously (Getman, 2021). Digital nomads typically include freelancers, entrepreneurs, remote workers, and individuals who earn income through online ventures. This group generally seeks flexibility, freedom, and new experiences (Ili, 2024).

Key characteristics of the digital nomad lifestyle include flexibility, constant travel, use of technology, and communities and networks (Cook, 2023; Zhou et al., 2024). Flexibility allows digital nomads to work from anywhere, enabling them to set their working hours and locations according to their preferences. Constant travel is central to their lives, allowing them to discover new places without being tied to a single location and engage with new cultures. The use of technology is critical, as digital nomads rely heavily on the Internet and mobile technologies for their work, requiring them to be connected and accessible at all times (Chevtaeva and Denizci-Guillet, 2021). Additionally, digital nomads often interact with others who share similar lifestyles, forming communities that facilitate information sharing and support networks.

Historical Development

The concept of digital nomadism emerged in the early 21st century with the widespread availability of the Internet and the advancement of mobile technologies. The first digital nomads took advantage of the flexibility provided by the Internet to live and work in different countries. By the mid-2000s, the term "digital nomad" had become widely known (Shawkat et al., 2021).

The development of digital nomadism reflects significant changes in the nature of work. The acceptance of remote working models in various sectors has facilitated the spread of digital nomadism (Kuzheleva-Sagan and Nosova, 2016). During this period, remote working and freelancing have become increasingly popular in the business world. Additionally, economic and social factors have played a role in the widespread adoption of digital nomadism. Young professionals in particular have sought flexibility and freedom in their careers. Digital nomadism has gained popularity by offering a lifestyle that meets these demands.

Technological Infrastructure

The advent of digital nomadism is contingent upon the advent of the internet and mobile technologies. The Internet provides digital nomads with the ability to work from any location, while mobile devices facilitate this process even further (Demaj et al., 2021). The daily lives of digital nomads are inextricably linked to broadband internet connections, cloud computing services, online collaboration tools, and mobile applications.

The expansion of technological infrastructure has rendered the digital nomad lifestyle more accessible and appealing. The aforementioned technological developments have enabled digital nomads to work from any location globally while exploring new cultures. The phenomenon of digital nomadism has emerged and rapidly spread as a consequence of the convergence of modern working life and technological advancements (Kuzheleva-Sagan and Nosova, 2016). This lifestyle affords digital nomads the opportunity to interact with diverse cultures and to promote local cuisines. Therefore, digital nomads play a significant role in gastronomy tourism and cultural exchange.

Gastronomy Tourism and Cultural Ambassadorship

Gastronomy Tourism

Gastronomy tourism is defined as travel undertaken with the objective of exploring a destination's culinary culture (Brisson, 2012). This type of tourism is centered on the experience of local foods and cuisines by tourists. Gastronomy tourism is not limited to the experience of eating; it also encompasses the processes of food preparation, local food production, markets, and the stories of chefs (Long, 2004; Everett, 2005). Gastronomy tourism offers tourists a multitude of enriching experiences from a multitude of perspectives, including cultural, historical, and social. Gastronomy tourism not only serves to promote a destination's culinary culture but also offers tourists a more profound cultural experience. In this framework, digital nomads play an important role in the promotion and dissemination of gastronomy tourism.

Cultural Ambassadorship

Cultural ambassadorship is the act of individuals acting as intermediaries between different cultures, with the objective of enhancing cultural understanding and interaction (Davari and Jang, 2023). Digital nomads fulfill this role through gastronomy. Cultural ambassadorship is generally understood to encompass activities designed to promote and disseminate a country's or region's cultural characteristics and values to others.

Digital nomads assume the role of cultural ambassadors in a number of ways:

• Promotion of Foods: Digital nomads experience local foods in the places they visit and share these experiences on digital platforms. Through blog posts, social media shares, and videos, they promote local foods, helping these cuisines reach broader audiences.
• Cultural Exchange: Digital nomads facilitate cultural exchange by engaging with diverse cultural communities. Furthermore, they disseminate information about the historical and cultural contexts of local cuisines, thereby fostering cultural understanding and tolerance.
• Education and Awareness: Digital nomads disseminate information to their followers regarding the historical development of local foods and culinary cultures. Such education serves to increase people's curiosity and respect for different cultures.

By disseminating information about the culinary cultures of the places they visit, digital nomads play a pivotal role in gastronomic tourism. The dissemination of local culinary traditions via digital platforms and social media facilitates cultural exchange and fosters mutual understanding between diverse cultural groups. This process contributes to the development and spread of gastronomy tourism.

The Cultural Communication of Food

Food is an integral component of a society's cultural heritage and identity (Almerico, 2014). The role of food in cultural communication allows individuals and communities to express themselves and share their histories and traditions (Beşirli, 2010). Digital nomads facilitate the dissemination of culinary culture to a global audience through the use of digital platforms.

The role of food in cultural communication is enacted in the following ways:

• Narrative: Foods frequently serve as a conduit for conveying the narrative of a specific cultural identity. Digital nomads disseminate the narratives and traditions associated with specific foods, thereby introducing these cultures to their followers.

- Cultural Bonds: The consumption of food can facilitate the formation of social connections. Digital nomads facilitate the establishment of connections between disparate cultures by disseminating information about local foods.
- Cultural Awareness: The act of sharing culinary cultures serves to increase people's awareness of different cultures. Digital nomads facilitate this process, thereby promoting cultural understanding and tolerance.

Digital nomads enhance the role of food in cultural communication by discovering local foods and sharing them on digital platforms. This process facilitates cultural exchange and facilitates the construction of bridges between different cultures (Yayla et al., 2024).

Gastronomy tourism and cultural ambassadorship are significant aspects of the digital nomad lifestyle. Digital nomads play an instrumental role in the promotion of local cuisines, thereby contributing to the growth of gastronomy tourism and fulfilling the role of cultural ambassadors. This process facilitates cultural understanding and tolerance, bolsters local economies, and stimulates the growth of gastronomy tourism (Yayla et al., 2024). As global culinary ambassadors, digital nomads facilitate the recognition and appreciation of local cuisines on a global scale.

Contributions of Digital Nomads to Gastronomy Tourism

Cultural Sharing

The contributions of digital nomads to gastronomy tourism can be observed in the sharing of cultural experiences. Digital nomads, who are often transient individuals who work remotely, engage in the discovery of local foods in the destinations they visit and subsequently disseminate these experiences on digital platforms (Ji et al., 2024). This sharing contributes to the cultural exchange and dissemination of knowledge about local culinary traditions. Such contributions are of great importance for gastronomy tourism. The social media accounts, blogs, and YouTube channels of digital nomads represent a powerful tool for introducing different cultures to their followers (Thompson, 2019; Bozzi, 2020).

Digital nomads disseminate images and videos of local foods on their social media accounts, thereby reaching a vast audience. The most frequently utilized platforms for these types of shares are Instagram, X (Ex-Twitter), and TikTok (Holleran, 2022). In contrast, blogs offer more detailed content, including recipes, histories, and stories about foods. Such posts not only capture the interest of followers but also motivate them to visit the destinations in question. Videos and vlogs are also utilized by digital nomads to promote local foods. Another significant avenue for digital nomads to disseminate information about local foods is through video-sharing platforms such as YouTube. These platforms serve as a conduit for the dissemination of information regarding the preparation, cooking techniques, and flavors of various foods. Such videos offer a visual feast to viewers, thereby encouraging them to try the foods in question.

In addition to promoting foods, digital nomads utilize these channels to disseminate information about local cultures and traditions. This contributes to an enhanced understanding and tolerance of cultural differences.

Economic Impacts

The economic impact of digital nomads on gastronomy tourism is also significant (Wang et al., 2018). Their contributions to local economies occur in various ways, both directly and indirectly:

- Support for Local Businesses: Digital nomads visit local restaurants, cafes, markets, and food producers in the places they travel to and share positive feedback about these places. This helps promote local businesses and expand their customer bases. In particular, social media shares can draw customers directly to these businesses and increase their revenues.
- Increase in Tourism Revenues: Digital nomads contribute to the discovery of new destinations and increase tourist interest in these places through their shares. Promoting local cuisines leads to the revitalization of gastronomy tourism and increases tourism revenues for these destinations. This provides significant contributions to local economies.
- Demand for Gastronomy Tours and Experiences: As digital nomads promote local cuisines, the demand for gastronomy tours and cooking classes in these regions increases. Such experiences encourage tourists to stay longer and spend more, thereby providing additional revenue to local economies.

Globalization of Local Cuisines

The globalization of local cuisines is facilitated by the contributions of digital nomads, who play a significant role in the recognition and appreciation of local cuisines on a global scale (Ünal, 2024). This process is enabled by the capacity of digital nomads to disseminate their content to a vast audience.

- Global Reach: The social media accounts and blogs of digital nomads have a significant global following. This enables the introduction of local foods and culinary cultures to global audiences. For example, the promotion of a

Japanese sushi restaurant by a digital nomad can increase global awareness of the restaurant and Japanese cuisine in general.

• Cultural Interaction and Adaptation: As digital nomads engage with various culinary traditions, they gain an understanding of the recipes and cooking techniques associated with these cuisines. They disseminate this knowledge by adapting it to their own cultural contexts. This process facilitates interaction between disparate culinary traditions, thereby fostering the emergence of novel fusion cuisines. For instance, a digital nomad's reinterpretation and dissemination of a culinary tradition learned in Thailand within their own country can result in the discovery of novel flavors and dishes.

• Promotion and Awards for Local Cuisines: Digital nomads can facilitate the promotion of local cuisines on international platforms and contribute to their recognition through awards. For example, the promotion of a local restaurant by a digital nomad may result in the restaurant being nominated for and subsequently winning international gastronomy awards.

By disseminating information about local cuisines to global audiences, digital nomads facilitate the recognition and appreciation of these cuisines on a worldwide scale. This process contributes to the enrichment of culture and the diversification of gastronomy. Consequently, digital nomads play a pivotal role in gastronomy tourism, as they facilitate cultural exchange, economic growth, and the global dissemination of local cuisines. These contributions significantly promote the development and spread of gastronomy tourism. As global culinary ambassadors, digital nomads help local cuisines gain recognition and appreciation worldwide. This new style of travel and work contributes to cultural understanding and tolerance, strengthens local economies, and promotes the development of gastronomy tourism.

The Role of Digital Platforms

Social Media

Social media represents one of the most significant avenues through which digital nomads contribute to gastronomic tourism. Digital nomads utilize digital platforms such as Instagram, Facebook, TikTok, and Twitter to disseminate their experiences to a vast audience. These platforms serve as a crucial conduit for the promotion of local cuisines and the facilitation of cultural interaction (Voll et al., 2022; Lacárcel et al., 2024). Social media represents an effective tool for digital nomads to promote local cuisines and enhance cultural interaction. The dissemination of information through these platforms contributes to the development of gastronomic tourism and the global recognition of local cuisines.

Digital nomads contribute to gastronomic tourism by employing creative and innovative methods in content production and sharing. The most common forms of media through which these contents are produced and shared are blogs, vlogs, and podcasts. Content production and sharing are effective methods employed by digital nomads to disseminate information about local cuisines and to support gastronomy tourism. Such content provides valuable information to followers, thereby encouraging them to explore new culinary experiences.

Interaction and Follower Base

Digital nomads have a wide follower base on social media and other digital platforms (Bozzi, 2020; Macgilchrist et al., 2020). The interaction they establish with these followers is crucial for the promotion and spread of gastronomy tourism.

- Interaction with Followers: Digital nomads continuously interact with their followers. They communicate directly with their followers through comments, messages, and live broadcasts. This interaction keeps the followers' interest alive and encourages them to consume more content.
- User-Generated Content (UGC): Followers contribute to the content shared by digital nomads by adding their own experiences. User-generated content helps spread the digital nomads' content and increases engagement. Hashtag campaigns and contests are methods that encourage users to produce content.
- Influencer Collaborations: Digital nomads can expand their influence by collaborating with other influencers. Joint projects, interviews, and guest blog posts contribute to the growth and diversification of the follower base.

The interaction and follower base of digital nomads contribute to the impact of their contributions to gastronomy tourism. The establishment of strong relationships with followers serves to promote local cuisines and facilitate cultural exchange (Mouratidis, 2018). Through these interactions, digital nomads play a pivotal role in the advancement and dissemination of gastronomy tourism.

Digital platforms represent the primary means through which digital nomads contribute to gastronomy tourism. The use of social media, content production and sharing, interaction, and the establishment of relationships with follower bases enables digital nomads to promote local cuisines and enhance cultural interaction. This process contributes to the development of gastronomy tourism and the recognition of local cuisines on a global scale.

Future Perspectives

The Future of Digital Nomadism

The future of digital nomadism is likely to be characterized by a continued increase in its prevalence, driven by the rapid advancement of technology and the evolution of work models. The adoption of remote work culture and the global spread of internet access will contribute to the increase in the number of digital nomads.

- Technological Developments: The widespread adoption of 5G technology will enhance internet speed and quality. This will enable digital nomads to work seamlessly in more locations. Additionally, the advancement of artificial intelligence and automation technologies will make the work processes of digital nomads more efficient.
- Changes in Work Models: As companies and organizations continue to adopt flexible work models, digital nomadism will become a more attractive lifestyle. The spread of remote work policies will make it possible for more people to become digital nomads.
- New Digital Platforms: The emergence of new social media platforms and digital collaboration tools will enable digital nomads to produce and share content more effectively. These platforms will facilitate digital nomads' reach to global audiences.

The Future of Gastronomy Tourism

The growth of gastronomy tourism will be further enhanced by the impact of digital nomads and technological advancements. This growth will result in an increased global recognition of local cuisines and a concomitant enhancement of the sustainability of gastronomy tourism.

- Globalization of Local Cuisines: The promotion of local cuisines through digital nomads will contribute to the growth of gastronomy tourism. This process will enable the recognition and appreciation of different cultures' foods worldwide.
- Sustainable Gastronomy Tourism: Trends in sustainable tourism will increase efforts to make gastronomy tourism sustainable as well. Local food production and consumption will reduce the carbon footprint and support local economies.
- Innovative Gastronomy Experiences: Technological advancements and the creative content of digital nomads will add innovative experiences to

gastronomy tourism. Virtual food tours, augmented reality (AR), and virtual reality (VR) technologies will offer unique culinary experiences to tourists.

Cultural Interaction and Tolerance

Digital nomads will continue to build bridges between different cultures, enhancing global understanding and tolerance. This process is important for the future of gastronomy tourism and cultural ambassadorship.

- Cultural Sharing and Understanding: By promoting local cuisines, digital nomads will enhance cultural sharing and understanding globally. This will contribute to peace and cooperation worldwide.
- Education and Awareness: The content produced by digital nomads will help people learn about different cultures and become more sensitive to these cultures. This process will contribute to the development of global citizenship consciousness.

The growth of digital nomadism and gastronomy tourism will continue to be influenced by technological advancements and changing work models. Digital nomads will contribute to the development of gastronomy tourism and enhance cultural interaction by promoting local cuisines. This process will enhance cultural understanding and tolerance globally, strengthen local economies, and promote the sustainability of gastronomy tourism. It is anticipated that digital nomads will continue to serve as culinary ambassadors in the future.

Conclusion

Digital nomads make significant contributions to gastronomy tourism through the opportunities provided by modern work life and technological advancements. This chapter has examined the ways in which digital nomads facilitate cultural exchange through their culinary experiences and has highlighted the significant role they play as cultural ambassadors. The contributions of digital nomads to gastronomy tourism can be evaluated according to three main headings: cultural sharing, economic impacts, and the globalization of local cuisines.

Digital nomads facilitate cultural exchange by disseminating information about local foods on social media and other digital platforms. Such exchanges facilitate the formation of connections between disparate cultural communities, thereby fostering a greater understanding and tolerance of cultural differences. Culinary cultures are disseminated to a vast audience through the medium of digital nomads, thereby significantly contributing to the development of gastronomy tourism.

From an economic standpoint, digital nomads serve to bolster the financial stability of local businesses and enhance the revenue streams of tourism destinations. Restaurants, cafés, and local food producers benefit from the promotional activities of digital nomads, which enable them to reach a larger customer base. Furthermore, the dissemination of information by digital nomads stimulates demand for gastronomic tours and experiences, thereby contributing to the growth of local economies.

Digital nomads facilitate the global recognition and appreciation of local cuisines. The promotion of local foods on international social media and blogs serves to disseminate information about these foods to a global audience. This process facilitates the global recognition and appreciation of local cuisines.

Future conceptual studies could explore the effects of digital nomads on different cultures in greater depth. Future studies could examine the role of digital nomads in cultural exchange and the challenges encountered in this process. Furthermore, theoretical research on the digitalization of gastronomy tourism and the impact of digital culture on gastronomy could provide a more comprehensive understanding of the role of digital platforms in gastronomy tourism.

Practical studies could include the creation of practical guides and resources to enhance the contributions of digital nomads to gastronomy tourism. These guides could assist digital nomads in promoting local cuisines more effectively. Furthermore, encouraging collaborations between digital nomads and local businesses could support gastronomy tourism. Such collaborations would benefit both digital nomads and local businesses. Gastronomy events organized with the participation of digital nomads could also contribute to the promotion of local cuisines. Such events would permit digital nomads to interact with their followers and disseminate their culinary experiences.

In essence, digital nomads facilitate cultural sharing, economic development, and the globalization of local cuisines through their contributions to gastronomy tourism. The effective utilization of digital platforms enables these contributions to reach a wider audience. Future conceptual and practical studies will assist in the elucidation of the impacts of digital nomads on gastronomy tourism and contribute to the advancement of this field. The role of digital nomads as culinary ambassadors will continue to enhance cultural understanding and tolerance, strengthen local economies, and promote the sustainability of gastronomy tourism.

References

Almerico, G.M. (2014). Food and identity: Food studies, cultural, and personal identity. *Journal of International Business and Cultural Studies*, 8, 1.

Beşirli, H. (2010). Yemek, Kültür ve Kimlik. *Milli Folklor, 22*(87), 159–169.

Bozzi, N. (2020). #digitalnomads, #solotravellers, #remoteworkers: A Cultural Critique of the Traveling Entrepreneur on Instagram. *Social Media+ Society, 6*(2), 2056305120926644.

Brisson, G. (2012). *Branding Prince Edward County as a Gastronomic Niche Tourism Destination: A Case Study.* Master Thesis, University of Ottawa, Ottawa, Canada.

Chevtaeva, E., and Denizci-Guillet, B. (2021). Digital nomads' lifestyles and coworkation. *Journal of Destination Marketing and Management, 21,* 100633.

Cook, D. (2023). What is a digital nomad? Definition and taxonomy in the era of mainstream remote work. *World Leisure Journal, 65*(2), 256–275. Doi: 10.1080/16078055.2023.2190608.

Davari, D., & Jang, S. (Shawn). (2023). Diaspora's intuitive role as cultural ambassador: toward a new cultural sustainability perspective. *Journal of Sustainable Tourism,* 1–18. https://doi.org/10.1080/09669582.2023.2225802.

Demaj, E., Hasimja, A. and Rahimi, A. (2021). Digital nomadism as a new flexible working approach: Making Tirana the next European hotspot for digital nomads. *The Flexible Workplace: Coworking and Other Modern Workplace Transformations,* 231–257.

Everett, H.J. (2005). *Class Acts: Culinary Tourism in Newfoundland and Labrador.* Doctoral Thesis, Memorial University of Newfoundland, Canada.

Getman, N. (2021). *Developing a digital nomads destination from the ground up.* Master of Science in Tourism Development and Culture, Instituto Universitario de Lisboa, Portugal. Retrieved from https://www.proquest.com/dissertations-theses/developing-digital-nomads-destination-ground-up/docview/2890691807/se-2.

Holleran, M. (2022). Pandemics and geoarbitrage: digital nomadism before and after COVID-19. *City, 26*(5–6), 831–847. Doi: 10.1080/13604813. 2022.2124713.

Ili, B. (2024). The Reflections of the Digital Nomad Community on Social Media: A Case Study on Twitter. In Ç. Topçu (Ed.), *Digital Capitalism in the New Media Era* (pp. 141–160). IGI Global. Doi: 10.4018/979-8-3693-1182-0.ch008.

Ji, Y., Kim, S-M. and Kim, Y.A. (2024). Way to Attract Digital Nomads to Tourist Destinations in the New Normal Era. *Sustainability,16*(6), 2336. Doi: 10.3390/su16062336.

Kuzheleva-Sagan, I. and Nosova, S. (2016). Culture of digital nomads: Ontological, anthropological, and semiotic aspects. K. Bankov (Ed.), *New semiotics between Tradition and innovation: Selected papers from 12th world Congress of the international Association for semiotic studies 2014*, IASS Publications & NBU Publishing House, pp. 131–140.

Lacárcel, F. J. S., Huete, R., and Zerva, K. (2024). Decoding digital nomad destination decisions through user-generated content. *Technological Forecasting and Social Change, 200*, 123098. Doi: 10.1016/j.techfore.2023.123098.

Liu, T. and Lin, W. (2017). Transnational work and workplace as infrastructure: Sino-British international branch campuses and academic mobilities. *Mobilities, 12*(2), 277–293.

Long, L.M. (2004). *Culinary Tourism*. Lexington: University Press of Kentucky.

Macgilchrist, F., Allert, H., and Bruch, A. (2020). Students and society in the 2020s. Three future 'histories' of education and technology. *Learning, Media and Technology, 45*(1), 76–89.

Makimoto, T. and Manners, D. (1997). *Digital nomad*. Wiley.

Mouratidis G. (2018) *Digital Nomadism: Travel, Remote Work and Alternative Lifestyles*. Lund University, Lund.

Özgen Çiğdemli, A.Ö., Yayla, Ş. and Çiğdemli, B.S. (2024). The world from the perspective of digital nomads: exploring sentiments in destination reviews. *Worldwide Hospitality and Tourism Themes*. Doi: 10.1108/WHATT-03-2024-0044.

Richards, G. (2002). Gastronomy: An essential ingredient in tourism production and consumption?. In *Tourism and Gastronomy* (pp. 3–20). Routledge. ISBN: 978-0415256227.

Richards, G. (2015). The new global nomads: Youth travel in a globalizing world. *Tourism Recreation Research, 40*(3), 340–352.

Setlak, S. (2018). *Exploring The Feasibility of Adapting A Digital Nomadic Lifestyle*. Retrieved from: https://repository.tcu.edu/bitstream/handle/116099 117/22419/Setlak Sarah-Honors_Project.pdf?sequence=1andisAllowed=y Date: 10.12.2023.

Shawkat, S., Abd Rozan, M.Z., Salim N.B. and Shehzad, H.M.F. (2021). *Digital Nomads: A Systematic Literature Review*. 7th International Conference on Research and Innovation in Information Systems (ICRIIS), Johor Bahru, Malaysia, pp. 1–6. Doi: 10.1109/ICRIIS53035.2021.9617008.

Thompson, B.Y. (2019). The Digital Nomad Lifestyle: (Remote) Work/Leisure Balance, Privilege, and Constructed Community. *International Journal of the Sociology of Leisure, 2*, 27–42. Doi: 10.1007/s41978-018-00030-y.

Ünal, G. (2024), The relationship between regional development and digital nomadism. *Worldwide Hospitality and Tourism Themes*. Doi: 10.1108/WHATT-03-2024-0056.

Voll, K., Gauger, F., and Pfnür, A. (2022). Work from anywhere: Traditional workation, coworkation and workation retreats: A conceptual review. *World Leisure Journal*, 1–25. Doi: 10.1080/16078055.2022.2134199.

Wang, B., Schlagwein, D., Cecez- Kecmanovic, D. and Cahalane, M.C. (2018).
Digital work and high-tech wanderers: Three theoretical framings and a
research agenda for digital nomadism. *ACIS 2018 Proceedings*, 2018, [online]
Available: https://aisel.aisnet.org/acis2018/55/.

Yayla, Ö., Özgür Göde, M. and Ekincek, S. (2024). Global palates: unraveling
digital nomads' culinary journeys and gastro-tourist profiles. *Worldwide Hospitality and Tourism Themes*. Doi: 10.1108/WHATT-03-2024-0045.

Zhou L. Buhalis D. Fan D. Ladkin A. and Lian X. (2024). Attracting Digital
Nomads: Smart Destination Strategies, Innovation, and Competitiveness.
Journal of Destination Marketing & Management, 31, 1–12. Doi: 10.1016/
j.jdmm.2023.100850.

Berrin Güzel[1] and Ilgaz Feray Demirağ[2]

Chapter 16 Artificial Meat as a Gastronomic Element

Introduction

At Milliways restaurant, a beefy cattle with big watery eyes and small horns approaches the table and introduces the most delicious parts of himself to the customers at the table. Those at the table begin to discuss the merits of eating an animal that is wanted versus one that is not wanted (Adams, 1980). It should be noted that this event takes place in a fictional story. Indeed, the concept of artificially producing meat was first proposed by the British politician Frederick Edwin Smith. Smith suggests that agricultural activities may decline by 2030, which could lead to the production of synthetic foods. He presents two potential approaches to protein production. These include the possibility of synthetic meat production, such as agricultural products, or the production of various high-priced animal foods, such as beef steak and chicken breast, in the laboratory with appropriate tools. He suggests that there is no need to feed a large cattle just for steak, and that in a future when the world's resources will not be enough to feed people, in vitro production of animal tissues and synthetic foods may be a possibility (Smith, 1930). It would appear that shortly after, in 1932, former British Prime Minister Winston Churchill expressed his thoughts on artificial meat as follows (Churchill, 1932: 299):

> '… We shall escape the absurdity of growing a whole chicken in order to eat the breast or wing, by growing these parts separately under a suitable medium. Synthetic food will, of course, also be used in the future. Nor need the pleasures of the table be banished. That gloomy Utopia24 of tabloid meals need never be invaded. The new foods will from the outset be practically indistinguishable from the natural products, and any changes will be so gradual as to escape observation…'.

Following the introduction of tissue culture techniques in the 1950s, the potential of using muscle tissue for the production of processed meat was recognised.

1   Prof. Dr., Aydın Adnan Menderes University, Faculty of Tourism, Food and Beverage Department, berrin.guzel@adu.edu.tr
2   Dr. Aydın Adnan Menderes University, Faculty of Tourism, Food and Beverage Department, ilgaz.feray.demirag@adu.edu.tr

This idea gained further traction in the 2000s, with the emergence of innovative approaches that utilised muscle tissue in the creation of meat products. Following a series of sensory analyses, it is believed that the product could potentially be consumed as food. The first ethical discussions regarding cultured meat began in 2008, when miniature steaks were produced using muscle tissue taken from frogs. In this discussion, artificial meat is seen as a potential option for consumers who wish to consume meat but do not wish to cause the animal any suffering. Since 2015 a number of start-up businesses are established (Zhang et al., 2021) with a view to producing artificial meat. Given that the world population is estimated to be 9.1 billion in 2050, it would be prudent to consider ways to increase both meat and grain production. It is estimated that 470 million tons of meat will need to be produced by 2050 (FAO, 2009).

The consumption of meat does not appear to be influenced by changes in disposable income in high-income countries. Factors such as human health, environmental impacts and animal welfare appear to be the main drivers of dietary change, with a reduction or change in meat consumption. In high-income countries, the preference for white meat is due to its perceived ease of preparation and perceived health benefits. In middle-income countries, however, significant changes occur due to economic growth, urbanisation and the growth of the fast-food industry. In low-income countries, the primary driver of meat consumption is population growth. However, limited access to meat in these countries prevents per capita meat consumption from increasing. This makes white meat the preferred choice in low-income countries due to its low price (OECD 2021, 2023).

Artificial Meat Production

The production of artificial meat is classified in a number of different ways. The first category of products is meat substitutes produced from alternative protein sources. These sources are plants and mushrooms. Secondly, and the focus of the current study, constructs are derived from tissues or cells that have been grown in vitro (Bonny et al., 2015). The quantity of meat produced from animal cells varies according to the type of animal used (poultry, fish, seafood and livestock) and the final product to be produced (burger steak or nugget). Nevertheless, despite these differences, the production process can be divided into four stages. The initial stage of the process is cell selection. This stage commences with the identification of the optimal cell source and cell type. Biopsies entail the removal of small tissue samples from either a living or slaughtered animal, which are then isolated and cultivated in a laboratory setting. Isolated tissues are then dissociated or processed by mechanical or enzymatic steps in order to separate the cells. It is possible that some cell lines may lack the physiological or genetic characteristics required to enable the desired growth and long-term functioning. In this context, the development of immortalised cell lines enhances reproductive capacity. It is of paramount importance that the resulting cell lines are not damaged and can maintain their properties. Consequently, the cells are observed following the addition of cryopreservation fluid. In the second stage, the cells are multiplied in large quantities and at high density. The cell source and types exhibit considerable variability. For instance, while mammalian cells reproduce optimally at 36.5–37.5 °C, fish cells can reproduce at 15–30 °C. In order to create the desired products, it is necessary to differentiate them according to cell types with the necessary properties. Nevertheless, it should be noted that differentiation of cells will not be 100 % successful, and thus the targeted cell type must be purified. The third stage is the harvesting stage. Once the cells have reached their maximum density in reproduction and transformed into the desired cell type, they are harvested in a manner that ensures the integrity of the tissue and cells and prevents microbial contamination. In the final stage of the process, the harvested cells/tissues are subjected to a specific type of processing in order to be transformed into a cell-based food product suitable for commercial production. In this context, sweetening and preservative ingredients are incorporated. Furthermore, the incorporation of distinct cell types enables the reconstruction of traditional meat structure and texture (FAO, 2023).

Source: FAO, 2023

The final category of artificial meat is meat derived from cloned animals. Although the cloning process was initiated by scientists, the resulting animal is a product of human intervention. This is because the clone is a copy of the mother, and therefore the cloning process is considered artificial (Bonny et al., 2015). It is important to note that in order for meat alternatives to be adopted by consumers and industrialised, they must be similar to real meat and ensure efficiency (Post, 2012).

However, there is no consensus on the degree of similarity between artificial meat and real meat (see Table 16.1 for comparison). Given that people consume real meat and artificial meat is promoted as an alternative, it is necessary for artificial meat to be similar to real meat. Conversely, a recently launched product must possess distinctive attributes to effectively compete in the market. For this reason, it is of the utmost importance that the new artificial meat is different (Bhat and Fayaz, 2011). Nevertheless, in both cases, the tissues must possess sensory properties such as colour, taste and softness that they exhibit in their natural state (Post and Hocquette, 2017).

Table 16.1. Difference between Real Meat and Artificial Meat

Real Meat	Artificial Meat
Obtained only from animal slaughter	Only a few animal slaughters are needed to collect stem cells
There are no meat quality checks	There are strict standards and hygiene controls for meat quality.
Exposure to pesticides is high	Exposure to pesticides is low
Animal biodiversity is not protected	Animal biodiversity is protected
Waste production is high	Waste production is low
Water consumption and carbon footprint are high	Water consumption and carbon footprint are low
Initial investment is low	Initial investment is high
A lot of resources are needed	Very few resources are needed
Animal welfare is problematic and there are ethical debates	It is subject to legal regulations and perceptual problems

Source: Mateti, Laha and Shenoy, 2022, p. 3429.

Additionally, there are some controversies associated with the manufacturing of synthetic meat. The first issue concerns the serum utilised in the production process. In order to facilitate the growth of cells, cell culture is conducted by extracting plasma from the cow fetus. Following the slaughter of the pregnant cow, the heart cells of the fetus, which is at least 2–3 months old, are extracted by inserting a needle into the heart (cardiopunctor). The issue arises from the fact that the fetus is not anaesthetised, which results in it experiencing pain. Nevertheless, a Mosa Meat has initiated the production process without the necessity of utilizing this serum. Secondly, the texture of the meat is a significant factor. While the texture of ground meat products, such as hamburgers, can be readily rendered realistic, this is less straightforward when it comes to pieces of meat. Indeed, the incorporation of fats into the meat is a crucial aspect of this challenge. Nevertheless, the issue is currently being addressed through the use of 3D printers. The final topic for discussion is the cost of production. The production of artificial meat is a costly process, which results in high prices in markets and restaurants (Robinson-Greene, 2023). The initial investment of $330,000 to produce the first burger with artificial meat, introduced in London in 2013, has decreased to $9.80 per burger. Nevertheless, Mark Post, the creator of the burger, and Bill Gates have stated that Memphis Meat, of which he is an investor, would not be economically viable in terms of cellular meat production. (Temple, 2021; Bandoim, 2022).

Furthermore, the religious and philosophical appropriateness of artificial meat is also a source of contention (Roy et al., 2021; Chriki and Hocquette, 2020). The differing religious compatibility debates that arise from the various methods utilised in the production process are further complicated by the fact that different details within these methods are open to differing interpretations (Dadon, 2022). Although it is commonly assumed that the absence of live animals in the production process eliminates the need to comply with religious rules (Bhat and Fayaz, 2011), this assumption is simplistic and requires further examination. For instance, the Qur'an (6:145) identifies certain animals as haram, or forbidden, to eat. These include pigs, animals slaughtered in the name of a deity other than Allah, animals not slaughtered in accordance with religious procedures, and animals that died spontaneously. Additionally, carcasses are included (The Qur'an). In contrast, the consumption of meat from domesticated donkeys, predatory animals, birds, hyenas, foxes, wolves, and cats is also prohibited by Muhammad, the Prophet (Hacıoğlu, 2018).

The production of artificial meat through the use of techniques such as embryonic and adult stem cells is a matter of contention within Islamic doctrine. In the context of embryonic stem cells, the focus is on the fetus. The development of the fetus is described in the hadiths as alaqah (blood clot) and mudghah (chewable-sized piece of meat). The consumption of alaqah is strictly prohibited due to the haram status of blood. The controversial nature of mudghah is due to the differing opinions on its acceptability. Some argue that it can be consumed, while others contend that it cannot be eaten, citing the absence of lanugo hairs in the fetus as a reason. Conversely, it is stated that the fetus can only be eaten when its mother is slaughtered and only when feathers are formed. In this context, the production of artificial meat, which will be derived from embryonic stem cells, is regarded as halal, provided that the embryo is at the mughdad stage and the mother is slaughtered. In the production of artificial meat from adult stem cells, the stem cells are obtained from live animals. In Islamic doctrine, the consumption of meat from live animals is prohibited on the grounds that the meat of such animals is deemed unclean. In this context, it is appropriate to slaughter the animal after it has died. Nevertheless, it should be noted that this does not apply to marine life, which is considered halal due to the purity of sea water (Directorate of Religious Affairs, 2024). Finally, although the serum technique involves the removal of blood cells and their subsequent separation just before the animal is killed, it is generally considered haram. However, it may be suitable for the production of artificial meat due to the change in quality that it brings about. Nevertheless, it is inadvisable to utilise serum derived from animals that are prohibited for consumption (Hamdan et al., 2018).

In Judaism, there are animals that are permitted and prohibited for consumption according to the kosher understanding. The specific animals that are permitted for consumption are clearly delineated in Leviticus 11. In order for an animal to be suitable for consumption as meat, it must possess both cloven hooves and the ability to chew cud. Furthermore, aquatic creatures must also possess scales and fins. In this context, shellfish, certain birds and four-legged and winged insects are prohibited (Leviticus: 11).

In Jewish belief, the most significant aspect is that the animal and the material used are kosher. In this context, a product obtained from an animal that is religiously kosher will also be kosher (Ottuh and Ihwighwu, 2023). Nevertheless, the question of whether artificial meat will be considered real meat and whether stem cells will be regarded as an animal remains open to debate (Krone, 2022). In accordance with the tenets of faith, the fetus utilised for the production of artificial meat is regarded as water during the initial forty days of pregnancy. In this context, despite the presence of stem cells, it is not considered meat according to some interpretations. Consequently, milk and meat can be consumed together, as the former is not yet a genuine and natural meat. During the production phase, although the stem cells were obtained from a piece of meat, they underwent a transformation as a result of the processes. Consequently, meat is also regarded as kosher provided that it has been derived from a kosher-compliant animal. Conversely, the consumption of blood is prohibited in Judaism. Given that blood is utilised in the production of artificial meat, it is therefore unsuitable to consume the meat produced. Nevertheless, this issue can be circumvented by utilising plant-based substrates (Dadon, 2022).

The Use of Artificial Meat

All processes related to the production of artificial meat have been developed with the intention of addressing the increasing global protein shortage, environmental concerns associated with animal farming, and social issues related to animal welfare and public health (Post, 2012). In this context, although the technology is still in its infancy, the development of artificial meat production will have a profound impact on the food industry in terms of production, quality and efficiency (Zhang et al., 2020; Chriki and Hocquette, 2020).

One of the principal challenges associated with the utilisation of artificial meat is the nomenclature employed to describe it. In studies conducted on this subject, consumers' sensitivity to the term and the emotions it evokes are evaluated (Li et al., 2024). For instance, the concept of '*lab-grown meat*' is predominantly associated with feelings of artificiality/unnaturalness and disgust. The term '*animal-free meat*' has been met with ambivalence among consumers, leading to the perception that it is a premium product for those who adhere to a vegetarian diet. Although '*cultured meat*' does not express negative emotions, it is associated with science and evaluated as distinct from natural meat. In contrast, '*clean meat*' was perceived as healthy, delicious, clean, and natural, with the most positive thoughts expressed (Byrant and Barnett, 2019). In this context, it is important to select the appropriate vocabulary for menu items carefully.

Artificial meat is particularly suited to the needs of food and beverage establishments. For example, Starbucks produces sausages made from plant-based ingredients. Dunkin' Donuts has entered into a partnership with Beyond Meat, a producer of plant-based meat, to produce hot dogs (Dunkin' Donuts, 2019). Additionally, McDonald's collaborated with the aforementioned company to develop a vegan burger (McDonald's, 2024). Burger King has also produced plant-based hamburger patties (Burger King, 2024). Nevertheless, although the products manufactured by Starbucks and Burger King are vegetarian, they are not vegan (Schlitz, 2021).

In the food and beverage industry, plant-based artificial meat is employed, rather than cell culture-based alternatives. These products have overcome the most fundamental obstacle to consumer acceptance. Nevertheless, it still constitutes a relatively minor proportion of a substantial market, given that the flavour and texture of these products differ significantly from those of real meat (Mateti et al., 2022). The preference for artificial meat derived from animals is driven by curiosity. The two main obstacles to the adoption of artificial meat are neophobic attitudes and emotional resistance. Even Weinrich et al. (2020) asserts that the perception of unnaturalness, disgust and the anticipation of bad taste are the primary reasons for emotional resistance. With the exception of curiosity, artificial meat can be preferred provided that it is cheaper than real meat (Zhang et al., 2020), as it does not replace real meat (Liu et al., 2021). Consequently, price is a significant factor, although this may vary according to cultural norms. Indeed, there are cultures where processed meat is more expensive than fresh meat, and there are also cultures where frozen meat is cheaper than fresh meat (de Araújo et al., 2022).

Those with nutritional knowledge are more inclined to consume and purchase artificial meat, given their greater familiarity with the product and its nutritional attributes. In this context, the adoption of healthier eating habits and an informed approach to new products is an effective strategy for influencing these preferences (Min et al., 2024). Those lacking information will evaluate their preferences for artificial meat based on the recommendations of their friends in social environments (Li et al., 2023), adopting a wait-and-see approach (Zhang et al., 2020).

The effect of age on the preference of artificial meat is somewhat contradictory, given that it was previously assumed that this product would be more popular and preferred among younger demographics. In contrast, however, younger people exhibited a less positive response to artificial meat. Consequently, it is crucial to develop it in accordance with modern eating habits (Liu et al., 2021). Nevertheless, other research findings appear to contradict this view (Min et al., 2024; Zhang et al., 2020; Mancini and Antonioli, 2019). One such example is the fact that young people tend to possess a more advanced scientific culture than the elderly, which in turn makes it easier for them to accept new technologies (Hocquette et al., 2015). Indeed, this situation can be explained by the difficulty in adapting to the rapid pace of technology advancement, which was first described by Toffler in his 1970s work titled Future Shock. (Thompson, 2014)

Results

One of the obstacles to the development of artificial meat is the lack of awareness among the general public about the issues currently facing the meat industry. Some of the reasons for this lack of knowledge include the need to improve the welfare of animals on farms, the necessity to regulate animal breeding in order to reduce greenhouse gas emissions, and the fact that there will be insufficient meat production to meet the increasing world population (Hocquette et al., 2015; Hocquette, 2015). Consequently, although it is imperative that governments raise awareness of this issue in order to increase the preference for artificial meat, the extremely rapid development of technology presents a significant challenge to governments (Thompson, 2014). It is of paramount importance for governments to elucidate and disseminate information regarding the environmental benefits that artificial meat will confer (Zhang et al., 2020). Nevertheless, it is important to acknowledge that the production of artificial meat does not automatically result in a net positive impact on the environment or animal welfare. Furthermore, there may be cultural differences in the perception of these issues (Pakseresth et al., 2022).

Those engaged in the food industry and those responsible for policymaking in the field of health communication should adopt different communication strategies in accordance with the type of consumer. For instance, those who are motivated by promotions should be targeted with gain-oriented messages. The choice of communication method should depend on the type of product. Avoidance-oriented messages, for instance, are more suitable for cultured meats (Shi et al., 2022).

It is similarly vital to enhance the nutritional awareness of the general public in order to reinforce the notion that artificial meat may prove advantageous in terms of nutrition (Zhang et al., 2020). Nevertheless, it is important to acknowledge that geographical factors can influence dietary habits in the dissemination of information. In light of the aforementioned considerations, it is imperative that efforts to popularise artificial meat be undertaken with great care in countries where cultural, religious and traditional influences exert a significant impact on meat consumption (Mancini and Antonioli, 2019).

It is challenging to anticipate the consumer response to the novel product, namely, artificial meat. In this context, the introduction of new products always carries an element of risk (Zhang et al., 2020). Consumer acceptance remains a controversial issue. Furthermore, the success of artificial meat is contingent not only on consumer acceptance but also on the enactment of requisite legal regulations by governments (Mancini and Antonioli, 2019).

References

Adams, D. (1980). The restaurant at the end of the universe. Pan MacMillan Pub.

Bandoim, L. (2022). Making meat affordable: Progress since the $330,000 lab-grown burger. https://www.forbes.com/sites/lanabandoim/2022/03/08/making-meat-affordable-progress-since-the-330000-lab-grown-burger/?sh=eb6f4ce46671 (Accessed: 13.05.2024).

Bhat, Z. F., & Fayaz, H. (2011). Prospectus of cultured meat—advancing meat alternatives. *Journal of Food Science and Technology*, 48, 125–140.

Bonny, S. P., Gardner, G. E., Pethick, D. W., & Hocquette, J. F. (2015). What is artificial meat and what does it mean for the future of the meat industry?. *Journal of Integrative Agriculture*, 14(2), 255–263.

Bryant, C. J., & Barnett, J. C. (2019). What's in a name? Consumer perceptions of in vitro meat under different names. *Appetite*, 137, 104–113.

Burger King (2024). Plant-Based Whopper. https://www.burgerking.ee/en/menu/meals/plant-based-whopper/ (Accessed: 11.03.2024).

Chriki, S., & Hocquette, J. F. (2020). The myth of cultured meat: a review. *Frontiers in Nutrition*, 7, 1–9

Churchill, W. (1932). Thoughts and Adventures. Churchill reflects on speis, cartoons, flying and the future. Thornton Butterworth: London.

Dadon, K. (2022). Lab-grown meat: A modern challenge in food production from the Jewish aspect. *Ekonomski İzazovi*, 11(22), 46–59.

de Araújo, P. D., Araújo, W. M. C., Patarata, L., & Fraqueza, M. J. (2022). Understanding the main factors that influence consumer quality perception and attitude towards meat and processed meat products. *Meat Science*, 193, 108952.

Directorate of Religious Affairs (2024). Din İşleri Yüksek Kurulu, Yengeç, istakoz, karides, kalamar ve midye gibi deniz ürünleri yenir mi?. https://kurul.diyanet.gov.tr/Cevap-Ara/987/yengec-istakoz-karides-kalamar-ve-midye-gibi-deniz-urunleri-yenir-mi (Accessed: 24.05.2024).

Dunkin'Donuts (2019). https://news.dunkindonuts.com/news/beyond-meat-dunkin#:~:text=Dunkin'%20today%20announced%20a%20new,for%20a%20future%20national%20rollout (Accessed: 22.05.2024)

FAO (2009). Global Agriculture towards 2050. https://www.fao.org/fileadmin/templates/wsfs/docs/Issues_papers/HLEF2050_Global_Agriculture.pdf (Accessed: 17.05.2024).

Hacıoğlu, N. (2018). Etlerinin yenilmesi yasaklanan hayvanlar ile ilgili hadis rivayetlerinin değerlendirilmesi. *Cumhuriyet İlahiyat Dergisi*, 22(2), 1191–1219.

Hamdan, M. N., Post, M. J., Ramli, M. A., & Mustafa, A. R. (2018). Cultured meat in Islamic perspective. *Journal of Religion and Health*, 57, 2193–2206.

Hocquette, A., Lambert, C., Sinquin, C., Peterolff, L., Wagner, Z., Bonny, S. P. & Hocquette, J. F. (2015). Educated consumers don't believe artificial meat is the solution to the problems with the meat industry. *Journal of Integrative Agriculture*, 14(2), 273–284.

Hocquette, J. F. (2015). Is it possible to save the environment and satisify consumers with artificial meat?. *Journal of Integrative Agriculture*, 14(2), 206–207.

Krone, A. (2022). Religion, animals, and technology. *Religions*, 13(5), 1–17

Leviticus (2024). 11: Eti yenen ve yenmeyen hayvanlar. https://kutsalkitap.info.tr/?q=Lev.11 (Accessed: 24.05.2024).

Li, H., Van Loo, E. J., van Trijp, H. C., Chen, J., & Bai, J. (2023). Will cultured meat be served on Chinese tables? A study of consumer attitudes and intentions about cultured meat in China. *Meat Science*, 197, 1–10

Liu, J., Hocquette, É., Ellies-Oury, M. P., Chriki, S., & Hocquette, J. F. (2021). Chinese consumers' attitudes and potential acceptance toward artificial meat. *Foods*, 10(2), 1–29.

Mancini, M. C., & Antonioli, F. (2019). Exploring consumers' attitude towards cultured meat in Italy. *Meat science*, *150*, 101–110.

Mateti, T., Laha, A., & Shenoy, P. (2022). Artificial meat industry: Production methodology, challenges, and future. *The Journal of The Minerals, Metals & Materials Society*, 74(9), 3428–3444.

McDonald's (2024). McPlant. https://www.mcdonalds.com/gb/en-gb/product/vegan-mcplant.html (Accessed: 11.04.2024).

Min, S., Yang, M., & Qing, P. (2024). Consumer cognition and attitude towards artificial meat in China. *Future Foods*, 9, 1–13.

OECD/FAO (2021). Meat. OECD Publishing.

OECD/FAO (2023). OECD-FAO Agricultural Outlook 2023–2032, OECD Publishing. Paris. https://doi.org/10.1787/08801ab7-en.

Ottuh, P. O., & Ihwighwu, J. O. (2023). An ethico-theological assessment of in-vitro meat in human society. *Ramon Llull Journal of Applied Ethics*, 14, 29–51

Pakseresht, A., Kaliji, S. A., & Canavari, M. (2022). Review of factors affecting consumer acceptance of cultured meat. *Appetite*, 170, 1–24

Post, M. & Hocquette, J. F. (2017). New sources of animal proteins: cultured meat. New aspects of meat quality – from genes to ethics. Woodhead Publishing Limited

Post, M. J. (2012). Cultured meat from stem cells: Challenges and prospects. *Meat Science*, 92(3), 297–301.

Robinson-Greene, R. (2023). Edibility and In-Vitro Meat, Ethical Considerations. UK: Lexington Books.

Roy, B., Hagappa, A., Ramalingam, Y. D., & Mahalingam, N. (2021). A review on lab-grown meat: Advantages and disadvantages. *Quest International Journal of Medical and Health Sciences*, 4(1), 19–24.

Schlitz, H. (2021). These are the fast-food chains where you can find fake meat on the menu. https://www.businessinsider.com/fast-food-chains-fake-meat-beyond-impossible-burger-menu-2021-7# (Accessed: 21.05.2024)

Shi, H., Ma, P., Zeng, Y., & Sheng, J. (2022). Understanding the interaction between regulatory focus and message framing in determining chinese consumers' attitudes toward artificial meat. *International Journal of Environmental Research and Public Health*, 19(9), 1–17.

Smith, F. E. (1930). The World in 2030. https://archive.org/details/in.ernet.dli.2015.527417/page/n3/mode/2up?view=theater (Accessed: 01.04.2024)

Starbucks (2024). Plant-Based Breakfast Sandwich. https://www.starbucks.com/menu/product/2123377/single?parent=%2Ffood%2Fhot-breakfast%2Fbreakfast-sandwiches-and-wraps (Accessed: 11.04.2024)

Temple, J. (2021). Bill Gates: Rich nations should shift entirely to synthetic beef. https://www.technologyreview.com/2021/02/14/1018296/bill-gates-climate-change-beef-trees-microsoft/ (Accessed: 10.05.2024)

The Qur'an. En'am, 145. https://kuran.diyanet.gov.tr/tefsir/En'%C3%A2m-suresi/934/145-ayet-tefsiri (Accessed: 24.05.2024).

Thompson, P. (2014). Artificial meat. In Ethics and Emerging Technologies (pp. 516–530). London: Palgrave Macmillan UK.

Weinrich, R., Strack, M., & Neugebauer, F. (2020). Consumer acceptance of cultured meat in Germany. *Meat Science*, 162, 1–6.

Zhang, L., Hu, Y., Badar, I. H., Xia, X., Kong, B., & Chen, Q. (2021). Prospects of artificial meat: Opportunities and challenges around consumer acceptance. *Trends in Food Science & Technology*, 116, 434–444.

Zhang, M., Li, L., & Bai, J. (2020). Consumer acceptance of cultured meat in urban areas of three cities in China. *Food Control, 118*, 1–7.

Vedat Kayiş[1] and Atif Akkil[2]

Chapter 17 Waste-Free Kitchen Management in Gastronomy

Introduction

In the industrial world, the gastronomy sector plays a critical role in terms of both economic and environmental sustainability. Waste generated due to the uninterrupted use of food every day is one of the main causes of environmental pollution and depletion of natural resources. In this context, due to the rapid consumption of resources, waste-free kitchen management is becoming increasingly important to achieve sustainability goals. Food waste brings with it serious environmental and socioeconomic problems (Stefan et al., 2013). Waste-free kitchen management includes strategies and practices developed to minimize food waste, optimize resource use and reduce environmental impacts.

This study aims to examine the principles and practices of waste-free kitchen management in gastronomy and the effects of these practices on sustainability. Waste-free kitchen management aims not only to reduce food waste, but also to increase economic efficiency and raise social awareness. In this regard, waste-free kitchen management is addressed with environmental, economic and social sustainability dimensions. The main purpose of the research is to disseminate waste-free kitchen management practices in the gastronomy sector and to reveal the benefits of these practices to the sector. In the study, waste-free kitchen management practices implemented in various restaurants and hotels were examined, and the results of these practices and the difficulties encountered were evaluated. In gastronomy, waste-free kitchen management not only ensures sustainability in food production and consumption, but also increases the competitiveness of businesses in the sector and helps them fulfill their social responsibilities. For this reason, it is of great importance to promote waste-free kitchen management and carry out comprehensive training and awareness studies on this subject (Kayış, 2023). The findings of the study include recommendations

1 Lecturer, Düzce University, Akçakoca Tourism and Hotel Management School, Department of Gastronomy and Culinary Arts, vadatkayis@duzce.edu.tr
2 Lecturer, Düzce University, Akçakoca Tourism and Hotel Management School, Department of Gastronomy and Culinary Arts, atifakkil@duzce.edu.tr

for strategic steps and policies required to increase the success of waste-free kitchen management practices. In this context, this study on waste-free kitchen management in gastronomy aims to make a significant contribution to achieving sustainability goals.

Food Concept

Solid and liquid nutrients taken by human beings to sustain their lives are defined as the basic elements for the body to continue its development, to provide the necessary energy, for the body organs to function regularly, and for the repair of damaged tissues and organs (Bender, 2006). In parallel, the concept of food defined by the Turkish Language Association (TDK) is stated as "all kinds of substances that are edible and used and consumed in nutritional activities" (Türk Dil Kurumu, 2021). According to the definition of Kesim (1995), the concept of food is defined as anything that can be consumed naturally and does not harm living things, except for the medicine required to complete the physical development of living beings, to repair worn-out tissues in the body, and to continue their lives. The most important issue generally focused on in food concept expressions is that food is the most basic consumption material needed for human life. In today's food consumption, the seasonal cycle of foods has changed, thanks to the availability of almost all foods in all seasons (Kayış and Akkil, 2023).

Sustainable Food

The agriculture and food sector, which has been affected by the changes brought about by globalization and has received its share, focuses on the issues that need to be emphasized in the sustainability system. Therefore, food, which is the most basic need for the continuation of human life, should be given importance in the field of sustainability, and as a result, sustainable food systems should be made necessary (Lentink et al., 2016). One third of the foods that are processed to make them ready for consumption are wasted or are wasted as a result of ignoring different factors. In parallel, according to FAO's World Food Security and Nutrition Status Report published in 2021, "there were approximately 828 million people on the hunger line, and this number increased even more during and after the pandemic process." Likewise, the number of people experiencing food insecurity, which was 2.3 billion in 2021, increased by 350 million with the pandemic. 11.7 % of the global population in the world experiences severe food insecurity (FAO, 2020).

Sustainable food; It is an approach that follows the same path as the sustainable development perspective in food systems, covering different stages such as food production, processing, distribution, preparation and consumption. According to Haspolat (2015), sustainable food emerged when it was determined that the process from production to consumption of food, which is mandatory to sustain human life as well as to protect human health, has a positive impact on natural resources and environmental dimensions. Ilbery and Maye (2005) list the criteria that should be focused on in sustainable food as follows:

- Saving energy use by using economically close resources,
- With the understanding of justice, paying attention to the rights of individuals working in the food industry and being fair in terms of wages and conditions,
- Following a diet program that does not contain harmful content in every respect,
- Avoiding the availability of food in terms of distance during the purchasing process of product supply,
- Providing comprehensive benefits for all members of society in terms of social sustainability,
- In the context of environmental sustainability, turning to environmentally beneficial products in production or paying attention to the production that does not harm the environment.

The World Food and Agriculture Organization states that the food value chain has been created based on the criteria that emphasize the importance of concepts such as economy, environment, production-consumption and social life in sustainable food (FAO, 2018).
In terms of sustainable food value chain;

- The aim of making profit at all stages from production to consumption process,
- Providing large-scale benefit opportunities for individuals in society,
- Not consuming unlimited natural resources,
- Ensuring sustainability after the production of agricultural raw materials,
- Processing agricultural raw materials into consumable foods and offering them for sale in line with demands.
- Evaluation of the waste produced during the process of making it suitable for consumption,
- The last stage means carrying out all processes systematically and within a plan (Neven, 2014).

Food Waste and Food Loss

Population growth throughout the world, increasing consumption rather than production, producers-consumers not using food effectively and efficiently, unconscious consumption reveal that waste and losses in food are excessive. Research has shown that an average of 13 million tons of food is left unused and thrown away every day in the world we live in, in addition to this, 5 million cubic meters of water is wasted in vain, and finally, 1.5 million tons of greenhouse gases are released into the atmosphere recklessly and recklessly (Çetinoğlu and Ünlüönen, 2020). Loss in food and unconscious waste of food during production and consumption; It poses a threat in terms of food security, environmental and economic aspects (Abiad and Meho, 2018).

It is estimated that 1/8 of the world's total population can be saved from malnutrition (Gustavsson et al., 2011) if all food loss and food waste around the world is evaluated in a planned and coordinated manner. Quantitatively, food loss and waste may vary depending on the economic situation of the countries, urbanization rates, as well as development, welfare and income levels (Chalak et al., 2016). When food waste and loss is examined in underdeveloped and developing countries, it generally occurs in the processing and storage stages of products produced in agricultural activities after harvest (Gustavsson et al., 2011). Losses during post-harvest storage and processing account for approximately 44 % of global food waste and loss Lipinski, B., Hanson, C., Lomax, J., Kitinoja, L., Waite, R. & Searchinger, T. (2018). Reducing Food Loss and Waste, Working Paper, Installment 2 of Creating a Sustainable Food Future (ss. 1-36). Washington DC: World Resouces Institute. The factors that caused this negative scenario to emerge are; logistics, technical and technological inadequacies, lack of infrastructure required for storage, workforce, bad agricultural practices, financial problems, etc. creates variables.

According to the research conducted by Lipinski et al. (2018), 56 % of food loss and waste is caused by developed countries in North America, Europe and Oceania, as well as industrialized countries such as South Korea, Japan and China (Lipinski et al., 2018). The behavior, attitudes and values of consumers are mostly effective in the emergence of this high rate of food loss and waste in industrialized and developed countries. Factors shaping consumer behavior can be listed as increasing the quality of life, increasing income and welfare levels, preferences for spending more time in social areas, and the increase in the participation of women in business life (Çetinoğlu and Ünlüönen, 2020).

The waste problem appears as a current global problem that brings economic, environmental and ethical issues to the agenda, and that every country should pay attention to. In order to produce permanent solutions to these problems, public institutions and non-governmental organizations in countries are carrying out studies on the edibility of food waste. In the light of these studies, promises of institutions and organizations in different geographies of the world to minimize food losses and wastes have led researchers in the field to conduct studies on sustainable foods and waste evaluation (Marthinsen et al., 2012).

Waste Concept

As stated in the Environmental Law, waste; It is defined as "any substance that is formed as a result of an activity, thrown into the environment or left somewhere". According to the regulation, it is defined as "any substance or material that is thrown or left into the environment or has to be thrown away by its producer or the real or legal person who actually possesses it" (Atık Yönetimi Yönetmeliği, 2015).

Waste-Free Kitchen

In recent years, the concept of zero waste has come to the fore frequently. The concept of zero waste, which is among the important elements of sustainability, means eliminating waste generation as much as possible or minimizing it, preventing waste, and collecting waste separately according to its characteristics and participating in the recycling process. Individual awareness of zero waste is as important as that of countries and governments. Because domestic wastes as well as commercial-industrial wastes harm the environment. According to World Bank reports, annual household waste, which is thought to be around 1.3 billion tons, is expected to reach 2.2 billion tons in 2025 (Wilson et al., 2015).

The fact that human beings continue their lives by forgetting that they are a part of nature causes brutal damage to the environment. Due to the impact of industrialization and urbanization, scarce resources are used unconsciously, and the amount of domestic waste calculated per person is increasing day by day as a result of changes in eating habits. In the context of sustainable development strategy, waste management strategies are being adopted around the world that aim to transform waste from being a threat to human health and the environment into an input for the economy. Considering waste management strategies, the issues that producers and consumers should pay attention to are stated below (Kayış, 2023).

- Limited Consumption Should Be Preferred

The main way to reduce waste is to limit consumption. Limiting consumption also paves the way for reuse in a positive way. In this context, some behavioral patterns at home should be revised. Glass jars, market and market bags, glass bottles, rechargeable batteries should be recycled for reuse, and old sheets, towels and fabric materials should be recycled. Obsolete products used in daily use should be recycled with personal efforts, otherwise they should be evaluated until it is time to recycle them. If not, it is important to be included in the system by dropping them at the right points and delivering them to the right addresses.

• Compost Should Be Created in Organic Waste

A zero waste approach has been adopted to encourage the effective and efficient use of natural resources, which are scarce in the intense global world. You will need to pay attention to the rules when getting a policy. This technology is used in daily use such as plastic-cardboard papers, tobacco-cutlery, etc. Products should be preferred in single technological packaging and similar quality, and should be used within the possibility of being used without running out. In addition to this, the ability to recycle organic waste in kitchens requires a method that complies with zero waste rules. The recycling process of organic waste generation is very important, especially within the framework of the 'Raw Food' system. Raw food menus include a wide range of foods, from starters to beverages (Kabacık and Bayram, 2023). The important aspect of this wide variety is creating a compost product. Compost, used to prevent food loss and waste, is expressed as the conversion of organic food waste into fertilizer by several different methods. Especially in professional kitchens, due to the large amount of food waste, the food waste generated in these kitchens is in an important position for composting. Thanks to composting, food loss in kitchens can be reduced to low levels. Food waste, which is treated as garbage with the composting method, is reused as fertilizer with proper composting. In the compost method, large-scale composting can be applied to almost all food waste, as well as small-scale composting. The simplest composting method is the compost formed by rotting unused vegetable and fruit residues in a compost container, which can be buried in the ground or used in pots (Tarım ve Orman Bakanlığı, 2020).

Kitchen Suggestions for Zero Waste

It is also necessary to pay attention to other elements that are constantly used in the kitchen. First of all, it should be waited until the existing products are finished and nothing should be wasted. For example, a kitchen cloth can be used instead of paper towels. Instead of napkins, fabric handkerchiefs can be preferred. Glass jars are also very suitable as storage containers. Some suggestions to prevent food waste in the kitchen can be listed as follows:

• Tea leaves or coffee grounds can be used as compost at the base of flowers and trees.
• The leftover cabbage leaves can be pickled or consumed by roasting them with onions and peppers.
• Stale bread can be made into breadsticks or baked with vegetables by adding eggs.
• The stems of the vegetables can be added to dishes prepared from spinach and celery.
• Stale bread can be cut into cubes and baked. Thus, it can be used as croutons in soups.
• Green leafy vegetables such as yellowed mint, parsley and dill should not be thrown away, they should be boiled and used. Boiled vegetable juices can be turned into a drink that relieves edema.
• Boiled beet juice can be drunk to make a salad or rice and couscous can be made.

Zero waste strategies are based on the principle of an environmentally friendly approach. Increasing social awareness on this issue is important in terms of leaving usable resources and a clean world to future generations. It should not be forgotten that the efforts made by individuals for zero waste can give a better direction to our environment and future (Kayış, 2023).

Sustainable Kitchen Practices

When the literature is examined, it is observed that sustainable restaurant practices and many similar classifications have been implemented in order to have a more livable environment and nature. A lot of food waste and waste occurs in the tourism industry. "Food Waste Prevention and Awareness Platform" was established in order to draw the attention of the society to this area. The slogan "Bon Appetit, No Waste" has started to be used with the "Orange Flag" application in order to raise awareness in the whole society in tourism enterprises, educational institutions, hospitals, military institutions and similar organizations where food waste is intense. The aim of these practices is to minimize food waste. In order to achieve this, various criteria have been created to raise awareness of business officials, employees and consumers participating in tourism (Turuncu Bayrak, 2019).

Some certificates are given to restaurants operating in order to prevent food waste and adopt the principle of sustainability, in accordance with their establishment purposes. These certificates are deemed appropriate for businesses with exemplary practices such as "Green Restaurants Association", "Green Generation Restaurants" and "Sustainable Food Services".

Table 17.1 presents the membership criteria and contents of the certification systems determined by the Sustainable Restaurants Association for businesses.

Table 17.1. Sustainable Practices in Restaurants

Organizations	Sustainable Practices
Sustainable Restaurants Association	• **Social Dimension:** Production of healthy and natural foods, marketing strategy responsibility, providing social benefit and increasing welfare • **Environmental Dimension:** Using resources effectively and efficiently, eliminating environmental damage (saving water, increasing energy efficiency, etc.) • **Resources-Related Dimension:** Environmentally friendly production, seasonal production, on-site production, fair trade and adoption of sustainability principles
Sustainable Food Services	• Equipment • Fats, oils and machine oils • Energy efficiency • Green cleaning • Disposable products • Food and food waste
Green Generation Restaurants	• Reduce chemical use and pollution • Water consumption • Sustainable food • Sustainable furniture and building materials • Waste management • Energy consumption • Communication and education
Green Restaurants Association	• Energy • This • Sustainable furniture and construction • Sustainable food • Chemical and pollution prevention • Disposable products • Waste

Source: Emirdağ, 2019.

When the aforementioned criteria and classifications are examined, the issues emphasized in sustainable restaurant practices are; These can be expressed as topics such as energy use, water and waste management practices, sustainability of buildings, employee training and social responsibility principle, chemical substance use, pollution prevention elements and sustainable food and beverage selection.

Environmentally Friendly Businesses

Sloan, Legrand and Chen, (2005) emphasize that hotels should take responsibility for the environment, as resource consumption creates huge negative ecological, social and environmental impacts worldwide.

Pineda and Brebbia (2004) claimed that financial savings are one of the most important reasons that inspire an organization to focus on the implementation of environmentally friendly practices in a hotel. This is especially important in a competitive environment where the costs of many processes such as energy, water and waste disposal are very high. By maximizing efficiency and reducing waste, the hotel can reduce energy consumption by 20–40 % without negatively impacting performance. Determining the motivations for becoming an environmentally friendly business has also been the focus of various studies (Tzschentke, Kirk and Lynch, 2004).

Environmentally friendly hotel practices also provide positive public relations activities through marketing, recognition and rewards, which increases customer demand in the market. Additionally, in order to support the implementation process, many national and international organizations provide awards to the businesses that best implement sustainability practices in the tourism industry, providing a great advantage in recognition and awareness. While being environmentally friendly largely means controlling and managing waste, it also relates to the types of products purchased. These include environmentally friendly products that are energy efficient, recyclable or locally grown (Kayış, 2023).

Results

In today's global world, in societies where the concept of waste has gained importance, ensuring that kitchens are waste-free is one of the most important issues emphasized. When a waste-free kitchen is evaluated in the context of sustainability, it also attracts the attention of industry representatives. Rating systems that evaluate tourism businesses around the world positively discriminate against businesses and producers that are sensitive to waste issues. Local and national press, public and private sectors make intense efforts to minimize waste.

Waste management in kitchens is an advantageous situation for sector representatives when evaluated from both a commercial, social and production perspective. However, in the world of gastronomy, the emergence of non-edible waste
is inevitable. At this point, kitchen waste can be minimized thanks to waste-free
kitchen practices. When the whole society adopts what needs to be done for a
waste-free kitchen, it will be possible to achieve economic advantage with less
waste and loss.

Positive results are observed in the studies carried out to recycle waste. Public
institutions, NGOs, media, educational institutions, and private sector representatives carry out R&D studies to minimize kitchen waste and recycle the resulting
waste, and these studies are promoted in the media. Thanks to these promotions,
sensitivity and sensitivity to the issue of waste in kitchens will be increased.

Sustainable gastronomy is among the trending trends in recent years. Waste
management and waste-free kitchen practices in kitchens can be found at the
core of sustainability. In order for trends to be accepted throughout society, the
concept of waste in the principle of sustainability will become more important
day by day. For a more livable future, it is necessary to protect food, reduce waste,
and develop conscious consumption behavior.

References

Abiad, M.G. & Meho, L.I. (2018). Food loss and Food Waste Research in the
Arab World: Systematic Review. Food Secur., 1–12

Anonim a, (2015). Atık Yönetimi Yönetmeliği, Resmî Gazete (29314, 2 Nisan 2015).
https://www.resmigazete.gov.tr/eskiler/2015/04/20150402-2.htm (Erişim Tarihi: 02.02.2024).

Anonim b, (2020). Tarım ve Orman Bakanlığı, Gıda Artık ve Atıklarından
Kompost Yapımı. Lojistik Sektöründe Gıda Kaybını Azaltmaya Yönelik Rehber Doküman. https://www.tarimorman.gov.tr/ABDGM/Belgeler/Uluslara
ras%C4%B1%20Kurulu%C5%9Flar/G%C4%B1dan%C4%B1%20Koru%20
Kompost.pdf (Erişim Tarihi: 07.02.2024).

Anonim c, (2019). Turuncu Bayrak. http://www.turuncubayrak.org/ (Erişim
Tarihi: 26.04.2024).

Atık Yönetimi Yönetmeliği, (2015). Resmî Gazete (29314, 2 Nisan 2015).
https://www.resmigazete.gov.tr/eskiler/2015/04/20150402-2.htm   (Erişim
Tarihi: 02.02.2024)."

Bender, D. A. (2006). Benders Dictionary of Nutrition and Food Technology.
Woodhead Publishing.

Chalak, A., Abou-Daher, C., Chaaban, J., & Abiad, M. G. (2016). The global economic and regulatory determinants of household food waste generation: A
cross-country analysis. Waste management, 48, 418422.

Çetinoğlu, D. & Ünlüönen, K. (2020). Otel İşletmelerinde Gıda İsrafını Önle-
meye Yönelik Turuncu Bayrak Uygulaması Üzerine Bir Araştırma. Sosyal,
Beşeri ve İdari Bilimler Dergisi, 3(5), 318–335.

Emirdağ, A. (2019). Restoran Yöneticilerinin Bakış Açısıyla Sürdürülebilir
Uygulamaların Önündeki Engeller: İzmir Örneği. (Yayımlanmamış Yüksek
Lisans Tezi), Dokuz Eylül Üniversitesi Sosyal Bilimler Enstitüsü, İzmir.

FAO (2018). Food loss and waste and the right to adequate food: Making the
connection https://www.fao.org/documents/card/en/c/ca1397en/ (Erişim
Tarihi: 12.03.2024).

FAO (2020). Dünyada Gıda Güvencesi ve Beslenme Durum Raporu. https://
www.fao.org/3/ca9692en/online/ca9692en.html (Erişim Tarihi: 13.03.2024).

Gustavsson, J., Cederberg, C., Sonesson, U., Otterdijk, R. & Meybeck, A. (2011).
Global Food Losses and Food Waste, FAO, Rome.

Haspolat, N.A. (2015). Gıda Güvenliğinde Sürdürülebilir Gıda Sistemleri (AB
Uzmanlık Tezi). Gıda Tarım ve Hayvancılık Bakanlığı Avrupa Birliği Dış
İlişkiler Genel Müdürlüğü, Ankara.

Ilbery, B. & Maye, D. (2005). Food Supply Chains and Sustainability: Evidence
from Specialist Food Producers in the Scottish/English Borders. Land Use
Policy, 22, 331–344.

Kabacik, M. & Bayram, F. (2023). "Raw Food Practices in Gastronomy". Ö. Yayla,
A. Işın, İ. Yazıcıoğlu ve F. Bayram (Ed.). Gastronomy Attractions and Practices in Tourism (s. 165–175) içinde. Berlin: Peter Lang.

Kayış, V. (2023). Gastronomik Akımlar-1, S. Türk Aslan (Ed.), Atıksız Mutfak
(s. 243–260). İksad Yayınevi.

Kayış, V. & Akkil, A. (2023). " Ready Food Sector In Gastronomy". Ö. Yayla, A.
Işın, İ. Yazıcıoğlu ve F. Bayram (Ed.). Current Trends and Practices in Tourism (s. 43–56) içinde. Berlin: Peter Lang.

Kesim, P.D.M. (1995). Gıda Teknolojisi. Eskişehir: Anadolu Üniversitesi Yayınları.

Lentink, A., Senders, A., Safa, A., Franchi, V., Lambert, S. & Laub, R. (2016).
FAO's Approach to Gender Sensitive and Sustainable Food Value Chains.
Sustainable Value Chains for Sustainable Food Systems, Meybeck, A. and
Redfern, S. (Edt.), a workshop of the FAO/UNEP Programme on Sustainable
Food Systems (ss. 117–127), 8–9 June 2016, Rome.

Lipinski, B., Hanson, C., Lomax, J., Kitinoja, L., Waite, R. & Searchinger, T. (2013).
Reducing Food Loss and Waste, Working Paper, Installment 2 of Creating a
Sustainable Food Future (ss. 1–36). Washington DC: World Resouces Institute.

Marthinsen, J., Sundt, P., Kaysen, O. & Kirkevaag, K. (2012). Prevention of Food Waste in Restaurants, Hotels, Canteens and Catering, Copenhagen: Nordic Council of Ministers

Neven, D. (2014). Developing Sustainable Food Value Chains-Guiding Principles. FAO, E-ISBN 978-92-5-108482-3, Rome.

Pineda F.D. & Brebbia C.A. (2004). Sustainable Tourism, Southampton, pp. 221–229.

Sloan, P., Legrand, W. & Chen, J.S. (2005). "Factors Influencing German Hoteliers' Attitudes Toward Environmental Management", Advances in Hospitality and Leisure (Advances in Hospitality and Leisure, Vol. 1), Emerald Group Publishing Limited, Bingley, pp. 179–188. https://doi.org/10.1016/S1745-3542(04)01011-2

Stefan, V., Herpen, E., Tudoran, A., & Liisa, L., (2013). Avoiding Food Waste by Romanian Consumers: The Importance of Planning and Shopping Routines, Food Quality and Preference, Volume 28, Issue 1, April 2013, Pages 375–38pp.

Tarım ve Orman Bakanlığı, (2020). Gıda Artık ve Atıklarından Kompost Yapımı. Lojistik Sektöründe Gıda Kaybını Azaltmaya Yönelik Rehber Doküman. https://www.tarimorman.gov.tr/ABDGM/Belgeler/Uluslararas%C4%B1%20Kurulu%C5%9Flar/G%C4%B1dan%C4%B1%20Koru%20Komp ost.pdf (Erişim Tarihi: 07.02.2024).

TDK (2021). http://sozluk.gov.tr (Erişim Tarihi: 23.03.2024).

Türk Dil Kurumu, (2021). "TDK" http://sozluk.gov.tr (Erişim Tarihi: 23.03.2024)."

Turuncu Bayrak, (2019). http://www.turuncubayrak.org/ (Erişim Tarihi: 26.04.2024).

Tzschentke, N., Kirk, D. & Lynch, P.A. (2004). "Reasons for going green in serviced accommodation establishments", International Journal of Contemporary Hospitality Management, Vol. 16 No. 2, pp. 116 124. https://doi.org/10.1108/09596110410520007.

Wilson, D. C., Rodic, L., Modak, P., Soos, R., Carpintero Rogero, A., Velis, C., & Simonett, O., (2015). Global Waste Management Outlook (GWMO); Prepared for United Nations Environment Programme (UNEP) and International Solid Waste Association (ISWA); Wilson, DC, Ed. UNEP International Environment Technology Centre (IETC): Osaka, Japan.

Ali Şen[1]

Chapter 18 Surimi as a Gastronomic Value: A Scientific Review of Gastronomy, Origin, and Technology

Introduction

The production process of surimi originated in Southeast Asia and significantly developed in Japan during the 16th century. While the term "surimi" in Japanese translates to "minced meat," it is expressed as "yú jiāng," meaning "fish puree," in Chinese. Presently, the United States, Japan, and Thailand stand as the largest surimi producers, with China, Vietnam, and Malaysia also holding significant positions in surimi production (Jeyakumari, 2014).

Although the history of surimi production began with Japan's processing industry, the rapid development of the surimi industry in the United States facilitated its spread to Korea and Southeast Asia. With the increasing production of surimi, Japan's share in global surimi production has decreased (Park & Lin, 2005). Surimi is defined as products obtained by mixing ground fish meats with seafood spices, hardeners, and other components, followed by thermal processes such as steaming, deep-frying, boiling, and smoking. Kamaboko, chikuwa, tempura, and hanpen are typical and traditional surimi products in Japan (Ooizumi & Park, 2013).

The global spread of surimi production and consumption has also influenced the integration of seafood into the culinary cultures of many countries. In this context, the entry and use of seafood in Turkish cuisine are noteworthy. Turkish cuisine experienced significant development, especially during the reign of Fatih Sultan Mehmet. Seafood inherited from Byzantine culinary culture was introduced into Turkish cuisine (Dilsiz, 2010). During the Fatih era, seafood such as oysters, shrimp, and fish were frequently brought to the palace and used in meals (Kahraman & Sönmezdağ, 2017). In this context, the main purpose of this section is to comprehensively examine the place of surimi derived from seafood in gastronomy, the production process, and surimi-based products. A thorough examination and evaluation of surimi in gastronomy and contributing to the literature in this field enhance the significance of the study.

---

1   Ph.D., Karamanoğlu Mehmetbey University, School of Applied Sciences, Department of Gastronomy and Culinary Arts, alisen@kmu.edu.tr

Gastronomy Concept

The term gastronomy is derived from the Greek words "gaster" (stomach) and "nomas" (law) (Güzel et al., 2015). Gastronomy refers to the culinary culture or the art of dining where food and beverages are prepared within the framework of health and hygiene rules, presented in an appealing manner to the eye and palate. It is also defined as healthy, well-organized, comforting, and delicious cuisine (Hatipoğlu, 2014). In some sources, gastronomy is considered a branch of science that utilizes both natural and social sciences and is expressed as the art of eating and drinking (Bayram & Işın, 2022; Sormaz et al., 2015).

Gastronomy is associated with various fields such as anthropology, sociology, economics, chemistry, agriculture, medicine, and modern technology. This indicates that gastronomy is not limited to food and beverages alone (Gülen, 2017). The roots of gastronomy tourism lie in agriculture, culture, and tourism. This allows gastronomy tourism to be marketed and positioned as a regional attraction and experience. All these elements are integrated under the umbrella of gastronomy and tourism. In other words, gastronomy is a discipline that examines the relationship between culture and all consumable food and beverages (Cömert & Durlu Özkaya, 2014).

In the modern world, gastronomy is not limited to preparing and presenting delicious meals. It also deals with issues such as sustainable food production, waste management, and environmental impacts. With the advancement of technology, gastronomy is enriched with new cooking techniques and innovative presentation methods. Molecular gastronomy is an example of these innovative approaches and involves the use of scientific principles in cooking (This, 2006; McGee, 2004).

Furthermore, gastronomy plays a significant role in preserving cultural heritage. Traditional recipes and cooking techniques contribute to preserving cultural identity by being passed down from generation to generation (UNESCO, 2020).

Gastronomy and Surimi

The industrial food sector has experienced rapid growth since the 1950s, further accelerated by globalization. Advances in the fields of chemistry and physics have led to further development of food processing and production techniques. For example, the transglutaminase method is one of the most commonly used methods in the food industry. However, this technique is still relatively unknown in Turkey. Transglutaminase enhances protein structure, allowing two proteins to stick together, and is therefore widely used in the production of sausages, deli meats, and imitation crab meat (surimi) sold in markets (Özdoğan, 2014).

Surimi is an intermediate product used in various products ranging from traditional "kamaboko" to shellfish. Technically, it is a stabilized myofibrillar protein obtained from washed and mechanically deboned fish meat, mixed with cryoprotectants, and stored by freezing. The quality of surimi is determined based on a range of characteristics such as gel strength, color, moisture content, contamination, and microbiological count. Other factors affecting the final quality include pH, protein content, fat content, cryoprotectants, and other food-grade additives. In addition to these quality attributes, the gel properties (especially gel strength) of surimi are among the most important factors in surimi production and trade. The gastronomic significance of surimi extends beyond its technical attributes, highlighting its integration into different culinary cultures and versatile usage. Modern gastronomy encourages the fusion of surimi products produced using traditional methods with new cooking techniques and presentation methods. Surimi serves as an important component in creating different tastes and textures, making it ideal for innovative gastronomic applications (Park & Lin, 2005).

Surimi: Origin and History

Surimi has a rich history dating back to the 16th century as a commercial product and fully developed in the 19th century. High-quality white fish is typically preferred for surimi production (Süle, 2011). Seafood has been consumed in various forms across cultures throughout history. The advancement of the food industry has standardized seafood, transforming surimi from traditional, regionally diverse products into a standardized commodity. Surimi, which means "ground fish meat" in Japanese, undergoes various processes to acquire its unique characteristics (Ercoşkun, 2003).

In Japan, surimi is a traditional method developed for the long-term preservation of fish meat, with a history spanning centuries. In the 1950s, American producers discovered this method, leading to surimi production finding a significant market in the United States and subsequently spreading worldwide. Frozen surimi is used as a raw material in many convenience food industries such as croquettes, hamburgers, meatballs, and sausages. Today, the Japanese produce hundreds of different products from surimi and consume an average of 6.80 kg of surimi per person per year, equivalent to the annual seafood consumption of Americans (Lanier & Lee, 1992).

Surimi Production: Key Players

Certain characteristics are required for fish used in surimi production. Desired attributes for surimi-based products include strong gel-forming properties, good organoleptic quality, white meat, year-round availability, efficiency, and affordability (Jeyakumari, 2014).

Various methods are employed for fish preparation in surimi production. One involves cutting off the fish head and separating the intestines from the carcass. Another method involves filleting the fish and removing bones and spines from the fillet. Both methods require careful execution. It is particularly crucial to remove internal organs entirely, as components like liver or intestines mixed in the mince can lead to shelf-life issues. Ample water and a brush are needed during the splitting and filleting steps to separate unwanted portions of fish meat (Park & Lin, 2005).

The quality and characteristics of surimi are influenced by various factors such as the types of fish used, the fishing season, and the freshness of the fish. The diversity of fish species and the influence of various factors notably determine the quality of surimi, especially in terms of gel-forming ability (Okazaki & Kimura, 2014).

Another crucial step in surimi production is the washing process. This step not only removes unwanted substances but also increases the concentration of myofibrillar proteins (Jeyakumari, 2014). The surimi production process begins with the procurement of fish and ends with freezing and storage stages (Park & Lin, 2005).

The freshness of the materials used in surimi production significantly impacts product quality. Effective cooling and low-temperature storage are necessary for preserving freshness. Freshness can affect gel strength, and controlling the freshness of fish material minimizes changes in surimi quality. Surimi quality can vary depending on the season and the sizes of fish species used, underscoring the importance of freshness control during the production process (Okazaki & Kimura, 2014).

Production Materials

Surimi is primarily a concentrate of myofibrillar proteins and is formed with a gel matrix. The interaction of myofibrillar proteins within surimi with the gel matrix depends on various factors, including added additives, pH, time/temperature relationship, and myofibrillar protein concentration (Lanier, 1990).

Salt (NaCl)

Salt is added during the final wash to enhance surimi's gel-forming ability. The optimum level is typically around 2 % (Jeyakumari, 2014).

Milk Protein Concentrates

Used as a filler material in surimi technique, milk protein concentrates function as water binders or gelling agents. Whey protein isolates and lactalbumin, among other milk protein concentrates, may reduce surimi gel strength (Bugarella et al., 1985; Chung & Lee, 1990).

Sugar

Sugar is used in surimi as a cryoprotectant and sweetener. It increases water-binding capacity by protecting protein from freeze denaturation (Jeyakumari, 2014).

Egg White

A common additive in surimi and similar products, egg white can enhance gel strength and is used in a range of 3 % to 10 % by weight (Chen, 1987).

Starch

Starch is frequently used in surimi and surimi-based products. The type of starch affects the strength of surimi gel and its freeze-thaw stability. The optimal usage rate is typically between 5 % and 8 % (Chen, 1987).

Color and Flavor Additives

Color and flavor additives are used for imitation seafood in surimi production. These additives help enhance the aesthetic and taste profile of the products (Jeyakumari, 2014).

Isolated Soy Protein (ISP)

Isolated soy protein, with its moisture and fat retention properties and gelling ability during cooking, is commonly used in surimi and similar products (Westeryl et al., 1980).

Surimi-Based Products and Production Techniques

Surimi-based products can be categorized into four groups based on their production technologies and structural properties: molded products, fibrous products, composite-molded products, and emulsified products.

Molded Products

These products are produced by shaping the kneaded surimi dough into the desired shape for elastic texture and good gel formation. Single extrusion or co-extrusion processes can be used. In single extrusion, the dough is shaped by a single head; co-extrusion involves multiple heads that create the texture during the folding stage (Yerlikaya & Gökoğlu, 2006).

Fibrous Products

Surimi dough is passed through a rectangular head to form a thin sheet. This sheet is then cut into strips using a cutting mechanism, which are then assembled, colored, wrapped, and cut. For example, thin strips are preferred in imitation crab sticks (Lee, 1984; Lee, 1986; Okazaki, 2002).

Composite-Molded Products

These products are created by breaking down the surimi gel block or adjusting the mixing ratios. Shrimp and lobster imitations are the most typical examples. Another type of composite molded product is fish ham (Jeyakumari, 2014).

Emulsified Products

Similar to red meat emulsions, these products have a low fat content. Animal fat is not necessary; vegetable oils are generally preferred. The emulsified dough prepared for sausages and sausage-like products is filled into casings and cooked with steam and smoking (Mansfield, 2003).

Advancements and Innovations in Surimi Technology

Advancements and innovations in surimi technology garnered significant interest in the seafood and food industry, particularly in the United States, in the early 1980s. Imitation crab sticks, especially in Europe, gained wide attention. Previously unused or rarely used raw materials were successfully utilized. Frozen surimi drew attention with its long shelf life and high functional protein content.

Various processing techniques and ingredients allowed for the production of surimi-based products with diverse appearances and qualities. In Japan, the surimi technique has been developed for centuries. The increase in raw material supply supported the development of new products, production techniques, and product storage systems. Learning from and understanding the principles of the Japanese surimi industry played a significant role in spreading the surimi industry to other countries (Lee, 1984; Park & Lanier, 2000).

Conclusion

Surimi production emerges as a rapidly evolving industry globally, contributing to the efficient and effective utilization of marine resources.

For countries like Turkey, endowed with rich marine resources, it should be noted that surimi technology presents significant opportunities. Despite the country's vast potential in fisheries, there is currently insufficient research and industrial application in surimi production. However, enhancing research efforts and developing surimi technology in this field could diversify Turkey's fishing industry and strengthen its economy.

In this context, further exploration and development of surimi technology could not only benefit the fishing industry but also make positive contributions to the food sector and the overall economy. Encouraging and supporting surimi production aligned with sustainable fishing principles could contribute to the sustainable management of marine resources and leave a healthier environment for future generations.

References

Bayram, F. & Işın, A. (2022). Sustainable gastronomy: the importance of local foods and geographical indications in gastronomic tourism. In Academic Studies in Gastronomy. Detay-Ankara.

Burgarella, J. C., Lanier, T. C., Hamann, D. D., Wu. M. C. (1985). Gel strength development during heating of surimi in combination with egg white or whey protein concentrate. *J. Food Sci. So*, 1595–1597.

Chen, J. S. (1987). Optimization in the formulation of surimi-based extruded products., University of Rhode Island, M.S. thesis, Kingston, Rhode-Island.

Chung, K. H. & Lee, C. M. (1990). Effect of water binding and dispersion pattern of ingredients the textural properties of surimi gel. Presented at the annual meeting at institute of food technologists. Anaheim, California.

Cömert, M. & Durlu Özkaya, F. (2014). The importance of Turkish cuisine in gastronomy tourism. *Journal of Tourism and Gastronomy Studies*, 2(2), 62–66.

Dilsiz, B. (2010). Gastronomy and tourism in Turkey: The Case of Istanbul. Master's thesis, Istanbul University, Istanbul.

Ercoşkun, H. (2003). Surimi: fish gel products. *Pamukkale University Journal of Engineering Sciences*, 22–28.

Gülen, M. (2017). Gastronomy tourism potential and evaluation of Afyonkarahisar. *Current Tourism Research Journal*, 1(1), 31–42.

Güzel Şahin, G. & Ünver, G. (2015). "Gastronomy tourism" as a destination marketing tool: A study on the gastronomy tourism potential of Istanbul. *Journal of Tourism and Gastronomy Studies*, 3(2), 63–73.

Hatipoğlu, A. (2014). *An examination of the ottoman palace cuisine in the context of gastronomy tourism.* Sakarya University, Social Sciences Institute Department of Tourism Management, Sakarya, 2014.

Jeyakumari, A. (2014). Surimi and surimi-based products. In G. Ninan, V. Ronda, & J. A (Eds.), Modern Food Processing Technology (pp. 169–175): Central Institute of Fisheries Technology, Cochin.

Kahraman, A. G. & Sönmezdağ, A. S. (2017). Fish consumption in ottoman cuisine and integration of pickled olive caviar into rural tourism gastronomy. *Journal of Agricultural Sciences Research*, 10 (1): 20–26.

Lanier, T. C. (1990). Interactions of muscle and nonmuscle proteins effecting heat-set gel rheology. In Macromolecular Interactions and Food Colloid Stabiliti. N.Parris and R.A.Barford, (Eds.), ACS Symposium Series, 268–284.

Lanier, T. C. & Lee, C. M., (1992). Surimi technology. New York: Marcel Dekker Inc.

Lee C. M. (1984). Surimi process technology. *Food Tech,* 38(11):69.

Lee, C. M. (1986). Surimi manufacturing and fabrication of surimi-based product. *Food Technol.,* 3, 115–124.

Mansfield, B. (2003). Fish, factory trawlers, and imitation crab: the nature of quality in the seafood industry. *J. Rural Studies*, 19, 9–21.

McGee, H. (2004). On food and cooking: the science and lore of the kitchen. Scribner.

Okazaki, E. (2002). Aplication of high technology to seafood processing. *Farming Japan*, 36(5), 17– 22.

Okazaki, E. & Kimura, I. (2014). Frozen surimi and surimi-based products. In Seafood processing technology, quality and safety (pp. 209–235).

Ooizumi, T. & Park, J. D. (2013). Manufacture of fish sausage. In surimi and surimi seafood (pp. 301).

Özdoğan, O. N. (2014). Trends, concepts, approaches, success stories in the food and beverage industry. Ankara: Detay.

Park, J. & Lin, T. J. (2005). Surimi: manufacturing and evaluation. In surimi and surimi seafood (pp. 33–105). New York: Taylor and Francis, Boca Raton.

Park, J. W. & Lanier, T. C. (2000). Processing of surimi and surimi seafood. "Marine freshwater products handbook". Technomic Publishing Company: Lancaster, NH, 417-445.

Sormaz, Ü., Özata, E. & Güneş, E. (2015). Gastronomy in tourism. *Journal of Social Sciences*, 1(2), 67–73.

Süle, Ö. (2011). *Production of surimi from carassius gibelio and determination of its chemical and microbiological quality*. Süleyman Demirel University, Institute of Science and Science Department of Features Capture and Processing Technology, Master's thesis, Isparta, 2011.

This, H. (2006). Molecular gastronomy: exploring the science of flavor. Columbia University Press.

UNESCO (2020). Representative list of the intangible cultural heritage of humanity. https://ich.unesco.org/en/lists/

Westerly, D. B., Decker, C. D., & Holt, S. K. (1980). Gelling proteins. In Third Nat. Tech. Seminar of Mechanical Recovery and Utilization of Fish Flesh, RE Martin (ed.), National Fisheries Enst. Washinghton, DC (pp. 324-347).

Yerlikaya, P. & Gökoğlu, N. (2006). Evaluation of surimi waste. In Proceedings of the 9th food congress of Turkey, May 24–26, Bolu.

Mustafa Yilmaz

Chapter 19 The Deep Roots of Coffee Culture/ A Tasting Journey around the World

Introduction

Looking back from the past to the present, the concept of consumption was initially used to meet physiological needs. However, with the influence of technology, consumption has now transformed into a means to fulfil cultural, social, and personal purposes. An example of this transformation is coffee, which has gained rapid popularity worldwide. The name coffee derives from the Arabic "gahwah" and has evolved into "kahve" in Turkish. Its meaning is "a drink that gives pleasure." Historically referred to as 'black pearl,' coffee has a long and complex history of both bitter and sweet experiences (Dalgıç, 2022). Throughout history, coffee has been the scene of many cultural and social interactions, leading to celebrations as well as bans. Today, coffee is cultivated on five continents, and each continent has developed its own unique flavors and consumption cultures. Although 85 species of coffee are known in nature, only three of them-Arabica, Canephora (Robusta) and Liberica-are grown commercially. (Wagner, Von Rothkirch, & Stull, 2001). Arabica, Robusta, and Liberica coffees are the most consumed coffee varieties in the global coffee market. Beyond being one of the most significant cultural elements of a country, coffee also has social and economic impacts. The enduring presence of coffee with its different varieties and modes of consumption spread over a vast geography makes it a unique cultural element. The multicultural nature of coffee highlights the regions where coffee is grown and the destinations with their own unique coffee varieties (Bohn, et al., 2012; Yılmaz, 2023). Coffee production encompasses a long process from the sowing of the seed to filling the cups, employing millions of people in the process. The culture of coffee has spanned from shepherds to Sufi lodges, merchants to palaces, and has become a widespread consumption item around the world today (Dalgıç, 2022; Yurt, 2023).

Historical and Cultural Journey of Coffee

Historians suggest that the origins of coffee date back to Old Testament stories. Some believe that the coffee bean is the same as the "parched corn" given by

Naomi to David and by Boaz to Ruth. Another group of researchers posits that the "black broth" consumed by the Spartans, known as Lacedaemonians, might have actually been coffee. The Italian traveller Petrus de Valle claims that the history of coffee dates back to the Trojan Wars (Atkinson et al., 2009). However, there is no definitive historical evidence regarding who first drank coffee. The most widespread legend is the story of Khaldi, a Yemeni shepherd. While grazing his flock under the moonlight, Khaldi observed that his goats became energetic after eating red berries from a bush. Intrigued, Khaldi tried the berries himself and experienced a similar surge of energy. This discovery led to the spread and popularity of coffee among monks and clerics (Heisse, 1996). Although coffee has been known since the 12th century, it began to be used as a pleasurable beverage in the 14th century. Despite differing rumours about the homeland of coffee, most historians and researchers agree that coffee spread worldwide from Southern Ethiopia. This claim is based on the similarity between the word coffee and the "Kaffa" region in Southern Ethiopia. The term coffee first appears in a medical book written in Arabic by the Turkish scholar Ebubekir, who lived between 1405 and 1525. This book mentions the use of coffee in Iran in 1420 and its subsequent export to Aden. Coffee, which spread from Ethiopia to Yemen, Mecca, and Medina, quickly gained popularity in the Islamic world (Bajmaku, 2014). It is known that before the 14th century, coffee beans in Yemen were used to make bread or consumed as a fruit. The written sources do not provide definitive information about the emergence of coffee as a beverage. The oldest and most comprehensive work related to coffee is the treatise "Umdati's-Saffe fi Hilli'i-Kahve" by Abdulkadir al-Jaziri. This work was published in Baron Silvestre de Sacy's book "Chrestomathie Arabe ou Extraites de Divers Auteurs Arabes" (Gürsoy, 2005). Even before coffee left its mark on global cuisine, trade, folklore, and culture, it was already a significant product. With a short leap across the Red Sea, coffee not only influenced social, political, and cultural life in Africa and Central Asia but also in Europe and America. Coffee has strengthened communication networks, inspired minds, revitalised tired spirits, and become an indispensable daily routine for countless people around the world (Bajmaku, 2014).

Before the 14th century, coffee beans were used in Yemen for making bread or consumed as a fruit. Written sources do not provide definitive information about coffee's emergence as a beverage before it left its mark on global cuisine, trade, folklore, and culture. The oldest and most comprehensive work on coffee is Abdulkadir al-Jaziri's treatise 'Umdati's-Saffe fi Hilli'i-Kahve'. This work was partially published in Baron Silvestre de Sacy's book 'Chrestomathie Arabe ou Extraits de Divers Auteurs Arabes' (Gürsoy, 2005). The food and beverages offered in a society are an important part of its cultural structure. In particular, eating and drinking activities have always been considered significant in Turkish society. The food and beverages consumed by a society are among the most important elements reflecting that society's religious beliefs, cultural values, and history (Sezgin & Onur, 2017; Yurt & Bayraklı, 2022). In Turkish culture, coffee has a deep-rooted history and remains significant as a beverage that upholds our cultural values and preserves our traditional values. Initially consumed in homes, coffee gradually moved to coffeehouses. With the Industrial Revolution, the French and Italians invented espresso machines to transform Turkish coffee into a beverage without grounds, while the Germans invented filter coffee machines. In the 19th century, Americans discovered instant coffee. Today, coffee has become one of the most important beverages consumed by more than one-third of the world's population. The primary reason for this widespread consumption is coffee's significant role in social life (Engelmann & Dulloo, 2007; Sökmen, 2008; Farah, 2009; Arslan, 2019; Onur & Ceylan, 2023).

Arabica Coffee

Arabica coffee originated in the mountains of Abyssinia (now Ethiopia) and is still cultivated in areas with tropical climates. Arabica coffee is the most common type of coffee in the world and was the first type of coffee to be cultivated. The birthplace of Arabica coffee is the highland forests of Ethiopia and South Sudan. These regions are known as the places where primitive peoples started their journey to conquer the world (Stoffelen, et al., 2008). Arabica coffee accounts for 64 % of global coffee production and has more than 200 varieties. This type of coffee is low in caffeine and high in aroma and is preferred for its taste profile. Arabica coffee has softer, floral and fruity flavors. These characteristics make it ideal for consumers looking for variety and rich flavors in their coffee. There are tall and short types of Arabica coffee trees. Tall Types: Typica, Bourbon, Mocha, Mundo Nova, Maragogype, Marella. Short Types: Caturra, Catuai, Catimor (Herman et Janssens, 2011). Growing Regions Arabica coffee is grown at higher altitudes. It is generally produced in Africa, Papua New Guinea and South America. Arabica beans are sweeter, softer to drink and generally have fruit flavored notes compared to Robusta (Güven, 2020). Arabica coffee trees grow at altitudes of 800–2,000 meters above ground level and yield an average of 5 kg of fruit per year. Approximately 1 kg of beans are obtained from this fruit. Arabica vs. Robusta Arabica beans contain less caffeine than Robusta beans, but are more aromatic and flavorful. Robusta coffee beans have stronger aromas and intense flavor. Robusta beans are also twice as high in caffeine as Arabica. Arabica, which has high acidity, is known for its fruity and floral flavors, while Robusta has more earthy and harsh flavors (Saltan and Kaya, 2018). Arabica is the most widely produced coffee type in the world. Arabica production is widespread in all coffee producing countries, especially in South America. Robusta is mostly produced in Africa and South Asia. Arabica coffee beans are the most popular type of coffee, accounting for more than 60 % of all cups drunk worldwide. Arabica coffee remains popular among coffee lovers for its low caffeine content, high aroma and diverse taste profiles. Its journey began in the highland forests of Ethiopia and South Sudan, and continues all over the world today. Grown in tropical climates, this coffee has an important place in the world coffee market.

Robusta Coffee

Robusta coffee is a type of coffee obtained from the beans of the plant 'Coffea canephora,' native to Africa, and is sometimes referred to as Coffee Canephora.' After Arabica, Robusta is the second most widely cultivated coffee species globally, known for its resilience to adverse natural conditions and diseases. Discovered in Uganda in 1862, it was traditionally used by local tribes in ceremonial practices. When the Arabica plant suffered significant damage from coffee rust disease, Robusta gained prominence for its distinctive characteristics. Predominantly grown in Asia, Africa, and Brazil, Robusta accounts for approximately one-third of global coffee production. This coffee is cultivated at altitudes up to 600 metres above sea level and is known for its high resistance to harsh climatic conditions. Robusta trees yield more produce than Arabica trees and have a higher caffeine content, which is its most notable feature. Robusta coffee is characterised by its pronounced bitterness and is often used as a filler in instant coffee, espresso, and some ground coffee blends. Due to its high caffeine content (twice as much as other coffee types), it is a particularly strong coffee and leaves a robust taste on the palate. However, excessive consumption can lead to palpitations and stomach pains, so it is advisable to consume it with caution. Robusta coffee beans are grown at lower altitudes compared to Arabica and are widely available. They are particularly produced in regions such as Africa, Indonesia, and India. With its durability and high yield, Robusta holds a significant place in the coffee industry. For both producers and consumers, Robusta coffee is an important coffee type. Its resilience, high caffeine content, and distinctive taste have secured a special place for it in the world of coffee.

Table 19.1. Coffee Producing Countries in the World and Their Production Amounts

Market	% of Global Production	Total Production (2023/2024, 60 KG Bags)
Brazil	39%	66.3 Million
Vietnam	17%	29.1 Million
Colombia	7%	12.2 Million
Ethiopia	5%	8.35 Million
Indonesia	5%	8.15 Million
Uganda	4%	6.4 Million
India	4%	6.1 Million
Honduras	3%	5.3 Million
Peru	2%	4 Million
Mexico	2%	3.87 Million

Source: USDA, 2023
Usda, (2024). 2023/2024 Coffee Production,
https://fas.usda.gov/data/production/commodity/0711100, Accessed Date: 01.05.2024..

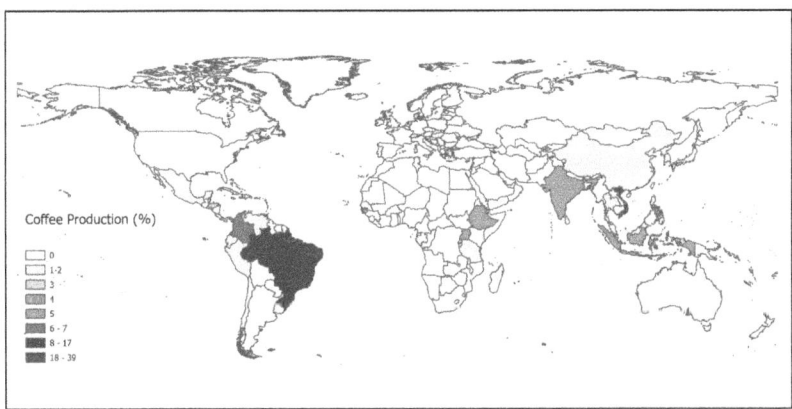

Figure 19.1. Coffee Growing Countries in the World
Source: Usda, 2024.

Liberica Coffee

Liberica coffee possesses an extraordinary flavour profile defined by a blend of floral, fruity, and smoky notes. One of the most distinctive features of Liberica coffee is its large, almond-shaped beans. These beans are larger in size and uniquely shaped compared to other coffee varieties. The unique taste of Liberica imparts a distinctive flavour profile to coffee blends. Dominant bitter chocolate notes, subtle woody aromas, and bold, robust flavours make this coffee exceptional. These characteristics offer a unique and unforgettable coffee tasting experience. The journey of Liberica coffee is intertwined with the coffee history of the Philippines in the late 19th century. Faced with a severe crisis due to coffee rust disease devastating Arabica coffee plantations worldwide, the American government introduced Liberica coffee to the Philippines in 1898. This move was seen as a lifeline, offering a resilient alternative crop. Liberica coffee adapted well to Philippine soil, and the country quickly became a leading producer of this special coffee. However, despite its initial success, the Liberica coffee industry gradually declined throughout the 20th century. The Philippines holds a special place at the heart of Liberica coffee production, considered a national treasure. The fertile soils and favourable climate of the Philippines nourished strong Liberica coffee crops, making it a significant player in the country's coffee industry. Beyond the Philippines, other countries also play a role in cultivating and processing Liberica coffee. Malaysia, Vietnam, Indonesia, and Liberia are among these countries, each contributing to the global supply of this unique coffee variety. These countries produce high-quality Liberica coffee thanks to their suitable climate and soil conditions. Liberica coffee is notable both for its flavour profile and its history. With its large almond-shaped beans and floral, fruity, smoky notes, it offers a distinctive tasting experience. Grown in the Philippines as well as in Malaysia, Vietnam, Indonesia, and Liberia, Liberica coffee holds a significant place in the global coffee industry. This unique coffee holds special significance for both coffee enthusiasts and coffee producers.

The development and rise in popularity of coffee, evolving into new trends, is a complex process shaped by various socio-cultural and economic dynamics. This evolutionary process is characterised by innovations and changes occurring at many stages, from coffee production to consumption. Coffee has transcended its role as a mere beverage to become central to social interaction, cultural expression, and economic activities over time. Historically, coffeehouses have functioned as centres for socialising, political discourse, and cultural interaction, contributing to the evolution of coffee as a social experience and cultural symbol.

The Evolution of Coffee Becoming a Trend

Coffee has gradually become a societal experience and cultural symbol, holding a significant place in the worlds of literature and art. For instance, many renowned writers and poets have composed works about coffee, drawing inspiration from its influence on intellectual and artistic processes (Tucker, 2017; Haktanir & Gullu, 2024). Even today, coffee culture remains a significant social activity. The industrial transformation of coffee has been realised through the processes of roasting, grinding, and packaging. The roasting process is a critical step that determines the aroma and flavour of coffee beans, which can be roasted lightly, medium, or dark to achieve different flavour profiles. The grinding process facilitates the brewing process by converting fresh coffee beans into finely or coarsely ground powder. The packaging process ensures the preservation of fresh coffee, providing consumers with fresher and higher-quality products.

The emergence of the first coffee chains at the beginning of the century played a crucial role in the development of the global coffee market. These chains, by offering a standardised coffee experience, have been instrumental in popularising coffee consumption and establishing globally recognised coffee brands. Today, the global coffee market serves a wide array of services through various coffee chains, local coffee shops, and online coffee retailers (Baggenstoss, Poisson, Kaegi, Perren, & Escher, 2008; Tadesse, Jemal, & Abebe, 2016; Tucker, 2017; Haktanir & Gullu, 2024).

Coffee is known to be the most valuable commodity in the world after crude oil. Coffee consumption has undergone specific stages since the 1900s, referred to as the First, Second, and Third Wave coffee movements. The First Wave coffee refers to the instant coffee culture of the early 1900s, typified by brands like Nescafé and Folgers. The Second Wave, emerging in the 1960s and beyond, is exemplified by chains like Starbucks, which introduced espresso-based drinks such as lattes and cappuccinos, enhancing the enjoyment of coffee. The Third Wave coffee movement, at its core, represents a respect for coffee, treating it akin to food or music. Understanding the origin of the coffee, including the specific farm and production parameters, roasting methods, and the best brewing techniques to achieve optimal aroma and flavour, is fundamental to the Third Wave coffee movement. This movement offers consumers a genuine experience through various roasting, grinding, and brewing techniques and specialised brewing equipment like Chemex, siphon, and Aeropress (Oral, 2016; Latif & Müge, 2018; USDA, 2023).

Global Coffee Market

Cultivated in over 70 tropical countries and consumed worldwide, coffee holds significant importance in international trade, being the second most traded commodity after oil. The annual production is approximately 8 million tonnes, with an annual export value recorded at around 20 billion dollars. In Turkey, coffee exports in 2019 amounted to 407 thousand dollars, placing the country 88th among coffee-exporting nations (Turkish Statistical Institute, 2020). Among the world's largest coffee producers, Brazil, Vietnam, and Colombia stand out, while the highest per capita coffee consumption is observed in Scandinavian countries. Notably, Finland ranks at the top globally, with a per capita consumption of approximately 12 kilograms of coffee (International Coffee Organization, 2021).

Although Turkey holds a small share in global coffee consumption, there has been a significant increase in recent years. In 2018, for the first time, per capita annual coffee consumption in Turkey exceeded 1 kilogram, rising from 350 grams to 1.1 kilograms over the past decade. This represents a notable 13.2 % increase (Kont, 2021).

Conclusion

Coffee, beyond being merely a commercial product, holds significant social and cultural symbolism. With its ability to adapt to various flavours and additives, coffee appeals to a wide culinary audience, fitting seamlessly into diverse food and drink themes. This flexibility allows coffee to cater to evolving tastes. Particularly, Turkish Coffee, following its unique roasting and grinding processes, acquires a distinctive aroma during the preparation and presentation stages. This special type of coffee occupies an essential place in our culture, featuring prominently in conversations, family gatherings, post-meal rituals, and general social life. The historical evolution and contemporary popularity of coffee have elevated it beyond a mere beverage, making it an important cultural, social, and economic commodity. The unique consumption practices of coffee across different cultures worldwide underscore its multicultural nature and global impact. This highlights coffee's impressive journey from past to present and its indispensable role for billions of people globally. Coffee continues to hold a significant position in both production and consumption worldwide. In Turkey, coffee consumption has significantly increased in recent years, nearing the global average. This trend indicates Turkey's potential to hold a stronger position in the global coffee market in the future.

References

Arslan, F. (2019). Tüketicilerin kahve tüketim alışkanlıkları ve kahve dükkânı tercihleri: Antalya ilinde bir araştırma. *International Journal of Contemporary Tourism Research*, 3(2), 224–234. https://doi.org/10.30625/ijctr.618828

Atkinson, C., Banks, M., France, C. and McFadden, C. (2009). "Çikolatalı ve Kahveli Tarifler", Türkiye İş Bankası Kültür Yayınları, Anness Pub., London, s. 266.

Baggenstoss, J., Poisson, L., Kaegi, R., Perren, R., & Escher, F. (2008). Coffee roasting and aroma formation: application of different time temperature conditions. *Journal of agricultural and food chemistry*, 56(14), 5836–5846.

Bajmaku, A. (2014). Kahve Kültürü Ve Kahvehane Mekanlarının Sosyo Kültürel Ve Politik Yaklaşımlar İle Popüler Kültür Çerçevesinde Değerlendirilmesi: Kosova Örneği. Mimar Sinan Güzel Sanatlar Üniversitesi Fen Bilimleri Enstitüsü.

Bohn, S.K., Ward, N.C., Hodgson, J.M.,Croft, K.D. (2012). Effects of tea and coffee on cardiovascular disease risk. Food Funct, 3 (6), 575–591.

Dalgıç, Z. (2022). Yorgun akşamların en vefalı sostu kahve. https://www.dytbanusalman.com/yorgun-aksamlarin-en-vefali-dostu-kahve-2/. Accesed Date: 12.05. 2024

Engelmann et al, C., Astorga, S., Dussertand F. A. (2007). Conserving Coffee Genetic Resources Bioversity International, Italya.

Farah, A. (2009). Coffee As a Speciality and Functional Beverage, Functional and Speciality Beverage Technology, Paul Paquin Published by Woodhead Publishing Limited, Cambridge, UK.

Gürsoy, D. (2005). "Sohbetin Bahanesi KAHVE", Oğlak yayımcılık ve Reklamcılık Ltd. Şti., s. 20.

Güven, D. (2020). Kahve Yetiştiriciliği, Tarım ve Orman Bakanlığı Tarımsal Araştırmalar ve Politikalar Genel Müdürlüğü Batı Akdeniz Tarımsal Araştırma Enstitüsü, https://arastirma.tarimorman.gov.tr/batem/Belgeler/Kutuphane/Teknik%20Bilgiler/Kahve%20Yetistiriciligi.pdf, Accessed Date: 21.05.2024.

Haktanir, M., & Gullu, E. (2024). Place attachment in coffee shops: a customer perspective study in North Cyprus. *Journal of Hospitality and Tourism Insights*, 7(1), 312–328.

Heisse U. (1996). " Kahve ve Kahvehaneler" Dost Kitabevi yayınları, Ankara, s. 46.

Kont, G. (2021). Kahve İhracat Pazar Araştırması, İzmir Ticaret Odası, https://api.izto.org.tr/storage/Documents/original/sftRqzhkUNkY3Hib.pdf Accessed Date: 27.05.2024.

Latif, Ö. B., & Müge, Ö. R. S. (2018). İkinci Dalga Kahve Tercihini Etkileyen Faktörler: İçtiğimiz Kahveleri Tanıyor muyuz?(Factors Affecting the Preference of 2nd Wave Coffee: Do We Recognize the Coffee We Drink?). *Journal of Tourism & Gastronomy Studies*, 6(4), 150–173.

Onur, M., Ceylan, F. (2023). Heritage of the Anatolian geography: registered varieties of ancestral wheat (siyez, gacer, and menceki). J. Ethn. Food 10, 36. https://doi.org/10.1186/s42779-023-00203-5

Saltan, F. Z., & Kaya, H. (2018). Kahve: Bir farmakognozik derleme. *FABAD Journal of Pharmaceutical Sciences*, 43(3), 279–289.

Sezgin, A. C. & Onur, M. (2017). Kültür Mirası Düğün Yemekleri'nin Gastronomi Turizmi Açısından İncelenmesi: *Erzincan İli Örneği, Erzincan Üniversitesi Sosyal Bilimler Enstitüsü Dergisi*, 203–214.

Sökmen, A. (2008). Yiyecek-İçecek Hizmetleri Yönetimi ve İşletmeciliği, Detay Yayıncılık, Ankara.

Stoffelen, P., Noirot, M., Couturon, E. & Anthony, F. (2008). A new caffeine-free coffee from Cameroon. Botanical Journal of the Linnean Society, 158(1), 67–72.

Tadesse, F. T., Jemal, Y., & Abebe, H. (2016). Effect of green coffee processing methods and roasting temperatures on physical and cup quality of Sidama coffee, Southern Ethiopia. *Journal of Nutritional Ecology and Food Research*, 3(1), 44–50.

Tucker, C. M. (2017). *Coffee culture: Local experiences, global connections.* Routledge.

USDA, (2023). Coffee: World Markets and Trade, United States Department of Agriculture Foreign Agricultural Service. https://apps.fas.usda.gov/psdonline/circulars/coffee.pdf, Accessed Date: 21.05.2024.

Usda, (2024). 2023/2024 Coffee Production, https://fas.usda.gov/data/production/commodity/0711100, Accessed Date: 01.05.2024.

https://fas.usda.gov/data/production/commodity/0711100, Accessed Date: 01.05.2024.

Yılmaz, A. Ş. (2023). Kahve Turizmine İlişkin Sistematik Bir Araştırma (A Systematic Research of Coffee Tourism). *Journal of Tourism & Gastronomy Studies, 11*(3), 2203–2222.

Yurt, İ. (2023). İsraf ve Tüketime Bir Tepki: Çöpteki Hazine "Freegan Food". ODÜ Sosyal Bilimler Araştırmaları Dergisi. 13 (1), 729–742. Doi: https://doi.org/10.48146/odusobiad.1179019.

Yurt, İ., & Bayraklı, B. (2022). Safranbolu'da yöresel bir lezzet: Peruhi. *Safran Kültür ve Turizm Araştırmaları Dergisi, 5*(2), 270–287.

Sibel Ayyildiz[1] and Ayşe Nur Uslu[2]

Chapter 20 Alternative Protein Sources for Individuals on a Vegan Diet; Meat Analogs

Introduction

Food refers to the nutritional elements needed to prevent diet-related diseases, improve human physical and mental health and slow down aging, and thus to ensure the survival of individuals (Valoppi, Agustin, Abik, & de Carvalho, 2021). The amount of food produced today needs to be doubled to provide for the population, which is anticipated to be just about 9.8 billion by 2050 (Caporgno & Mathys, 2018). This situation gradually increases the importance of global food security (Valoppi et al., 2021). The production and consumption of environmentally sustainableland healthy food is growing in importance as a critic topic for global population and health (Ayyıldız, 2023). A global nutrition transition has taken place in the last few decades as a result of developments in the food system chain, urbanisation and incremental revenues (Cliceri, Spinelli & Dinnella, 2018).

Plant-based diets are lately have the world at one's feet for their well-beings to, the environment, animal welfare, and public health. The most important motivations of individuals who abstain from meat are especially environmental awareness and animal rights (Dhont & Ioannidou, 2024). Numerous studies have found that individuals who don't use animal products are more ethically motivated than individuals who consume animal products (Rosenfeld, Rothgerber & Tomiyama, 2020). However, The health risks associated with the production and consumption of animal foods (e.g. cardiovascular diseases, infectious diseases, colorectal cancer, etc.) are one of the main reasons why people prefer more plant-derived products (Hayek, 2022; Dhont & Ioannidou, 2024). Food-related promoters and manners have been coralated with different system in food

---

1   Asst. Prof., Karabuk University, Safranbolu Tourism Faculty, Department of Gastronomy and Culinary Arts, sibelayyildiz@karabuk.edu.tr
    [2] R.A. Karabuk University, Safranbolu Tourism Faculty, Department of Gastronomy and Culinary Arts, aysenuruslu@karabuk.edu.tr

preferences. People who were more uneasy about health liabled to incorporate into fruit and vegetables in their diet, while abstaining fats and highly processed carbohydrates. Vegetarians are more conscious of health than omnivores and more uneasy about the natural content of food commodities come in the diet (Cliceri, Spinelli & Dinnella, 2018).

In the recent times, the numbers of consumers tailer a vegan diet and the request vegan food have heighten significantly in many developed countries. The locution vegan food express to products without animal-based food components. Veganism is the refusal to consume not only products obtained after the animal has been killed but also eggs, dairy products and other animal food ingredients. Although vegans present only a small proportion of the population, it is believed that their impact on the food sector will continue to grow (Janssen, Busch, Rödiger & Hamm, 2016). Impediments hindering heightened consumption of plant-based food are designate as meat delightfulness, food habits, fear of protein lack, lack of vegetarian choices, and challenges in preparing grain legumes and other vegetarian foods, especially lack of implementation knowledge (Varela, Arvisenet, Gonera & Myhrer, 2022). Many studies have questioned why meat continues to be an important part of the diet. The results were determined as the inability to give up meat in dietary habits, liking the taste of meat, identification of meat with masculine characteristics and denial of animal rights (Markowski & Roxburgh, 2019). When the researches analysing the consumers who prefer meat are examined, the findings denote that there is a disparity relate the genders and that the group of consumers who prefer meat come under by men. The main motivations for replacing meat with protein sources that are meat substitutes are associated with gender (Spendrup & Hovmalm, 2022).

Plant-Based Nutrition within the Scope of Sustainability

High speed global population growth has led to an increased need for protein-containing products (Sun, Ge, He, Gan & Fang, 2021). Just about one billion people at present have insufficient protein intake; It is also conjectured that traditional protein resources are inefficient (Caporgno & Mathys, 2018). Twentieth century nutritional transition that made livestock the significant source of protein in many countries is inducing growing pressures on the health of animals, human and the planet (de Boer, Schösler & Aiking, 2017). Investigating on many studies conventional meat production systems have determined that they use high quantity of earth, water, and energy. If it look from the viewpoint of sustainability, livestock is pass for a substantial cause of greenhouse gas emissions at the present time (Hwang, You, Moon and Jeong, 2020). Animal-based diets have been associated with a considerable raise in greenhouse gas emissions on a globularly (Cliceri et al., 2018). Reach sustainability, food security, environmentally friendly and public health objectives necessitate a modulation to a less meat-based diet, which is supported by many scientists (Schösler, de Boer, Boersema & Aiking, 2015; Hartmann & Siegrist, 2017).

Shifting from animal-based to plant-based diets offers the potential to reduce greenhouse gas emissions while benefiting human health (Grasso, Roos, Crowley, 2021). Reducing meat consumption has also become important against zoonotic disease risks (Hayek, 2022). Foodborne pathogens are frequently found in meat and are responsible for millions of diseases (Sun et al., 2021). Additionally, reducing meat consumption contributes to the protection of the environment. In theory, global dietary amendments are enough to send converse ongoing deforestation trends (Hayek, 2022). For these reasons, finding alternatives to animal protein is of great importance (Goyal, Thakur &Yadav, 2022).

Some Important Alternative Protein Sources Used as Meat Analogs

Proteins are indispensable in our diets and play a crucial role in preserving health generally. Muscle mass is essential for various bodily functions such as mediating hormone synthesis, immune responses, repairing cells and improving signalling pathways within the body (Goyal et al., 2022). Animal-based diets have been identified to be associated with diseases such as cardiovascular diseases, obesity, type 2 diabetes, and various types of carcinogenicity (Goyal et al., 2022; Zhang, Guan, Yu, Zhou & Chen, 2022). Many animals live under a bad situation and to be slaughtered, give ethical problem. The meat paradox is defined as wanting to consume meat but not wanting to face any health, ethical or animal welfare issues (Hwang et al., 2020). Plant foods with a balanced amino acid composition are healthy, high in protein, low in saturated fat and cholesterol-free. Due to these characteristics, plant foods have a great potential to replace meat with the development of meat-like products (Sun et al., 2021). Plant-based diets have become popular because they help decrease the environmental footprint of the diet and develop human health and animal welfare. Though the percentage of vegetarians and vegans is low compared to others, in recent years their number has increased significantly (Alcorta, Porta, Tárrega, Alvarez & Vaquero, 2021). According to research on veganism, which is a plant-based diet, the proportion of people who prefer this type of nutrition is increasing worldwide. (Bagci ve Olgun, 2019). Veganism is a social justice movement that aims to create a world where animals are not exploited in any form. It recognizes the inherent value and rights of animals, and encourages individuals to abstain from using animal products for food, clothing, entertainment, or any other purpose (North, Kothe, Klas & Ling, 2021). For this reason, the most important source that can be used as a substitute for animal products is plant products. Plant sources are nowadays turning into products in demand in different forms and have started to take their place in food markets as meat analogues or meat substitutes. Meat analogues are meat-like protein products that can be processed by using plant sources as raw materials, the addition of auxiliary additives and different processing methods. During production, many plant raw materials such as legumes, oil seeds, wheat, mushrooms and algae can be used together with auxiliary additives for different purposes (Künili, Dinç & Çolakoğlu, 2023).

Plant-based meat analogs are vegetative products that imitation the appearance, fibrous texture, and flavor of animal meat. Various non-animal protein sources (e.g. legumes, vegetables, grains, fungi and microalgae) are used instead of animal proteins in the production of a wide variety of meat-free products such as sausages, burgers, and nuggets (Boukid, 2020). Alternative meat technologies are shown as a good opportunity to solve the problems caused by conventional meat. Important alternative protein sources include plant-based, insect-based and cell-based food products. Especially plant-based meat alternatives and cell-based substitute meat are more popular (Hwang et al., 2020).

Since the study was conducted within the scope of vegan individuals, meat analogues were examined within the framework of plant-based protein sources. In a widespread manner vegetable protein sources used by individuals on a vegan diet: wheat, quinoa, chia, oat flakes, cashew, nuts, walnut, hazelnut, sesame, and psyllium seeds etc. (Jappe, 2023).

Wheat Gluten Protein: The gluten found in wheat can produce the desired dough for the development of meat analogues (Ahmad, Qureshi, Akbar, Siddiqui & Gani, 2022). Gluten is used to improve the textural integrity of bakery products and to strengthen flours with low protein content. Sources of gluten are associated with vegetarian meats, processed meats and reconstituted seafood. Gluten, which also acts as an emulsifier, thickener and gelling agent, is used in the production of butter, ice cream, condiments, marinades and sauces (Biesiekierski, 2016). Both processed and unprocessed foods (tofu and tempeh, etc.) are also produced from wheat protein sources selected as substitutes (Jappe, 2023). Wheat gluten, also known as seitan, is a protein derived from wheat that is commonly used as a meat substitute in vegetarian and vegan cooking. The dough obtained from wheat is washed with water until all starch granules are removed and a sticky structure is left behind. This highly elastic and chewy substance can then be seasoned, shaped, and cooked to resemble various meat products (Alcorta et al., 2021).

Legume Proteins: Legumes belong to the Leguminosae family, which is wealthy in terms of fiber, protein and starch. Recently, legumes such as peas, lupines, lentils, chickpeas and beans have been commonly used in the preparation of meat analogues (Singh, Trivedi, Enamala, Kuppam, Parikh, Nikolova & Chavali, 2021). Legumes, with their high protein content, are of private importance due to their well beings for agricultural product systems by biological nitrogen-fixation (Thompson, Öning,Holmgren, Strandler & Hultberg, 2020). Although most of the vegetable proteins are of low quality, comparison with the animal protein legumes are fine source of protein including approximately 25–50 % protein (Joshi & Kumar, 2015).

Legume proteins from peas, lupins, lentils or chickpeas are used as raw materials in meat alternatives. Among these, pea-based protein is the most hopeful (Alcorta et al., 2021). Pea ingredients are softer than soy products. It has been determined that legume proteins, especially obtained from peas, form fibrous meat structures. Protein isolates with high protein content have been found to increase firmness and chewiness in meat analogues (Ahmad et al., 2022). Soy protein products have become more and more popular because of their high nutritional quality, low price, and versatile functional properties (Joshi & Kumar, 2015). Soybeans and products made from them are considerable part of a vegan diet (Jappe, 2023). Soybeans are also rich in vitamins, fiber content, fat and carbohydrates, micro and micronutrients. They imitate the fibers found in chicken within the scope of protein concentrates. Soy protein concentrate gives the meat analogue a fibrous texture, chewiness and firm feel (Singh et al., 2021).

Tempeh and Tofu products derived from soybeans are well-known plant-based meat substitutes (Ahmad et al., 2022). Tofu obtained from soybeans is maybe the most commenly known meat alternative; it is a perfect source of protein, iron, and calcium (Joshi & Kumar, 2015). Soy is utilized for its superior nutritional value in creating protein-rich products, like tofu, which is made by coagulating and pressing soy curds into a dense block (Alcorta et al.,2021). Tempeh is a staple food that is especially rich in high protein and fiber sources. It also has the advantage of containing Vitamin B12, which is released through the fermentation process. Textured vegetable protein (Soymeat-TVP) is produced mainly from soybeans. The production process is a bit difficult, but the final product has a fibrous degree of maturity that resembles meat. Many different flavors can be achieved with different spices (Joshi & Kumar, 2015).

Some Seeds (Canola, Sunflower, Quinoa and Chia etc.): Recently, within the scope of the search for new protein sources, high-quality protein sources that are frequently textured to obtain a desired fiber-like structure are mentioned. Some of these sources (hemp, sunflower, rapeseed and sesame, etc.) contain protein (Benkovic, et al., 2023). Rapeseed (or canola) is a highly promising alternative source of a new protein that can be used as a meat substitute in the plant-based food products market (Banovic & Sveinsdotti, 2021). Containing easily digestible high-quality storage proteins (globulins and albumin), hemp seeds are rich in sulfur-containing amino acids, arginine and glutamic. Numerous studies have shown that hemp seed protein has high protein quality and functionality (Zahari, Rinaldi, Ahlstrom, Östbring, Rayner, & Purhagen, 2023). Canola and rapeseed are notable sources of protein with good emulsifying and foaming qualities (Ahmad et al., 2022). Oilseed proteins obtained from rapeseed and canola can be used as configurator agents when it is heated, constitutive meat-like textures (Alcorta et al., 2021). Diverse oils attained from rapeseed/canola, sunflower,palm, corn, peanut/groundnut, cottonseed, and soybean, are used to preserve the essence of the meat analogues by redound its volatile flavour intact (Singh et al., 2021).

Quinoa, the world's most popular plant-based healthy food, is a complete protein. This means that quinoa has all the essential amino acids. Quinoa is high in fiber, low on the glycemic index, gluten-free, and contains vitamins such as Fe, Mg, K, P, Ca, B_1, B_2, B_3, B_6) E and various beneficial antioxidants. Chia Protein is obtained from the seeds of Salvia hispanica, a native plant of South Africa. It is used to make ready popular nutrition food products such as baked goods, porridges, chia powder, and smoothies. Chia contains high amounts of vitamins, antioxidants and minerals. Since it has a quality nutritional fiber, it increases digestibility (Singh et al., 2021).

Mushroom Proteins: Mushroom-based meat substitutes; Increasing consumer demand is rapidly developing due to its marketability, environmental friendliness and ethical nutritional suitability. To meet the growing demand for plant-based proteins, mushroom-based meat analogs are considered both a viable and sustainable option (Singh & Sit, 2024). Mushrooms have many benefits for human nutrition. Mushrooms have high protein content. Mushrooms contain 19 %-35 % protein based on their dry weight. It has been stated that it contains a much higher amount of protein compared to vegetables, pork, beef and other livestock products (Wang & Zhao, 2023). Since mushroom has a fibrous structure, it is easy to chew. Mushrooms could conduce fulfill our daily needs of protein and vitamins (Kumar, Chatli, Mehta, Singh, Malav & Verma, 2016).

Edible mushrooms have recently been used as textured protein sources in an alternative formulation to meat (Zhang et al., 2022). The original commercial meat analogues such as burger patties and sausages with mycelia were done from the edible fungi Fusarium graminearu (Kumar et al., 2016). It gives meat-like flavor and umami taste (Singh & Sit, 2022). Mushroom is one of the important options used in the production of meat analogue. Because mushrooms contain amino acids with rich sulfur content that help obtain meat flavor ((Mishal, Kanchan, Bhushette, & Sonawane, 2022).

Algae (Spirulina): Algae have executed potential to meet the population's need for a more sustainable food procurement, especially in terms of protein request. These promising protein resources present several vantages over other at present used raw materials from an environmental perspective. Microalgae are microscopic algae wealthy in point of protein, lipids and other bioactive compounds (Caporgno & Mathys, 2018; Alcorta et al., 2021). Microalgae-derived proteins have complete essential amino acids profiles. Their protein content is higher than that of traditional sources, such as meat, poultry and dairy products. These proteins also head a source of polyunsaturated fatty acids (Alcorta et al., 2021). In addition, spirulinas are a potentially rich and highly bioavailable iron source for human diets (Gurney & Spendif, 2020). Therefore, microalgae have been in recent years used as dietary supplements and sources. Furthermore, microalgae have been recently accepted by 130 national academies of science and medicine as one of the innovator foods that can be source provider to human health and today's world in the near future (Alcorta et al., 2021). Algae, which is Introduced as one of the best protein sources, has been identified by the World Health Organisation as the best health product of mankind (Lafarga, Fernández-Sevilla, González-López, & Acién-Fernández, 2020; Ayyıldız, 2024). Algae, which is an important meat substitute (Lafarga et al., 2020), is used in the production of soups, pasta, bread, biscuits, cakes, beverages and sauces (Alçay, Bostan, Dinçel, & Varlık, 2017; Costa, Freitas, Rosa, Moraes, Morais, & Mitchell, 2019; Ayyıldız, 2023). Reasons for using algae in foods; It is easy to consume due to its accepted taste, versatility, ease of storage and transportation, texture and appearance (Caporgno & Mathys, 2018).

Consumer Approaches to Meat Analogs

Increases in meat prices, vegetarian and vegan diets, concerns about animal suffering, and sustainability issues have led market trends towards meat substitutes derived from plant sources (Ibrahim & Faujan, 2023). There is an increasing demand for high-quality and more functional proteins that can successfully replace or compete with proteins derived from animal sources. (Goyal et al., 2022). However, consumers' perspectives may contain some limitations. Most meat eaters are aware of the benefits of switching to a more plant-based diet but find vegetarianism and veganism troublesome, expensive, or unappealing. This prevents the purchase and consumption of these products, even if there is awareness about their environmental and health benefits. It is thought that preparing meals by vegetarians and vegans is troublesome and that food ingredients cannot always be found in markets. Food neophobia, however, is characterized by disinclination to deplete new or unusual foods. Meat substitutes obtained from soy, legumes, and grains may be a good alternative to give a knockdown to consumers to plant-based diets. Because they are less likely to trigger feelings of refusal and suspicion than more unusual alternatives (Alcorta et al., 2021).

The marketing expectation of meat analogue is very shiny due to its immanenet qualities of very cheap source of protein, lactose intolerant person, appropriate for health conscious non-vegetarians, or ethical qualities and nutritional issues for vegetarians. Thus meat analogues have a far better fighting chance than other products as some consumer desire charming and nutritious product completely free of meat (Kumar et al., 2016). Moreover cost plays an important role in the success of the meat analogs alternate among consumers (Ishaq, Irfan, Sameen & Khalid, 2022).

Results

Due to the rapid increase in the world population and limited natural resources, there is a protein deficiency with high biological value. In addition, approximately 30 per cent of global warming and climate change is caused by the food industry. There is a clear concern about animal-based protein, as the use of animal protein causes climate change and disruption of the phosphorus cycle, as well as water depletion. As a result, researchers around the world are constantly examining meat alternatives that are considered richer sources of protein, sustainability, and healthier.

Meat analogues have become popular in the food industry in recent years due to reasons such as production not depending on seasonality, durable shelf life and low cost. Meat analogs are plant-based food alternatives that approximate the organoleptic qualities and/or chemical properties of certain types of meat. In addition to being derived from non-animal proteins, these products are very similar to meat in appearance, smell and taste. Important motivations for using meat analogs are; It provides a wider range of proteins for human nutrition and supports animal welfare and ethical, sustainable nutrition and sustainable environmental models.

Meat is at the basis of human nutrition. However, vegetarian individuals and people who are sensitive to healthy nutrition and the environment use plant-based food alternatives instead of meat to meet their protein needs. It is essential to consume more plant-based foods, as reducing meat consumption contributes to the environment and health. Plant-based meat analogues are considered more acceptable, environmentally sustainable and cost-effective foods among consumers. It will accelerate the transition to a sustainable food system with increased support from food companies, food suppliers, gastronomy chefs, public authorities and environmental associations. Therefore, developing strategies for the production, development, improvement and sustainability of meat analogues is very important for planetary health.

References

Ahmad, M., Qureshi, S., Akbar, M. H., Siddiqui, S. A., Gani, A., Mushtaq, M., … & Dhull, S. B. (2022). Plant-based meat alternatives: Compositional analysis, current development and challenges. *Applied Food Research*, 2(2), 100154.

Alcorta, A., Porta, A., Tárrega, A., Alvarez, M. D., & Vaquero, M. P. (2021). Foods for plant-based diets: Challenges and innovations. *Foods*, 10(2), 293.

Alçay, A. Ü., Bostan, K., Dinçel, E., & Varlık, C. (2017). Alglerin insan gıdası olarak kullanımı. *Aydın Gastronomy*, 1(1), 47–59.

Ayyıldız, S. (2023). Su Ürünleri. Gıda Coğrafyası (Ed: Deniz, T. ve Kırmacı, H.A.), Detay Yayıncılık, Ankara, 1. Baskı, s. 235–276.

Ayyıldız, S. (2024). Spor alanında kullanılan gıda takviyeleri yerine gastronomik ürün önerileri. *Nevşehir Hacı Bektaş Veli Üniversitesi SBE Dergisi*, 14(1), 15–41.

Bagci, S. C., & Olgun, S. (2019). A social identity needs perspective to Veganism: Associations between perceived discrimination and well-being among Vegans in Turkey. *Appetite*, 143, 104441.

Banovic, M., & Sveinsdóttir, K. (2021). Importance of being analogue: Female attitudes towards meat analogue containing rapeseed protein. *Food Control*, 123, 107833.

Benković, M., Jurinjak Tušek, A., Sokač Cvetnić, T., Jurina, T., Valinger, D., & Gajdoš Kljusurić, J. (2023). An Overview of Ingredients Used for Plant-Based Meat Analogue Production and Their Influence on Structural and Textural Properties of the Final Product. *Gels*, 9(12), 921.

Biesiekierski, J. R. (2017). What is gluten?. *Journal of gastroenterology and hepatology*, 32, 78–81.

Boukid, F. (2021). Plant-based meat analogues: From niche to mainstream. *European food research and technology*, 247(2), 297–308.

Cliceri, D., Spinelli, S., Dinnella, C., Prescott, J., & Monteleone, E. (2018). The influence of psychological traits, beliefs and taste responsiveness on implicit attitudes toward plant-and animal-based dishes among vegetarians, flexitarians and omnivores. *Food Quality and Preference*, *68*, 276–291.

Caporgno, M. P., & Mathys, A. (2018). Trends in microalgae incorporation into innovative food products with potential health benefits. *Frontiers in nutrition*, *5*, 58.

Costa, J. A. V., Freitas, B. C. B., Rosa, G. M., Moraes, L., Morais, M. G., & Mitchell, B. G. (2019). Operational and economic aspects of Spirulina-based biorefinery. *Bioresource technology*, *292*, 121946. 1–10.

de Boer, J., Schösler, H., & Aiking, H. (2017). Towards a reduced meat diet: Mindset and motivation of young vegetarians, low, medium and high meateaters. *Appetite*, *113*, 387–397.

Dhont, K., & Ioannidou, M. (2024). Similarities and differences between vegetarians and vegans in motives for meat-free and plant-based diets. *Appetite*, *195*, 107232.

Grasso, N., Roos, Y. H., Crowley, S. V., Arendt, E. K., & O'Mahony, J. A. (2021). Composition and physicochemical properties of commercial plant-based block-style products as alternatives to cheese. *Future Foods*, *4*, 100048.

Goyal, N., Thakur, R., & Yadav, B. K. (2024). Physical approaches for modification of vegan protein sources: a review. *Food and Bioprocess Technology*, 1–24.

Hartmann, C., & Siegrist, M. (2017). Consumer perception and behaviour regarding sustainable protein consumption: A systematic review. *Trends in Food Science & Technology*, *61*, 11–25.

Hayek, M. N. (2022). The infectious disease trap of animal agriculture. *Science Advances*, *8*(44), eadd6681.

Hwang, J., You, J., Moon, J., & Jeong, J. (2020). Factors affecting consumers' alternative meats buying intentions: Plant-based meat alternative and cultured meat. *Sustainability*, *12*(14), 5662.

Ibrahım, H. S. S., & Faujan, N. H. (2023). potential use of underutilised mushroom stems in meat products and meat analogues: A mini review. *Malaysian Journal of Science Health & Technology*, *9*(2), 147–152.

shaq, A., Irfan, S., Sameen, A., & Khalid, N. (2022). Plant-based meat analogs: A review with reference to formulation and gastrointestinal fate. *Current Research in Food Science*, *5*, 973–983.

Janssen, M., Busch, C., Rödiger, M., & Hamm, U. (2016). Motives of consumers following a vegan diet and their attitudes towards animal agriculture. *Appetite*, *105*, 643–651.

Jappe, U. (2023). Vegan diet-alternative protein sources as potential allergy risk. *Allergo Journal International, 32*(7), 251–257.

Joshi, V. K., & Kumar, S. (2015). Meat Analogues: Plant based alternatives to meat products-A review. *International Journal of Food and Fermentation Technology, 5*(2), 107–119.

Kumar, P., Chatli, M. K., Mehta, N., Singh, P., Malav, O. P., & Verma, A. K. (2016). Meat analogues: Health promising sustainable meat substitutes. *Critical Reviews in Food Science and Nutrition, 57*(5), 923–932. https://doi.org/10.1080/10408398.2014.939739

Lafarga, T., Fernández-Sevilla, J. M., González-López, C., & Acién-Fernández, F. G. (2020). Spirulina for the food and functional food industries. *Food Research International, 137*, 109356. 1–43.

Markowski, K. L., & Roxburgh, S. (2019). "If I became a vegan, my family and friends would hate me:" Anticipating vegan stigma as a barrier to plant-based diets. *Appetite, 135*, 1–9.

Mishal, S., Kanchan, S., Bhushette, P., & Sonawane, S. K. (2022). Development of Plant based meat analogue. *Food Science and Applied Biotechnology, 5*(1), 45–53.

North, M., Kothe, E., Klas, A., & Ling, M. (2021). How to define "Vegan": An exploratory study of definition preferences among omnivores, vegetarians, and vegans. *Food Quality and Preference, 93*, 104246.

Nowacka, M.; Trusinska, M.; Chraniuk, P.; Drudi, F.; Lukasiewicz, J.; Nguyen, N.P.; Przybyszewska, A.; Pobiega, K.; Tappi, S.; Tylewicz, U. (2023) Developments in plant proteins production for meat and fish analogues. *Molecules, 28*, 1–27.

Rosenfeld, D. L., Rothgerber, H., & Tomiyama, A. J. (2020). From mostly vegetarian to fully vegetarian: Meat avoidance and the expression of social identity. *Food Quality and Preference, 85*, 103963.

Schösler, H., de Boer, J., Boersema, J. J., & Aiking, H. (2015). Meat and masculinity among young Chinese, Turkish and Dutch adults in the Netherlands. *Appetite, 89*, 152–159.

Singh, M., Trivedi, N., Enamala, M. K., Kuppam, C., Parikh, P., Nikolova, M. P., & Chavali, M. (2021). Plant-based meat analogue (PBMA) as a sustainable food: A concise review. *European Food Research and Technology, 247*, 2499–2526.

Singh, A., & Sit, N. (2022). Meat analogues: Types, methods of production and their effect on attributes of developed meat analogues. *Food and bioprocess technology, 15*(12), 2664–2682.

Singh, A., & Sit, N. (2024). Fungi-based meat analogs. In *Handbook of Plant-Based Meat Analogs* (pp. 99–119). Academic Press.

Spendrup, S., & Hovmalm, H. P. (2022). Consumer attitudes and beliefs towards plant-based food in different degrees of processing-The case of Sweden. *Food Quality and Preference, 102,* 104673.

Sun, C., Ge, J., He, J., Gan, R., & Fang, Y. (2021). Processing, quality, safety, and acceptance of meat analogue products. *Engineering, 7*(5), 674–678.

Thompson, H. O., Önning, G., Holmgren, K., Strandler, H. S., & Hultberg, M. (2020). Fermentation of cauliflower and white beans with Lactobacillus plantarum–impact on levels of riboflavin, folate, vitamin B 12, and amino acid composition. *Plant Foods for Human Nutrition, 75,* 236–242.

Wang, M., & Zhao, R. (2023). A review on nutritional advantages of edible mushrooms and its industrialization development situation in protein meat analogues. *Journal of Future Foods, 3*(1), 1–7.

Valoppi, F., Agustin, M., Abik, F., Morais de Carvalho, D., Sithole, J., Bhattarai, M., … & Mikkonen, K. S. (2021). Insight on current advances in food science and technology for feeding the world population. *Frontiers in sustainable food systems, 5,* 626227.

Varela, P., Arvisenet, G., Gonera, A., Myhrer, K. S., Fifi, V., & Valentin, D. (2022). Meat replacer? No thanks! The clash between naturalness and processing: An explorative study of the perception of plant-based foods. *Appetite, 169,* 105793.

Zahari, I., Rinaldi, S., Ahlstrom, C., Östbring, K., Rayner, M., & Purhagen, J. (2023). High moisture meat analogues from hemp–The effect of co-extrusion with wheat gluten and chickpea proteins on the textural properties and sensorial attributes. *Lwt, 189,* 115494.

Zhang, C., Guan, X., Yu, S., Zhou, J., & Chen, J. (2022). Production of meat alternatives using live cells, cultures and plant proteins. *Current Opinion in Food Science, 43,* 43–52.

Sevil Atalay Tohumcu[1] and Gencay Saatci Savsa[2]

Chapter 21 Geographical Indications and Gastronomic Value Sustainability: Sherbets

Introduction

Food culture not only makes individuals in the society physically connected to an area and geography, but also teaches them a lot about who they are and which culture they are from (Delind, 2006). Many factors are important in the formation of the food and beverage culture of societies. Traditional ceremonies, social structure, customs, traditions, customs, religion and beliefs constitute the unique culinary culture of societies (Aydın, 2023). In addition, food and beverages have multidimensional meanings ranging from the process of nutrition, culture, spending quality time together, gaining experiences and preserving traditions (Avcıkurt & Sarıoğlan, 2019). The belief patterns of societies also play a major role in the formation and shaping of culinary culture. Indeed, after the Turks adopted Islam, they stopped eating donkey, horse and pork meat, and drinking wine and koumiss, which were forbidden by the religion. As a result of this effect, a rich culture of sherbet and pleasantries has been formed (Kızıldemir, Öztürk & Sarıışık, 2014). While sherbets, which have a prominent place in Turkish culture, are in the group of non-alcoholic beverages that can be consumed with sugar, hot and cold, in Turkish cuisine, beverages are prepared by various methods such as distillation, brewing, fermentation with the addition of various nutrients according to their properties (Aktaş & Özdemir, 2005; Özkan, Erçetin & Güneş, 2019). The preparation of sherbets, whether hot or cold, the way they are served, to whom they are served and with what rituals show that they are an essential gastronomic value in Ottoman cuisine. Sherbets that have been consumed during the Ottoman period are generally; honey, jujube, sugar, sirkencübin, redbud, rose, rose, basil, violet, grape, lotus, chicory, chicory, suvye, sour cherry, dinar, pomegranate blossom (gülnâr), fukaʾa, anber (Aydın, 2023), lily, rose, violet, jasmine, fulia, spindle, lovage and lotus flowers, and koruk sherbet, saffron, lohusa

---

1   Ph.D. Student, Çanakkale OnSekiz Mart University, Tourism Faculty, sevilatalay_90@hotmail.com
2   Assoc. Prof. Dr., Çanakkale OnSekiz Mart University, Tourism Faculty, gencaysaatci@comu.edu.tr

sherbet, liquorice, hollyhock, tamarind, mint (Özkan, Erçetin & Güneş, 2019), fig, quince, peach, black and red grape, molasses, lemon (Obuz, 2024).

Geographical Indications and Sustainability

There are some opinions on the concept of geographical indication. According to one perspective, it is stated that it is used as a quality marker of goods in Egypt (Kanberoğlu & Yıldırımçakar, 2022), while according to another perspective, it is stated that it dates to the 12th century. It was used by weavers in Central Europe and England to indicate the geography of the product. Geographical indications are the first form of trademarks to specify the origin and characteristics of the product to distinguish it (Gündoğdu, 2006). A geographical indication is a sign that indicates the quality, recognition or other characteristics of a product and identifies it as belonging to the territory, region, or locality to which it is attributed (Giovannucci, Josling, Kerr, O'Connor & Yeung, 2009). The geographically indicated product provides a quality criterion for the product by differentiating it from other similar products in the region (Toklu, 2016). Although the concept of geographical indication is subject to more than one arrangement, it was first included in Council Regulation No. 2081/92 and then in TRIPS (Trade-Related Aspects of Intellectual Property Rights) (Yalçın, 2009). The first international legislation on geographical indication was made with the Paris Treaty of 1883 and the implementation of the decision was put into practice with the new legislation in 1925 (Tekelioğlu, 2019). Geographical indications in Turkey have been protected under the 'Decree Law on the Protection of Geographical Indications' numbered 555 published in the Official Gazette in 1995 (Decree Law on the Protection of Geographical Indications, 2024). The Turkish Patent and Trademark Office (TURKPATENT) is the official institution for the registration of geographical indications and traditional product names in Turkey (Türk Patent 1, 2024). According to Law No. 6769 on Industrial Property, Article 34, geographical indications are registered as origin sign and appellation of origin.

A geographical indication is a sign that is integrated with a specific geographical region with a distinctive feature, reputation, or other characteristics. In addition, geographical indications are geographical indications that include products where at least one of the processing, production or other applications is required to take place within the designated geographical region. One of the raw material and processing or production stages can be realized in the region, while the applications for the other production and processing stages can be carried out outside the region to which they belong (Türk Patent 2, 2024).

The originating region, area or locality name of a product indicates the 'Name of Origin' if the following conditions are met together:

- Region, area, locality or, in very special cases, country with defined geographical boundaries.
- The whole or the main characteristics or qualities are derived from natural and human factors specific to this region, area or locality.
- It is required to be a product whose production, processing and other operations are carried out entirely within the borders of this region, area or locality (Decree Law on the Protection of Geographical Indications, 2024).

In addition to the designation of origin and the sign of origin, the Traditional Product Name, which is not included in the scope of the designation of origin and the sign of origin, includes the names produced from traditional raw materials or substances, consisting of traditional processing or production methods or traditional composition, and proven to be used traditionally for at least 30 years to identify the product in the relevant market (Türk Patent 3, 2024).

Consumers prefer geographically indicated products with the idea that the naturalness of the products needs to be protected. In addition, their confidence in geographically indicated products is higher and they do not hesitate to search for products to reach them (Güler & Benli, 2021). Geographical indications, which have become widespread in recent years, also encourage consumers of many gastronomic products to trust local gastronomic values and these values. In addition, geographical indications are considered as a legal and economic instrument for the development of rural areas and the preservation of gastronomic values and cultural heritage (Caso & Giordano, 2022) It also offers important opportunities in terms of sustainable gastronomy (Richardson & Fernqvist, 2022), which means not to waste natural resources at any stage from the preparation to the presentation of food and beverages.

Sustainability, which is defined by the World Commission on Environment and Development as meeting the needs of individuals today without compromising the ability of future generations to meet their needs (Pittel, 2002), is widely accepted to have three main dimensions: economic, social/social and ecological/environmental (Batat, 2020). *In the social dimension of sustainability*, geographical indications describe the formation of trust between producers and consumers, the preservation of cultural heritage and the transfer of traditional experiences and knowledge to future generations by documenting them (YÜCİTA, 2024), *In the economic dimension*, geographical indications contribute to increasing economic activities by increasing employment, making investments in the region and promoting tourism in the region (Da Silva & Peralta,

2011), increasing trade by providing more opportunities for the product to find a place in foreign markets (Gökovalı, 2007) and in the socio-economic field, it also contributes to the migration phenomenon and women's employment (Doğan, 2015). *In the ecological / environmental dimension*, by determining the boundaries in agricultural production areas, overproduction and environmental devastation are eliminated and biodiversity is protected, enabling the traditional knowledge to be carried to future generations. (Doğan, 2015). In addition, geographical indication is important for recording the products with unique characteristics because of the consumption behavior of a region over the years, establishing a standard in their production, and sustaining their production without changing the characteristics of the product. It also provides direct information to consumers about raw materials and production methods (Özen & Karaca, 2021).

Sherbet and Sherbet Types

Sherbet is prepared with water and sugar or by adding sugar, water and fruit juice (Halıcı, 2012). Sherbet, meaning to drink, derives from the Arabic word *şerben* (Oğuz, 2002; Oğan, 2020). Sherbet is defined as a liquid viscous base prepared by dissolving honey or sugar in water (Akçiçek, 2002; Sırıklı & Özkanlı, 2021), whereas it is defined by the Turkish Language Association as a beverage made by mixing sugar water and fruit juice (Turkish Language Association, 2024). It is also defined as the reconstituted form of syrups made by adding sugar to the bark, root or seeds of various flowers, plants, fruits (Akçiçek, 2002; Gedük, 2016). Sherbets, which have an important role in Turkish culinary culture, can be consumed during meals, to quench thirst, to cool down, as well as in periods of transition and in various disease states (Sürücüoğlu, 1997; Sarıoğlan & Cevizkaya, 2016).

Sherbet, which has an important place in beverage culture, has reached the current period by developing in the process from Central Asian Turkish societies to the Turkish society of the Republican period. As a result of nomadic life, although the sherbet culture was not very diverse in the Central Asian period, advances were made during the Seljuk period and the highest point was reached during the Ottoman period. Rose sherbet, sirkencubin and honey sherbets are the most prominent sherbets during these three periods (Çelik, 2020). In the Ottoman period, when the sherbet culture reached the highest point, the Ottoman palaces were the top-level representatives of the culture (Bilgin, 2020). Sherbet, which is thought to have spread from Arab culture to the East during the nomadic times of the Turks, is considered to have reached India, Pakistan, Iran and Mongolian lands through trade routes and even further to China (Bilgin, 2012; Sırıklı & Özkanlı, 2021).

As a result of the fact that sherbet was included as a cultural heritage in the Ottoman Empire and its consumption increased over time and it was consumed and known by the Europeans coming to the country, sherbet started to spread in European countries with different names (Ünal, 2023) and it is called sorvete in Portuguese, šérbe in Serbian and Croatian, sorbeto in Spanish (Bilgin, 2020), sorbetto in Italian, sorbet-sherbet in English, scherbett in German, sorbet in French (Ergin, 2022). The spread of sherbet in Europe is estimated to have been quite short. Therefore, it is not unusual to encounter sherbet sellers on the streets of London and Paris in the 17th century (Bilgin, 2012; Çelik, 2020). Nowadays, in the United Kingdom, sherbet is known as a kind of frozen dessert (Kilara & Chandan, 2006). Evliya Çelebi stated that there were 500 sherbet shopkeepers and 300 sherbet shops in Istanbul in the 17th century (Bilgin, 2020).

Sherbets are among the most consumed beverages in the Ottoman Palace Cuisine alongside water (Hatipoğlu & Batman, 2014). The 1620 Es'âr book contains the names of sherbet tools and utensils such as a footed sherbet bowl, sherbet jar, embroidered spring plate, sherbet sieve, sherbet bowl, crystal musehhep, sherbet cup, embroidered lid sultani sherbet bowl and sherbet bottle (Sürücüoğlu, 1997; Gedük, 2016). Sherbets, to which sugar, amber, musk and various fruit pieces were added for flavor and fragrance, were preserved in crystal jugs (Haydaroğlu, 2003), treat in precious vessels such as crystal, silver and gold. (Sarıoğlan & Cevizkaya, 2016). Sherbets are served in silver glasses to keep them cold (Yar, 2008), but they are also served in bowls. The snow used for cooling the sherbet to be consumed cold is filled into the lower bowl with a bowl called snow holder in order not to disturb the consistency of the sherbet (Sürücüoğlu, 1997; Aydın, 2023). In addition to these forms of service and offerings, it is noted that in the Ottoman Empire ever and anon, meals were accompanied by sherbets made from various fruits and flowers instead of water (Yar, 2008) that spoons with round and finely cut handles, which were circular in shape and had a greater depth than other spoons, were also placed on the table to be used while drinking sherbet (Oğuz, 1976; Ceyhun Sezgin & Durmaz, 2019). In the Ottoman period, sherbet was one of the main beverages at events such as circumcision ceremonies, weddings, mawlids, banquets for the reception and reception of statesmen, picnics and baths (Obuz, 2024). Lemonade, pear, grape, grape, quince, apple, plum, plum, coruk, pomegranate, walnut and mulberry are among the sherbet varieties that reflect the richness of the Ottoman meals (Ergin, 2022).

It is stated that in addition to sherbets that stand out with their cooling and refreshing properties, sherbets to be used as medicine were also produced in the helvahane (Bilgin, 2020). Sherbets produced for this purpose have been used to cure common ailments in daily life such as headaches, weakness and fatigue (Kuzucu, 2008; Çelik, 2020). It is also stated that women who fell ill in the harem were given sherbet as medicine (Gedük, 2016). According to the information obtained; while pomegranate flower sherbet treats tooth inflammation and gingival disorders, tamarind sherbet cleanses the blood (Oğuz, 1976; Aydın, 2023). Whereas Gülbeşeker is given to pregnant women and puerperal women who are weak after giving birth. While strengthening the stomach and lungs, it is good for indigestion when crushed and consumed in hot rose water, and the sherbet made with anise and gum is good for diarrhea (Yıldırım, 2008; Aydın, 2023). Tamarind sherbet, which contains 41 kinds of spices and was the favorite drink of Suleiman the Magnificent, regulates the digestive system and intestines with its blood-forming properties. Reyhan sherbet, on the other hand, provides many benefits such as stopping cough, relieving indigestion, dizziness, relieving mouth sores, stopping hair loss, increasing breast milk, relieving nausea. Koruk sherbet is effective in digestive system disorders and skin diseases such as eczema (Sarıoğlan & Cevizkaya, 2016). Mevlana emphasized the importance of sherbet by saying "we have chosen three things in the world, semai, sherbet and Turkish bath" (Çelik, 2020), while Evliya Çelebi described sherbet, which is frequently consumed in the summer period, as "peace to the spirit, food for the soul" (Yar, 2008).

Table 21.1 includes the types of sherbet registered with a geographical indication under the soft drinks group in the geographical indication system and in the application process. An application has been made for Sirkencübin sherbet to be registered as a traditional product.

Table 21.1. Sherbets Registered with Geographical Indication and in Application Process

Product Name	Application-Registration Date	Type	City	Situation
Urfa Licorice Sherbet (Biyanbalı)	02.05.2013 08.12.2016	Protected Geographical Indication	Şanlıurfa	Registered
Antep Licorice Sherbet	20.07.2017 01.07.2019	Protected Geographical Indication	Gaziantep	Registered

Table 21.1.   Continued

Product Name	Application-Registration Date	Type	City	Situation
Konya Reyhan Sherbet	24.09.2020 06.08.2021	Protected Geographical Indication	Konya	Registered
Maraş Ravanda Sherbet	12.11.2020 15.04.2022	Protected Geographical Indication	Kahramanmaraş	Registered
Bademli Koruk Sherbet	26.11.2020 08.05.2023	Protected Geographical Indication	İzmir	Registered
Konya Rose Sherbet	29.07.2022 -	Protected Geographical Indication	Konya	Application
Sirkencübin Sherbet	06.12.2022 -	Traditional Product Name	-	Application
Diyarbakır Licorice Sherbet	03.09.2023 -	Protected Geographical Indication	Diyarbakır	Application
Diyarbakır Reyhan Sherbet	05.09.2023 -	Protected Geographical Indication	Diyarbakır	Application
Hatay Licorice Sherbet	27.11.2023 -	Protected Geographical Indication	Hatay	Application
Arapgir Purple Reyhan Sherbet	09.02.2024 -	Protected Geographical Indication	Malatya	Application

Source: Turkish Patent 4, (2024).

Looking at the sherbets in the table, it is seen that the cities in the Southeastern Anatolia region have taken steps to register them with a geographical indication.

Conclusion

Popular culture, which we encounter in all areas of daily life, is seen as the culture preferred by many people today as a culture of rapid production and consumption. Food and beverage culture is also influenced by popular culture and negatively affected by competition. These effects can be seen as the replacement of foods and beverages of our culture such as lahmacun, pita, sherbet with foods and beverages of popular culture such as pizza, waffles and lattes (Yılmaz & Bekar, 2019).

While sherbet was frequently produced and consumed in the past, today it does not come to mind first due to the abundance of varieties such as fruit juices and carbonated drinks (Tezcan, 1990; Sırıklı & Özkanlı, 2021). The industry that emerged in the 1960s and afterwards as a result of the production of carbonated drinks in factories, which adversely affect health, is shown as evidence that the sherbet culture has changed. With the increasing influence of popular culture, sherbet consumption has decreased significantly after the 2000s compared to the Ottoman and early Republican periods (Sırıklı & Özkanlı, 2021).

Kayabaşı & Bucak (2022), in their research on the role and importance of sherbets in Turkish culinary culture, concluded that the participants today include sherbets only as an accompaniment to special days and rituals, and that the influence of family elders and personal research are effective in the tradition of making and consuming sherbets at these times. Büyükşalvarcı, Şapçılar & Yılmaz (2016) in their study titled "The Use of Local Dishes in Tourism Enterprises: The Case of Konya", it was stated that rose sherbet was used in two enterprises and sour cherry, black mulberry, black cherry and syrup were used in one enterprise. It was argued that the reason for not including local food and beverages or including them less is commercial considerations. Sırıklı & Özkanlı (2021) analyzed sherbet consumption after the 2000s in their study. The results obtained were not surprising in general. Despite the fact that sherbet consumption is almost non-existent, it is seen that the participants have knowledge about what sherbet is. Nowadays, the fictionalized presentation of the Ottoman period in the form of TV series was mentioned by the participants as one of the sources where sherbet is heard the most. As can be understood from this situation, the inclusion of traditional culinary culture in productions in visual media creates positive results.

Like many gastronomic values, sherbets have an important position in our culture. As discussed in this chapter, geographical indication registration is recognized as an important factor in the protection, sustainability and transfer of cultural heritage to future generations. However, this alone is not sufficient. A multi-faceted perspective should be created by giving great importance to the transfer of this cultural element to future generations without being forgotten and to be kept alive by future generations. Sherbet is a drink that can be consumed not only during Ramadan but also in daily life, and it is thought that it would be beneficial to convey this situation to young generations through visual media and social media. Identifying and inventorying the forgotten sherbets of our culture, including them in educational programs and conducting studies on their importance in the tourism sector will be important steps in keeping this gastronomic heritage element alive.

References

Akçiçek, E. (2002), "Dünden bugüne şerbetçiliğimiz", Yemek Kitabı (Yay. Haz. M. Sabri Koz), Çalış Ofset.

Aktaş, A & Özdemir, B (2005) İçki teknolojisi. Detay Yayıncılık.

Avcıkurt, C. & Sarıoğlan, M. (2019). Gastronomi olgusuna sosyolojik bakış. C. Avcıkurt ve M. Sarıoğlan (Edt.), *Gastronomi sosyolojisine genel bakış* (ss. 1–14). Detay Yayıncılık.

Aydın, F. (2023), Divan şiirinde şerbet, *Littera Turca, Littera Turca Journal of Turkish Language and Literature*, 9(3), 411–428.

Batat, W. (2020). Pillars of sustainable food experiences in the luxury gastronomy sector: A qualitative exploration of Michelin-starred chefs' motivations. *Journal of Retailing and Consumer Services*, 57(3), 1–13.

Bilgin, A. (2012), Osmanlılarda şerbet kültürü ve tatlıhâne-i amire'de üretilen şerbetler, *Yemek ve Kültür Dergisi*, (29).

Bilgin, A. (2020). Osmanlı kültüründe şerbet. *Toplumsal Tarih, Mayıs,* 50–57.

Büyükşalvarcı, A., Şapcılar, M. C. & Yılmaz, G. (2016). Yöresel yemeklerin turizm işletmelerinde kullanılma durumu: Konya örneği. *Journal of Tourism and Gastronomy Studies*, 4(4), 165–181.

Caso, A. & Giordano, S. (2022). Cross-border territorial development through geographical indications: Gargano (Italy) and Dibër (Albania). Encyclopedia, 2, 1845–1858.

Ceyhun Sezgin, A. & Durmaz, P. (2019). Osmanlı mutfak kültüründe şerbetlerin yeri ve tüketimi. *Journal of Tourism and Gastronomy Studies, 7* (2), 1499–1518.

Coğrafi İşaretlerin Korunması Hakkında Kanun Hükmünde Kararname (2024). *Amaç, kapsam, korumadan yararlanacak kişiler, tanımlar.* http://www.icc.tobb. org.tr/spot/docs/cografi-isaretler/555%20say%C4%B1l%C4%B1%20Co% C4%9Frafi%20%C4%B0%C5%9Faretlerin%20Korunmas%C4%B1%20Hakk% C4%B1nda%20Kanun%20H%C3%BCkm%C3%BCnde%20Kararnameye%20 %C4%B0li%C5%9Fkin%20Uygulama%20Y%C3%B6netmeli%C4%9Fi.pdf.

Cömert, M. & Kaya, Ü. C., (2021). Sürdürülebilir gastronomi içinde destinasyon yönetimi. F. Durlu Özkaya, F. Özkök, A. Sünnetçioğlu ve S. Sünnetçioğlu (Edt.), *Sürdürülebilir gastronomi* (ss. 137–155). Detay Yayıncılık.

Çelik, (2020). *19.ve 20. yüzyılın Türk kültür hayatında şerbet.* [Yüksek Lisans Tezi]. Anadolu Üniversitesi.

Da Silva, E. F. & Peralta, P. P. (2011). Collective marks and geographical ındications - competitive strategy of differentiation and appropriation of ıntangible heriage. Journal of Intellectual Property Rights, 16, 246–257.

Decree Law on the Protection of Geographical Indications, (2024).

Delind, L.B. (2006). Of bodıes, place, and culture: re-sıtuatıng local food. *Journal of Agricultural and Environmental Ethics*, 19, 121–146.

Doğan, B. (2015). Coğrafi işaret korumasının gelişmekte olan ülkeler için önemi. *NWSA-Social Sciences, 10* (2), 58–75.

Ergin, Y. B. (2022). Mutfağın sarayı seyahatnemelerde Osmanlı mutfağı. Cezve Kitap Yayınları. İstanbul.

Gedik, Y. (2020). Sosyal, ekonomik ve çevresel boyutlarla sürdürülebilirlik ve sürdürülebilir kalkınma. *International Journal of Economics, Politics, Humanities & Social Sciences, 3*(3), 196–215.

Gedük, S. (2016), "Osmanlı saray geleneğinde şerbet ve şerbet kapları", 2. Sağlık Tarihi ve Müzecilik Sempozyumu, 03–05 Haziran, İstanbul, s. 275–292.

Giovannucci, D., Josling, T., Kerr, W., O'Connor, B. & Yeung, M. T. (2009). Guide to geographical ındications: linking products and their origins. *International Trade Centre*.

Gökovalı, U. (2007). Coğrafi işaretler ve ekonomik etkileri: Türkiye örneği. *İktisadi ve İdari Bilimler Dergisi, 21* (2), 141–160.

Güler, O. & Benli, S. (2021). Sürdürülebilir gastronomi. F. Durlu Özkaya, F. Özkök, A. Sünnetçioğlu ve S. Sünnetçioğlu, (Edt.), *Sürdürülebilir gastronomi ve tüketici davranışları* (ss. 211–245). Detay Yayıncılık.

Gündoğdu, G., 2006. *Türk hukukunda coğrafi işaret kavramı ve korunması.* [Yüksek Lisans Tezi]. Marmara Üniversitesi.

Halıcı, N. (2012). Açıklamalı yemek ve mutfak terimleri sözlüğü, Oğlak Yayıncılık.

Harris, J. M. (2000). Basic principles of sustainable development. *Dimensions of Sustainable Developmnet, 1*(1), 21–41.

Hatipoğlu, A. & Batman, O. (2014). Osmanlı saray mutfağı'na ait gastronomik unsurların günümüz Türk mutfağı ile kıyaslanması. *Seyahat ve Otel İşletmeciliği Dergisi, 11* (2), 62–74.

Haydaroğlu, İ. (2003). Osmanlı saray mutfağından notlar. *Tarih Araştırmaları Dergisi, 22*(34), 1–10.

Kanberoğlu, Z. & Yıldırımçakar, İ., 2022. Coğrafi işaretlerin bölgesel gelişmedeki rolü: Van kahvaltısı örneği. *Van Yüzüncü Yıl Üniversitesi Sosyal Bilimler Enstitüsü Dergisi, 58.* 23–39.

Kayabaşı, A. & Bucak, T., (2022). Şerbetlerin Türk mutfak kültüründeki yeri ve önemine dair bir araştırma, *ODÜSOBİAD, 12* (1), 71–96.

Kaypak, Ş. (2011). "Küreselleşme sürecinde sürdürülebilir bir kalkınma için sürdürülebilir bir çevre". *Karamanoğlu Mehmetbey Üniversitesi Sosyal ve Ekonomik Araştırmalar Dergisi, 13*(20), 19–33.

Kızıldemir, Ö., Öztürk, E. & Sarıışık, M. (2014). Türk mutfak kültürünün tarihsel gelişiminde yaşanan değişimler. *AİBÜ SBE Dergisi, 14* (3), 191–210.

Kilara, A. & Chandan, R. C. (2006). Ice craem and frozen desserts. Y. H. Hui (Edt.), *Handbook of food products manufacturing.* (ss. 593–633).

Kuzucu, K. (2008), Türk mutfağı, A. Bilgin- Ö. Samancı, (Edt). *Osmanlı içecek kültüründe yeni bir tat olarak çay* (ss.243-259). T.C. Kültür ve Turizm Bakanlığı Yayınları.

Obuz, M. (2024). Osmanlı mutfak kültüründe şerbet. *Uludağ Üniversitesi Fen-Edebiyat Fakültesi Sosyal Bilimler Dergisi, 25*(46), 255–266.

Oğan, Y. (2020). Gastronomi sözlüğü (A' dan Z'ye). M. Sarıışık, G. Özbay ve V. Ceylan (Edt.), *Şerbet,* Detay Yayıncılık.

Oğuz, B. (1976). Türkiye Halkının Kültür Kökenleri, İstanbul: 1. İstanbul Matbaası.

Oğuz, B. (2002). Türkiye halkının kültür kökenleri 1. Anadolu Aydınlanma Vakfı Yayınları

Özen, N. D. & Karaca, O. B. (2021). Sürdürülebilir gıda üretimi. F. Durlu Özkaya, F. Özkök, A. Sünnetçioğlu ve S. Sünnetçioğlu (Edt.), *Sürdürülebilir gastronomi* (ss. 27–56). Detay Yayıncılık.

Özkan, M., Erçetin, H. K. & Güneş, E. (2019). Türk mutfak kültürüne ait kaynar (lohusa) şerbeti üzerine bir değerlendirme. *Journal of Tourism and Gastronomy Studies, 7* (3), 2310–2320.

Pittel, K. (2002). Sustainability and Endogenous Growth, Cheltenham, UK and Northampton. MA, US: Edward Elgar.

Richardson, L. & Fernqvist, F. (2022). Transforming the Food System through Sustainable Gastronomy—How Chefs Engage with Food Democracy. J. Hunger. Environ. Nutr., 1–17.

Sarıoğlan, M. & Cevizkaya, G. (2016). Türk mutfak kültürü: şerbetler. *Sosyal Bilimler Araştırması Dergisi. 6* (14), 237–250.

Sırıklı, İ. K. & Özkanlı, O. (2021). Türk mutfağında şerbet geleneği ve 2000'den sonra Türkiye'de şerbet tüketiminin durumu. *International Social Sciences Studies Journal, 7*(81), 1832–1839.

Sürücüoğlu, M.S. (1997). Türk mutfağında şerbetlerin yeri ve önemi, *Anayurttan Atayurda Türk Dünyası,* 4(11), 26–33

Tekelioğlu, Y. (2019). Coğrafi işaretler ve Türkiye uygulamaları. *Ufuk Üniversitesi Sosyal Bilimler Enstitüsü Dergisi*, 8(15), 47–75.

Tezcan, M. (1990). Geleneksel Türk içecekleri (meşrubatları). *Türk Halk Kültürü Araştırmaları* (Türk Mutfağı Özel Sayısı), 118–127.

Toklu, İ. T. (2016). Tüketiciler coğrafi işaret için daha fazla ödemek ister mi? Artvin balı üzerine bir araştırma. *Karadeniz Araştırmaları*, (52), 171–190.

Türk Dil Kurumu. (2024). Şerbet. *Türk dil kurumu sözlükleri*. sozluk.gov.tr (Erişim Tarihi: 05.07.2024).

Türk Patent 1, (2024). Coğrafi İşaret. https://ci.turkpatent.gov.tr/sayfa/hakk%C4%B1m%C4%B1zd (Erişilme Tarihi: 07.05.2024).

Türk Patent 2, (2024). *Coğrafi işaret nedir?* https://ci.turkpatent.gov.tr/sayfa/co%C4%9Frafi-i%C5%9Faret-nedir. (Erişilme Tarihi: 07.05.2024).

Türk Patent 3, (2024). *Geleneksel ürün adı nedir?* https://ci.turkpatent.gov.tr/sayfa/geleneksel-%C3%BCr%C3%BCn-ad%C4%B1-nedir (Erişilme Tarihi: 07.05.2024).

Türk Patent 4, (2024). *Coğrafi işaret ile tescillenmiş ve başvuru sürecindeki şerbetler.* https://ci.turkpatent.gov.tr/veri-tabani (Erişim Tarihi: 20.04.2024).

Turkish Language Association (2024) Şerbet. *Türk dil kurumu sözlükleri.* sozlukgovtr (Erişim Tarihi: 05.07.2024)

Ünal, D. C. (2023). *Sürdürülebilir gastronomi kapsamında gıda atıklarından şerbet üretimi.* [Yüksek Lisans Tezi]. İstanbul Gelişim Üniversitesi.

Yalçın B., 2009. *Yöresel ürünlerin pazarlamasında e-ticaretin etkisinin incelenmesine yönelik bir araştırma.* [Yüksek Lisans Tezi]. Çanakkale Onsekiz Mart Üniversitesi.

Yar, H. S. (2008). *Osmanlı sarayında mutfak kültürü ve sofra gelenekleri.* [Yüksek Lisans Tezi]. Beykent Üniversitesi.

Yıldırım, N. (2008). 14. ve 15. yüzyıl Türkçe tıp yazmalarında hastalıklara tavsiye edilen çorbalar, aşlar ve tatlılar. Türk Mutfağı. Kültür ve Turizm Bakanlığı Yayınları.

Yılmaz, H. & Bekar, A. (2019). Gastronomi olgusuna sosyolojik bakış. C. Avcıkurt ve M. Sarıoğlan (Edt). *Popüler kültür ve gastronomi* (ss. 47–58). Detay Yayıncılık.

YÜCİTA 1, 2024. *Kültürlerin parmak izleri: coğrafi işaretler* https://yucita.org/page_15_Kulturel-Boyut. (Erişim Tarihi: 11.05.2024).

Irfan Yurt[1]

Chapter 22 The Meeting Point of Flavors: Gastronomy Festivals

Introduction

Gastronomy is one of the most fundamental elements in human history, and the act of eating has been a vital necessity since the dawn of human existence. Over time, consumption habits and culinary culture have evolved and taken shape (Pederson, 2012). Throughout this evolution, food consumption has transcended the mere satisfaction of a basic need, becoming a significant means for people to come together, establish relationships, and share cultural expressions (Sağır, 2012).

Throughout history, Türkiye has been a meeting point for diverse cultures, facilitating the emergence of a rich culinary culture (Onur & Ceylan, 2023). With its various geographical regions, climates, and cultural interactions, Turkish cuisine has become a globally recognised and cherished treasure of flavours. Today, the cultural significance and social function of food are also manifested in gastronomy festivals. Gastronomy festivals are events that showcase and promote the food and drink culture of a region or country. These festivals not only highlight local food and beverage traditions but also reflect the cultural identity and heritage of the region. Gastronomy festivals contribute positively to the local economy, tourism, and regional development. Furthermore, they attract tourists and promote gastronomy tourism, thereby enhancing the allure of the destination (Sormaz, Yılmaz & Pala, 2023).

These festivals, where local delicacies, international cuisine, and unique flavours converge, serve as platforms not only for culinary events but also for bringing cultures (Lee & Arcodia, 2011) and people closer together. Featuring regional specialities from all corners of Türkiye as well as examples from world cuisines, these festivals are akin to a feast. They also provide an opportunity to promote Turkish cuisine and local products, share traditional recipes, and discover new trends in the field of gastronomy. Gastronomy festivals offer a delectable journey and an unforgettable experience to better understand culinary culture and to

---

1 Ph.D., Karabuk University, Safranbolu Tourism Faculty, Gastronomy and Culinary Arts, irfanyurt@karabuk.edu.tr

explore new tastes. This section focuses on the culinary encounters at Türkiye 's gastronomy festivals.

Gastronomy Themed Festivals

Gastronomy is a discipline that guides the discovery, procurement, and preparation of food. Gastronomy tourism is a form of tourism that influences travel motivation and behaviours based on food and drink experiences. Additionally, gastronomy tourism reflects the cultural identity and heritage of a tourist region, providing a competitive advantage (McKercher et al., 2006). By combining food and tourism, gastronomy tourism offers alternative tourism opportunities to promote economic and social growth (Sormaz, Yilmaz, Özata, & Büyükyildirim, 2023).

Festivals provide significant contributions to local economies, offering various benefits to the local population. The increase in the number and diversity of festivals is known to be organised by communities to promote local tourism and generate economic benefits (Çevik, Şimşek & Yilmaz, 2017). Furthermore, festivals serve as examples of sustainable tourism practices (Yoon et al., 2010). Festivals contribute to the enhancement of communal culture, the development of cultural heritage, the preservation of traditions and the strengthening of intercultural relations.

Festivals are categorised according to their purposes. These categories include agricultural festivals, youth festivals, religious festivals, celebratory events, gastronomy festivals, film festivals, balloon festivals, and kite festivals, among many others (Yeoman et al., 2012). Among these, gastronomy festivals have particularly attracted attention in recent years. Focusing on food and beverage products made, grown, and produced at regional and local levels, these festivals are of great importance for regional promotion and sustainability (Doğdubay & İlsay, 2016). These festivals enhance people's knowledge and interest in the gastronomic values of the regions they visit and contribute to highlighting these values (Cohen & Avieli, 2004). Furthermore, these events significantly contribute to the development of a destination by stimulating tourism in tourist regions through direct contributions to the use of transportation services by visitors, the rental of hotel rooms for accommodation needs, and the use of venues for various purposes (Atak, 2009: 41).

Gastronomy festivals have become a significant means of promoting the gastronomy and culture of tourism destinations (Ottenbacher & Harrington, 2010). However, there is no specific classification for evaluating the quality of services offered at such festivals (Campoverde-Aguirre et al., 2022). As events where local foods and cultural experiences are showcased, gastronomy festivals are gaining increasing importance in tourism and gastronomic promotion activities (Björk & Kauppinen- Räisänen, 2016). These festivals provide accessible entertainment for individuals regardless of demographic differences and offer tourists the opportunity to experience authentic cultural encounters (Wan & Chan, 2013). Furthermore, adherence to food safety standards at these events is critical to protecting participants' health and ensuring the success of the festivals (Onur & Ceyhun-Sezgin, 2024). Studies on the quality of gastronomy festivals have examined visitor behaviour and the impact of these events on tourism and the economy. Crompton and Love (1995) evaluated festival quality through a four-dimensional structure: unique entertainment, general attributes, information, and comfort services. Lee et al. (2008) developed the term 'festivalscape' using the concept of servicescape. Chang, Gibson & Sisson (2014) noted that the quality of a festival is assessed through sub-dimensions such as hospitality, location, product, convenience, and programme, and that these factors influence satisfaction and loyalty towards the festival. According to Vesci and Botti (2019), the quality of food and beverages, the service provided by staff, and the information given significantly determine participants' attitudes towards local festivals and their intentions to revisit.

Gastronomic events are a significant attraction for tourism (UNTWO, 2024) and play a key role in the development of many tourist destinations. These festivals contribute to economic growth by fostering the development of new businesses and increasing tourism revenues (Cleave, 2020). Additionally, they provide an ideal platform to strengthen regional and local identity and showcase the community's local products. According to Getz (2008), food festivals help destinations differentiate themselves from other locations and create an objective image and brand for the region. Three key elements stand out in the organisation of a gastronomic festival (Organ et al., 2015):

(a) *Flavour:* The variety, quality, and authenticity of the food offered at the festival are of great importance. Flavour is a fundamental element that determines participants' taste experiences throughout the festival.

(b) *Location:* The choice of venue and its atmosphere affect how participants experience the festival. Reflecting the local culture and ambiance enhances the festival's success.

(c) *Tradition:* In terms of tradition, it is important that the food served at a festival is in keeping with the traditional culinary culture of the region or country. Showcasing traditional dishes reinforces the local identity of the festival and helps to provide an experience for the participants.

Recently, gastronomy festivals are one of the first activities of local governments in (Litvin & Fetter, 2006) the promotion and marketing of local products. Because gastronomy-themed festivals offer the opportunity to reveal the authenticity of food and to introduce and discover new places to tourists (Özdemir, 2008). Gastronomy festivals related to food cultures include many elements such as subunu, product promotion and production. The dishes presented at the festival reflect the situation, traditions and customs of the cultural environment and serve as a means of communication with tourists. Festivals organised in this way are also important in the formation and protection of gastronomic identity (Dredge & Whitford, 2011).

Gastronomy Festivals in Türkiye

Gastronomy festivals in Türkiye offer a unique opportunity to experience the local culture. While showcasing the region's gastronomic products, these festivals also highlight its rich cultural life. Traditional gastronomy festivals held in Türkiye are of great significance for both tourism and culture (Büyükşalvarcı & Akkaya, 2018). Table 22.1 presents an example of a gastronomy festival from one of Türkiye's various provinces. These festivals play a crucial role in preserving cultural heritage and supporting economic development.

Table 22.1. Traditional Gastronomy Festivals in Türkiye

Plaka No	İl	Gastronomi Festivalleri
01	Adana	Adana Kebab and Turnip Festival, Orange Strawberry Festival
02	Adıyaman	Çiğ Köfte Festival
03	Afyonkarahisar	GASTRO Afyon International Tourism and Taste Festival
04	Ağrı	Ağrı Honey Festival
05	Amasya	Amasya Apple Festival
06	Ankara	International Kalecik Karası Grape Festival
07	Antalya	Antalya Coffee and Chocolate Festival
08	Artvin	Artvin Kafkasör Culture and Tourism Festival
09	Aydın	Aydın Olive and Olive Oil Festival
10	Balıkesir	International Ayvalık Olive Harvest and Tourism Festival
11	Bilecik	Bilecik Gastoronomy Festival
12	Bingöl	Yedisu Dry Bean Festival
13	Bitlis	MoNE Gastronomy Festival
14	Bolu	Mengen International Cooking and Tourism Festival

Table 22.1.   Continued

Plaka No	İl	Gastronomi Festivalleri
15	Burdur	19th Söğüt Traditional Tomato and Culture Festival
16	Bursa	Bursa Gastronomy Festival
17	Çanakkale	Umurbey Traditional Peach Festival
18	Çankırı	International Çankırı Salt Festival
19	Çorum	Iskilip Dolma Pickle and Strawberry Festival
20	Denizli	Denizli Tavas Zeybek Festivali
21	Diyarbakır	Diyarbakır Karpuz Festivali
22	Edirne	Edirne Ciğer Festivali
23	Elazığ	Elazığ Coffee and Chocolate Festival
24	Erzincan	Erzincan Tulum Cheese Festival
25	Erzurum	Erzurum Cag Kebab Festival
26	Eskişehir	Sivrihisar Dövme Sausage Festival
27	Gaziantep	Gaziantep International Gastronomy Festival
28	Giresun	Giresun Hazelnut Festival
29	Gümüşhane	Gümüşhane International Rosehip, Pestil, Culture and Tourism Festival
30	Hakkâri	Hakkari Local Food Festival
31	Hatay	Hatay Taste Festival
32	Isparta	Eğirdir Apple Harvest Festival
33	Mersin	Mersin Tantuni Festival
34	İstanbul	Istanbul International Gastronomy Festival
35	İzmir	Izmir Boyoz Festival
36	Kars	Kars Cheese Festival
37	Kastamonu	Kastamonu Gastronomy Festival
38	Kayseri	Manti, Sausage, Pastrami (MA-SU-PA) Culture Festival
39	Kırklareli	Traditional Demirkoy Strawberry Festival
40	Kırşchir	Traditional Bulgur Festival
41	Kocaeli	Izmit Pişmaniye Festival
42	Konya	Konya GastroFest
43	Kütahya	Kütahya Gastronomy Festival
44	Malatya	Malatya Apricot Festival
45	Manisa	International Mesir Macunu Festival
46	Kahramanmaraş	Kahramanmaraş Ice Cream Festival
47	Mardin	Mardin Gastronomy Festival
48	Muğla	Muğla Olive and Olive Oil Festival

(continued on next page)

Table 22.1.   Continued

Plaka No	İl	Gastronomi Festivalleri
49	Muş	Local Flavors Festival
50	Nevşehir	Cappadocia Traditional Food Festival
51	Niğde	Niğde Apple Festival
52	Ordu	Ordu Zümrüt Hazelnut Festival
53	Rize	Uluslararası Rize Çay, Turizm ve Yaz Sporları Festivali
54	Sakarya	Agora Pumpkin Festival
55	Samsun	Pita, Rice and Fish Festival
56	Siirt	Siirt Peanut Festival
57	Sinop	Sinop Lakerda Festival
58	Sivas	Sivas Madımak Festival
59	Tekirdağ	Tekirdag Cherry Festival
60	Tokat	Tokat Gastronomy Festival
61	Trabzon	Trabzon Anchovy Festival
62	Tunceli	Tunceli Munzur Culture and Nature Festival
63	Şanlıurfa	Halfeti Fruit Food Festival
64	Uşak	Usak Tarhana Festival
65	Van	Van International Gastoronomy Festival
66	Yozgat	Yozgat Gastoronomy Festival
67	Zonguldak	Zonguldak Gastoronomy Festival
68	Aksaray	Traditional Ağaçören Walnut Festival
69	Bayburt	Bayburt Gastoronomy Festival
70	Karaman	Ayranci Divle Berendi Obruk Cheese Festival
71	Kırıkkale	Arıcan 97 Pumpkin Festival
72	Batman	Gercüş Vintage Gastronomy Festival
73	Şırnak	Şırnak Gastro Fest
74	Bartın	Bartın Gastronomy Festival
75	Ardahan	Göle Culture and Kashar Festival
76	Iğdır	Igdir Apricot Festival
77	Yalova	Yalova-Subasi Kiwi Festival
78	Karabük	Saffron Festival
79	Kilis	Kilis Gastoronomy Festival
80	Osmaniye	Osmaniye Flavor Festival
81	Düzce	Traditional Duzce Herbs Abundance Festival

Table 22.1 includes a selection of gastronomic festivals held in various provinces of Türkiye. Additionally, the Turkish Cuisine Week events, coordinated by the

Ministry of Culture and Tourism, are organised annually in all 81 provinces and across all international representations. These events showcase the unique flavours of each province.

In their study, Ekerim and Tanrısever (2020) identified 367 gastronomy festivals in Türkiye. They found that the Mediterranean Region hosts 53 festivals, the Eastern Anatolia Region 25, the Aegean Region 59, the Southeastern Anatolia Region 16, the Central Anatolia Region 46, the Black Sea Region 51, and the Marmara Region 84.

Aslan et al. (2021) reported a total of 389 gastronomy-themed festivals held in Türkiye. According to their findings, the regions with the highest number of festivals are: the Aegean Region with 93, the Marmara Region with 92, the Mediterranean Region with 57, the Central Anatolia Region with 53, the Black Sea Region with 51, the Eastern Anatolia Region with 28, and the Southeastern Anatolia Region with 15 (Aslan, Akoğlu, and Şengül, 2021).

It was found that most of the gastronomy festivals in the Aegean Region are predominantly fruit and vegetable-themed. Furthermore, a significant number of these festivals are observed to be organised by municipalities and public institutions.

Results

In recent years, there has been a notable increase in the number of gastronomic festivals organised at local, national, and international levels. These festivals not only contribute to the entertainment and cultural understanding of the local population but also play a significant role in the development of a tourism destination and in attracting visitors. Consequently, the importance of gastronomic festivals in tourism destinations is steadily increasing (Yurt & Sağır, 2023). Correspondingly, there has also been a rise in the number of studies on this subject in the national and international literature. Gastronomy festivals allow visitors to taste foods and beverages they have not experienced before, learn about the culture and traditions of the regions they visit, and develop social bonds by interacting with the local population (Mason & Paggiaro, 2012). Through these festivals, food and beverages gain greater significance, the number of visitors to the region increases, and the strengthening of social bonds within communities is encouraged (Dredge & Whitford, 2011). Additionally, gastronomy festivals offer visitors the opportunity for on-site experiences and bring together producers and consumers. Visitors can gain knowledge about the food and beverages offered at the festivals and directly observe the processes of growing, producing, and cooking the products (Mason & Paggiaro, 2012).

In Türkiye, most festivals are held in the spring and summer months, typically aimed at promoting local products, fostering community cohesion, and facilitating trade. However, it has been observed that the international promotion of festivals in Türkiye is insufficient in terms of gastronomy tourism. These festivals are generally aimed at the local population, with limited potential for attracting tourists. As evaluated in this study, gastronomic festivals in Türkiye largely focus on promoting local foods and products. Therefore, to enhance the effectiveness of gastronomic festivals in Türkiye, it is necessary to ensure continuity and implement effective promotional strategies.

References

Aslan, E., Akoğlu, A. and Şengül, S. (2021). Gastronomi Festivali Tercihinde Ziyaretçilerin Memnuniyet ve Bağlılık Düzeylerini Etkileyen Faktörler: Ege Bölgesi Örneği. *Manisa Celal Bayar Üniversitesi Sosyal Bilimler Dergisi,* 19 (1); 77–94.

Atak, O., (2009). Türk turizminin tanitiminda festivallerin yeri ve önemi: Antalya örneği, *Yayınlanmamış Yükseklisans Tezi, İstanbul Üniversitesi Sosyal Bilimler Enstitüsü, Turizm İşletmeciliği Anabilim Dalı,* İstanbul.

Björk, P. & Kauppinen-Räisänen, H. (2016). Local food: A source for destination attraction. *Int. J. Contemp. Hosp. Manag.,* 28(1), 177–194.

Büyükşalvarcı, A. ve Akkaya, A. (2018). The Evaluation of gastronomy festivals as events tourism. *Akademik Sosyal Araştırmalar Dergisi,* 6(67), 452–467.

Campoverde-Aguirre, R.; Carvache-Franco, M.; Carvache- Franco, W.; Almeida-Cabrera, M. (2022). Gastronomi Festivallerinde Hizmet Kalitesinin Analizi. *Sustainability,* 14(21), 14605. https://doi.org/10.3390/su142114605.

Çevik, H.; Şimşek, K. Y. & Yılmaz, İ., (2017). The Evaluating of Service Quality in Recreatio-nal Sport Events: Kite Festival Sample. *Pamukkale Journal of Sport Sciences,* 8 (1), 73–93.

Chang, S.; Gibson, H.; Sisson, L. (2014). The loyalty process of residents and tourists in the festival context. *Curr. Issues Tour.* 17(9), 783–799.

Cleave, P. (2020). Food as a leisure pursuit, a United Kingdom perspective. Ann. Leis. Res., 23(4), 474–491. https://doi.org/10.1080/11745398.2019.1613669.

Cohen, E., & Avieli, N. (2004). Food in tourism: attraction and impediment. *Annals of Tourism Research,* 31(4), 755–778.

Crompton, J.L.; Love, L.L. (1995). Predictive validity of alternative approaches of evaluating quality of a festival. *J. Travel Res.,* 34(1), 11–24. https://doi.org/ 10.1177/004728759503400.

Doğdubay, M., & İlsay, S. (2016). *Bir iletişim biçimi olarak gastronomi konulu festivaller.* Hakan Doğdubay ve İlsay (Ed.), Bir iletişim biçimi olarak gastronomi. Ankara: Detay Yayıncılık

Dredge, D.; Whitford, M. (2011). Event tourism governance and the public sphere. *Journal of Sustainable Tourism*, 19 (4–5), 479–499.

Ekerim, F., & Tanrısever, C. (2020). Türkiye gastronomi festivalleri ve haritalandirilmasi (Gastronomy festivals and their). *Journal of Tourism and Gastronomy Studies*, 8(3), 2277–2297

Getz, D. (2008). Event tourism: Definition, evolution, and research. *Tour. Manag.*, 29 (3), 403–428.

Lee, I., & Arcodia, C. (2011). The Role of Regional Food Festivals for Destination Branding. International Journal of Tourism Research, 13, 355–367. https://doi.org/10.1002/jtr.852.

Lee, Y.K.; Lee, C.K.; Lee, S.K. & Babin, B.J.(2008). Festivalscapes and patrons' emotions, satisfaction, and loyalty. *J. Bus. Res.*, 61(1), 56–64.

Litvin, S. W. & Fetter, E. (2006), Can A festival be too successful? A review of spoleto, USA. *International journal of contemporary hospitality management*, 18 (1), 41–49.

Mason, C. M. ve Paggiaro, A. (2012). Investigating the role of festivalscape in culinary tourism: the case of food and wine events. *Tourism Management*, 33, 1329–1336.

McKercher, B.; Mei, W. S.; Tse, T. S. (2006). Are short duration cultural fastivals tourist attractions? *Journal of Sustainable Tourism*, 14 (1), 55–66.

Onur, M., & Ceyhun-Sezgin, A. (2024). Determination of food safety knowledge level and practice behaviors of chef candidates within the scope of occupational standard. Nevşehir Hacı Bektaş Veli Üniversitesi SBE Dergisi, 14(1), 42–55.

Onur, M., Ceylan, F. (2023). Heritage of the Anatolian geography: registered varieties of ancestral wheat (siyez, gacer, and menceki). *J. Ethn. Food*, 10, 36.

Organ, K.; Koenig-Lewis, N.; Palmer, A.; Probert, J. (2015). Festivals as agents for behaviour change: A study of food festival engagement and subsequent food choices. *Tour. Manag.*, 48, 84–99.

Ottenbacher, M.C.; Harrington, R.J. (2010). Strategies for achieving success for innovative versus incremental new services. *J. Serv. Mark*, 24(1), 3–15.

Özdemir, G. (2008). Destinasyon Pazarlaması, Detay Publishing, Ankara.

Pederson, L. B. (2012). Creativity in gastronomy- exploring the connection between art and craft, (Unpublished Thesis), Copenhagen Business School, Frederiksberg.

Sağır, A. (2012). Bir yemek sosyolojisi denemesi örneği olarak tokat mutfağı. Turkish Studies, International Periodical For The Languages, Literature and History of Turkish or Turkic, 7(4).

Sormaz, Ü., Yılmaz, M., & Pala, K. (2023). An evaluation of the gastronomy tourism potential of Amasya from a sustainable tourism perspective through SWOT analysis. *Journal of Tourism & Management Research*, 8(2), 1169–1179.

Sormaz, U., Yilmaz, M.,Özata, E. & Büyükyildirim, C. (2023). Evaluation of the Gastronomic Tourism Potential of Burdur Province By Swot Analysis. *Journal of Tourism & Gastronomy Studies*, 11(2), 1262–1279.

Vesci, M.; Botti, A. (2019). Festival quality, theory of planned behavior and revisiting intention: Evidence from local and small Italian culinary festivals. *J. Hosp. Tour. Manag.*, 38, 5–15. https://doi.org/10.1016/j.jhtm.2018.10.003.

Wan, Y.K.P. & Chan, S.H.J. (2013). Factors that Affect the Levels of Tourists' Satisfaction and Loyalty towards Food Festivals: A Case Study of Macau. Int. J. Tour. Res., 15(3), 226–240.

World Tourism Organisation (UNTWO). Affiliate Members Report; Global Report on Food: Madrid, Spain, 2012; Volume 4, Available from Tourism. Available online: https://www.unwto.org/archive/global/publication/unwto-amreport-vol-4-global-repor (accessed on 15 March 2024).

Yeoman, I., Robertson, M., Ali-Knight, J., Drummond, S., & Mcmahon-Beattie, U. (2012). Festival and events management. *New York, United States of America: Routledge*.

Yoon, Y. S.; Lee, J. S. and Lee, C. K., (2010). Measuring Festival Quality and Value Affecting Visitors' Satisfactio and Loyalty Using a Structural Approach. *International Journal of Hospitality Management*, 29 (2), 335–342.

Yurt, İ and Sağır, Y. E. (2023). The Effect of Staff Behaviours in Food and Beverage Establıshments On Customer's Eating and Drinking Experience. Gastroia: Journal of Gastronomy and Travel Research, 7(2), 448–460.

Ibrahim Çekiç

Chapter 23 Intangible Cultural Aspects of the Gastronomic Product

Introduction

Gastronomy is a complex process that includes all the artistic and scientific elements it contains, starting from the historical development process of food and beverages, and the detailed understanding, application, and development of all their features and adaptation to today's conditions (Eren, 2007). This process includes not only cooking techniques, but also nutritional science, cultural and social interactions shaped around food, the precursors that trigger the emergence of eating and drinking behavior, and social sensitivities such as sustainability and environmental awareness. In this context, gastronomy focuses not only on the taste and nutritional values of food and beverages but also on factors such as the visual aesthetics and presentation of meals (arrangement of ingredients from a creative perspective, color harmony, plate layout, and use of decorative elements) and aims to visually enrich the dining experience (Coşkun and Özata, 2024). In this context, it is possible to state that gastronomy stands out as both an art form and a scientific discipline.

The most important output of gastronomy is food and beverage-themed products. These outputs, which we can describe as gastronomic products, can also be considered as cultural indicators that shed light on the social characteristics of societies (Yıldız and Aksoy, 2018). These indicators, which give meaning to the characteristic codes of the societies to which they belong and help us to get to know societies or communities closely, like other cultural elements, have two different forms according to their shape and content. The first is the basic form of the gastronomic product and includes all the eating and drinking elements and the physical formations that can be associated with these elements. The second form of gastronomic product consists of gastronomy-themed intangible cultural heritage elements. Intangible cultural heritage is defined as "the practices, representations, expressions, knowledge, skills and related tools, equipment and cultural spaces that communities, groups and, in some cases, individuals define as a part of their cultural heritage" (UNESCO, 2003). Gastronomy-themed intangible cultural heritage elements cover all social perceptions and practices with food and beverage elements at their core. The Turkish coffee tradition and the custom of setting the table can be a good example in this context. In Turkey, coffee is not perceived just as a beverage but is seen as a symbol of hospitality and goodness (Balcı, 2019). Similarly, in various regions of Anatolia, the tradition of setting the table is not only associated with eating but is also perceived as a practice that paves the way for families to come together, socialize, and transmit culture (Çerikan, 2019). This study focuses on the second form of gastronomic product, that is, the intangible cultural heritage aspect. In this context, the traditions, rituals, and cultural practices behind gastronomic products were discussed in detail, and how these elements were preserved and transferred as cultural values were examined. Additionally, how intangible cultural heritage can be used in destination marketing and how it can contribute to sustainability in tourism has been examined.

Gastronomic Product

Gastronomic product is the whole of the eating and drinking elements that reflect the cultural, historical, and geographical characteristics of any geography and the outputs shaped around these elements. These outputs not only represent a culinary culture but also offer visitors the opportunity to discover the rich heritage and cultural diversity of the region. This makes gastronomic products an important element that reflects the characteristic features and cultural identity of a region. Therefore, it is possible to say that gastronomic products are among the motivational sources that shape tourists' behavioral intentions. Smith and Xiao (2008) classified gastronomy tourism resources under four headings:

- Facilities: Buildings and structures, land use, routes
- Activities: Consumption, tours, education, and observation
- Events: Consumer shows, festivals
- Organizations: Systems – organizations

The classification in question expands the range of the gastronomic product concept and also emphasizes the cultural characteristics of the concept. This shows that gastronomic products are a rich and complex experience that includes not only flavors but also people's interactions and cultural ties with each other. Gastronomic products have a structure that can appeal to different types of tourists. Therefore, it is possible to say that gastronomy is seen as a marketing element in the tourism sector, creating a competitive advantage and as a tool for economic development (Akgöz, 2021). Destinations that are aware of this situation are trying to highlight their gastronomic knowledge and trying to develop touristic products that center on food and beverage elements.

Intangible Cultural Heritage

Although there are different classifications of culture today, it is possible to say that one of the most general classifications is material culture and spiritual culture. While concrete assets such as buildings, equipment, clothes, etc. owned by society are discussed under the title of material culture, concepts such as the beliefs, traditions, norms, and ways of thinking of the society are discussed under the title of spiritual culture elements. Although culture can be classified in different ways, one of the most common approaches is the distinction between material culture and spiritual culture. Material culture covers the physical and tangible assets of a society. This category includes buildings, equipment, clothing, technological tools, works of art, and all physical objects used in daily life. Material culture includes elements that reflect the economic, technological, and artistic development of society (Türker and Çelik, 2012). Spiritual culture covers the abstract values and norms of society. In this context, there are elements such as beliefs, traditions, customs, moral values, language, literature, music, myths, and religious rituals. These two categories provide an important analytical framework for understanding and examining cultural elements. While material and spiritual cultural elements reflect the identity and history of a society, the interaction of these two dimensions plays a critical role in understanding the processes of cultural change and continuity.

The concept of cultural heritage has a meaning that reflects the common history of a society and strengthens the feelings of solidarity and unity among the members of this society. This concept can also be defined as a set of resources that have survived from the past to the present and include people's values, beliefs, knowledge, and traditions, which are constantly changing but have an ownership bond (İSPEM, 2014). As can be seen, the concept of cultural heritage has a complex structure that includes all cultural elements. The concept of intangible cultural heritage is a point of distinction that has emerged as a result of this situation. Intangible cultural heritage is nourished by social perception shaped around concrete cultural elements and practices that have become traditional in the process. In this context, it is possible to list the study areas that can be evaluated within the concept of intangible cultural heritage in general categories (UNESCO, 2003):

- Oral traditions and narratives,
- Performance arts,
- Social practices,
- Information and applications about nature and the universe
- Handicraft tradition

In this context, it is possible to list the epics, legends, folk tales, proverbs, fairy tales, village theatrical plays such as karagöz and meddah, rituals, feasts, and traditional dishes that societies have shaped from the past to the present under these categories. Food and beverage elements are not only a part of material culture but also one of the starting points of intangible cultural heritage. These elements make an important contribution to the preservation of social memory through rituals and traditions that reflect the history, beliefs, and values of the society. Eating and drinking practices and the social context of these practices serve as a source of understanding the history of the society.

Dimensions of the Gastronomic Product

Gastronomy is an interdisciplinary field of study. Recommendations on the preparation, cooking, and presentation of food and the nuances of what, where, when, and in what way to consume constitute the general structure of gastronomy (Santich, 2004). The gastronomic product is constantly shaped within this structure and introduces new products in line with changing consumer expectations. These products may sometimes be the food itself, and sometimes they may be traditional and modern practices formed around the specific characteristics of eating and drinking elements. Technological developments, cultural interactions, and environmental factors also play an important role in the continuous shaping of these products. Innovative trends such as molecular cuisine and fusion cuisine, conscious consumption movements, and the tendency towards healthy and organic foods can be considered as reflections of these factors.

Gastronomic product contains various interrelated dimensions due to its structure. In his study, Çekiç (2021) grouped these dimensions under two categories. The figure for these categories, which was created by taking into account the shape and content characteristics of the gastronomic product, is given below.

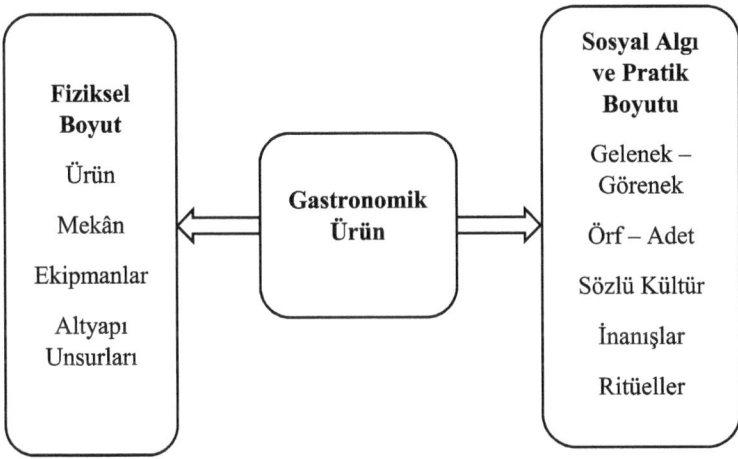

Figure 23.1. Dimensions of the Gastronomic Product. Reference: Çekiç (2021)

When the figure is examined, it is seen that a cultural approach is taken when sizing the gastronomic product. This approach highlights food and other physical elements associated with food, as well as intangible elements other than these elements. In this context, the focus is on the physical dimension of the gastronomic product, the eating and drinking elements, and the technical components in the preparation and service process of these elements. The social perception and practical dimension of the gastronomic product are associated with practices that include the cultural codes of the society beyond the physical existence of the food, such as traditions-customs, manners-formalities, oral culture, beliefs, and rituals.

Intangible Cultural Aspects of the Gastronomic Product

The social perception and practical dimension of gastronomic products represent their intangible cultural aspect. It can be said that this dimension, the preparation and consumption processes of food, includes elements that reflect the social norms, values and identity of the society. At the same time, the intangible cultural dimension of the gastronomic product carries food beyond its physical existence, making it a motivational element for tourists who want to recognize, experience, and compare the cultural aspects of different geographies.

Traditions – Customs

Tradition, which is a versatile concept, has different meanings depending on the field in which it is used but generally refers to the whole of cultural elements that continue from the past to the present (Hancıoğlu, 2016). Custom, on the other hand, is a phenomenon that individuals internalize by seeing some dynamics in the society they belong to during the socialization process. Traditions and customs are among the building blocks of culture and contribute to individuals learning appropriate forms of behavior through rules and norms (Luthans & Doh, 2012). There are many traditions regarding eating and drinking in Turkish culture. One of these traditions is the practice of hosting guests. The tables prepared for the guests are prepared completely. The basis of being generous to guests lies in the perception that guests are guests of God. It is also possible to say that this situation takes hosting guests to a divine dimension.

The expression "The son does not set the table unless he sees it from the father…" in Dede Korkut refers to the fact that hosting guests is a custom. Again, as stated in the Book of Dede Korkut, "The basis of the house is that if a guest comes to the house from the countryside or the wild, and her husband is not at home, she feeds him, gives him drink, hosts him and sends saints." The expression is important as it emphasizes the value given to hosting guests (Ergin, 2005). In most parts of Anatolia, opening the table to guests without asking whether they are hungry or full is remarkable as it shows the hospitality of the Anatolian people. The perfection of the table served to the guest is expressed by the sentence "There was a piece of bird's milk missing from the table." (Toprak, 2019).

Traditions regarding the cooking and sharing process of Turkish coffee in Anatolia are also remarkable. Turkish coffee has always become an indispensable part of some social events such as engagement ceremonies, holidays, and socializing meetings (Kültür ve Turizm Bakanlığı, 2024). Offering salted coffee to the groom-to-be during the marriage ceremony, fortune-telling with coffee grounds, associating coffee offerings with memory, and starting from the right side in the coffee presentation can be counted among the perceptions and practices encountered in daily life.

Sira nights held in the eastern and southeastern regions of Turkey are also among the events shaped around food. Sira nights are entertainment ceremonies held by groups of friends close in age, especially on winter nights, at a different friend's house every week. Sıra nights are a verbal conversation with instruments. Çiğköfte (steak tartar a la turca) is the gastronomic item at the center of these assemblies. During the entertainment, a piece of çiğköfte is thrown onto the ceiling to control the consistency of the çiğköfte kneaded using traditional methods. If the çiğköfte sticks to the ceiling, it indicates that it is ready to be served. Sira nights are also a tradition where norms and values are transferred (Kaya, 2015). This tradition was included in the list of intangible cultural heritage in 2010.

Manners – Formalities

Manners and formalities are two sociological terms used together, making definition difficult (Yanardağ, 2017). In general terms, manners refer to the actions that most people adopt and make a habit of or the words that they habitually use in such a special sense that no other meaning comes to mind when heard (Zekiyyüddîn, 2000). Formalities, on the other hand, are unwritten rules that have been applied in a society for a long time, generally passed from generation to generation, applied among the public, and specifying the actions that should and should not be done according to the value provisions of good and evil (Yanardağ, 2017). Manners and formalities, which are one of the defining characteristics of Turkish society, are encountered at almost every stage of social life. One of these stages is related to eating and drinking elements. The situations like bread is seen as a symbol of abundance, bread on the ground in an open area is kissed, touched to the head, and placed on a high place, the guest is not asked if he or she is hungry, the elder of the family is the first to start eating, meatless food is not served to the guest, getting up after the guest, not talking while there is food in the mouth can be listed among the manners and formalities related to eating and drinking (Göktaş, 2011; Çetin, 2020). In addition, in Turkish culture, "Water is for the younger, the table is for the elder." There is also a manner like this (TDK, 2024). This manner is important in that it emphasizes the understanding that elders should be respected and minors should be protected. The phrase "water is for the younger" is related to the fact that water is one of the most indispensable elements of life. The phrase "the table is for the elder" refers to the fact that everything has an order and that people should be included in this order according to their age, culture, etc. (NTV, 2023).

The practice called eye right in Turkish culture also appears as a reflection of helpfulness and the tendency to share. This trend, nourished by religious sensitivity, is based on the principle of offering consumed food and beverage items to people around them. In this context, families with traditional sensibilities advise their children to eat ice cream, candy, etc. at home in case other children want them, or they ask them to give even a piece of what they have to other children (Korukcu, 2016).

Oral Culture

Oral culture is a concept that covers all the elements that societies' knowledge, experience, beliefs, feelings, and traditions are transferred from generation to generation through non-written means. Myths, legends, epics, folk tales, jokes, idioms, proverbs, swear words and slang words, oaths, expressions of greetings, names, and nicknames, oral history, and folk poetry are known forms of oral expression (Kültür Portalı, 2024). These forms of expression can be shaped around many elements that societies have shaped from the past to the present. When Turkish culture is examined, it is seen that there are many oral culture products about food. The cultural products in question are related to the fact that Turks do not see food only as a consumption element. For Turks, food is a part of unity, brotherhood, sharing, and cultural transfer. Food epics are the most obvious extension of this understanding, and together with the types of dishes they contain and the foods related to them, they are, in a way, valuable as a document in terms of local culture and history. Food epics also vary in terms of their subjects. These epics are categorized as follows according to their content characteristics:

- Epics about various dishes and foods,
- Epics that deal with just one food, drink, or dessert,
- Humorous food epics (Kaya, 2008).

A stanza from the praise written by Kadir Gürsoy, pseudonymous Gülebi, for the dishes of his region is given below.

> Baklava kadayıf then tulumba
> Revani jams after these
> Don't forget our omac
> Our meals are very delicious.

Cooking meals, especially wedding meals, in cooperation is among the traditions kept alive by the Anatolian people. The chansonettes performed among women during the meals prepared by the imece (collective work) method are also remarkable due to the social references they contain (Çekiç, 2022).

> I have a loved one at the wedding
> She has my tissue in her hand
> Before eating the keşkek
> I want to enter your bosom

Gastronomic products are frequently included in the ending forms of fairy tales, which are oral culture products of Turkish literature. One of these is apple. Some of the Turkish fairy tales end with the words "Three apples fell from the sky, one for the teller, one for the teller, and one for me." The frequent use of apples in oral culture products is associated with the creation myth, that is, the apple is the forbidden fruit that caused people to be expelled from heaven (Özkaynak, 2013).

Beliefs

Beliefs are among the dynamics that regulate social life. Beliefs about what to eat and how to eat also form part of these regulatory dynamics. These beliefs appear in two dimensions: religious and cultural, and shape the food culture of the society. The religious dimension includes divine laws. The perception of haram and halal is an extension of these laws. In this context, it is possible to say that each society has different definitions for universal edibility (Sırıklı, 2023). For example, it is among the religious-based beliefs of Turkish society that the meat of an animal that is not slaughtered in the name of Allah cannot be eaten and that pork is haram. The cultural dimension of beliefs includes social perceptions or superstitious tendencies that societies have developed over the historical process, apart from religious rules. Many elements that center on food are mentioned in the literature. Some of these are listed below.

- It is believed that the chickpeas in the keşkek eaten on the eve of Ramadan will bring Salawat throughout Ramadan (Tokuz, 2002).
- For the good and evil spell, fruit is read and fed to the person on whom the spell is cast; for the good and evil spell, soap and beans are read and thrown into a glass of water; for the love spell, red pepper is thrown into the oven (Artun, 1978).
- Keeping bread next to the newborn baby to protect it from the evil spirit, also called red-woman (Göktaş, 2011).
- In Anatolia, salt, sugar, flour, dough, yeast, bread, and vinegar are seen as symbols of abundance and abundance in terms of their structures, shapes, and functions, and after reading the Holy Quran, salt and sugar are blown into it to be blessed, so that newly married people can live in abundance; dough and sugar are placed in front of their houses, and it is believed that bread crushed with a knife robs the house of its abundance (Okuşluk, 2011).
- On the first day of Hıdırellez, due to the belief that the whole nature will start a new and vibrant life, the first lamb of the year is taken to the countryside and the lamb is slaughtered for the sake of Hızır, and the tables are filled with rice, with the idea that Hıdırellez tables will increase fertility (Aktürk, 2014).

Rituals

Rituals are fixed forms of behavior that express symbolic values. Transitions of life stages, important social or religious times, and periods of crisis are exhibited through these rituals. Transition rituals indicate the passage through stages, calendar rituals are performed at certain times, and crisis period rituals provide emotional support during traumatic periods (Karaman, 2010). Rituals, in a way, are the practical implementation of behavioral patterns shaped by cultural codes in the process. Food rituals are frequently encountered during the preparation and presentation stages of food. The keşkek (a dish of mutton or chicken and coarsely ground wheat) agha ritual performed by the residents of Kazancılı Village in Ordu's Perşembe District is a good example in this context. In this ritual, the keşkek aga, chosen by auction, turns the environment into a visual feast with his traditional clothes and fixed behavioral patterns (Çekiç, 2022). Another example of food rituals in Turkish culture is the mesir paste ceremony. This paste is a mixture prepared using forty-one types of spices (Sarıca and Özbay, 2023). A festival is held regularly every year in Manisa to keep the mesir paste tradition alive. Mesir Paste Festival consists of three basic elements: praying, mixing, and throwing. The festival also includes practices such as cortege formation, parades, and general entertainment. Praying is a duty performed before and during the mixing process. During this process, various prayers are recited and the manifestation of Allah's name "Shafi" and his consent is prayed for. During the mixing stage, forty-one spices and other elements, whose names are spoken out loud, are added to the symbolic paste cauldron in a certain order and mixed carefully with wooden mixers. In the scattering stage, the prepared pastes are thrown to the public from the domes and minarets of the Sultan Mosque (Çekiç, 2021b).

Conclusion

Gastronomic products are not only nutrients but also important values that reflect the cultural identity, history, and traditions of a society. Elements such as recipes, cooking techniques, ways of sitting at the table, and rituals accompanying meals are transferred from generation to generation and become an important part of social memory. Gastronomic products have two basic dimensions. Firstly, the gastronomic product, which is its basic form, includes eating and drinking elements and all the physical formations that can be associated with these elements. The second form creates gastronomy-themed intangible cultural heritage elements. The intangible cultural aspect of gastronomic products is of great importance in understanding and preserving a society's identity and cultural heritage. Local cuisine reflects the cultural identity and heritage of a destination, providing tourists with authentic and unforgettable experiences. These gastronomic experiences enable tourists to connect deeply with the traditions, lifestyles, and values of the places they visit. Therefore, the intangible aspect of gastronomic products should not be ignored when determining tourism strategies. Integrating local dishes and the rituals that accompany these dishes into tourism activities can increase the cultural richness and attractiveness of a destination. Promotion and preservation of gastronomic heritage can contribute to sustainable tourism development and provide a significant boost to local economies. Turkish cuisine has a rich knowledge regarding the intangible cultural aspect of food. It is important for future studies to focus on these elements, both for the tourism sector and for the sustainability of culture.

References

Akgöz, E. (2021). *Gastronomi turizminde güncel konular.* Karaman, A., Şalvarcı, Ş.ve Aylan, F. K. (Editorler). Destinasyon Pazarlama Aracı Olarak Gastronomi Turizmi. Konya: Eğitim Yayınevi.

Aktürk, S. (2014). *Türkiye'de Hıdırellez etrafında oluşan folklorik unsurlar üzerine bir inceleme.* (Yayımlanmamış Yüksek Lisans Tezi). İstanbul Üniversitesi Sosyal Bilimler Enstitüsü, İstanbul.

Artun, E. (1978). Tekirdağ *Folklor Araştırmaları.* İstanbul: Tem Ofset.

Balcı, F. (2019). Cezveden kültüre 40 yil: Türk kahvesi ve geleneği. *The Journal of Academic Social Science, 87*(87), 315–328.

Coşkun, S., & Özata Şahin, E. (2024). Gastronomide görsellerle yiyecek içecek stilistliği. *USBAD Uluslararası Sosyal Bilimler Akademi Dergisi,* 6(14), 149–164.

Çekiç, İ. (2021). *Gastronomi şehirlerinin algılanan mutfak imajı ile davranışsal niyet arasındaki ilişki.* (Yayımlanmamış Doktora Tezi). Gazi Üniversitesi Sosyal Bilimler Enstitüsü, Ankara.

Çekiç, İ. (2021b). *Gastronomi temalı somut olmayan kültürel miras unsurlarının turizmde kullanımı.* Karabulut, Ş. (Editör). İçinde İktisadi sosyal ve kültürel yönleriyle turizm. Ankara: Gazi Kitabevi.

Çekiç, İ., & Özkan, A. (2022). Geleneksel tören keşkeğinin Türk gastronomisindeki yeri ve önemi. *Uluslararası Türkçe Edebiyat Kültür Eğitim (TEKE) Dergisi, 11*(1), 522–435.

Çerikan, F. U. (2019). Türk ailesinde sofra adabı, Denizli örneği ve işlevselliği. *Uluslararası Türkçe Edebiyat Kültür Eğitim (TEKE) Dergisi, 8*(1), 481–511.

Çetin, K. (2020). *Medeniyet değerlerimiz mutfak ve yemek kültürü.* İstanbul: Ravza Yayıncılık Matbaacılık.

Eren, S. (2007), *Türk mutfağı ve Haccp sistemi; Mutfak profesyonellerinin Haccp bilgilerinin ölçülmesi,* I. Ulusal Gastronomi Sempozyumu. Antalya, Türkiye.

Ergin, M. (2005). *Dede Korkut Kitabı.* İstanbul: Boğaziçi Yayınları.

Göktaş, Ö. (2011). *Türk Kültüründe Ekmekle İlgili İnanışlar.* (Yayımlanmamış Yüksek Lisans Tezi). Sakarya Üniversitesi Sosyal Bilimler Enstitüsü, Sakarya

Hancıoğlu, H. (2016). Gelenek üzerine. *Littera Turca Journal of Turkish Language and Literature, 2*(1), 1–14.

İSPEM (2014). Kültürel Mirasın Korunması. Retrieved from: https://www.guven liyasam.org, Access Date: 16.03.2024.

Karaman, K. (2010). Ritüellerin toplumsal etkileri. *Süleyman Demirel Üniversitesi Fen-Edebiyat Fakültesi Sosyal Bilimler Dergisi, 2010*(21), 227–236.

Kaya, D. (2008). Halk edebiyatında yemek destanları. *Motif Akademi Halkbilimi Dergisi, 1*(1), 77–90.

Kaya, M. (2015). *Bir şehir kültürü olarak Şanlıurfa sıra gecesi geleneği.* 3. Milletlerarası Şehir Tarihi Yazarları Kongresi, Ankara: Türkiye Yazarlar Birliği Yayınları.

Korukcu, A. (2016). *Peygamberimizin sünnetinde değerler eğitimi örnekleri.* Hasan Hüseyin Bircan, H.H. ve Dilmaç, B. (Editörler). Değerler bilançosu. Konya: Çizgi Kitabevi.

Kültür Portalı (2024). Sözlü anlatımlar. Retrieved from: https://www.kulturport ali.gov.tr/ Access Date: 19.03.2024

Kültür ve Turizm Bakanlığı (2024). Türk Kahvesi Kültürü ve Geleneği. Retrieved: https://yakegm.ktb.gov.tr/TR-345122/turk-kahvesi-kulturu-ve-gelenegi.html, Access Date: 22.04.2024.

Luthans, F., & Doh, J. P. (2012). *International management: culture, strategy, and behavior.* New York: Mcgraw-Hill.

NTV (2023). Su küçüğün sofra büyüğün. Retrieved from: https://www.ntv. com.tr/atasozleri/su-kucugun-soz-sofra-yemek-buyugun-2025,   Access Date: 26.04.2024.

Okuşluk, R. Ş. (2011). Türk halk kültüründe bolluk ve bereketle ilgili inanç ve uygulamalarda eski Türk kültürü izleri. *folklor/edebiyat, 17*(66), 209–228.

Özkaynak, E. (2013). *Masal formellerinin sembolik çözümlemesi.* Yayımlanmamış Yüksek Lisans Tezi. Fırat Üniversitesi Sosyal Bilimler Enstitüsü, Elazığ.

Santich, B. (2004). The study of gastronomy and its relevance to hospitality education and training. *International Journal of Hospitality Management, 23*(1), 15–24.

Sarıca, V., & Özbay, G. (2023). Somut Olmayan Kültürel Miras Kapsamında Fonksiyonel Gıdalar: Mesir Macunu Örneği. *MANAS Sosyal Araştırmalar Dergisi, 12*(2), 665–676.

Sırıklı, İ. K. (2023). *Dinsel İnanışlar ve Beslenme Kültürü.* Mankan ve Saygı Y.B. (Editörler). Yemek, Kültür ve Toplum (Beslenme Antropolojisi). Ankara: Detay Yayıncılık.

Smith, S. L. & Xiao, H. (2008). Culinary tourism supply chains: a preliminary examination. *Journal of travel research*, 46(3), 289–299.

TDK (2024). Türk Dil Kurumu Sözlükleri. Retrieved from: https://sozluk.gov.tr/, Access Date: 15.05.2024.

Tokuz, G. (2002). *Gaziantep ve Kilis mutfak kültürü.* Gaziantep: Gaziantep Üniversitesi Vakfı Yayınları

Toprak, A. (2019). Türk kültüründe misafirperverlik ve sofra açmak/sofra çekmek (Samsun örneği). *Mecmua*, (7), 74–81.

Türker, A., & Çelik, İ. (2012). Somut olmayan kültürel miras unsurlarının turistik ürün olarak geliştirilmesine yönelik alternatif öneriler. *Yeni Fikir Dergisi*, 9, 86–98.

UNESCO (2003). Somut Olmayan Kültürel Mirasın Korunması Sözleşmesi. Retrieved from: https://www.unesco.org.tr/Pages/181/177/ Acces Date: 16.03.2024.

Yanardağ, A. (2017). Örf ve adetler sosyolojisi. *Iğdır Üniversitesi İlahiyat Fakültesi Dergisi*, (9), 39–63.

Yıldız, M. Z., & Aksoy, S. (2018). *Vakıflı köyü yeme-İçme kültürü.* TÜCAUM 30. Yıl Uluslararası Coğrafya Sempozyumu, 734–747.

Zekiyyüddîn, Ş. (2000) *İslâm hukuk ilminin esasları.* Ankara, Türkiye Diyanet Vakfı Yayınları.

Çağlar Bayar[1]

Chapter 24 The Effects of Tablecloth Selection on Consumer Feelings in Gastronomy

Introduction

Gastronomy is not only about the taste of food, but also about the experience of eating as a holistic art (Uçuk & İlhan, 2021). In this context, even relatively small details such as tablecloths can have a big impact on consumer sentiment. The tablecloth plays a critical role in setting the atmosphere of a restaurant and shaping the customer's dining experience (Ölmez, 2023). Elements such as color, texture, pattern, and material can influence the consumer's psychological reactions, and these reactions can shape the overall dining experience positively or negatively. Restaurants pay serious attention to aesthetic details to increase customer satisfaction and attract them back again and again. Strategic choices in tablecloth selection shape consumer perceptions and emotions. For example, a high-quality, elegant tablecloth used in an upscale restaurant can evoke a sense of prestige and care in guests, while comfortable and colorful tablecloths used in a more intimate café create a warm and inviting atmosphere (Akay & Yılmaz, 2021). Enriching gastronomy with aesthetic elements has become an important strategy to deepen the customer experience and make it more memorable. In this context, in addition to tablecloths, table arrangements, lighting, music and paintings hanging on the walls of the restaurant are among the critical factors that determine the atmosphere of restaurants. For example, napkins, cutlery and plates that match the tablecloth visually enrich the dining experience, making the customer's time spent in the restaurant more enjoyable and at the same time, they enjoy the food they have eaten more. Psychological research on how different colors and patterns affect the emotional state and perception of the consumer shows that choosing the right tablecloth can positively affect customer psychology (Bingöl & Özkaya, 2020). In particular, tablecloths in neutral tones give a feeling of calmness and tranquility, while vibrant colors lead to feelings of energy and joy. These elements should be carefully selected and applied according to the target audience and concept of the restaurant. Thus, a simple detail such as a

---

1   Research asistant, Gaziantep Islam Science and Technology University, Faculty of Fine Arts Design and Architecture, caglar.bayar@gibtu.edu.tr

tablecloth plays a strategic role as an integral part of the gastronomic experience and keeps customers connected to the restaurant. In this section, we will examine how tablecloth selection is used as a strategic tool in the gastronomy sector and its impact on consumer sentiment. Whether or not tablecloths are used, their color, patterns and motifs, thickness and thinness, and the type of material used for the cover are discussed and their effects on consumer psychology are emphasized.

Whether the Tablecloth Is Used or Not

Whether or not to use tablecloths in a restaurant or other food service venue is an important decision that greatly affects the overall atmosphere of the venue, the perception of customers and the dining experience (Spence et al., 2013). Venues where tablecloths are not used usually aim to create a more relaxed and intimate environment. Such venues can range from a rustic café to a modern bistro. Tables without tablecloths emphasize the naturalness and intimacy of the space. Especially businesses that want to bring out the natural texture and beauty of wooden tables can avoid using tablecloths. Tables made of quality materials such as wood, marble or metal stand out for their aesthetic value and offer customers a tactile and visual richness (Söderlind, 2011). However, not using tablecloths also offers practical and economic advantages. Regular cleaning and maintenance of tablecloths can be time-consuming and costly. Uncovered tables require less effort in terms of cleaning and maintenance. Quick and easy cleaning of tables can increase the speed of service and reduce staff workload, especially during peak hours. This can positively affect service quality by increasing customer satisfaction. The comfort and naturalness created by an environment without tablecloths can also affect customer behavior (Deveci et al, 2017). Customers who dine in a more relaxed atmosphere rather than a formal and elegant restaurant may feel more comfortable and be more open to social interactions. This can be especially attractive for families, groups of friends and young customers. In an intimate and relaxed environment, customers are more likely to stay longer, which means potentially higher sales for the business. However, not using tablecloths may not always be the best option. Luxury restaurants and hotels often choose to use tablecloths. In such places, tablecloths symbolize elegance and refinement. Tablecloths in white, cream or pastel colors evoke a sense of cleanliness and order, which increases customers perception of quality (Stoopendaal & Bal, 2013). Tablecloths also emphasize food presentation and enhance the aesthetic value of the dishes. A sophisticated table setting gives customers a sense of a carefully crafted experience. Tablecloths also play an important role in terms of hygiene. Especially in luxury and high-standard venues, tablecloths are changed after each customer, which raises hygiene standards. Tablecloths also protect the surface of the table, ensuring its longevity. This is an important advantage, especially for tables made of valuable materials (Gürpınar et al., 2020). Not using a tablecloth can create a negative experience for some customers. In particular, customers with a more formal and traditional dining culture may find a table without a tablecloth inadequate and sloppy. Such customers may consider a clean and neat tablecloth as an indicator of quality service. Therefore, businesses need to analyze their target audience well and make an informed decision about the use of tablecloths.

Color of Tablecloth

The color used for the tablecloth is an important element in determining the atmosphere of the place to eat. Colors significantly affect the overall style of the space and the customer experience (Özdemir, 2020). Each color has its own unique connotations. Due to these associations, the business owner should make choices in accordance with the concept of the business and the expected customer portfolio (Kaya & Epps, 2004). White color on a tablecloth is an indicator of cleanliness, quality and elegance. Therefore, white tablecloths are mostly preferred in luxury and formal places. The feeling of hygiene provided by the white color provides guests with a sense of confidence in the food they eat. In addition, white tablecloths make the color of the dishes served to the guests more prominent, and offer a more elegant appearance in terms of presentation and aesthetics. The white simplicity makes the atmosphere of the restaurant more prosperous and bright for the customers. Black tablecloths are associated with elegance, grace and mystery (Gonzalez, 2023). The sophisticated and elegant air that the color black provides is especially preferred by businesses that want to create a complete and elegant atmosphere, such as nightclubs, luxury restaurants or high fashion venues. Black tablecloths emphasize the prestige of the dining space and offer customers a luxurious experience. In addition, the powerful and impressive look of the black color gives customers an unforgettable experience. Red tablecloths are associated with vitality, passion and energy. Therefore, red tablecloths are often preferred in vibrant and energetic environments such as fast food restaurants or casual dining venues. Red tablecloths offer customers an energetic atmosphere and make the dining experience more enjoyable. The appetizing effect of red color makes customers more interested in the food, which can increase the sales of the business (Casales-Garcia et al., 2020). Blue tablecloths are associated with calmness, serenity and tranquility. Therefore, blue tablecloths are often preferred in relaxing and peaceful environments such as beach restaurants, seaside cafes or spa restaurants Blue color is known as a calming color that puts the person in a calm mood. Blue tablecloths are often encountered in places where seafood is sold as a main course. Beach restaurants are preferred in small and medium food establishments near the sea to reflect the atmosphere and menu of the region (Cifci et al., 2023). Green tablecloths are mostly seen in restaurants that sell organic products in places that encourage healthy eating. Green tablecloths are often preferred in picnic areas, mountain hotels and restaurants, and businesses located in the highlands (Akdeniz & Temeloğlu, 2022). The choice of color is a very vital element for a food business. The psychological connotations that each color evokes in people are different, and business owners have to consider them.

Patterns and Motifs Used in Tablecloths

The patterns and motifs on the tablecloths affect the tastes of the consumers and enable them to form a certain judgment about the restaurant. A number of patterns are in harmony with the concept of the restaurant and strengthen the pleasure experienced by the consumer (Kencana & Rahmanita, 2024). The flower motif is frequently used in tablecloths because they look aesthetically pleasing and are associated with romance by people. Such motifs; roses, tulips, daisies, etc. add a lively atmosphere to the business, and in some cases, create authentic atmospheres for businesses that offer romantic dinners (Emodi, 2022). Covers using geometric patterns are used by smaller and smaller venues. It is used in picnic areas, family businesses and beach restaurants to add a relaxed and calm atmosphere. Squares, circles, rectangles, and symmetrical lines are among the most commonly used (Trautmann, 2021). In addition to these, the use of traditional motifs can also increase consumer preferences according to the concept of the restaurant business. In a restaurant with an Asian cuisine concept, the use of texts or letters written in the alphabets of those regions on the tablecloths, and the inclusion of animal or plant motifs that evoke that region are highly appreciated by the consumer and enable them to connect more with the plate they come across. This is also true for spaces that conceptualize more specific places. The use of motifs reminiscent of that specific place on the tablecloths of businesses located in cities and neighborhoods that stand out with a certain feature or in a different place and determines its concept there causes positive feedback for the business (Wu et al., 2022). To explain with an example for a better understanding, it is not absurd for a café or restaurant in Paris to include Eiffel tower motifs on its tablecloths in order to attract local and foreign tourists in the region where it is located. Or, for a business that does not exist in Italy but sells in the concept of Italian cuisine, it is quite normal for the Leaning Tower of Pisa to be on the tablecloths. These tactics and strategies, which seem small, enable the customers who come to the business to establish a bond with the restaurant and the food eaten, consciously or unconsciously (Gaver et al., 2006). Tablecloths should also not contradict the decoration of the space. If there is an interior design of the business, the decorations used, the paintings, the carpets should be in harmony and harmony. Contradictory situations that evoke contradictions in the customer cause dissatisfaction in the consumer (Gabaccia & Pilcher, 2011). In food establishments that appeal to children, they prefer appropriate motifs on tablecloths that can attract the attention of children and make it easier for their families to feed their children. Businesses that include superheroes, cartoon characters, cute animals and motifs that can attract the attention of their children have come a long way in gaining customers (Eren, 2018). Simple lines, dots, zigzags and similar patterns that do not have a direct meaning but are used on tablecloths are used to create a modern impression in city restaurants. These shapes, which do not attract attention at first glance but draw stylish and harmonious lines instead of a plain flat image, are used in restaurants and other food establishments in big cities (Grömer, 2018).

Thickness and Thinness of the Tablecloth

It may create hesitations about whether there is a connection between the thick or thin tablecloth and the consumer's relationship with the food. However, recent studies show that the thickness or thinness of the tablecloth in the selection of tablecloths in restaurants significantly affects the consumer food relationship (Spence, 2017). The thick tablecloth creates the image of quality in the minds of the customers who come to the business. Thin fabrics are mostly preferred by restaurants that are cheaper and weaker in terms of prestige. Considering the cost of the thickness of the fabric, business owners should make appropriate decisions by considering their target customer portfolio and general concepts (Doğan, 2023). In addition, the thick tablecloth affects the sound of the products being placed on the table while serving, and this sound begins to affect the thoughts of the guest about the food before they have even tasted it. Since the sound of placing materials such as plates, forks or knives on thick tablecloths is a fuller sound, this creates a positive impression on the customer (Tonus & Kaynar, 2015). The fact that thick tablecloths make less noise when materials are placed on them is a priority for luxury and quality restaurants. Because these places have a quieter atmosphere and lower decibel levels. Business owners do not want their guests to be exposed to unnecessary sound pollution. They aim to better enjoy their meals and improve their experience in a quiet environment (Soysaldı, 2020). Although thin tablecloths are not very suitable for such luxury places, they are a very suitable choice for places with smaller budgets, middle and low-income customers. Cafes and bistros often prefer tablecloths that are as thin as possible. The reason for this is to offer a more intimate environment to its guests. For customers who want to spend time comfortably, they aim to create a calm environment where they can come together with their family and friends and spend time peacefully (Çağlayan, 2018). While thin tablecloths create a more comfortable and intimate environment, they are also advantageous in terms of storage and cleaning. They take up less space and are practical to use. On the other hand, thin tablecloths are less effective in protecting the surface of the table. They increase the risk of stains and damage to the table. The business owner aims to make the right decision by considering his budget, concept and customer target audience (Ünlü et al., 2022).

Material Used for Tablecloth

The choice of material for tablecloths significantly affects the general atmosphere of the restaurant, its customer base, its concept and general psychological approaches to the guest. In the previous topic, we touched on how the thinness and thickness of the cover have an effect. In direct proportion to this, of course, the type of material chosen is also a vital issue (Force, 2023). Fabric tablecloths are among the most preferred. Although the type and quality of the fabric differs from business to business, the first choice that comes to mind for tablecloths is fabric covers. In fact, when many people think of covers, fabric covers come to mind. Since we have mentioned the quality of the fabric and its varying thinness and thickness in the previous section, we will not include it here. Here, tactile sensations that change with the type of fabric, aesthetic elements, and impressions of the consumer will be emphasized. Food businesses, which we can define as luxurious, upper segment, prefer cotton, soft, eye-smooth covers. Tablecloths are often the first stage where businesses can make physical contact with their guests. It has been observed that when the guests feel the texture of the soft, smooth, quality fabric when they put their hands on the table, even without realizing it, there are positive changes in their mood (Ulasewicz & Baugh, 2017). Of course, the impressions and feelings evoked by tablecloths with harder, rougher protrusions and serrated surfaces are in different directions. This does not mean that the consumer is getting a bad impression of the business. It varies according to the structure of the business and what they expect from their customers. If the restaurant does not want to host its customers at their tables for a long time, if it wants a quick turnover, it can choose this type of cover. Large food companies that are sensitive to this issue often do not include tablecloths in their businesses, even if they do, they do not want their customers to be very comfortable, to relax and spend long hours there, and they make choices accordingly. They are not only limited to covers, but they do not want even the chairs of the guests to be very comfortable, they prefer chairs that are hard and uncomfortable and cannot be spent on them for a long time (Ceven & Gürarda, 2017). In addition to cotton fabrics, polyester fabrics are also frequently encountered in amsa covers. Although polyester is not a very preferred choice in garment making due to some chemicals in its content, it is used abundantly in tablecloths. Polyester fabric stands out here with its strength and durability (Liu at al, 2019). The fact that it can be used for long periods of time without wearing out too much brings financial profit for the business. Considering its features such as not being at a very uncomfortable level in terms of comfort and feel, being affordable and durable, polyester becomes an important option for serious business owners. Cotton fabrics may also have disadvantages in some cases due to the fact that they can wrinkle easily, require regular ironing and some stains cannot be cleaned completely. However, the resistance of polyester fabric to stains is more advantageous in a number of cases because it does not wrinkle easily (Murdoch, 2021).

Results

Under the heading of gastronomy, we focused on the feelings of tablecloths on consumers in the food and beverage sector. We have shown that not only good food and good presentation are not enough, but there are also side factors that need extra attention, which seem small but have a big impact when they come together. Among these, we tried to deal with the tablecloths and give as much concise information as possible. We explained what the use of tablecloths can change and affect from business to business. We explained what the color of the selected cover evokes and which colors are more suitable for which businesses. We talked about what colors evoke, what they symbolize, and what they activate in human psychology. In addition to the color, we discussed how the patterns and motifs on the cover will contribute, what they can and cannot affect. We mentioned that with a motif on the tablecloth of the business, it can lead to serious meaningful changes in the concept of the business. We have included many detailed studies, from the thickness of the cover to its thinness, and we have taken it as a subject. We explained how the sounds of plates, forks, spoons and knives due to the thinness of the thickness change the feelings of the customers.

We talked about how the material chosen for the cover can benefit the reputation and goals of the business. We talked about the different reasons why cotton tablecloths and polyester tablecloths are selected and not selected for businesses. When we bring all these together, tablecloths are a factor that appeals to all the sensory organs of the consumer and has important effects on the enjoyment of the food eaten. Direct visual, auditory and tactile effects can be observed. Although the consumer is not aware of the effects of this situation on food and beverage, even the smallest detail is of great importance for businesses and companies. This study we have done is a pioneer in the literature in terms of directing to a single title under the field of gastronomy. Although the effects of tablecloths on gastronomy are mentioned in a number of studies, it has been determined that there is no study focusing directly on this subject. I anticipate that these and other inconspicuous issues will be discussed and researched in more detail in the future, and I believe that this study will make important contributions to this process.

References

Akay, E., Yılmaz, İ., & Er, A. (2021). Nörogastronomi. Aydın Gastronomy, 5(2), 143–156.

Akdeniz, D., & Temeloglu, E. (2022). How Color-Harmony on a Food Plate Affects Consumers' Perceptions? International Journal of Gastronomy Research, 1(1), 16–25.

Bingöl, M. P., & Özkaya, F. (2020). Gastronomi ve mutfak sanatları alanında temel sanat eğitimi uygulamaları. İnönü Üniversitesi Kültür ve Sanat Dergisi, 6(1), 175–192.

Casales-Garcia, V., Museros, L., Sanz, I., Falomir, Z., & Gonzalez-Abril, L. (2020). Extracting feeling from food colour. In Advances in Tourism, Technology and Smart Systems: Proceedings of ICOTTS 2019 (pp. 15–24). Springer Singapore From HYPERLINK "https://link.springer.com/chapter/10.1007/978-981-15-2024-2_2%20%20Accessed%20on%2026.10.2024" https://link.springer.com/chapter/10.1007/978-981-15-2024-2_2 Accessed on 26.10.2024.

Ceven, E. K., & Gürarda, A. (2017). An investigation of performance properties of curtain fabrics produced with different types of polyester yarns. Textile and Apparel, 27(2), 131–138.

Cifci, H., Gok, I., Atsiz, O., & Cifci, I. (2023). Insights into the art of plating in gastronomy: A content analysis of master chefs' perspectives. Journal of Culinary Science & Technology, 21(2), 238–263.

Çağlayan, A. F. (2018). Resim sanatında plastik öge olarak doku ve doku-anlam ilişkisi (Master's thesis, Güzel Sanatlar Enstitüsü).

Deveci, B., Deveci, B., & Avcıkurt, C. 2017). Yeme davranışı: Gastronomi ve mutfak sanatları öğrencileri üzerine bir araştırma. Journal of Tourism & Gastronomy Studies, 5(3), 118–134. https://dspace.balikesir.edu.tr/xmlui/handle/20.500.12462/3639 Accessed on 26.10.2024

Dolanbay Doğan, S. (2023). Kişisel Özelliklerin Dokunsal Konfor Algısına Etkisi ve Kumaş Tercihinin Tahminlenmesi Üzerine Model Önerileri.

Emodi-Nnoruka, M., Chudi-Duru, C., & Okpalauba, V. (2022). Texture, Repeat Pattern System as Formal Elements of Design. Books/feschschrıfts. https://nigerianjournalsonline.com/index.php/Feschschrifts/article/view/3118 Accessed on 26.10.2024

Eren, S. (2018). Ekolojik restoranlar ve perma-kültür uygulamaları: Ekbiçyeiç restoranı üzerine bir araştırma. Güncel Turizm Araştırmaları Dergisi, 2(Ek1), 534–552.

Gabaccia, D. R., & Pilcher, J. M. (2011). "Chili Queens" and Checkered Tablecloths: Public Dining Cultures of Italians in New York City and Mexicans in San Antonio, Texas, 1870s–1940s. Radical History Review, 2011(110), 109–126.

Gaver, W., Bowers, J., Boucher, A., Law, A., Pennington, S., & Villar, N. (2006, June). The history tablecloth: illuminating domestic activity. In Proceedings of the 6th conference on Designing Interactive systems (pp. 199–208).

Gonzalez-abrıl, L. (2023, November). Sentiment Analysis of Gastronomic Posts from Colour Palettes and Narrative Content. In Artificial Intelligence Research and Development: Proceedings of the 25th International Conference of the Catalan Association for Artificial Intelligence (Vol. 375, p. 311). IOS Press.

Grömer, K. (2018). Textiles: pattern, structure, texture, and decoration (pp. 247–263). Cambridge.

Gürpınar, S., Ağan, C., & Özer, Ç. (2020). Gastronomi Ve Mutfak Sanatlari Öğrencilerinin El Hijyen Uygulamalari: İstinye Üniversitesi Örneği. Turizm Ekonomi ve İşletme Araştırmaları Dergisi, 2(1), 5–17.

Kaya, N., & Epps, H. H. (2004). Relationship between color and emotion: A study of college students. College student journal, 38(3), 396–405.

Kencana, M., & Rahmanita, N. (2024, March). Crochet Fashion Innovation for Improving the Creative Industry and Developing Pariaman Tourism, in West Sumatra, Indonesia. In Talenta Conference Series: Local Wisdom, Social, and Arts (LWSA) (Vol. 7, No. 2, pp. 251–256).

La Force, T. (2023). A Tablecloth as Source Material. International New York Times, NA-NA.

Liu, J., Petit, E., Brit, A. C., & Giboreau, A. (2019). The impact of tablecloth on consumers' food perception in real-life eating situation. Food quality and preference, 71, 168–171.

Murdoch, T. (2021). "A Performance for the Service of a Table": New Light on Eighteenth-Century Dining. Getty Research Journal, 14(1), 181–190.

Ölmez, M. (2023). Gastronomik sunum teknikleri. Gastronomi ve Mutfak Sanatları Temel Kavramlar ve Güncel Konular, 239.

Özdemir, B. (2020). Gastronomi Akimlarinda Sağlikli Mor Yiyecekler. GSI Journals Serie B: Advancements in Business and Economics, 3(1), 16–30.

Soysaldı, A. (2020). Gönen iğne oyaları ve oya pazarı. Folklor Akademi Dergisi, 3(4), 159–172.

Söderlind, P. U. (2011). The Gastronomic man and Georgia s food culture. Review of Applied Socio-Economic Research, 1(1), 97–122.

Spence, C. (2017). Gastrophysics: The new science of eating. Penguin UK.

Spence, C., Hobkinson, C., Gallace, A., & Fiszman, B. P. (2013). A touch of gastronomy. Flavour, 2, 1–15.

Stoopendaal, A., & Bal, R. (2013). Conferences, tablecloths and cupboards: How to understand the situatedness of quality improvements in long-term care. Social Science & Medicine, 78, 78–85.

Tonus, e., & Kaynar, h. (2015). Zonguldak Ereğlisi elpek bezi dokumacılığı'nın gelişiminde yeni tasarımların önemi ve örnek çalışmalar. Motif Akademi Halkbilimi Dergisi, 8(15), 31–60.

Trautmann, L. (2021). Emotions evoked by geometric patterns. J, 4(3), 376–393 From https://www.mdpi.com/2571-8800/4/3/29 Accessed on 26.10.2024.

Uçuk, C., & İlhan, İ. (2021). Gastronomi perspektifinden estetik ve yemek. Aydın Gastronomy, 5(1), 35–44.

Ünlü, H., Kıvanç, M. İ., & Apak, Ö. C. (2022). Yiyecek içecek işletmelerinde müşterilerin temizlik algısı: bayburt ili örneği. Safran Kültür ve Turizm Araştırmaları Dergisi, 5(3), 402–417.

Wu, Y., & Kyungsun, K. (2022). Decorative Image and Cultural Implication of Embroidery in Jinnan (Southern Shanxi). Fibres & Textiles in Eastern Europe, 30(2), 112–122.

Özge Adan Gök[1] and Ceren Miral Çavdirli[2]

Chapter 25 Storytelling as a Marketing Tool in Gastronomy Tourism

Introduction

For centuries, people have told each other stories about the places they came from, the places they lived and the places they visited. Because people establish a bond with the place as a result of their experiences (Bassano et al., 2019: 11). Storytelling is an important part of communication (Bury, 2020). Storytelling can be defined as sharing knowledge, experience or traditions in a more understandable, meaningful and memorable narrative format (Kim et al., 2020:681). The role of storytelling is to stimulate desire, stimulate imagination, and create empathy. Tourism storytelling means making the tourists' potential and/or real experience through narration and by this way activating their desires (Bassano et al., 2019: 18). According to Manthiou et al. (2017), positive emotions have a positive effect on storytelling, and negative emotions have a negative effect on storytelling. Research results also found that storytelling had a positive impact on repurchase intention (p. 1081). Research shows that storytelling can be used in various areas. For example, according to the research conducted by Bury (2020), it shows that the introduction of storytelling has achieved this, as students think that storytelling helps them improve their English skills. Thus, it can be said that using storytelling as an education method is also beneficial (p. 147).

Digital Storytelling

Digital storytelling can be defined as a new multimedia format that reveals the creativity of ordinary people by putting a 2–5minute film based on personal stories on digital platforms (Qiongli, 2006). Through modern digital media, share their experiences of the destinations they love. Shared feelings and stories can stimulate interest in these places. Thus, it can motivate tourists (and even local residents) to visit the region (Bassano et al., 2019: 11). Storytelling is a unique

---

1 Ph.D., Dokuz Eylul University, School of Applied Sciences, Department of Tourism Management, ozge.adan@deu.edu.tr
2 Ph.D., Dokuz Eylul University, Faculty of Business, Department of Tourism Management, ceren.miral@deu.edu.tr

phenomenon to human society. The power of storytelling has not diminished for thousands of years. Nowadays, with the new media age, storytelling has become stronger with digital multimedia tools (Qiongli, 2006: 383).

Narratives on the digital platform can be a strategic tool for tourism sector to provide products that address the environmental interests of tourists and thus contribute to greater sustainability in the sector (Paiva et al, 2023: 14439). For instance, tourist selfies provide an opportunity to understand tourists' selfie storytelling by recognizing what interests tourists have about destinations during their holidays (Elshaer et al., 2022:15). In this regard, the research conducted by Fusté-Forné, F. (2022) in Greenland towns shows that people and experiences in digital storytelling are limited. Digital posts show individuals performing outdoor activities such as cycling, canoeing or trekking. Additionally, it seems that posts about animals and gastronomy are very limited. Regarding gastronomy, a single post displaying cheering cups was observed. It demonstrated the opportunity to communicate 'food' as a cultural and natural element within the Greenland tourist experience (p. 1700). The concept of tourists' selfie storytelling actually describes tourists'concerns about taking selfies (Elshaer et al., 2022:3). Considered from this perspective, digital storytelling can be an important tool in analyzing consumers.

The benefit of digital storytelling is not only about understanding tourist behavior and creating marketing strategies for them. It is also important to evaluate the destination from the perspective of the local people who are its stakeholders. According to Tosun et al. (2024), digital storytelling components positively affect residents' place attachment (p. 15). Digital storytelling can contribute to local people's loyalty to the destination, which can increase residents' value creation behavior in tourism. Local managers can include stories that appeal to local people in their marketing efforts to support local people's participation (Petek et al., 2024:16). In addition, the way digital storytelling is done can also increase the impact of storytelling. According to the study of Tosun et al. (2024), it was found that a chatbot's speaking style (emotional and neutral) is related to the elements of digital storytelling (p. 15). Storytelling styles and the way they are told on digital platforms can change the perceptions of tourists. Storytelling should also be carefully selected on digital platforms and arranged in a way that allows tourists to perceive it positively.

Storytelling in Tourism

Place storytelling is a concept that allows local stakeholders to identify themselves and tell their personal testimonies about the destinations which they like

(Bassano et al., 2019: 15). Place has geographical, spatial, human and social and psychological dimensions (Cheng-Yi Luo et al, 2023: 730). Place storytelling is considered within the scope of new communication methods. It is destination's ability to reach its target market by telling its stories which is related to its ability to gain competitive advantage (Bassano et al., 2019: 11). If tourists discover the unique meaning and value of a place they will intend to revisit the destination. They will also recommend this place to the other people (Cheng-Yi Luo, 2023: 732). Considered from this perspective, the concept of place story telling is an important issue for touristic places.

The concept of storytelling in tourism communication serves as a component that includes emotional and symbolic elements (Kim et al., 2020: 679). Narrative storytelling, on the other hand, is a type of tourism in which visitors become active participants of the narrative rather than passive observers, taking on roles in the story and interacting with the characters and their environment. In this way, they can shape the story and, as a result, engage in deeper interaction and emotional connection with the destination or theme. Examples of narrative storytelling experiences include the Ghost Tour at the Edinburgh Dungeon, Colonial Williamsburg in Virginia and the Underground Railroad immersive experience at the National can be given (Whalen and Dunlap, 2024: 4).

Stories about tourism marketing is between destination marketing organizations, the tourism industry, and tourists. Stories are used to create and manage tourist experiences (Moscardo, 2020: 2). In other words, storytelling is used as a tool to increase the participation of visitors in destinations and provide an unforgettable experience (Campos, 2023: 1). It is important to ensure customer overall satisfaction to improve destination experiences (Guleria, 2024: 294). Moreover, tourists can convey the places they experience to their immediate surroundings. Elshaer et al. (2022) revealed that it is preferred to take photographs especially about the society, the destination-specific social environment, cultural heritage and leisure activities. This finding proves that tourist selfie storytelling is related to the characteristics of these local destinations and shows that tourists document all the places, events and interactions they experience (p. 13).

In tourism so many research has been conducted in various areas regarding storytelling. These studies focus on tourist destinations (Guleria, 2024; Jo et al., 2022), tourist businesses (Floricic and Jurica, 2023; Whalen and Dunlap, 2024), tourists (Guleria and Adil, 2024; Elshaer et al., 2022) and various tourism types (Kim et al., 2020; Campos et al., 2023). Studies have shown that storytelling consists of various dimensions. Moscardo (2002) made a conceptual framework for stories and storytelling in tourism. Three main types of the framework are the pre-experience, emerging experience and post-experience of the story. There are

elements under these types. Three key cross-cutting elements have been identified for each of these story types. At the heart of pre-experience stories are the
stories that attract the attention of tourists and/or are sought by tourists (p. 2).

In the researches which are conducted on storytelling has also found that storytelling consists of various dimensions. For instance, in the study conducted by
Cheng-Yi Luo (2023), it was found that storytelling consists of four dimensions
(p. 733). The results of the empirical study by Kim et al. (2020) revealed five
storytelling features for medical tourism. These are authenticity and educability for story features and enjoyability, descriptiveness, and emotionality features
are for telling (Kim et al., 2020:689). In the study of (Jo et al, 2022), the relationship between five dimensions of tourism storytelling, interestingness, educability, sensibility, descriptiveness, uniqueness, and brand value and lovemarks
were examined. According to the research results, tourism storytelling in interestingness, educability and uniqueness dimensions has a significant influence
on brand value. Additionally, tourism storytelling in interestingness, sensibility,
descriptiveness dimensions have a significant influence on lovemarks.

It is important to evaluate storytelling in tourism in terms of tourists' perceptions and experiences. Because storytelling should allow tourists to perceive the
destination or tourist products in a different and unique way. When evaluated
from this perspective, the impact of storytelling on the minds of tourists and the
factors affecting this should be examined in detail. Campos et al. (2023) conducted research on tourists on this subject. When the people who participated
in the research talked about storytelling, they mostly talked about imagination.
Thus, this experience allowed participants to think about the past and become
more interested in the history shared by the tour guide (p. 12). Storytelling
affects the heritage experience for tourists in three ways. These can be listed as
emotional engagement, imagination and memorability. Stories underpin the
connections visitors make with museum exhibits or heritage sites. It has been
revealed that emotional engagement through storytelling can be the result of
human empathy or personal connections. In other words, emotional engagement can occur by establishing connections with one's own life, identity or culture (Campos, 2023:11).

When storytelling in tourism is examined in terms of touristic supply, it can
be considered as a marketing tool that will create a competitive advantage for
both touristic businesses and destinations. For instance, storytelling strategies
Airbnb hosts use online aren't just about narrative. These stories also create originality. This authenticity is intricately linked to the host's socio-economic identity, with elements such as usernames, profile photos, age, gender, location, and
occupation (Lu and Wang, 2024: 13). Floricic and Jurica (2023) examined some

wine hotels. In the case study used in the research, themed rooms, wine tasting, tours, wine spa treatments and innovative experiences are implemented in the wine hotel. According to the results of the research, it is stated that unique wine tourism themed hotels can gain a competitive advantage in unique destinations where wine culture stands out with organizations such as tourism animation, storytelling and gamification (p. 3001).

Storytelling in Gastronomy

In recent years, the number of tourists traveling with the motivation of eating and drinking has been increasing around the world. Individuals travel to see and taste both the local cuisines of the places they live in and the cuisines of different cultures. Travels made for this purpose are called gastronomy tourism. In literature gastronomy tourism is defined as 'a type of tourism activity which is characterized by the visitor's experience linked with food and related products and activities while travelling' (UNWTO, 2024). Gastronomy tourism is a tourism activity characterized by visitors' experience of food-related products and activities while traveling (İstanbul İl Kültür ve Turizm Müdürlüğü, 2024). Gastronomy tourism includes food and beverage festivals, restaurant visits, local markets and cooking courses, observing its production and preparation process (Hall and Mitchell, 2005). Moreover, gastronomy tourism supports protecting culture by preserving the unique texture of food and beverages belonging to a region and bringing them to the present day (Albayrak, 2013: 248). It also contributes to the authenticity of the destination. The origins of gastronomy tourism lie in agriculture, culture and tourism. These three elements provide the opportunity to market and position gastronomy tourism as a regional attraction and experience (Birdir ve Akgöl, 2015; 58). Local food and beverages, which are an important element of attraction for destinations to be perceived as different from their competitors, add value to the regions where they are located (Haven-Tang and Jones, 2006: 71).

Gastronomy tourism is a tool for the promoting the regional tourism and competitive target marketing (Hall et al., 2003). Ethnic foods mean foods originating from the beliefs and beliefs of ethnic people who have lived in the region for a long time. Local cuisine refers to foods created by local people using locally sourced agricultural products, whose taste has become characteristic of the local people and creates a cultural continuity (Jongsuksomsakul, 2024:6). With unique resources gastronomy tourism can be used as a marketing tool for local markets. According to Guzman and Canizares (2011), local dishes ensure the satisfaction of tourists and gastronomy creates motivation to travel (p. 63–72).

It will be beneficial for tourism destinations to make an effort to reveal their gastronomic values and to use these values in the promotion and marketing of the destination in order to gain a competitive advantage (Yaşar and Tekeler, 2023; 823). For instance, according to the research conducted by Guleria (2024), customer-based destination brand equity has a significant impact on tourists' storytelling intentions. The research also confirms that customer-based brand equity contributes to increased tourists' intention to share stories both online and offline. (p. 292–293). Fusté-Forné, F. (2020) conducted research on the current and potential relationship between tourism and the cheese-making processes of agricultural food producers in the Roncal region in northern Spain. According to the results of the research, the land and historical, cultural and natural production and distribution processes related to cheese making in rural and mountainous regions are of critical importance. In addition, rural lifestyle, which includes tangible and intangible elements, and the origin and story content of the cheese and its transfer to visitors and tourists are other critical issues in tourism. In the research, which investigates the use of food stories by Kardeş and Sarıışık (2021) in gastronomy marketing, is a literature review study on the culinary culture of the first Turkish Civilizations established in Anatolia, foods developed and preserved since the nomadic period, Ottoman culinary culture, culinary culture of the Republican Period, ethnic diversity and cuisine, which was enriched thanks to relations with neighboring countries, were examined. At the end of the research, it was concluded that gastronomic products/services enriched with stories will increase cultural quality and awareness and will have a positive impact on the country's economy (p. 739). In the research of Michael and Fusté-Forné, F. (2022), Al Arab, Emirates Palace, St. It analyzes how luxury hotels such as St. Regis Saadiyat Island and Atlantis support gastronomy by determining the visual characteristics of social media posts. According to the results, the essential drivers of luxury gastronomy are about the discovery of cultures, experiences in the hotel environment, and local peoples lifestyle that is seen as authentic. In general, social media platforms that use storytelling techniques allow the narrative to identify foods that suit visitors' tastes and encourage the active participation of young people in local areas (Jongsuksomsakul, 2024:12).

Results

Gastronomy tourism can be defined as a tourism type that includes food-related activities in destinations. As it is known, destination attractions differ according to the characteristics of the destinations. The uniqueness of these features and the correct transfer of their features to tourists are also important in terms of destination marketing. In this context, it is important to convey stories about touristic products to tourists. Because stories contain the originality, uniqueness and authenticity of products or places and are conveyed to people in a way that attracts their attention. When the products in question are gastronomic values, their transfer through storytelling provides a unique experience for tourists. Storytelling should be developed using various material and spiritual resources such as monuments, statues, myths, legends, old sayings, historical events found in the destination that create the uniqueness of the destination (Jo and Kim, 2022: 12). Destination marketing experts can develop a sense of loyalty through storytelling (Tosun et al., 2024: 16). In addition, the content of the stories changes as they are passed on to others, making them dynamic. For this reason, local government should try to strategically influence the communication within the narrative structure of the stories and constantly monitor the development of their content (Bassano et al., 2019: 16). Storytelling also affects the brand value of destinations. Tourists may perceive the brand value of a tourist destination different depending on the storytelling. Thus if each tourist destination creates its own unique storytelling and is well planned to arouse interest and include educational content, its brand value will increase (Jo and Kim, 2022:12). Storytelling is also conveyed digitally to tourists. Within the scope of gastronomy tourism, food-related stories can also be conveyed to tourists digitally. According to Michael and Fuste-Forne (2022), the selected digital story can depict moments prepared through special meals in a place that brings guests together with hedonic and unique experiences (p. 835). More tourists can be reached through food storytelling on digital platforms. This can have an increasing effect on awareness of both local dishes and the destination. Stories and digital storytelling through artificial intelligence can be used effectively in destination marketing for domestic markets. Thus, tourism managers can increase the awareness of local residents and fill the knowledge gaps regarding the history and legends about the destination. These contents can be used as a good marketing tool to differentiate the destination in destination marketing. Using stories about local dishes, which will be evaluated within the scope of gastronomy, on digital platforms, social media accounts and destination web pages will improve the brand image of the destination and reveal its uniqueness.

References

Albayrak, A. (2013) Alternatif Turizm. Detay Yayıncılık: Ankara.

Bassano, C., Barile, S., Piciocchi, P., Spohrer, J. C., Iandolo, F., & Fisk, R. (2019). Storytelling about places: Tourism marketing in the digital age. Cities, 87, 10–20.

Birdir, K. and Akgül, Y. (2015). Gastronomi Turizmi ve Türkiye'yi Ziyaret Eden Yabancı Turistlerin Gastronomi Deneyimlerinin Değerlendirilmesi. İşletme ve İktisat Çalışmaları Dergisi, 3(2), 57–68.

Bury, J. (2020). Introducing storytelling into tourism and hospitality courses: students' perceptions. Journal of Teaching in Travel & Tourism, 20(2), 135–155.

Campos, A. C., Guerreiro, M. M., and Beevor, M. C. (2023). Storytelling in heritage tourism: an exploration of co-creative experiences from a tourist perspective. Museum Management and Curatorship, 1–26.

Cheng-Yi Luo, Chin-Hsun (Ken) Tsai, Ching-Hui (Joan) Su and Ming-Hsiang Chen (2023) From stage to a sense of place: the power of tourism performing arts storytelling for sustainable tourism growth, Journal of Travel & Tourism Marketing, 40:8, 728–743, DOI: 10.1080/10548408.2023.2293012

Elshaer, A., Huang, R., and Marzouk, A. (2022). Tourists' selfies storytelling: Preferences, intentions, and concerns for practise in the tourism and hospitality industry. Journal of Vacation Marketing, 13567667221145712.

Floricic, T. and Jurica, K. (2023). Wine Hotels-Intangible Heritage, Storytelling and Co-Creation in Specific Tourism Offer. Heritage, 6(3), 2990–3004.

Fusté-Forné, F. (2020). Developing cheese tourism: A local-based perspective from Valle de Roncal (Navarra, Spain). Journal of Ethnic Foods, 7(1), 26.

Fusté-Forné, F. (2022). The portrayal of Greenland: a visual analysis of its digital storytelling. Current Issues in Tourism, 25(11), 1696–1701.

Guleria, A., Joshi, R., and Adil, M. (2024). Impact of memorable tourism experiences on tourists' storytelling intentions: an empirical investigation. International Journal of Tourism Cities. 10 (1), 280–301.

Guzman, T. L. and Canizares, S. S. (2011), Gastronomy, Tourism and Destination Differentiation: A Case Study in Spain, Review of Economics & Finance, 2 (1), ss. 63–72.

Hall, C.M., Sharples, L., Mitchell, R., Macionis, N., Cambourne, B. (eds.) (2003). Food Tourism Around the World. Boston: Butterworth-Heinemann.

Hall, M., Mitchell, R. (2005), Gastronomic tourism: comparing food and wine tourism experiences, In M. Novelli (Editor), Niche Tourism,Contemporary Issues, Trendsand Cases, ss. 89–100 .

Haven-Tang, C. and Jones, E. (2006). Using Local Food and Drink to Differentiate Tourism Destinations Through a Sense of Place: A Story From Wales-Dining at Monmouthshire's Great Table, Journal of Culinary Science & Technology, 4(4), 69–86.

İstanbul İl Kültür ve Turizm Müdürlüğü (2024). Gastronomi Turizmi. Access Date: 26.05.2024:https://istanbul.ktb.gov.tr/TR-276239/gastronomiturizmi. html#:~:text=Gastronomi%20turizmi%2C%20ziyaretçilerin%20seyahat%20 ederken,karakterize%20edilen%20bir%20turizm%20faaliyetidir.

Jo, M., Cha, J., and Kim, J. (2022). The effects of tourism storytelling on tourism destination brand value, lovemarks and relationship strength in South Korea. Sustainability, 14(24), 16495.

Jongsuksomsakul, P. (2024). Culinary Storytelling About the Local Cuisine of Phitsanulok, Thailand. SAGE Open, 14(1), 21582440241233451.

Kardeş Çolakoğlu, N., and Sarışık, M. (2021). Yerel Gastronomi Ürünlerine Ait Hikâyelerin Destinasyon Pazarlamasında Kullanılmasına İlişkin Bir Değerlendirme. Afyon Kocatepe University Journal Of Social Sciences, 23(2).

Kim, S. H., Song, M. K., and Shim, C. (2020). Storytelling by medical tourism agents and its effect on trust and behavioral intention. Journal of Travel & Tourism Marketing, 37(6), 679–694.

Lu, Y. and Wang, Y. C. (2024). Online Hosts' Storytelling Strategies: A Narrative Analysis of Mindfulness-Themed Airbnb Online Experiences. Journal of Travel Research, 00472875241237259.

Manthiou, A., Kang, J. and Sean Hyun, S. (2017) An integration of cognitive appraisal theory and script theory in the luxury cruise sector: the bridging role of recollection and storytelling, Journal of Travel & Tourism Marketing, 34:8, 1071–1088, DOI: 10.1080/10548408.2016.1277575

Michael, N. and Fusté-Forné, F. (2022). Marketing of luxurious gastronomic experiences on social media: The visual storytelling of luxury hotels. International Journal of Tourism Research, 24(6), 827–838.

Moscardo, G. (2020). Stories and design in tourism. Annals of tourism research, 83, 102950.

Paiva, D., Carvalho, L., Brito-Henriques, E., Sousa, A. M., Soares, A. L., and Azambuja, S. T. (2023). Digital storytelling and hopeful last chance tourism experiences. Tourism Geographies, 25(5), 1428–1444.

Petek Tosun, Abdullah Uslu & Emrullah Erul (2024): Connecting through chatbots: residents' insights on digital storytelling, place attachment, and value co creation, Current Issues in Tourism, DOI: 10.1080/13683500.2024.2316857

Qiongli, W. (2006). Commercialization of digital storytelling: An integrated approach for cultural tourism, the Beijing Olympics and wireless VAS. International Journal of Cultural Studies, 9(3), 383–394.

Tosun, P. Uslu, A. and Erul, E (2024): Connecting through chatbots: residents' insights on digital storytelling, place attachment, and value cocreation, Current Issues in Tourism, DOI: 10.1080/13683500.2024.2316857

UNWTO (2024) Gastronomy and Wine Tourism. Access Date: 27.05.2024: https://www.unwto.org/gastronomy-wine-tourism#:~:text=The%20Committee%20on%20Tourism%20and,products%20and%20activities%20while%20travelling.

Whalen, E. A., & Dunlap, R. (2024). Hotel innovation and novelty: a case study of Disney's Star Wars Galactic Starcruiser. Current Issues in Tourism, 1–14.

Yasar, I., Tekeler, M. C. (2023). Destinasyon Pazarlama Aracı Olarak Gastronomi Turizmi: Bir Literatür İncelemesi. Uluslararası Anadolu Sosyal Bilimler Dergisi, 7(3), 812–826. https://doi.org/10.47525/ulasbid.1327953

Eda Güneş[1] and Doğukan Bayesen[2]

Chapter 26 Introduction to Pastry Making: History, Classification, Education, and Pastry Making Practices

François Vatel/*born in 1631 and died in 1671*
"Inventor of whipped cream"

Introduction

The pastry sector has developed as a dynamic field reflecting the cultural, economic, and technological traces of societies from past to present. Historically, the origins of pastry making date back to the processing of the first grain products and their inclusion in the production process according to the baking techniques of ancient civilizations. However, it should not be forgotten that the development of the pastry sector has been pivotal around various revolutionary events. For example, the discovery of the Americas brought new ingredients to Europe, significantly contributing to the sector's development.

Pastry making, which appears as an art that leaves its mark on each era, has evolved from ancient times to the present day. From Egypt to Rome, from Medieval Europe to Ottoman cuisine, pastry making has been shaped over a wide time span through factors such as the expansion of trade routes, cultural interactions, and the increase in material diversity. The emergence of innovative approaches and new recipes, as mentioned above, occurred through ingredients such as cocoa, vanilla, and sugar brought to Europe via the discovery of America.

The emergence of pastry businesses, which accompanied the spread of food and beverage establishments, significantly contributed to the development of the sector. This led to standardization in pastry products and the emergence of new recipes and trends, providing substantial gains to the sector.

---

1   Assoc. Prof. Dr., Necmettin Erbakan University, Faculty of Tourism, Department of Gastronomy and Culinary Arts, egunes@erbakan.edu.tr
2   Lecturer, Istanbul Rumeli University, Vocational School, Department of Hotel, Restaurant and Catering Services, dogukan.bayesen@rumeli.edu.tr

The topics addressed in this chapter aim to contribute to the development of an academic perspective in the field of pastry making. Additionally, it is intended to offer readers a comprehensive insight into the rich and diverse depths of the pastry field.

History of Pastry

The concept of pastry is not as new as it might be thought; it dates back as far as the art of cooking itself. It is known that the first pastry practices began with bread. People created sweets by blending breads with various fruits and sugary mixtures similar to molasses. It can be said that different types of cakes emerged during this process. For example, it is known that the Hittites living on Anatolian soil added sweet products to bread and called it cake. Especially with the gradual inclusion of sugar in kitchens and the preparation of special doughs for cakes, it is possible to say that the products began to distinguish themselves from bread (Teyin, 2018).

This distinction became particularly evident with the development of the oven. The development of the oven laid the foundation for the concept of pastry, playing a role in the creation of equipment, baking methods, and even table settings suitable for this art. Pastry practices gained momentum among the Romans and Ancient Greeks, known for the widespread use of ovens and the importance given to sweets and pastries at their tables. However, the fall of the Roman Empire dealt a significant blow to the pastry sector (Oğan, 2020).

The discovery of the Americas changed everything and revitalized the pastry sector. The main reason for this was the discovery and increased spread of ingredients such as vanilla, cocoa, and sugar, which form the basis of the pastry sector. It is known that modern pastries emerged around the mid-19th century. Particularly in America, "society" women were known to hire their own pastry chefs, doing so as a display of wealth.

The pastry revolution brought about by the French Revolution is notable for supporting the ingredient revolution that occurred with the discovery of America. So why is the French Revolution important for pastry? The French Revolution, which began with the uprising of the poor and hungry, made us better understand the importance of the need for food. Despite the debated accuracy, Marie Antoinette, who is thought to have had the audacity to say "let them eat cake" in the face of the misery during the French Revolution, highlights the importance of pastry in the palace. The fact that only pastry chefs were expelled from the palace after the revolution is an interesting development that supports this statement. However, it can be said that this was a positive development for the pastry sector. The pastry chefs, who became unemployed after the revolution, opened various shops in Paris, thus making a significant contribution to the pastry sector. This is how modern pastry began to develop in France.

Another event that can undoubtedly be described as a revolution is the discovery of whipped cream. This legendary cream found by Vatel not only enhanced the taste and texture of cakes but also added a new dimension to presentation. Besides this discovery, it can be said that the Industrial Revolution brought many innovations in terms of presentation and production. For example, the transition to mass production and the gradual emergence of pastry cream, sauces, and glazes during this period added a different dimension to pastry presentation. Additives are also included in these developments. The pastry sector gained significant advantages with the use of these substances, such as extending the shelf life of products, marketing them to distant countries, and enabling mass production.

Today, pastry work is "special." As is known, meals are often concluded with a dessert or pastry. We also celebrate special occasions like birthdays with a "special" food such as cake. This explains why the cake is special. The reason for the special status of cakes is thought to be the difficulty of making or accessing them in the past.

Finally, it should be noted that with the ever-evolving gastronomy and new trends added to the literature, the concept of pastry has gone beyond imagination and continues to develop constantly.

Classification in Pastry

Pastry businesses, like food and beverage establishments, are also classified. These businesses can be categorized into three groups based on their size, product variety, and establishment type.

Pastry Shop Businesses Based on Their Sizes

In our country and around the world, it is possible to see pastry businesses of various sizes. These businesses can be simply classified as small, medium, and large enterprises.

Small businesses are those that obtain their products from external sources, either as dough or already baked, and sell them at their counters. These businesses are generally small shops established solely for sales. The products are sold daily and fresh, allowing the businesses to avoid the cost burden associated with production. The ability for customers to choose products from the counters provides an additional advantage.

Despite these advantages, these businesses have some disadvantages. For example, problems that may arise from the dough or products purchased externally affect these businesses. Additionally, if small businesses employ personnel who are not well-informed, they may not be able to provide necessary information to their customers about the products.

Medium-sized businesses can be defined as those that produce goods daily to meet daily sales. In these pastry businesses, dough products, cakes, and sweets are produced daily and offered for sale. Like small businesses, the products sold at the counters are produced in the kitchens of these businesses. Since medium-sized businesses have to cover their production costs, they do not have the production advantages that small businesses do. However, businesses with an on-site production kitchen have significant advantages in understanding and addressing customer complaints related to production issues. These advantages allow them to more easily build a loyal customer base and ensure that most customers leave satisfied.

It is possible to mention that large businesses also produce their products on-site, but these businesses consist of chain establishments. It is known that they distribute raw materials via shipment to ensure product standardization. This method allows them to maintain consistent taste across all products. The advantages of standardization include cost control and consistent product quality.

Classification of Pastry Shops According to Product Varieties

As is known, pastry businesses offer a wide range of products to consumers, from sweets to breakfast pastries. The variety in the number of products sold naturally leads businesses to specialize in certain products. For example, it is possible to see pastry shops that only sell cakes, as well as those that sell breakfast pastries or sweets.

Cake shops display the cakes they produce daily in glass counters for customers. These businesses can either prepare the products in their own kitchen or sell products purchased from another company.

In businesses that produce breakfast pastries and bread, external purchases are generally not made. The reason is that these products are more appealing to customers when they are fresh and warm. However, these businesses should not be confused with mobile street vendors. In these businesses, breakfast pastries are produced until a certain hour, after which the focus shifts to bread production.

The situation is the same for businesses that sell sweets. They serve sweets produced either by external procurement or by their own production.

Types of Pastry Shops According to Their Establishment Forms

If we were to evaluate pastry businesses based on their establishment type, it would be more appropriate to consider both the target market they serve and the way they provide services. Pastry businesses can cater to various markets.

To define pastry businesses serving a limited market, we can refer to establishments that target specific customer groups and aim to produce and serve products accordingly. Examples of such businesses include those located around terminals, rest stops, schools, hospitals, and factories, serving the customer base in these areas. On the other hand, there are pastry businesses that do not have a specific market boundary. These establishments are located in various areas, from busy streets to residential neighborhoods, and they do not target any particular customer group.

How does a pastry business provide service? There are pastry businesses with seating areas inside where customers can select their products, as well as those that only offer products in packaged form. These businesses are differentiated based on the way they provide services.

Patisserie Training

Pastry making has been a profession of great cultural and gastronomic significance throughout history. This special branch of the food and beverage industry requires both artistic and technical knowledge, making it a complex field.

Pastry making has existed since ancient times, evolving into its current professional level over the centuries. In medieval Europe, when pastry guilds first emerged, training was conducted through a master-apprentice relationship. In the late 19th and early 20th centuries, pastry schools and academic programs began to develop. During this period, countries such as France, Italy, and Germany played pioneering roles in pastry education.

One of the cornerstones of pastry education is theoretical training. Students gain knowledge in areas such as food safety, hygiene, nutrition, and material science. They also receive education on the history of pastry and its place in various cultures. This knowledge helps to deepen and broaden students' professional understanding.

Supporting theoretical knowledge with practical applications is an indispensable part of pastry education. Students work with real ingredients in kitchens, learning basic techniques and recipes. During practical training, students develop skills in dough kneading, cake decorating, chocolate, and sugar craft.

Modern pastry education benefits from the opportunities provided by technology. Computer-aided design programs and advanced kitchen equipment support students' creative processes. Additionally, thanks to online education platforms, students have the opportunity to take lessons from experts around the world.

In recent years, there has been a greater emphasis on sustainability and the use of local products in pastry education. This approach not only increases environmental awareness but also contributes to local economies. Students are taught sustainable material use and eco-friendly production techniques.

Another important component of pastry education is gaining real-world experience. Internship programs and on-the-job training enable students to apply their theoretical and practical knowledge in real-world settings. This process also helps students expand their professional networks and find their place in the job market.

Continuous education and development are crucial in the pastry profession. In Türkiye, a new program called the Pastry and Bakery program is a two-year university program that specializes in pastry education.

Pastry Practices Around the World

As mentioned in the history of pastry making, practices that spread over time have evolved into different forms in modern times. Previously, pastry products were produced in a more uniform manner with minor variations. However, with the discovery of new products and emerging trends, pastry making has evolved into a completely different dimension.

Today, in the production of fresh pastries, product aesthetics are as important as taste. The introduction of many decorative elements, especially the use of chocolate for decorative purposes, has led to the emergence of modern fresh pastry models. For example, the introduction of fondant has brought a new dimension to pastry making. Pastry chefs have been able to eliminate the laborious effort of cream preparation and create various shapes for decorative purposes.

Mechanization is another significant development in the production of pastry products worldwide. Advances in the production process following the Industrial Revolution have facilitated the assurance of standards, quality, and hygiene in products. It should be noted that this advancement has also changed the visual appeal of products and made them more enticing in terms of presentation.

Historical events have also influenced pastry making practices. For instance, pastry chefs expelled from the palace during the French Revolution established various businesses within Paris, contributing to the development of the sector.

It is important to reiterate the significant effects of the Industrial Revolution. Another important development was the impact of World War I and II. This significance lies in the food items provided to soldiers. Biscuits and similar items given to soldiers during the war, due to their ease of transportation and slow deterioration, served as a guiding light for the pastry sector.

Today, pastry making stands out as a constantly evolving sector with new emerging trends. With advancements in various aspects from presentation to aesthetics, and the opening of many new businesses, it is possible to see a pastry business in every neighborhood.

Pastry Practices in Türkiye

It is possible to say that the culture of sweets has developed significantly in the Anatolian region. Especially during the Hittite period, it is important to note that there were around 300 types of bread. So why is bread production important for pastry practices in Anatolia? The Hittites, rather than consuming bread in its plain form, enriched it by adding various sweeteners such as fruits and honey. Thus, the Hittite civilization, which laid the foundation for pastry making, introduced the culture of sweets to the Anatolian lands.

Another civilization that ruled the Anatolian lands, the Roman Empire, advanced pastry practices further. During this period, it is known that not only bread was sweetened but also special pastry doughs were produced and consumed. In fact, it is even possible to see mobile pastry vendors in the streets of Rome.

The sweet culture of Central Asian Turks continued to exist in these lands with the arrival of Turks to Anatolia. Turks pioneered pastry practices in this geography. When we consider the sweet culture of Central Asian Turks, it is seen that the emphasis was on the use of raw materials rather than product production during this period. Especially, it is known that molasses and honey were consumed in a simple form. However, when they arrived in Anatolian lands, they encountered more fertile soils and many new products. Additionally, they developed many new products by cooking and mixing new ingredients with each other. It is observed that halva first found its place in the kitchen during this period. The reason for this is thought to be to meet the energy needs of the Turkish, who were a warrior society, and to obtain products that are easy to preserve. Halvas made by mixing honey or molasses began to be made.

During the Ottoman period, we see that trade flourished and products not grown in Anatolian lands began to be used in the kitchen. Especially, this empire with vast territories was affected by this situation in the kitchen as well. In addition to milk-based sweets and fruit-based sweets being made in the kitchen, significant developments were experienced in the field of pastry making. The immigrants to Russia and the Black Sea in the 19th century made significant contributions to the advancement of the pastry sector. The request for help from Russia during the uprisings in the 19th century led to the rapprochement between the Ottoman Empire and Russia. As a result of this rapprochement, the Russians, who wanted to support the Tsarist economy in the Black Sea region, opened their borders to the Ottoman people. The immigrants from the Black Sea region (especially eastern Black Sea) and the Balkans who went to Russia progressed in this field by working in bakeries, restaurants, and pastry shops. Those who returned home after the October Revolution pioneered this sector in Türkiye. The initiation of production activities by opening various bakeries and pastry shops explains why the foundations of this sector are in the Black Sea. In the Balkans, advancements in milk-based sweets continue to this day.

It is possible to say that Turks are experiencing a golden age in the pastry sector today. Skilled hands that blend traditional flavors with contemporary and global techniques and equipment create new and delicious modern Turkish pastry products. However, if we were to make a negative inference, it is possible to say that with globalization, we are slowly abandoning traditional flavors. This situation not only leads us to forget our cultural heritage but also results in uniform production in pastry products (Delil, 2021).

Conclusion

This section of the book addresses the history of pastry making, the classification of pastry businesses, and the examinations of practices in both the world and Türkiye, demonstrating that the sector is not just a production process but also a cultural and social phenomenon. It is shown how historical events and the discovery of the New World led to a turning point in the evolution of pastry making with the inclusion of new ingredients.

With the arrival of key ingredients such as cocoa, vanilla, and sugar in Europe, fundamental changes have occurred in pastry making techniques and flavor perceptions worldwide. As a result, pastry businesses emerged, which were subsequently categorized into various classes, bringing about changes and developments in many areas, from marketing strategies to customer relations, product variety, and operational structure.

For instance, while small businesses create customer loyalty with unique products, large-scale enterprises have established standardization and extensive distribution networks to reach different markets. Medium-sized businesses have managed to serve a wide range of customers by balancing both ends.

In conclusion, the art of pastry making is a global field constantly shaped by changing material access, technological innovations, and cultural exchanges. This dynamic structure has facilitated the evolution of pastry making as both a craft and an art. With increasing awareness of health and sustainability in the coming years, it is believed that new trends and materials will emerge in the pastry industry, enriching it further with innovation.

References

Delil, S. (2021). *Türkiye'de bulunan gastronomi ve mutfak sanatları bölümleri için pastacılık ve ekmekçilik ön lisans programı önerisi.* Master's thesis. Başkent University Institute of Social Sciences.

Oğan, Ö. G. Y. (2020). Yiyecek İçecek Hizmetleri. Ankara: Nobel Publishing.

Teyin, G. (2022). Pasta Tüketen Bireylerin Pasta Tercihleri Üzerine Bir Araştırma. Aydın Gastronomy, 6(2), 191–200

Mehmet Fatih Kayran[1]

Chapter 27 Gastronomy Photography

Introduction

Photographs have a significant impact on individuals' travel preferences, especially in the pre-travel stage. These visuals, which influence travel decisions, play a crucial role in promoting tourism destinations. The photographs used in promotional and advertising activities generally highlight the attractiveness of tourism destinations, including natural and historical beauties, local events, regional food and beverages, indoor recreation facilities, and the products and services offered by tourism enterprises. At this stage, it is understood that photographs serve an important promotional function for tourism stakeholders. These visuals, which enhance the attractiveness of tourism destinations, help potential tourists form positive impressions of the destination (Karayılan, Akın & Gukuzade, 2017).

Professional photographers and stylists play a significant role in the capturing and usage of these photographs. Various presentation methods have been developed to make food and beverages look more attractive and appealing in photographs. Gastronomy photography is an art that aims to visually present food and beverages in an appealing way. Photographers specializing in this field use various techniques and tools to capture the colors, textures, and details of food in the best possible way (Andrews, 2014). Gastronomy photography has become an important part of the culinary world and is used in many areas, from restaurant menus to food magazines, social media posts, and advertising campaigns (Haines, 2017). Photography is one of the most effective visual arts for evoking a wide range of emotions in people. Food companies and food and beverage businesses utilize the power of photography over food to take advantage of this visual art's impact (Custer, 2010).

As the aesthetic images of food have become more prominent and social media platforms have developed, interest in food photography has increased. Social media allows food photographers to reach a wider audience and ensures that food photographs are seen by more people (Özdoğan, 2014). In this context,

1   Assist. Prof., Harran University, Halfeti Vocational School, Department of Hotel, Restaurant and Catering Services, fatihkayran@harran.edu.tr

the study discusses the purpose and importance of gastronomy photography, the techniques and equipment used, and the relationship between gastronomy photography and social media.

Gastronomy Photography: Purpose and Importance

Photography is one of the most effective visual arts that evokes emotions and connotations. The food industry benefits from this art by making food and beverages visually appealing. Gastronomy photography is a branch of art where food is designed, staged, and photographed using light, angles, and shooting techniques (Karakulak, 2006). This form of photography adds a new dimension to the culinary world, treating taste and visual appeal in an aesthetic dimension (Eryılmaz, 2017).

Gastronomy photography goes beyond simply photographing food in a mundane way; it presents photos that are specially designed for a specific purpose, taken with a professional approach, and carefully created with attention to detail. These photos are prepared considering composition, light, content, aesthetics, and technical aspects. The purpose of the photograph is directly related to where it will be used. For example, there are significant differences between a photo taken for a food magazine and one designed for a restaurant menu (Eryılmaz, 2017).

A professional approach begins with knowing and applying basic photography techniques. Experienced photographers consciously take shots, rather than randomly, and achieve the desired image through their photography knowledge (Custer, 2010). Food photos shared by consumers on the internet and social media are generally considered amateur efforts.

Gastronomy photography aims not only to make food visually appealing but also to evoke the taste and aroma of the food, thereby stimulating the viewer's desire to consume. Photographers use various techniques to enhance the visual appeal of food, making the photos more aesthetic and inviting (Fisher, 2012). The development of social media platforms has increased interest in food photography. Social media allows food photographers to reach wide audiences and ensures that food photos are seen by more people (Özdoğan, 2014).

Gastronomy photography emphasizes creativity and innovation when photographing food and beverages. Therefore, it is constantly evolving with technological advancements and changing consumer demands. New photography techniques, higher resolution cameras, and advanced editing software enable food photographers to produce more creative and impressive images (Manna and Moss, 2005).

Gastronomy photography has gained significant importance in today's world, where technology and consumer habits are rapidly changing. This art form aims to appeal to consumers' visual senses by presenting food and beverages in an aesthetic and visually appealing manner (Haines, 2017). The main purpose of gastronomy photography is to stimulate people's consumption impulses and increase the consumption of food (Andrews, 2014). With the development of social media and digital platforms, the aesthetic images of food have become even more important, leading to an increased interest in food photography (Özdoğan, 2014). Gastronomy photography plays an important role in the preferences of consumers by visually presenting the final form of food and beverages. This process typically continues with the consumer developing a sympathy towards the brand or establishment featured in the photograph. Therefore, gastronomy photography aims not only to increase consumers' appetite and desire to eat in the short term but also to contribute to the brand's long-term preference and recognition (Fisher, 2012).

The primary task of food photographers is to make food more attractive by using specific techniques to attract the attention of consumers (Custer, 2010). Gastronomy photography involves arranging and photographing food and beverages using light, angle, and shooting techniques (Karakulak, 2006). This art form makes food images more attractive, captures consumers' attention, and helps companies in the food and beverage sector to promote their products more effectively. Gastronomy photography has the ability to appeal to consumers' emotions and evoke a desire to taste. This desire is an instinct that the human body cannot ignore. Although initially seeming costly, the areas of use for food photographs should be considered broadly. Gastronomy photography not only emphasizes the power of a menu but also helps a brand provide customers with a story that conveys depth and value. Each restaurant has its unique personality, and gastronomy photography is a tool that helps showcase this personality in a meaningful way. In an environment where competition is intense, attracting the attention of customers is of great importance. (Fisher, 2012).

In summary, gastronomy photography is an art form that aims to attract consumers' attention by presenting food and beverages in an aesthetic and visually appealing manner. This art form has become increasingly important with the changing technology and consumer habits, and has become an important marketing tool in the food and beverage sector.

The Emergence of Gastronomy Photography

Food photography, one of the most challenging and lucrative forms of photography, is predominantly seen in advertising and editorial formats such as books, magazines, newspapers, blogs, and more. When we look at the history of food photography, it dates back thousands of years. In ancient times, humans depicted food on cave walls, and in ancient Rome, markets, hunts, and ceremonies involving food were depicted in art (Armendariz, 2013; Özdoğan, 2016).

The first photograph related to food photography is considered to be taken in 1832 by a French inventor named Joseph Nicephore Niepce. It was a black and white photograph featuring a bowl, a glass, and a piece of bread (Glyda, 2019: 1; Blanchard, 2020: 3). Subsequently, in 1845, William Henry Fox Talbot took a photograph that focused entirely on food, specifically peaches and pineapples in a basket, rather than a still life. This photograph marked the beginning of food photography history. Additionally, upon careful examination of the piece, it can be observed that the pineapple in the photograph is positioned leaning to the right, indicating early signs of food styling in photography (Turshen, 2017).

In 1906, WK Kellogg published the first printed advertisements created using food photography for Corn Flakes (Glyda, 2019: 1).Food photographs first appeared in the 1910s as visuals created for advertising films, followed later by images in cookbooks. Today, new trends have emerged in response to changing demands, leading to the creation of food photographs using different techniques (Sosef, 2019). However, food photography has faced some challenges in the past. Particularly, in the late 1960s and early 1970s, it gained a bad reputation due to food manipulation. For instance, a lawsuit was filed against Campbell's due to the use of marbles in their soup advertisement. Such incidents diminished consumers' trust in products advertised and highlighted the importance of ethical standards (Custer, 2010).

In the 1980s, the use of a black background became popular in food photography. With a black background, the colors of the food became more vivid, making the photos more appealing (Glyda, 2019: 1). In the 1990s, food photography started to be influenced by fashion and commerce. Publications specializing in food shifted from informing consumers to selling. In recent years, food photography has started to bring back its classic style. Photos featuring carefully crafted, elegant dishes have become popular again. This change indicates that food photography is an ever- evolving field (Duman ve Eryılmaz, 2021).

Basic Equipment Used in Gastronomy Photography

Although photography can be performed anytime and anywhere, the rules of photography are not always the same in every situation. The ability to make the right choices based on experience is crucial for taking good photographs. In other words, to be a good photographer, one needs to have a blend of science, art, technical knowledge, talent, and experience (MEGEP, 2012).

To take a good food photograph, the primary requirements are a high-resolution camera and a strong light source. Food items naturally reflect their aesthetic appeal under natural light. However, the time window for capturing food photographs with natural light is very limited. Therefore, in a studio setting, it is possible to create the impression of natural light using various equipment (De Bruin, 1999: 2).

The tools and equipment used in food photography are described in detail. These tools are essential for presenting and photographing food in the best possible way. High-resolution cameras, appropriate lenses, light sources, reflectors, backgrounds, and various photography accessories play a critical role in capturing high-quality food photographs. When combined with the photographer's skill and experience, these elements result in aesthetic and appealing food photographs (MEGEP, 2012; De Bruin, 1999).

The most important elements of the technical infrastructure required for food photography include the camera, lenses, tripod, and light sources (Eryılmaz, 2017).

With the development of digital cameras, a variety of cameras with different features capable of meeting various expectations have been produced in the post-film era. (Sarıtaş, 2022).In food photography, it is crucial to use high-resolution cameras. The technical features of the camera are of utmost importance to ensure that the food being photographed appears sharp and clear. While various types of cameras exist, they all share common operational mechanisms. The selection of the right equipment in food photography directly influences the quality of the shots (Akyol, 2010).

A lens is a collection of glass elements that ensure light from the subject is accurately transmitted onto the film or sensor, and it is the most crucial part of a camera. High-resolution photographs are achieved through high-quality lenses. (Akyol, 2010; Sarıtaş, 2022). In professional photography, including food photography, one of the essential requirements is the variety of lenses that the camera can use. A camera that can utilize different types of lenses is considered professional, and the availability of various lens options facilitates the photographer's work. Since lenses determine how the camera captures the subject, they are often considered more important than the camera itself (Gisseman, 2016).

Another important element that should be included in the technical equipment of a food photographer is a tripod, also known as a camera stand. The stand is crucial in photography and video shooting. Tripod, photography is a three-legged equipment used for stabilizing the camera and determining the shooting angle. The main reason for using a tripod in photography is to prevent slipping and shaking in both video and photo shoots while carrying the camera by hand. With this equipment, since the camera is fixed, clearer photos and videos will be obtained. An important feature that should be found on a tripod is the spirit level. The spirit level is an adjustment that allows us to see if the camera is balanced on the tripod (Akyol, 2010: 302).

Lighting is one of the most crucial elements in food photography, as in other types of photography. Food photography is a specialized field that aims to represent food and beverages in the best possible way, leveraging the power of visual storytelling. The most effective photographs in this field are often achieved through proper lighting. Lighting should be adjusted to accurately reflect the texture, color, and flavor of the food. Therefore, a food photographer should have a good understanding of lighting techniques (Manna ve Moss, 2005).

In food photography, the direction of light is as important as the light source itself. Lighting techniques, depending on the direction of light, are among the most crucial factors determined by the photographer's personal preferences. These techniques can vary based on the photographer's creativity and experience, and are often defined using specific positions on a clock face, which are commonly used in food photography (Gisseman, 2016):

The use of these techniques plays a crucial role in achieving the desired atmosphere and effect in food photography. Especially for beginners, practicing and experimenting with different lighting techniques is important (Gisseman, 2016).

In summary, using the right lighting techniques is crucial in food photography, as it plays a significant role in determining the quality of the photographs. Photographers should skillfully use different lighting methods to ensure that the food is represented in the best possible way.

Points to Consider in Gastronomy Photography

When taking food and beverage photographs, there are some important points to consider regarding the product. When products are placed in front of the camera, errors that the photographer may not notice but others might become apparent. Therefore, it is important for food photographers to have a detailed knowledge of photography techniques (Custer, 2010). There are many points to consider in order to create a successful photograph in food photography. These include; professional and technical knowledge, correct use of light and angle, effective composition, focusing on the food in the photograph, creativity, post-processing editing of the photograph, and others (Custer, 2010).

Food photography starts its journey with the food stylist and ends with the food photographer. A person working professionally in this field needs to have a solid grasp of the basic professional and technical knowledge in the kitchen. A food photographer should be knowledgeable about light and heat-sensitive products, as well as determining the key points where the product should stand out, similar to a food stylist. It is essential for a food photographer to understand the function of each ingredient used in a dish from an artistic perspective in order to create impressive compositions. Therefore, it is important for food photographers to receive basic training in this field. Having knowledge in this field during the shoot will ensure that the resulting photograph is nearly flawless and will also facilitate the work of the food stylist (Vogel, 2007).

One of the most essential elements for a photograph to be successful is light. Although details about light source and direction were discussed in detail in the previous section, it is worth mentioning here as well. In food and beverage photography, light is crucial for presenting food and drinks in a clear and appealing manner. The texture of food and the consistency of drinks can be better reflected with proper lighting (Young, 2012). Photographers should ensure that the light comes from the right direction to enhance the quality of the images. Proper lighting ensures that food and drinks are seen clearly (Parks-Whitfield, 2012).

The foundation of a good photograph lies in establishing the correct angle and light source, followed by creating an effective composition. Composition, one of the fundamental elements of a photograph, is the process of bringing together many parts to form the integrity of the photograph. These parts are formed through colors, textures, and shapes, and are arranged in harmony (Chang et al., 2017). In gastronomy photography, creating the right composition is of great importance (Young, 2012). In photography literature, composition is defined as the process of combining parts that do not express themselves individually to form an expression in a photograph (Chang et al., 2017). The elements that make up the composition in a photograph are the fundamental elements that determine the aesthetics and meaning of the photograph. Bringing these elements together correctly enhances the attractiveness of the photograph and attracts the viewer's attention. In gastronomy photography, creating the right composition is an important element that enhances the attractiveness of the photograph. Factors such as how products will be placed, how the background will be arranged, and how the focal point will be determined need to be taken into account when creating the right composition (Campbell, 2013).

Another important aspect to consider in gastronomy photography is creativity. Consumers tend to gravitate towards the unusual and different. While technically proficient photographs may be produced when conventional or ordinary elements are involved, they may be considered unsuccessful if they fail to capture consumers' attention. This is because the primary goal of a food photographer is to encourage consumers to purchase the product through their photographs. Therefore, food photographers must continuously improve themselves and keep up with innovations. While taking photos, they will encounter many moments that will require them to engage their creativity. In these moments, they should focus on what will surprise the consumer. A food photographer should aim to take photos that reflect their creativity and talent and that will inspire consumers to read a recipe found in magazines or books (Uygun, 2007).

A photograph is a visual material that requires post-processing and the involvement of different professional fields to be prepared for publication. One important aspect to consider in gastronomy photography is the post-processing edits. Variable conditions can make it challenging to achieve the desired image during the shoot. Therefore, photographs intended for professional use are often subjected to a process called "post-production," where aspects such as contrast, tone, color, exposure, and framing are adjusted to prepare the image for printing. Depending on the desired outcome, different professional fields may be involved, with graphic design and retouching being crucial components of this process. While in some cases, only the intervention of a graphic designer may be sufficient, in others, a more detailed retouching process may be necessary (Eryılmaz, 2017).

Gastronomy Photography and Social Media

Social media offers a diverse range of formats and content, with platforms such as Instagram, Facebook, Twitter, Youtube, Pinterest, Google, and blogs becoming integral parts of daily life. These platforms provide users with the ability to share what they eat and drink, places they visit, things they like or dislike, follow various topics of interest, and engage in discussions. Gastronomy photography has significantly evolved with the rise of social media. Restaurants, chefs, and food brands now aim to reach large audiences by sharing their delicious dishes and drinks on these platforms. This trend highlights that gastronomy photography requires more than just capturing photos of tasty food and drinks (Sabimbona, 2013).

With the popularity of gastronomy photography, social media users have also joined the trend by capturing and sharing images of their meals on their social media accounts. These food posts have become a trend on social media platforms, facilitating interactions among people worldwide. Users often strive to highlight the ambiance and presentation of the food in their photos.

This trend has intensified competition among restaurants, prompting them to achieve professionalism in food photography to attract customers' attention. Overall, the impact of gastronomy photography on social media continues to be felt in three main areas: professional, commercial, and hobbyist (Akkuş, 2020).

As a result, social media has revolutionized gastronomy photography, turning it into a dynamic and captivating field of art. These platforms provide an opportunity to reach a wide audience, allowing restaurants, chefs, and food enthusiasts to showcase their creativity and delicious dishes to the world. Gastronomy photography on social media has become a storytelling tool that goes beyond the taste of food. The photos show viewers that food culture is not just about flavor but also a cultural and historical experience. With the popularity of this trend, social media users have also joined in by photographing their meals and sharing them on their social media accounts. These posts have become a trend on social media platforms worldwide, facilitating interaction among people globally (Şener, 2014).

Result

Gastronomy photography is an important art form that enables food and drinks to be presented in an aesthetic and appealing manner. In this study, the basic concepts, techniques, and relationship with social media of gastronomy photography have been examined.

Gastronomy photography is an important tool for documenting and promoting food culture. Photos emphasize the taste and presentation of food and drinks, providing viewers with a visual feast. With the development of technology and the widespread use of social media, gastronomy photography has become even more important. Restaurants and food brands seek to gain a competitive edge by using social media platforms to promote and market their products with the help of professional photographers.

Gastronomy photography not only involves photographing food and drinks but also serves as a storytelling tool. Photos carry a cultural and historical value as part of food culture and culinary tradition. Photographers can be successful in gastronomy photography by developing their creative and technical skills. Proper use of light, composition, and color enhances the appeal of photos.

In the future, gastronomy photography is expected to become even more important and develop further. With advances in technology and the influence of social media, food culture and gastronomy photography will become even more popular.

In conclusion, gastronomy photography is an important tool for documenting and promoting food culture and culinary tradition. Those interested in this field should develop their creative and technical skills and take advantage of the power of social media. Whether done for commercial purposes or as a hobby, gastronomy photography offers a delicious journey for everyone.

References

Akkuş, M. (2020). The Importance of Social Media Promotions as a Visual Communication Medium and Gastronomy Photography (Unpublished master's thesis). Yeditepe University, Institute of Social Sciences, Istanbul.

Akyol, O. (2010). Temel Photography, Istanbul University Open and Distance Education Faculty Radio TV Cinema Program Lecture Notes.

Andrews, P. (2014). *Food Photography: From Snapshots to Great Shots*. Peachpit Press.

Armendariz, M. (2013). Focus on food photography for bloggers (Focus on Series): Focus on the fundamentals. Focal Press, UK.

Blanchard, M.S. (2020). Appetizing foods the creation of an appetizing image, (HonorsThesis), Appalachian State University, USA.

Campbell, T., (2013). Food Photography &Lighting: A Commerical Photographer's Guide to Creating Irresistible Images. New Riders Publishing, Berkeley.

Chang, Y. B., Ciampo, M., ve Mitchell, H. (2017). "Creating Images with Impact: Food Photography Tips from MyPlate", Journal of Academy of Nutrition and Dietetics, 117(8), 1171–1173

Custer, D. (2010). *The Power of Food Photography: Capturing the Essence of Food*. Gastronomy Journal, 15(3), 334–341.Eryılmaz, A. (2017). *The Art of Gastronomy Photography: Aesthetic and Technical Aspects*. Journal of Culinary Arts, 20(3), 112–125.

De Bruin, N. (1999). The Art Of Food Photography. Central University of Technology, Departm

Duman, D., & Eryılmaz, G. (2021). Food Styling and Photography. In D. Çanakçı (Ed.), Within Neogastronomic Trends (pp. 437–455). Nobel Yayıncılık, Ankara.

Eryılmaz, M. (2017). *The Relationship Between Gastronomy and Art: The Role of Photography*. Culinary and Art Studies, 30(5), 84–97

Fisher, L. (2012). The Art of Food Styling and Photography. Culinary Arts Review, 22(1), 19–28.

Gisseman, C. (2016). Food photography a beginner's guide to creating appetizing ima-ges. Rocky Nook Inc. USA.

Glyda, J. (2019). Food photography: Creating appetizing images (1st ed.). Routledge.

Haines, B. (2017). *Plate to Pixel: Digital Food Photography & Styling*. Wiley.

Karakulak, M. (2006). *Gastronomy Photography: Designing and Photographing Food and*

Karayılan, M., Akın, A., & Gukuzade, A. (2017). The Role of Photography in Tourism Promotion. *Tourism Research Journal*, 25(4), 863–880.

MEGEP (2012). Food and Beverage Services - New Recipe Module. Ankara.

Manna, J., & Moss, L. (2005). *Creating Delicious and Aesthetic Food Photos*. Journal of Food Aesthetics, 18(4), 83–92.

Özdoğan, A. (2014). The Impact of Social Media on Food Photography. *Gastronomy Journal*, 10(2), 161–174.

Park-Whitfield, A. (2012). Food styling & photography for dummies. John Wiley&SonInc. Hoboken, New Jersey.

Sabimbona, S. (2013). Evaluation of Social Networks as a Learning Tool: A Comparison of Burundi and Turkey. Unpublished Master's Thesis, Istanbul University, Institute of Science, Istanbul.

Sarıtaş, A. (2022). Kitchen Managers' Interest, Usage Status, and Knowledge Levels in Food Styling and Photography: The Case of Istanbul. Unpublished Master's Thesis, Necmettin Erbakan University, Institute of Social Sciences.

Sosef, G. (2019). History and Evolution of Food Photography. Journal of Culinary Arts, 25(3), 37–50.

Şener, N. (2014). The Menu of the Day on Social Media: An Evaluation of "Shared" Food Photographs on Social Media. *Erciyes Journal of Communication Akademia*, 3(3), 72–78.

Turshen, J. (2017). "Food Photography, Over the Years." The New York Times, Erişim adresi https://www.nytimes.com/2017/05/18/t-magazine/food-photography-history.html, Erişim tarihi: 15.05.2024.

Uygun, S. (2007). Advertising photography and creativity. [Unpublished master's thesis]. Marmara University.

Vogel, A. (2007). Food Photography. M. R. Peres (Ed.), The Focal Encyclopedia of Photography (ss. 323–324). Elsevier.

Young, N.S., (2012). Food Photography: From Snapshots to Great Shots. Peachpit Press, California, USA.

S. Ceylin Şanli Kayran[1]

Chapter 28 Gastronomy Museum

Introduction

Gastronomy museums stand out as significant cultural heritage sites that carry traces of dietary habits, culinary cultures, and food production throughout human history. These museums showcase local culinary diversity, traditional cooking techniques, regional products, and the history of industrial food production in many countries and regions. Gastronomy museums not only present the history of food and beverages to visitors but also offer an educational and enjoyable experience by presenting their cultural and societal context.

Gastronomy museums play important roles such as promoting tourism, contributing to the local economy, and increasing awareness of gastronomy in society, not just introducing local culinary cultures. These museums encourage awareness and experience in gastronomy by organizing various activities such as events, educational programs, and tasting tours for local residents and visitors.

This section of the book provides information on the concepts of museums and museology, as well as insights into gastronomy and gastronomy museums. Within this framework, the classification of gastronomy museums, examples of gastronomy museums, and studies conducted in the literature will be examined in this section.

The Concept of Museology and Museum

The concept of Museology and Museum The word "museum" is derived from the Greek word "Mouseion," meaning "a place where the Muses live," referring to the inspirational goddesses of the arts. The origins of museums trace back to the nine daughters of Zeus and Mnemosyne in Greek mythology, known as the Muses. These goddesses represented various creative domains such as music, dance, and poetry (Keleş, 2003; Kandemir & Uçar, 2015).

Museology encompasses a wide range of activities from prehistoric periods to the modern era. Activities within museology include the preservation and

---

1   Assoc. Prof., Harran University, Halfeti Vocational School, Department of Travel, Tourism and Entertainment Services, HYPERLINK "mailto:ceylinsanli@harran.edu.tr" ceylinsanli@harran.edu.tr

exhibition of artifacts obtained from archaeological excavations, the collection and display of artworks, the gathering and presentation of ethnographic materials, as well as the conservation and opening to the public of historical buildings or cultural sites. Within this framework, museology is closely related to various disciplines such as archaeology, art history, anthropology, history, and cultural studies (Okan, 2018; Okan, 2015).

The International Council of Museums defines a museum as "A museum is a not-for-profit, permanent institution in the service of society that researches, collects, conserves, interprets and exhibits tangible and intangible heritage. Open to the public, accessible and inclusive, museums foster diversity and sustainability. They operate and communicate ethically, professionally and with the participation of communities, offering varied experiences for education, enjoyment, reflection and knowledge sharing" (ICOM, 2024). Another definition states that a museum is "an institution managed for the public benefit, which continuously manages to preserve, examine, evaluate, and display a whole consisting of elements carrying cultural value in various forms" (Okan, 2015). Based on these definitions, it can be observed that museums play a key role in preserving, safeguarding, and transmitting both tangible and intangible cultural heritage of humanity to future generations. By carrying out activities such as preservation, research, exhibition, and promotion of artworks, museums serve as a bridge spanning from the past to the future, raising awareness among people and preserving cultural values (Kervankıran, 2014).

The roots of modern museology can be traced back to ancient Greece with the establishment of treasure structures where private items were collected. In France, private studios where collections were preserved and exhibited formed the initial steps of modern museology. By the 17th century, collected collections gained societal value beyond being mere hobbies (Ersoy, 2022). As museology evolved towards contemporary times, museums began to offer visitors various experiences. These experiences often go beyond visual presentations and include activities such as hands-on or three-dimensional films. Thus, sensory experiences of visitors are enhanced, promoting social interaction and knowledge sharing (Okan, 2018; Kandemir & Uçar, 2015).

The Concept of Gastronomy and Gastronomy Museum

The term "gastronomy" is derived from the Greek words "gastros" (stomach) and "nomos" (law, rule) (Scarpato, 2002; Kivela & Crotts, 2006). This concept is simply defined as "the science and art of good eating" (Gillespie & Cousins, 2001). In other words, gastronomy encompasses all processes related to people's eating habits (Savarin, 2009). It covers a wide range of topics, including the art and science of cooking and eating, as well as the relationship between food and culture (Kivela & Crotts, 2006). Gastronomy can be understood as a concept related to the technical and standards of the process of transforming raw products into new products after being organized aesthetically, nationally, regionally, and culturally (Santich, 2004; Gillespie & Cousins, 2001). Additionally, gastronomy, although inherently related to the study of food and drink, according to contemporary gastronomic understanding, encompasses processes from the production and preparation of food and beverages to how, where, when, and why they are consumed (Santich, 2004). Herbst & Herbst (2007) define gastronomy as the art of good eating and the science of gourmet food and beverages. Therefore, gastronomy is not only related to eating and drinking but also to natural history, physics, chemistry, cuisine, commerce, and political economy (Savarin, 2009).

The development of gastronomy tourism and the increasing interest of tourists in this type of tourism, particularly in the cultures of countries, have led to innovations in this field. Especially for the preservation and promotion of local cuisines and the unveiling of forgotten dishes, gastronomy museums have begun to be established. These museums play a significant role in preserving and transmitting the regional culinary culture, which is an important attraction for gastronomy tourism, allowing visitors to learn about the culinary culture and history of the region and experience tasting local flavors. Accordingly, there is increasing interest in kitchen museums in line with the demands of tourists (Yeşilyurt & Arıca, 2018).

Gastronomy museums, also known as food museums (Kim, Park, Xu, 2020; Park, Kim & Xu, 2022; Williams, 2013; Kurniawati & Lestari, 2016), gastronomy museum, or museum of gastronomy (Lam, 2011), food and beverage museum (Smith, 2008; Edwards, 2013), are institutions that collect all kinds of tangible and intangible knowledge and objects related to the phenomenon of human nutrition, reduce or present this knowledge and objects on the development of the society to which they belong, organize exhibitions and educational programs on this subject, research, preserve, and archive information about culinary cultures that are part of the society (Koz, 2009). Llerena (2009) lists the importance of gastronomy museums as shedding light on all of humanity's history, art, and science, contributing to visitors' awareness, providing education about their rich living histories, encouraging food sustainability, and providing an opportunity for discussion on food-related issues.

The introduction and transmission of the culinary heritage of countries or regions to both domestic and foreign tourists are achieved through gastronomy museums. Gastronomy museums provide information about the history of foods specific to a country or region, the production of these foods, the prepa-ration process, and the tools used in these stages (Kurniawati & Lestari, 2016). Gastronomy museums, as symbols of the history and culture of a destination, serve as centers for learning and preserving regional and traditional dishes. These museums also present the origin, history, region-specific tools, produc-tion, consumption, and distribution processes of food. Therefore, gastronomy museums are also connected to other disciplines such as agriculture, art, sci-ence, and technology (Çakıcı et al., 2021; Kurniawati & Lestari, 2016). The mul-tidisciplinary nature of food and gastronomy offers extensive opportunities for museum practices. The growing interest in gastronomy has influenced the estab-lishment of gastronomy-themed museums. Worldwide, especially gastronomy museums attract visitors interested in food, often referred to as "foodies." These museums play an important role in expressing the identity, meaning, history, and memory of food through tangible objects (Park, Kim & Xu, 2020).

Gastronomy museums, reflecting culinary culture, are seen as one of the most important tools of gastronomy tourism for introducing and preserving the culi-nary heritage of regions. The presence of gastronomy museums and the promo-tion of these museums are attractiveness factors for destinations. Gastronomy tourism, with its local foods, local culinary culture, and stories related to culi-nary culture, provides special information representing local cultures and iden-tities (Sarı Gök & Şalvarcı, 2021).

Museums not only present the values they possess but also have an important function in transmitting these values to future generations. Gastronomy-themed museums, in particular, serve to introduce suitable values while revitalizing tourism in their regions (Demirci, 2021). Gastronomy museums are established to support sustainable eating habits and the sustainability of culinary culture, as well as to strengthen the intergenerational transmission of cultural values. Additionally, gastronomy museums enhance the attractiveness of destinations by introducing local culinary culture to both domestic and foreign tourists and serve as an effective marketing tool. Furthermore, gastronomy museums play an important role in highlighting the importance of culinary culture by reveal-ing the culture of the kitchen. They are also seen as effective tools in promot-ing regional culinary culture and guiding visitors in acquiring knowledge about regional gastronomy (Özdemir, 2021).

Gastronomy-themed museums are important indicators of the gastronomic development of a region or country. Tourists traveling for gastronomy tourism purposes prefer these museums to learn more about the gastronomic history, traditions, and culture of the places they visit and to taste local products (Aksoy ve Sezgi, 2015). Generally, gastronomy museums can be defined as areas where information about food can be obtained. The ways in which foods are displayed in these museums are quite diverse. Throughout history, various subjects related to gastronomy have been exhibited in gastronomy museums and cultural areas, ranging from cooking vessels to historical recipes and foreign culinary cultures. Gastronomy museums showcase gastronomic culture in many areas, from plants to wine, from kitchen culture to chocolate, from olive oil to aromatic plants (Çekal, Doğan & Aktürk, 2022).

Formun Üstü
Classification of Gastronomy Museum

Gastronomy museums can be classified in various ways based on examples of implementation and their functions. Yılmaz and Şenel (2014) examined gastronomy museums under the headings of cultural heritage, industrial heritage, rural tourism, and popular culture. Accordingly:

- Cultural Heritage-based Gastronomy Museums: These museums reflect the food and drink, eating habits, and cultural values of a region or culture.
- Industrial Heritage-based Gastronomy Museums: These museums reevaluate old factories or industrial facilities to present the history and processes of food and beverage production to visitors.
- Rural Tourism-based Gastronomy Museums: These museums aim to introduce visitors to the cultivation of agricultural products and the production processes of food and beverages in rural areas.
- Popular Culture-based Gastronomy Museums: These museums showcase the history and development of fast-food chains or brands that are part of popular culture.

Akyürek and Erdem (2019), on the other hand, classified museums into agriculture-focused, beverage-focused, kitchen culture-focused, and production area-focused categories. Accordingly:

- Agriculture-focused Gastronomy Museums: The content of these museums generally includes agricultural products, agricultural equipment, and agricultural areas.
- Beverage-focused Gastronomy Museums: These museums primarily educate visitors about wine production but also provide information about the production, packaging, and storage processes of beverages such as tea, coffee, apple juice, cola, and beer.

- Kitchen Culture-focused Gastronomy Museums: These museums represent the culinary culture of the region in which they are located, showcasing kitchen tools and equipment, foods, tables, etc.
- Museums focused on production areas: This typically entails the conversion of food and beverage production areas into museums. Examples of such museums include salt mines, olive oil factories, wind-water mills, honey production, etc.

Examples of Gastronomy Museums

Gastronomy-themed museums are widely present in various countries worldwide, with different themes. These museums offer visitors different experiences by showcasing local culinary cultures, production processes of food and beverages, their historical origins, and cultural significance. Especially in countries like Italy and France, which have rich culinary heritages in Europe, gastronomy museums hold great importance.

Italy's cheese, wine, and olive oil museums emphasize the country's rich gastronomic heritage. France, on the other hand, is renowned for its gastronomy museums with themes such as chocolate, wine, and cheese. These museums not only introduce the country's rich cuisine and culture but also host gastronomy-related education and events.

In multicultural countries like the United States, there are museums focused on various ethnic cuisines as well as local food and beverage production. Museums with themes such as fruits and vegetables, coffee, beer, bread, etc., convey the history, production processes, and cultural significance of these products to visitors (Akbıyuk, 2021).

Gastronomy museums also support social responsibility projects in addition to promoting local culinary cultures. Some museums engage in activities for the benefit of society by donating a portion of their income to purposes such as education or fighting hunger (Yıldırım Sarıhan, 2021).

Studies on Gastronomy Museums

Sarı Gök and Şalvarcı (2020) examined online visitor experiences of gastronomy-themed museums. They found that visitors made the most comments regarding the aesthetic theme of gastronomy museums, while the fewest comments were made regarding the employee theme. Savaşkan and Çavuş (2021) analyzed the reviews left by visitors of the Adatepe Olive Oil Museum on TripAdvisor and found that visitors to the olive oil museum were mainly influenced by education and aesthetic experiences. They also determined that visitors generally expressed positive views about their experiences. Similarly, Bekar Şimşek and Ayyıldız (2023) conducted a study in which visitor experiences at gastronomy-themed museums in Turkey were examined in terms of service errors. It was observed that service errors in gastronomy-themed museums were related to visitors, service system, employees, museum management and organization, and environment.

Bekar, Arman, and Sürücü (2017) investigated the use of the Marmaris Honey House as an attraction in tourism and its contribution to the region's tourism activities. The study revealed that the Marmaris Honey House has become a tourist attraction as a gastronomy museum, and since its opening, visits to the museum have increased. Aydınlı and Bulut Solak (2023), on the other hand, aimed to determine the use of the Atatürk Forest Farm Museum and Exhibition Hall as a destination attraction and its contribution to the region's tourism potential.

Çakıcı, Sırtlı, and Korkmaz (2021) attempted to determine the gastronomic values of Gökçeada and how the sustainability of these values could be ensured. Through interviews with local stakeholders, it was concluded that opening a gastronomy museum in Gökçeada was seen as a necessity for ensuring the sustainability of the island's local, cultural, and gastronomic values, and that the museum should be located in the town center. Similarly, Kırbaç and Bucak (2022) investigated the sustainability impact of gastronomy museums on local food products through discussions with stakeholders. Baycar (2022) focused on the proposal of an Apiculture Museum as a means of promoting local products through museums.

Sandıkçı, Mutlu, and Mutlu (2019) demonstrated the presentation differences of gastronomy museums. In the study, selected gastronomy museums' presentation differences were identified, and information was obtained from museum officials about how the exhibited objects were collected and the problems encountered in the museum. Ceyhun Sezgin and Akbıyuk (2021) evaluated gastronomy museums around the world thematically in terms of the general characteristics of kitchen cultures and dining habits. The research determined that due to the complex cultural structure of the United States, it hosted many different themed gastronomy museums, while countries around the Mediterranean were dominated by olive oil museums, and France and Italy had many gastronomy museums with different themes.

Demirci (2021) analyzed gastronomy museums' websites using content analysis. Ağcakaya and Can (2019) demonstrated the contribution of gastronomy museums in Turkey to the concept of sustainability through a literature review.

Similarly, Kurniawati and Lestari (2016) conducted a study where the potential of gastronomy museums in Indonesia was investigated as a cultural heritage of regional foods.

Kim, Park, and Xu (2020) examined the factors influencing tourists' perception of food experiences at gastronomy museums. The study found that tourists seek knowledge and gastronomic experiences when visiting gastronomy museums, and each experience is shaped by both tourist and environmental factors. Another study investigated visitors' motivations for visiting gastronomy museums. According to the research results, the most dominant motivation at the individual level comes from seeking education and information (Park, Kim, and Xu, 2020).

In general, studies on gastronomy museums focus on analyzing online visitor reviews. However, there are also studies in the literature that include evaluations of the potential use of museums through interviews with museum employees or stakeholders. Furthermore, studies examining the websites of gastronomy museums are also present in the literature. Additionally, it is observed that studies on gastronomy museums have intensified particularly since 2019.

Results

Gastronomy museums can be defined as institutions that convey food culture, local cuisines and food and beverage production processes to visitors, and host gastronomy-related training and events. These museums offer a wide range of information, from kitchen utensils to local recipes, reflecting the development of eating and drinking habits throughout history.

Gastronomy museums can have various themes and focus points, from reflecting the eating and drinking habits of a culture to the cultivation of agricultural products, from the development processes of fast food brands to the evaluation of industrial facilities. This diversity allows gastronomy museums to expand in a wide perspective. Gastronomy museums can present the history, production processes and cultural values of local foods to their visitors within the framework of educational programs and events.

In addition to the experiences they provide to visitors as an attractive element in tourism, gastronomy museums also offer important regional contributions such as preservation of local culture, sustainability and promotion. Gastronomy museums, which are opened to promote gastronomy tourism, on the one hand, introduce the local culinary culture to the visitors, and on the other hand, attract the attention of tourists to the region, promote local products, contribute to sustainability and support local development.

Studies conducted on gastronomy museums have revealed that museums are important cultural and economic resources within the framework of the potential and sustainability of gastronomy museums. For this reason, it is important to support and develop gastronomy museums, taking into account their contributions to preserving local culture, transferring it to future generations, and supporting local development.

References

Ağcakaya, H. & Can, I. I. (2019). Somut olmayan kültürel miras kapsamında mutfak kültürünün sürdürülebilirliği: Türkiye'deki gastronomi müzeleri örneği. Gastroia: Journal of gastronomi and travel research, 3(4), 788–804.

Akbıyuk, T. (2021). "Turizm Potansiyeli Açısından Türkiye'deki Gastronomi Müzelerinin Analizi". Yayınlanmamış Yüksek Lisans Tezi. Gazi Üniversitesi Sosyal Bilimler Enstitüsü. Ankara.

Aksoy, M., & Sezgi, G. (2015). Gastronomi turizmi ve Güneydoğu Anadolu Bölgesi gastronomik unsurları. Journal of Tourism & Gastronomy Studies, 3(3), 79–89.

Akyürek, S., & Erdem, B. (2019). Gastronomy museums as sustainable hangouts in gastronomy tourism: a gastronomy museum proposal for Gümüşhane city, Turkey. Turizam, 23(1), 17–33.

Aydınlı, F., & Bulut Solak, B. (2023). Atatürk Orman Çiftliği Müze ve Sergi Salonu'nun Türkiye'deki gastronomi müzeleri açısından değerlendirilmesi. Aydın Gastronomy, 8(1), 43–64.

Baycar, A. (2022). Yerel ürünlerin müze aracılığıyla turizme kazandırılması: Siirt arıcılık müze önerisi. GSI Journals Serie A: Advancements in Tourism Recreation and Sports Sciences, 5(2), 242–254.

Bekar, A., Arman, M. S. & Sürücü, Ç. (2017). Turizmde çekicilik unsuru olarak gastronomi müzeleri: Marmaris bal evi örneği. The Journal of Academic Social Science, 42(42), 468–477.

Bekar Şimşek, G. & Ayyıldız A. Y. (2023). Gastronomi temalı müzelerdeki ziyaretçi deneyimlerinin hizmet hataları yönünden incelenmesi. Türk Turizm Araştırmaları Dergisi, 7(2), 266–283.

Ceyhun Sezgin, A. & Akbıyuk, T. (2021). Thematic analysis of gastronomy museums in the world. Journal of Tourism & Gastronomy Studies, 9(1), 153–184.

Çakıcı, S., Sırtlı, A., & Korkmaz, M. (2021). Gökçeada'ya ait gastronomik değerlerin sürdürülebilirliğinin sağlanmasına yönelik bir araştırma: Gastronomi müzesi önerisi. Gastroia: Journal of Gastronomy And Travel Research, 5(2), 302–335.

Çekal, N., Doğan, E., & Aktürk, H. (2022). Türkiye'de gastronomi müzeleri ve özellikleri. *Sosyal, Beşeri ve İdari Bilimler Dergisi, 5*(11), 1655–1673.

Demirci, B. (2021). Türkiye'deki gastronomi müzelerinin web sitelerinin içerik analizi. *Türk Turizm Araştırmaları Dergisi, 5*(2), 1184–1199.

Edwards, Jennifer Stierman, "From So-So to SoFABulous: Southern Food and Beverage Museum" (2013). Arts Administration Master's Reports. 150.

Ersoy, H. (2022). "Modern Gastronomi Müzeciliğinde Kültürel Miras Yaklaşımları" Hamdullah Emin Paşa Üniversitesi Lisansüstü Eğitim Enstitüsü,

Gillespie, C. ve J. A. Cousins (2001). European gastronomy into the 21st century. Butterworth- Heinemann.

Herbst, S. T., & Herbst, R. (2007). new food lover's companion. Barron's Educational Series. Yayınlanmamış Yüksek Lisans Tezi, Alanya.

ICOM (2024). Museum Definition. https://icom.museum/en/resources/standa rds-guidelines/museum-definition/ Erişim Tarihi: 20.05.2024.

Kandemir, Ö., & Uçar, Ö. (2015). Değişen müze kavramı ve çağdaş müze mekânlarının oluşturulmasına yönelik tasarım girdileri. *Sanat ve Tasarım Dergisi, 5*(2), 17–47.

Keleş, V. (2003). Modern müzecilik ve Türk müzeciliği. *Atatürk Üniversitesi Sosyal Bilimler Enstitüsü Dergisi, 2*(1–2).

Kervankiran, I. (2014). Dünyada değişen müze algısı ekseninde Türkiye'deki müze turizmine bakış. *Electronic Turkish Studies, 9*(11), 345–369.

Kim, S., Park, E., & Xu, M. (2020). Beyond the authentic taste: The tourist experience at a food museum restaurant. *Tourism Management Perspectives, 36*, 100749.

Kırbaç, K., & Bucak, T. (2022). The importance of gastronomy museums in the sustainability of local food products: the case of Kars Zavot Eco-Museum.

Kivela, J. ve Crotts, C.J. (2006). Tourism and gastronomy: gastronomy"s ģnfluence on how tourists experience a destination, *Journal Of Hospitality & Tourism Research, 30*(3), 354–377.

Koz, G. F. (2009). "Osmanlı Mutfak Kültürünün Saray Müzelerde Sergilenmesi", Yıldız Teknik Üniversitesi Sosyal Bilimler Enstitüsü, Yayınlanmamış Yüksek Lisans Tezi, İstanbul.

Kurniawati, R., & Lestari, S. (2016, May). Preserving Indonesian traditional food an overview of food museum attraction. In *Asia Tourism Forum 2016-the 12th Biennial Conference of Hospitality and Tourism Industry in Asia* (pp. 431–434). Atlantis Press.

Llerena, Z. (2009). Food Conjures Memory: Making Memory in The Museum. *Faculty of Information Quarterly, 1*(2).

Okan, B. (2015). Günümüzde müzecilik anlayışı. *Sanat ve Tasarım Dergisi, 5*(2), 187–198.

Okan, B. (2018). Günümüz müzecilik anlayışındaki yaklaşımlar ve müze oluşumunu etkileyen unsurlar. *Tykhe Sanat ve Tasarım Dergisi, 3*(4), 215–242.

Özdemir, S. (2023). *Gastronomi müzeleri: Mutfak Kültürü Mirasının Keşfi.* In *Gastronomi ve Mutfak Sanatları Üzerine Güncel Araştırmalar-I.* içinde Ed. K. Grençer & H. Yazıt. Özgür Yayınları. Gaziantep. 165–184.

Park, E., Kim, S., & Xu, M. (2020). Hunger for learning or tasting? An exploratory study of food tourist motivations visiting food museum restaurants. *Tourism Recreation Research,* 1–15.

Sandıkcı, M., Mutlu, A. S., & Mutlu, H. (2019). Gastronomi temalı müzelerde sunum farklılıkları. In *International Marmara Social Sciences Congress (Autumn 2019)* (P. 540).

Santich, B. (2004). The study of gastronomy and its relevance to hospitality education and training. International Journal of Hospitality Management, 23(1), 15–24.

Sarı Gök, H. & Şalvarcı, S. (2021). Türkiye'deki gastronomi temalı müzelere yönelik çevrimiçi ziyaretçi deneyimlerinin incelenmesi. *Seyahat ve Otel İşletmeciliği Dergisi, 18*(1), 120–140.

Savarin, B. (2009). *The Physiology of Taste: Or Transcendental Gastronomy.* The Floating Press.

Savaşkan, Y., & Çavuş, Ş. (2021). Gastronomi temalı müzelerin ziyaretçi deneyimlerinin incelenmesi: Adatepe Zeytinyağı Müzesi örneği. In *2nd International Congress of New Generations and New Trends in Tourism Proceeding Book içinde* (pp. 93–114).

Scarpato, R. (2002). Gastronomy studies in search of hospitality, *Journal of Hospitality & Tourism Management,* 9: 152–163.

Smith, Chris, "Southern food and beverage museum" (2008). Arts Administration Master's Reports. 1.

Williams, E. (2013). Food museums. In K. Albala (Ed.), Routledge International Handbook of Food Studies (pp. 229237). New York: Routledge.

Yeşilyurt, H., & Arıca, R. (2018). Mutfak müzesi ziyaretçilerinin deneyimlerinin incelenmesi: Emine Göğüş Mutfak Müzesi örneği. *Türk Turizm Araştırmaları Dergisi, 2*(1), 60–70.

Yıldırım Sarıhan, Ç. (2021). "Sürdürülebilir Gastronomi Turizminde Gastronomi Müzelerinin Rolü: Türkiye Örneği". Yayınlanmamış Yüksek Lisans Tezi. Bolu Abant İzzet Baysal Üniversitesi Lisansüstü Eğitim Enstitüsü. Bolu.

Çağri Sürücü[1]

Chapter 29 Gastronomic Tourism Products within the Scope of Intangible Cultural Heritage

Introduction

The United Nations Educational, Scientific and Cultural Organization (UNESCO) convenes numerous conventions with the objective of safeguarding and maintaining cultural heritage, which represents one of the primary justifications for its establishment. The Convention for the Safeguarding of the Intangible Cultural Heritage is a pioneering instrument that seeks to preserve a society's traditional knowledge and culture and to facilitate its transmission from generation to generation (Kurt, 2023). In other words, the objective is to ensure the continued preservation of a society's cultural identity from the present day onwards. Intangible cultural heritage is observed in five principal domains: oral traditions and narratives (epics, legends, fairy tales), performing arts (puppetry, karagöz, folk theater), rituals and feasts (engagement, wedding, birth), knowledge and practices related to nature and the universe (traditional food), and handicraft traditions (weaving, coppersmithing) (Ministry of Culture and Tourism, 2024). From an analysis of these areas, it can be discerned that intangible cultural heritage is essentially a reflection of the values of folk culture, which are based on local culture and tradition.

The foundation of tourism is the combination of natural and cultural attractions. These attractions are observed in a multitude of locations, including historical heritage, crafts, rituals, festivals, and culinary culture. Tourists are motivated to engage with the local culture in depth while undertaking tourism activities in the destination they have chosen (Çapar & Yenipınar, 2016). One of the most crucial aspects of immersing oneself in the local culture is to engage in gastronomic tourism (Stone, Soulard, Migacz & Wolf, 2018). Gastronomic tourism products are defined as products, services, and their combinations that tourists can consume during their travels, use for a certain period of time, or carry forward to the post-travel period. These products are centered on gastronomic

1   Asst. Prof. Ph.D., Çankırı Karatekin University, Ilgaz Tourism and Hotel Management School, Department of Tourism Management, cagrisurucu@gmail.com

products such as local foods and beverages, gastronomic festivals, and cooking courses (Yılmaz, 2021). In this context, examples of local attractions include restaurants, local foods, local dishes, wineries, festivals, cooking courses, local products and farmers' markets, vineyards, gastronomy routes, local product farms and gastronomy museums (Ignatov & Smith, 2006; Smith & Xiao, 2008). For instance, tourists engage in gastronomic tours with the objective of discovering, becoming acquainted with, and experiencing the distinctive food, beverages, and culinary traditions specific to the destination they are visiting during their travels. Consequently, tourists have the chance to gain a deeper understanding of the region's culture by sampling its cuisine and observing the local market (Wolf, Spittler & Ahern, 2005; Suntikul, Agyeiwaah, Huang & Pratt, 2020). Local food can be a significant motivating factor for tourists when planning travel itineraries (Stone & Migacz, 2016). Recently, destination managers have been emphasizing destinations by using local food, local dishes and food-related activities to attract tourists to the destination (Lai, Lattimore & Wang, 2018; Hsu & Scott, 2020). These activities allow tourists to get to know the local culture up close. Local food and drinks offer tourists a different, unique and authentic experience (Stone, Migacz, Garibaldi & Wolf, 2020). Gastronomy museums, also known as food museums (Kim, Park, Xu, 2020; Park, Kim & Xu, 2020. For this reason, gastronomy museums offer tourists a cultural experience.

Destinations offer a variety of products, services and experiences to tourists in order to attract tourists. Destinations with a strong gastronomic identity can attract more tourists to their destinations with a variety of gastronomic tourism products. They can also offer tourists a unique cultural experience with these products. However, gastronomic tourism products can be evaluated within the scope of intangible cultural heritage and can be preserved and transferred to future generations. In this study, the concepts of intangible cultural heritage and gastronomic tourism products will be explained in detail and examples of gastronomic tourism products will be provided. In this context, studies on intangible cultural heritage and gastronomic tourism products will be analyzed. Finally, a framework will be presented by examining the relationship between cultural heritage and gastronomic tourism products as a consequence of the analyzed studies.

Intangible Cultural Heritage and Gastronomic Tourism Products

Local cuisines are intangible elements that contribute to the cultural values and characteristics of the region (Timothy & Ron, 2013). Gastronomic heritage represents the lifestyle, traditions and customs, cultural values and activities of the region (Kaşlı, Cankül, Köz & Ekici, 2015). Thus, gastronomic heritage is a holistic concept that includes the eating and drinking habits of the people living in the region, the tools used in the production of local dishes, presentation styles and festivals (Bayram, 2018). Gastronomic tourism products are of crucial importance for the protection of culinary culture. In other words, it is a crucial element in the transmission of culinary culture to future generations. In this context, the sustainability of culinary culture and its transmission to future generations can be achieved by the protection of gastronomic heritage (Fereli & Alyakut, 2018; Duman & Avcıkurt, 2023).

Local products and local cuisine represent experiential products that are at the center of tourists' travels and contribute to the enrichment of their tourism experience (Ellis, Park, Kim & Yeoman, 2018; Jeaheng & Han, 2020; Lee, 2022). From a cultural perspective, food plays an important role in enabling tourists to gain an understanding of the culture of the community in the destination they are visiting (Tse & Crotts, 2005; Kivela & Crotts, 2009). In essence, local cuisine offers tourists the opportunity to not only satisfy their hunger during their travels, but also to experience a dining experience that extends beyond the mere satisfaction of hunger (Lee, 2023). For instance, the preparation, cooking, and presentation of food offer tourists an immersive experience of the culinary arts. In addition to local cuisine, gastronomic museums, festivals, courses, and routes, as well as gastronomic tours, are regarded as the most effective means of conveying cultural heritage to tourists.

Gastronomy museums, are institutions dedicated to the display and promotion of local gastronomic products, including dairy products such as cheese, chocolate, olive oil, wines, and coffees (Yılmaz, 2021). Museums play a pivotal role in the recognition and preservation of regional heritage and culture. Museums are also seen as a primary source of attraction for tourist destinations (Moreno Gil, Ritchie & Almeida-Santana, 2019). Museums serve as repositories for cultural heritage and the distinctive attributes of destinations. For example, coffee and tea museums play an important role in understanding and promoting cultural heritage. In this context, the importance of the relationship between tea, coffee, tourism and hospitality comes to the front (Jolliffe, 2006).

Museums are an important tourist attraction used to reflect the cultural assets of the region. Tourists visit museums to have a cultural experience during their travels. In this sense, museums offer tourists a unique and unique experience (Falk & Dierking, 2016; Bideci & Albayrak, 2018). Therefore, museums have an important potential for tourists to learn about cultural heritage during their travels. Therefore, museums are recognized as an important dimension of tourism (Trinh & Rayan, 2016). Gastronomy museums reflect the culinary culture of the region. In additional, local products of the region and the tools, equipment and equipment of these products are exhibited in these museums. In this respect, gastronomy museums constitute a different element of attraction for many local and foreign tourists (Kim, Park & Xu, 2020). Therefore, there is an increase in the number of tourists visiting gastronomy museums. There are many gastronomy-themed museums in Turkey. Some of these are Emine Göğüş Culinary Museum, the Adatepe Olive Oil Museum, the Turkish Flavor Museum, the Gastronomy Museum, and the Çaykur Tea Museum. To illustrate, the Emine Göğüş Culinary Museum is situated in Gaziantep. In 2016, Gaziantep was designated as a UNESCO Creative City of Gastronomy. The Emine Göğüş Culinary Museum has as its objective the promotion of the culinary culture of Gaziantep. Furthermore, the museum displays a variety of tools and equipment utilized in Gaziantep cuisine. Additionally, the museum presents visual representations of local dishes. Consequently, the Emine Göğüş Culinary Museum is the inaugural culinary museum established in Turkey (Ministry of Culture and Tourism, 2024). In conclusion, gastronomy museums facilitate the memorization of local foods and regional dishes in the region by showcasing them prominently.

Gastronomy festivals are events that are organized with the theme of local food and drink. Events represent a significant draw for the tourism sector. Festivals represent a significant factor in the development of tourist destinations (Getz, 2008). Furthermore, festivals and other special events held in tourist destinations exert a considerable influence on the local economy (Smith & Costello, 2009). Gastronomy festivals typically showcase regional dishes and local foods from the region in question. Furthermore, these festivals provide an ideal setting for showcasing local gastronomic products to tourists in a distinctive manner. In this context, destination managers and local governments organize gastrono-mythemed festivals with the objective of promoting and marketing the destination (Kömürcü, 2013).

Gastronomy festivals offer a valuable opportunity to reinforce and enhance regional and local identity. Furthermore, they serve to disseminate the gastronomic heritage culture (Hubbard et al., 2012; Hollows et al., 2014). The presentation of local gastronomic products at gastronomy festivals serves an important function in the promotion of the lifestyle, traditions, customs, and culinary culture of the local population. Furthermore, these festivals provide tourists with a diverse range of experiences (Wu et al., 2014). Festivals organized in the destination are generally closely related to the culture of the people living in that region. Thus, festivals generally reflect the lifestyle of the local people. In this regard, gastronomy festivals are significant (Seçim, 2020). Culinary culture and rituals are among the intangible cultural heritage elements of society. Getting to know these cultural elements is through experiencing and tasting by visiting the destination. Therefore, gastronomy festivals provide the opportunity to experience the culinary culture of the destination on site. They also play an important role in the promotion of culinary culture (Sandybayev, 2018; Choo, Park & Petrick, 2022).

Gastronomy festivals can be organized in various themes. In different themes, festivals are organized by emphasizing only local gastronomic products specific to the region. Lately, it is seen that the interest in gastronomy festivals has also increased due to the increasing interest in gastronomy tourism. Tourists also experience food through gastronomy festivals. In other words, tourists enrich their experience with gastronomy festivals. (Everett & Aitchison, 2007; Lee & Arcodia, 2011). In Turkey, gastronomy-themed festivals are held in various regions. These include the Gaziantep International Gastronomy Festival, the Yeşilüzümlü and its surrounding area Morel Mushroom Festival, the International Adana Flavor Festival, and the Gastro Afyon International Tourism and Flavor Festival. These festivals highlight the local gastronomic products of the region and promote them. They also include culinary culture in their promotions.

Local foods and beverages are regarded as distinctive and traditional products of the region (Seyitoğlu, 2020). Furthermore, local food is a significant motivator for tourists seeking to visit the destination. In other words, it is utilized as a pivotal factor in attracting tourists traveling to the destination to experience gastronomy. While tourists consume local products during their travels, they also engage with the culture of food (Ignatov & Smith, 2006; Sanchez-Canizares & Castillo-Canalejo, 2015). The consumption of local foods is inextricably linked to the history, traditions, and customs of the destinations visited.

Local food and regional cuisine represent a significant aspect of the tourist experience (Harrington & Ottenbacher, 2010). Local food has emerged as a pivotal tourism resource. Local food serves as a pivotal element of the cultural heritage of the destination that tourists visit. Consequently, for tourists, gastronomy represents a crucial element in comprehending the intangible heritage or culture of the destination (Chen & Huang, 2015; Björk & Kauppinen-Räisänen, 2016). Consequently, local food is a crucial component that contributes to the allure and reputation of a destination (Chang & Yuan, 2011; Lee & Scott, 2015).

Gastronomy tours are defined as tours that are organized on a specific route with the objective of discovering local gastronomic products and culinary culture specific to a particular region. The primary objective of gastronomy tours is to visit local gastronomic products at their source. The primary motivation of tourists participating in these tours is the gastronomic experience. Tourists have the opportunity to experience local dishes, local food, and the culinary culture of a region during their travels. Furthermore, gastronomy tours serve to promote the preservation of the culinary culture of a region and the development of sustainable tourism activities (Onur, 2021; Belber & Kamış, 2022). In conclusion, gastronomy tours facilitate an increase in tourist movements and gastronomy tourism activities in the region.

Results

The demand for gastronomic tourism is on the rise, with an increasing number of tourists seeking out culinary experiences on their travels. Gastronomy travels basically focus on local gastronomic products and culinary culture. Culinary culture is one of the most important elements in gastronomy tourism. Specifically, destinations provide local gastronomic products and services to attract tourists to the region. These products and services offer tourists a unique and memorable gastronomic experience. Gastronomy deals with issues such as the preparation, presentation, historical and cultural context of meals using local gastronomic products as a whole. In this perspective, gastronomy tourism creates a power of attraction for domestic and foreign tourists It is very important to transfer the gastronomic cultural heritage to future generations. For instance, gastronomy museums play an important role in ensuring the sustainability of intangible cultural heritage. These museums protect the culinary culture of the region and pass it on to future generations. In gastronomy museums, the history of local gastronomic products, preparation processes and the tools used in cooking are exhibited.

Gastronomy festivals are activities organized to promote rich cultural heritage and local flavors. In these festivals, local gastronomic products and local foods are introduced. There is an increase in the number of tourists due to festivals. In the same, local food is an equally factor in tourist attraction. In this regard, tourists can enhance their travel experience by experiencing a cultural experience. Gastronomy tours are tours to explore local food and local products in the region through gastronomy routes. These tours are designed to experience food, explore gastronomic delicacies in the region and learn about the local food culture. Tourists have an memorable travel by experiencing cultural experience and local flavors together with gastronomy tours. In summary, culinary culture should be learned authentically and transferred to future generations.

References

Bayram, Ü. (2018). Gastronomik kültürel miras olarak Buldan Günbalı. Journal of Tourism and Gastronomy Studies, 6 (1), 361–371.

Belber, B. G. & Kamış, M. D. (2022). Gastronomi Turizminin Sürdürülebilirliğinde, Gastronomi Rotalarının Önemi, Cukurova 8th International Scientific Researches Conference, 15–17 April, Adana, Turkey.

Bideci, M. & Albayrak, T. (2018), "An investigation of the domestic and foreign tourists' museum visit experiences", International Journal of Culture, Tourism and Hospitality Research, Vol. 12 No. 3, pp. 366–377.

Björk, P. & Kauppinen-Räisänen, H. (2016), "Local food: a source for destination attraction", International Journal of Contemporary Hospitality Management, Vol. 28 No. 1, pp. 177–194.

Çapar, G., & Yenipınar, U. (2016). Somut olmayan kültürel miras kaynağı olarak yöresel yiyeceklerin turizm endüstrisinde kullanılması. *Journal of Tourism & Gastronomy Studies*, 4(Special Issue 1), 100–115.

Chang, W. &Yuan, J. (2011), "A taste of tourism: visitors' motivations to attend a food festival", Event Management, Vol. 15 No. 1, pp. 13–23.

Chen, Q. & Huang, R. (2015), "Understanding the importance of food tourism to Chongging (China)", Journal of Vacation Marketing, Vol. 22 No. 1, pp. 42–54.

Choo, H., Park, D. B., & Petrick, J. F. (2022). Festival tourists' loyalty: The role of involvement in local food festivals. *Journal of Hospitality and Tourism Management*, 50, 57–66.

Duman, H., & Avcıkurt, C. (2023). Evaluation of Local Dishes as An Intangible Cultural Heritage Value In Terms of Gastronomy Tourism: The Case of Ayvalık. *Journal of Gastronomy, Hospitality and Travel*, 2023, 6(2), 548–557.

Ellis, A., Park, E., Kim, S., & Yeoman, I. (2018). What is food tourism? *Tourism Management*, 68, 250–263.

Everett, S., & Aitchison, C. (2007). Food tourism and the regeneration of regional identity in Cornwall: An exploratory case study. In *Festivals and events: Culture and identity in leisure, sport and tourism* (pp. 167–192). Eastbourne.

Falk, J.H. & Dierking, L.D. (2016), The Museum Experience Revisited, Routledge, New York, NY.

Fereli, S. & Alyakut, Ö. (2018). Dünya kültür mirası listesine alınan tarihi Uzunköprü ilçesinin somut olmayan kültürel mirası: Geleneksel yemekleri. *Uluslararası Turizm, İşletme, Ekonomi Dergisi*, 2(2), 476–494.

Getz, D. (2008). Event tourism: Definition, evolution, and research. *Tourism management*, 29(3), 403–428.

Harrington, R.J. and Ottenbacher, M.C. (2010), "Culinary tourism. A case study of the gastronomic capital", Journal of Culinary Science and Technology, Vol. 8 No. 1, pp. 14–32.

Hollows, J., Jones, S. & Taylor, B. (2014), "Making sense of urban food festivals: cultural regeneration, disorder and hospitable cities", Journal of Policy Research in Tourism, Leisure & Events, Vol. 6 No. 1, pp. 1–14.

Hsu, F. C., & Scott, N. (2020). Food experience, place attachment, destination image and the role of food-related personality traits. *Journal of Hospitality and Tourism Management*, 44, 79–87.

Hubbard, K.W., Mandabach, K.H., McDowall, S. & Vanleeuwen, D.M. (2012), "Perceptions of quality, satisfaction, loyalty, and approximate spending at an American wine festival", Journal of Culinary Science & Technology, Vol. 10 No. 4, pp. 337–351.

Jeaheng, Y., & Han, H. (2020). Thai street food in the fast growing global food tourism industry: Preference and behaviors of food tourists. *Journal of Hospitality and Tourism Management*, 45, 641–655.

Jolliffe, L. (2006), "Tea and hospitality: more than a cuppa", International Journal of Contemporary Hospitality Management, Vol. 18 No. 2, pp. 164–168.

Kaşlı, M., Cankül, D., Köz, E.N. & Ekici, A. (2015). Gastronomik miras ve sürdürülebilirlik: Eskişehir örneği. Eko-Gastronomi Dergisi, 1 (2), 27–46.

Kim, S., Park, E., & Xu, M. (2020). Beyond the authentic taste: The tourist experience at a food museum restaurant. *Tourism Management Perspectives*, 36, 100749.

Kivela, J.J. & Crotts, J.C. (2009), "Understanding travelers' experiences of gastronomy through etymology and narration", *Journal of Hospitality & Tourism Research*, Vol. 33 No. 2, pp. 161–192.

Kömürcü, G. B. (2013). Etkinlik Turizmi Çeşidi Olarak Festivaller: Bozcaada Yerel Tatlar Festivali Örneği (Yayımlanmamış Yüksek Lisans Tezi), Çanakkale, Çanakkale Onsekiz Mart Üniversitesi.

Kurt, S. (2023). Somut Olmayan Kültürel Miras ve Turizm İlişkisi. A. Türker, S. Kurt & G. Köksal (Eds.), Anadolu'nun Somut Olmayan Kültürel Mirası (ss. 1–7). Detay Yayıncılık, Ankara.

Lai, M. U., Lattimore, C. K., & Wang, Y. (2018). A perception gap investigation into food and cuisine image attributes for destination branding from the host perspective: *The case of Australia. Tourism Management*, 69, 579–595.

Lam, A (2011). Designing is Cooking: A Museum of Gastronomy, Virginia Polytechnic Institute, Master's Dissertation, Virginia.

Lee, I., & Arcodia, C. (2011). The role of regional food festivals for destination branding. *International Journal of Tourism Research*, 13(4), 355–367.

Lee, K. S. (2022). Culinary aesthetics: World-traveling with culinary arts. *Annals of Tourism Research*, 97, Article 103487.

Lee, K. S. (2023). Cooking up food memories: A taste of intangible cultural heritage. *Journal of Hospitality and Tourism Management, 54*, 1–9.

Lee, K.-H. & Scott, N. (2015), "Food tourism reviewed using the paradigm funnel approach", Journal of Culinary Science & Technology, Vol. 13 No. 2, pp. 95–115.

Moreno Gil, S., Ritchie, J.B. & Almeida-Santana, A. (2019), "Museum tourism in canary islands: assessing image perception of directors and visitors", Museum Management and Curatorship, Vol. 34 No. 5, pp. 501–520.

Onur, N. (2021). Gastronomi turizmi ve Hatay lezzet rotası. *Turizm Ekonomi ve İşletme Araştırmaları Dergisi, 3*(2), 150–162.

Şahin, A. (2021). Gastronomi Müzeleri. G. Yılmaz & A. Şahin (Eds.), Örnek Olaylarla Gastoronomi Turizminde Yeni Eğilimler (ss. 95–109). Detay Yayıncılık, Ankara.

Sanchez-Can˜izares, S. & Castillo-Canalejo, A.M. (2015), "A comparative study of tourist attitudes towards culinary tourism in Spain and Slovenia", British Food Journal, Vol. 117 No. 9, pp. 2387–2411, doi: 10.1108/BFJ-01-2015-0008.

Sandybayev, A. (2018). The impact of street and food festivals in gastronomic tourism through visitor's emotions and satisfaction. A case of Abu Dhabi Food Festival. *International Journal of Research in Tourism and Hospitality, 4*(1), 27–32.

Seçim, Y. (2020). Gastronomy festivals in Turkey. *Selected Academic Studies from Turkish Tourism Sector*, 223–234.

Seyitoglu, F. (2020). "Tourist experiences of guided culinary tours: the case of Istanbul", Journal of Culinary Science and Technology, pp. 1–22.

Smith, S. L. J., & Xiao, H. (2008). Culinary tourism supply chains: *A preliminary examination. Journal of Travel Research, 46*(3), 289–299.

Smith, S., & Costello, C. (2009). Culinary tourism: Satisfaction with a culinary event utilizing importance-performance grid analysis. *Journal of Vacation Marketing, 15*(2), 99–110.

Stone, M. J., & Migacz, S. (2016). The American culinary traveler: Profiles, behaviors, & attitudes. Portland, OR: World Food Travel Association.

Stone, M. J., Migacz, S., Garibaldi, R., & Wolf, E. (2020). 2020 Food Travel Monitor. Portland, OR: World Food Travel Association.

Stone, M., Soulard, J., Migacz, S., & Wolf, E. (2018). Elements of memorable food, drink, and culinary tourism experience. *Journal of Travel Research, 57*(8), 1121–1132.

Suntikul, W., Agyeiwaah, E., Huang, W. J., & Pratt, S. (2020). Investigating the tourism experience of Thai cooking classes: An application of Larsen's three-stage model. *Tourism Analysis, 25*(1), 107–122.

T.C. Kültür ve Turizm Bakanlığı (2024). Gaziantep İl Kültür ve Turizm Müdürlüğü, Emine Göğüş Mutfak Müzesi https://gaziantep.ktb.gov.tr/TR-174064/emine-gogus-mutfak-muzesi.html (erişim tarihi: 01.05.2024).

T.C. Kültür ve Turizm Bakanlığı (2024). Somut Olmayan Kültürel Miras Nedir? https://yakegm.ktb.gov.tr/TR-345089/somut-olmayan-kulturel-miras-nedir.html (erişim tarihi: 01.05.2024).

Timothy, D. J., & Ron, A. S. (2013). Understanding heritage cuisines and tourism: Identity, image, authenticity, and change. *Journal of Heritage Tourism, 8*(2–3), 99–104.

Trinh, T.T. & Ryan, C. (2016), "Heritage and cultural tourism: the role of the aesthetic when visiting Mỹ Sơn and Cham Museum, Vietnam", Current Issues in Tourism, Vol. 19 No. 6, pp. 564–589.

Tse, P. & Crotts, J.C. (2005), "Antecedents of novelty seeking: international visitors' propensity to experiment across Hong Kong's culinary traditions", *Tourism Management*, Vol. 26 No. 6, pp. 965–968.

Wolf, M. M., Spittler, A., & Ahern, J. (2005). A profile of farmers' market consumers and the perceived advantages of produce sold at farmers' markets. *Journal of food distribution research, 36*(1), 192–201.

Wu, H.-C., Wong, J.W.-C. and Cheng, C.-C. (2014), "An empirical study of behavioural intentions in the food festivals: the case of Macau", Asia Pacific Journal of Tourism Research, Vol. 19 No. 11, pp. 1278–1305.

Yılmaz, G. (2021). Gastronomi Turizmi ve Gastronomik Turizm Ürünleri. G. Yılmaz & A. Şahin (Eds.), Örnek Olaylarla Gastoronomi Turizminde Yeni Eğilimler (ss. 1–23). Detay Yayıncılık, Ankara.

Elif Zeynep Özer[1] and Alper Çevik[2]

Chapter 30 Taste and Flavor Perception

Introduction

Taste creates physical perception through pure sensations. Flavor perception can be formed both by the effect of taste sensation and by psychological factors. Generally accepted taste sensations include: Sour, Bitter, Sweet, Salty, and Umami flavors. The 'Taste and Flavor Perception' section discusses these generally accepted taste sensations. In addition to these, other taste senses are mentioned. The first part of the section discusses the factors affecting flavor perception and flavor perception itself.

Taste Sensations

The surface of our tongue is covered with many small folds known as papillae. These papillae act as body sensors that allow us to detect the flavors of the food we eat. The functioning of these sensors is provided by taste buds. When food is broken down in the mouth, the chemicals released are detected by the taste buds. The resulting signals are then sent to the taste center in the brain, and we taste the food. Accordingly, the taste senses consist of five basic tastes: sour, bitter, sweet, salty, and umami, along with the vaguely defined tastes of kokumi, alkaline, fatty, and metallic.

Sour Taste

It is widely accepted that the sour taste is produced by acids (Breslin & Huang, 2006). Acidity (sourness) is not as highly appreciated as sweet and salty tastes, but it is still an important element in flavor. The sour taste induced by acids is not associated with a specific food group; however, it is still highly preferred in foods, and acidic additives are often used by people to make foods sour (Roper,

---

1 Assistant Professor, Kastamonu University Faculty of Tourism, Gastronomy and Culinary Arts, elifozer@kastamonu.edu.tr
2 Lecturer, Kastamonu University Daday Nafi ve Ümit ve Çeri Vocational School, Department of Hotel, Restaurant and Catering Services, Cookery Program, alpercevik@kastamonu.edu.tr

2007). Acidic products are often refreshing and are judged to be light and crisp. In terms of mouthfeel, acidity tends to be astringent and stimulates saliva flow. Acids can also be used as preservatives, similar to salt. Pickles are the most common example of this (Klosse, 2010).

Bitter Taste

A number of chemicals are associated with bitterness. The bitterness of phenolic compounds and some inorganic salts is perceived by the taste buds at the back of the tongue. The bitterness of these compounds is expressed by a threshold (perception) value (Karadeniz, 2000). The lower the threshold value, the more effective the compound, and bitterness is actually experienced as a burning sensation. Various spices and chilies create a bitter and burning sensation, but they are not flavors. The bitterness in chili is due to its capsaicin content. In other words, the bitter taste lingers on the tongue longer than other flavors. The receptors that detect sour and bitter foods are located at the back of the tongue (Batu, 2017).

Bitter is an interesting classification and can be defined as a taste that is astringent or sharp in nature. It is often considered an undesirable flavor, although it is sometimes intentionally added to foods. Most of the 'bitter' components found in plants such as coffee, cocoa, lemon peel, and olives are glycosides, and some are toxic. Despite this, bitter flavors are still used in our food and drinks. This is because very few of the toxic glycoside substances found in foods are absorbed by the body. Moreover, it is considered that the proportion of bitter-tasting molecules is not intense enough to poison people but rather only adds flavor to the food (Kaynar, 2013).

Sweet Taste

It is generally accepted that we are born with a preference for sweetness. This taste is, of course, directly related to sugar. Sugar is a water-soluble crystalline carbohydrate, primarily derived from sugar beet and sugar cane. The most common types are the monosaccharides glucose and fructose, and the disaccharides sucrose (a combination of glucose and fructose), lactose (found in milk), and maltose. Additionally, there are more complex polysaccharides such as pectins, gums, starches, and cellulose. Sugars serve other functions as well: they act as natural preservatives and contribute to the sensation of fullness or coating in the mouth (Klosse, 2010).

Sugar is not only indispensable for the sector. Today's young cooks tend to use more sugar in the kitchen than in the past. For example, it is noticeable that sugar has become an almost ordinary ingredient in mayonnaise and salad dressings (Klosse, 2010).

Salty Taste

In human history, sodium chloride (NaCl), also known as table salt, has traditionally been one of the most widely used condiments in daily life. NaCl is a neutral inorganic compound with a salty taste that plays an important role in maintaining the osmotic pressure balance in the human body. The purposes of salt used during food processing mainly include sensory, technological, and preservative functions. Meanwhile, as a fundamental ingredient in food processing, salt can enhance the flavor of pickled vegetables, bacon, and ham, and extend the shelf life of various foods (Le ve diğerleri, 2022).

Salt is a mineral that can be obtained from seawater or rock deposits. It is the world's oldest food condiment and is utilized across the globe. Serving as a flavor enhancer, it is responsible for the improved taste of many foods with just a pinch added. Consequently, it wields significant influence over the richness of flavor (Klosse, 2010).

Umami Taste

Umami, originating from Japan, is described as a "pleasant taste, delicious, or meaty" flavor (Cömert & Güdek 2017). It is a taste sensation elicited by various substances, particularly the amino acid glutamate, and 5'-ribonucleotides such as inosinate and guanylate (Ninomiya, 2015).

While traditional Western cuisine predominantly relies on animal fat for its sensory qualities, traditional Japanese cuisine features less fat and instead utilizes "dashi" or Japanese broth to enhance flavor. In the West, Brillat-Savarin introduced the term "osmasome" in his classic 1825 work "The Physiology of Taste" to describe the basis of meaty flavor but failed to identify the essential component. Conversely, in Japan, the discovery of umami is attributed in part to the simplicity of "dashi," which is made by steeping dried seaweed (konbu) in boiling water. In the early 20th century, Ikeda noticed an indistinct taste quality in savory foods, distinct from the four basic tastes (sweet, salty, sour, and bitter), particularly evident in soups and "dashi" made from seaweed (konbu) or dried fish (katsuobushi), both staples in Japanese cuisine. Upon studying the constituents of dried konbu, he identified glutamate as the source of this flavor and named it "umami." (Shizuko, Kumiko 2000).

Other Tastes

The four recognized basic tastes along with umami are commonly referred to as the five taste senses in literature. However, a new flavor was identified in a study conducted in 2015. This flavor is called "Oleogustus." It derives from the Latin words "oleo" (oil, fat) and "gustus" (taste), signifying the taste of oil (Süren, 2022).

In addition to being a taste, kokumi serves more as a flavor enhancer, amplifying the perception of other basic tastes, particularly sweet, umami, and salty. Kokumi taste is triggered by amino acids or small peptides. One of the most potent Kokumi compounds known is γ-glutamyl-valyl-glycine, which is present in foods like fish sauce, yeast, soy sauce, shrimp-paste, cheese, and beer. Kokumi peptides are also naturally found in protein-rich foods. Kokumi strengthens the calcium receptors on the tongue, resulting in a denser, more balanced, and mouth-coating sensation (Yılmaz and Altuntaş, 2022).

Flavor and Factors Affecting Flavor Perception

For thousands of years, humans have relied on their senses to assess food. Even before Homo sapiens evolved, sensory evaluation played a crucial role, as many plant-derived toxins and bacterial ingredients are perceived as bitter, sour, or rancid (Clark et al., 2009).

Flavor represents one of our most multisensory everyday experiences. Recent studies by psychologists and neuroscientists have unveiled the intricate interactions that contribute to the taste experiences we cherish, demonstrating how cues from all human senses are amalgamated. These academic advancements are now translating into real-world applications, with chefs and the food industry progressively incorporating the latest scientific discoveries into their food production processes (Spence, 2015).

The biting and chewing sounds of food are assumed to provide important information about the firmness of a vegetable, the ripeness of a fruit, or the texture of a piece of fish. In our everyday lives, we often consider the sound of food as part of its flavor. The 'crunch, crackle, and pop' of a breakfast cereal are as important an attraction as its flavor, while the crunch of a fried potato or chicken nugget can be an integral part of the chewing experience (Shepherd, 2011:144).

What we hear when we eat, drink, and even decide what to eat and drink plays a much more important role in our food and drink choices, taste, and flavor experiences than we might think. From the sounds of food preparation (food packaging, Akkuş, 2019) to the sounds of eating, and from background sounds to background music, food preparation can significantly influence the flavor of food. It also contributes to making food and beverages appear more valuable (Piqueras-Fiszman and Spence, 2016).

The appearance of food elicits a variety of physiological, emotional, and cognitive responses. Firstly, it serves as an indicator for the body's preparation for subsequent food intake and is accompanied by expected physiological responses such as the cephalic phase release of insulin and changes in heart rate (Drobes et al., 2001; Wallner Liebmann et al., 2010). Secondly, it can evoke emotional responses such as the desire to eat (Ouwehand and Papies, 2010). Thirdly, the image of food activates cognitive processes such as memorization and hedonic evaluation based on information stored during previous experiences with the food (Van der Laan et al., 2010: 296).

There are two aspects of olfaction: orthonasal and retronasal olfaction. The former is the most familiar, originating from the outside and registered through the nose during breathing. Retronasal odor refers to odors perceived from inside the mouth. Both 'smells' are crucial for assessing the characteristics, richness, and complexity of a particular aroma. However, the two parts of the olfactory system serve markedly different functions. Orthonasal perception is used to identify distant objects and provides information about potential palatability in both positive (attractive odor) and negative (unpleasant odor) situations. The retronasal sense (also known as the inner nose) directly contributes to tasting and thus to food identification in the mouth. From an evolutionary perspective, we can infer that our nose (and eyes) have always aided us in making the right food choices in the absence of packaged, safe foods with detailed labels (Klosse, 2010).

The sense of smell is the only sense that is often conflated with the sense of taste. For this reason, it is believed that the distinctive flavor of the foods we perceive and experience primarily originates from the sense of smell (Boyacı, 2019).

Associative learning is believed to play a key role in flavor perception. The basic understanding is that when an unfamiliar food is ingested, a cortical process is initiated, creating an associative link between the odor and taste components. With continued exposure to the food, these associations eventually lead to a strong flavor memory that modulates subsequent interactions between the monosensory components. Many observed features of flavor are thought to result from this modulation. Furthermore, once a flavor memory is firmly encoded, the presentation of odor components alone is sometimes sufficient to activate the entire flavor memory (Fondberg, 2021).

he label on the food we purchase, the price, and the brand of the products we consume can influence our perception of taste and may alter the taste of the food either positively or negatively (Ağan and Doğan, 2022). Consequently, the distinct flavor profiles of brands allow consumers to differentiate between brands without relying on brand names or images (Büdün, E, 2020).

Results

Flavor perception involves a complex sensory system. Food marketers (markets, food and beverage businesses, etc.) can manipulate flavor perception to ensure that the food consumed is perceived more favorably.

On the other hand, taste perception is a simpler process, primarily arising from the perception of the food item taken into the mouth by various taste receptors.

Taste perception may vary depending on sensory sensitivity, health status, and age. In contrast, flavor perception may vary depending on factors such as ambiance, sound, associations with the food consumed, and the consumer's memories of the food (such as comfort food). The common factor between these two perceptions is odor. Both flavor perception and taste perception can be altered by changes in smell.

References

Ağan, C., & Doğan, M. (2022). Lezzet ve Lezzetin Bilimi: Mutfak Şeflerinin Lezzet Algıları Üzerine Bir Araştırma. Safran Kültür ve Turizm Araştırmaları Dergisi, 5(2), 199-219.

Akkuş, Ç. (2019). Restoran atmosferi algısının sosyal medya paylaşımlarına etkisi: bir temalı restoran örneği. Manas Sosyal Araştırmalar Dergisi, 8(1), 628-642.

Ariffin, Batu, A. (2017) Taste and Aroma Perceptions of Foods from the Perspective of Molecular Gastronomy. Aydin Gastronomy, 1 (1):25–36, 2017.

Bei Le, Binbin Yu, Muhammed Sadık Emin, Ruixi Liu, Na Zhang, Olugbenga P, Soladoye, Rotimi E Aluko, Yuhao Zhang (2022). Salt taste receptors and associated salty/salt taste-enhancing peptides: A comprehensive review of structure and function Trends in Food Science & Technology Volume 129, November 2022, Pages 657–666

Boyacı, D. 2019. The Effect of Senses on Flavour Perception and Purchase Intention: Aydın Adnan Menderes University, Institute of Social Sciences, Master's Thesis, Aydın.

Breslin, P. A., & Huang, L. (2006). Human taste: Peripheral anatomy, tastetrans-duction, and coding. Taste and Smell, 63, 152–190.

Büdün, E, 2020. The Role of Sensory Branding Stimuli in Creating Attitude Towards a Brand: A Research on the Home Textiles Sector: Istanbul University Institute of Social Sciences PhD Thesis, Istanbul.

Clark, S, l Costello, M, Drake, M, Bodyfelt, F, (2009). The Sensory Evaluation of Dairy Products

Cömert, M., Güdek, M. (2017) Fifth Taste: Umami (Fifth Taste: Umami) Journal of Tourism and Gastronomy Studies 5/3 (2017) 397–408

Drobes, D. J., Saladin, M. E., & Tiffany, S. T. (2001). Classical conditioning mechanisms in alcohol dependence. In N. Heather, T. J. Peters, & T. Stockwell (Eds.), International handbook of alcohol dependence and problems (pp. 281–297). John Wiley & Sons Ltd.Cömert, M., Güdek, M. (2017) Beşinci Tat: Umami (Fifth Taste: Umami) Journal of Tourism and Gastronomy Studies 5/3 (2017) 397-408.

Fiszman, p, Spence, C, Multisensory Flavour Perception From Fundamental Neuroscience, Through to the Marketplace, 2016

Fondberg, R. (2021). Mechanisms of flavour perception: how odour and taste interact when we eat. Unpublished Ph.D., Karolinska Institutet Department of Clinical Neuroscience, Stockholm.

Food Cues. NeuroImage, 55, 296–303.

Karadeniz, F. (2000). Flavour Perception Mechanism. Food 25(5): 317–324

Kaynar, K. (2013). Taste of our mouth. http://www.acikbilim.com/2013/09/dosyalar/agzimizin-tadi.html. Access date: 30.05.2024.

Klosse, P. (2010). The Essence of gastronomy: Understanding the Flavour of Foods and Beverages. New York, Taylor & Francis Group

Ninomiya, K. (2015). Science Of Umami Taste: Adaptation To Gastronomic Culture. Flavour, 4(13), 1–5

Ouwehand, C., & Papies, E. K. (2010). Eat it or beat it. The differential effects of food temptations on overweight and normal-weight restrained eaters. Appetite, 55(1), 56-60.

Piqueras-Fiszman, B., & Spence, C. (Eds.). (2016). Multisensory flavor perception: From fundamental neuroscience through to the marketplace. Woodhead Publishing.

Roper, S. D. (2007). "Signal Transduction and Information Processing in Mammalian Taste Buds", Pflügers Archiv: European Journal of Physiology, 454(5), 759–776.

Shepherd, G., M., (2011). Neurogastronomy How The Brain Creates Flavor And Why It Matters, Columbia University Press.

Shizuko Y., Kumiko N. "Umami ve Gıda Lezzeti" The Journal of Nutrition Cilt 130, Sayı 4, Nisan 2000, Sayfa 921S-926S

Spence, C. (2015). Çok Duyulu Lezzet Algısı

Süren, T. (2022). Altıncı Tat Oleogustus: Gastronomideki Yeri. Konferans: Korku Ata Bilimsel Araştırmalar Kongresi: Osmaniye/Türkiye Cilt: 2

Tat Her Zaman Gözlerdedir: Görsel İşlemenin Nöral İlişkileri Üzerine Bir Meta-Analiz

Van der Laan, L. N., De Ridder, D. T., Viergever, M. A., & Smeets, P. A. (2011). The first taste is always with the eyes: a meta-analysis on the neural correlates of processing visual food cues. Neuroimage, 55(1), 296–303.

Wallner-Liebmann, S., Koschutnig, K., Reishofer, G., Sorantin, E., Blaschitz, B., Kruschitz, R., Unterrainer, H. F., Gasser, R., Freytag, F., Bauer-Denk, C., Mangge, H. & Mangge, H. (2010) Insulin and hippocampus activation in response to images of high-calorie food in normal weight and obese adolescents. Obesity, 18(8), 1552–1557.

Yılmaz, İ, Altuntaş, N, "Kokumi Tat Algısı Üzerine Bir Değerlendirme". Journal of Food and Feed Science - Technology 27: 13–19 (2022/1)

Emel Kaynakci[1] and Irem Serra Pekşen[2]

Chapter 31 The Role of Mass Nutrition Systems in Food Allergen Management

Introduction

Food and Food Allergies

Allergy, a dysfunction of the body's biological processes in response to foreign substances, is often accompanied by an abnormal immune response mediated by IgE and T-helper (Th)2 cytokines. The symptoms of allergy can range from mild (atopic dermatitis, rhinitis, etc.) to severe (anaphylaxis, anaphylactoid, etc.). Food allergy, a prevalent condition, affects around 8– 10 % of children and 5 % of adults (Blázquez &Berin, 2017; Sicherer& Sampson, 2018). The most common allergens are food, drugs, and insect stings (Dougherty et al., 2023; Zhang, 2023; Nutrition, 2024). The role of various nutrients and dietary components, such as vitamins A and D, minerals A, D, Zn, and iron, dietary fiber, fatty acids, and phytochemicals, in all stages of allergic inflammation is significant. They alter membrane lipid composition, key inflammatory and metabolic pathways, and gene expression at the transcriptional level through epigenetics. As climate change has an epigenetic effect, allergies that were not seen before may become apparent (Zhang, 2023; Lee & Ramsey, 2024). The climatic conditions experienced may also contribute to the observation of allergic conditions in the local population. Figure 31.1 below illustrates the distribution of food allergies by country for peanuts and tree nuts [combined], seafood, cow's milk, wheat, egg, soya, fruit [combined], and sesame. The darker the color, the higher the incidence of allergy (Conrado et al., 2021).

---

1   Asst. Prof. Dr., Akdeniz University, Faculty of Health Science, Department of Nutrition and Dietetics; Institute of Health Science, Department of Medical Biotechnology, ekaynakci@akdeniz.edu.tr
2   Bachelor degree, Akdeniz University, Institute of Health Sciences, Department of Medical Biotechnology, 202250014008@ogr.akdeniz.edu.tr

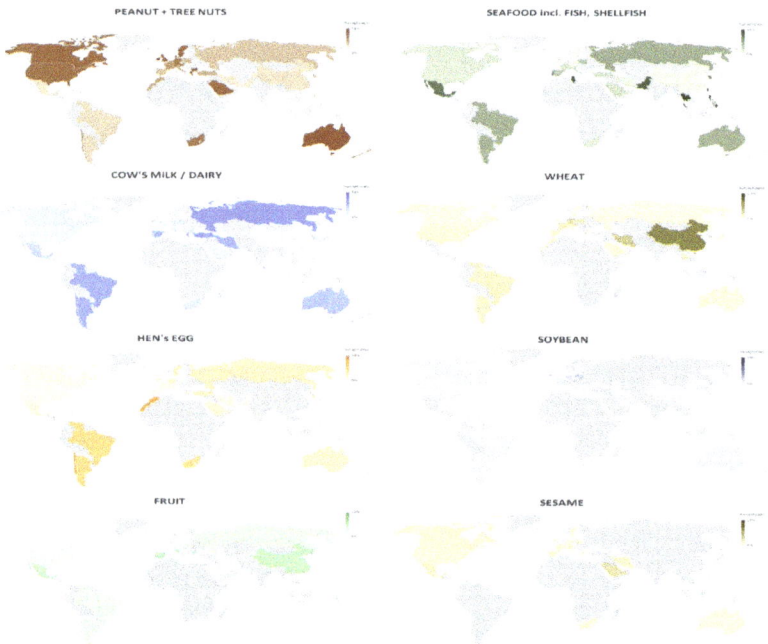

Figure 31.1. Global Maps Showing Changes in Relative Proportions of Reported Food Anaphylaxis from Common Allergens (Peanuts/Nuts [all], Soya, Cow's Milk, Wheat, Egg, Seafood, Fruit [all] and Sesame) by Country (Conrado et al., 2021).

Following the industrialization era, the incidence of food allergy has increased worldwide. This is because of the differentiation of the world's climates with industrialization. This can lead to the observation of previously unknown allergic symptoms. These symptoms develop as tourists with different geographical knowledge adapt to the region. Tourists who come to experience local culture tend to focus on local flavors. The occurrence of unexpected allergic symptoms in tourists who want to try local flavors puts tourists with allergic symptoms in a dangerous situation (Türker & Süzer, 2022; Yazicioğlu et al., 2022). Yazicioğlu et al., 2022). The tourism sector, which is interested in local cuisine, should be prepared for such situations. The importance of this preparation cannot be overstated. It ensures the safety of tourists and protects the image of local cuisine (Kaur & Kaur, 2022). The tourism sector plays a crucial role in managing food allergies, and it's essential for them to be proactive in their approach to ensure the safety and satisfaction of their customers.

In addition, the nutrients and metabolites consumed can regulate the metabolism and function of the structural cells and the various immune system cells (Zhang, 2023; Lee & Ramsey, 2024). In this way, dietary patterns influence the development and course of allergic diseases. In addition, food allergies may also develop with epigenetic factors (Chun et al., 2024). Diets high in energy, protein, saturated fat, n-6 fatty acids, medium chain fatty acids, cholesterol, and simple sugars; low in total dietary fiber, vegetables, and fruits, Zn, Fe, vitamin A, vitamin D, vitamin E, and processed foods trigger the risk of allergy (Zhang, 2023). The prevalence rate is uncertain, but it is estimated that about 6 % of children develop a food allergy in the first three years of life when they are introduced to new foods. Of these allergic foods, 2.5 % are cow's milk, 1 % are peanuts and 1.5 % are eggs. Studies have shown that children with milk and egg allergy can recover from allergic symptoms by school age, but for children with allergy to peanuts, nuts, and seafood, it has been reported to be lifelong, and different strategies have been implemented in different countries in the last 20 years (Sakihara, 2024; Jefferson et al., 2024). Any food can cause an allergy. However, milk, eggs, peanuts, shellfish, crustacean shellfish, wheat, and hazelnuts account for most food allergies (Lopez et al., 2023). In Turkey, lentils, cow's milk, eggs, hazelnuts, peanuts, walnuts, wheat protein, rice, buckwheat in the Far East, and sesame in the Middle East are the most common foods causing anaphylaxis. (Tercanlı ve Atasever, 2021). The main foods containing allergens are given in Table 1.(Sudharsonet al., 2021; Food Allergy Research & Education, 2020; WHO/IUIS Allergen Nomenclature Sub-Committee, 2021).

Table 31.1. Prevalent Types of Food Allergies and Food Sources

Allergen Name	Source	Group of Food	Allergen Type
Mal d 1	Malus domestica (apple)	Fruit	PR-10 protein
Act d 1	Actinidia deliciosa (kiwi)	Fruit	Actinidin
Pru p 3	Prunus persica (peach)	Fruit	Lipid Transfer Protein
Cuc m 2	Cucumis melo (melon)	Fruit	PR-10 protein
Api g 1	Apiaceae (celery)	Vegetable	Profilin
Lyc e 1	Lycopersicon esculentum (tomato)	Vegetable	LTP (Lipid Transfer Protein)
Cap a 1	Capsicum annuum (bell pepper)	Vegetable	Profilin
Lyc e 2	Lycopersicon esculentum (tomato)	Vegetable	Profilin

(continued on next page)

Table 31.1. Continued

Allergen Name	Source	Group of Food	Allergen Type
Api g 4	Apiaceae (celery)	Vegetable	Non-specific lipid transfer protein (nsLTP)
Bos d 6	Bos domesticus (cow's milk)	Dairy	Casein
Gad m 1	Gadus morhua (cod fish)	Fish	Parvalbumin
Pen a 1	Penaeus (shrimp)	Seafood	Tropomyosin
Hel a 1	Helianthus annuus (sunflower)	Seed	2S Albumin
Sin a 1	Sinapis alba (mustard)	Seed	2S Albumin
Ses i 1	Sesamum indicum (sesame)	Seed	2S Albumin
Jug r 1	Juglans regia (walnut)	Nut	2S Albumin
Cor a 9	Corylus avellana (hazelnut)	Nut	Cor a 9 (lipid transfer protein)
Ara h 1	Arachis hypogaea (peanut)	Legume	Storage protein
Lup a 5	Lupinus albus (lupine)	Legume	Beta-conglutin
Ara h 8	Arachis hypogaea (peanut)	Legume	PR-10 protein
Bet v 1	Betula verrucosa (birch)	Pollen	PR-10 protein
Phl p 1	Phleum pratense (timothy grass)	Pollen	Group 1 grass allergen
Bet v 2	Betula verrucosa (birch)	Pollen	Profilin
Zea m 1	Zea mays (corn)	Grain	Profilin
Tri a 19	Triticum aestivum (wheat)	Grain	Alpha-amylase inhibitor
Sec c 1	Secale cereale (rye)	Grain	Pollen allergen
Tri a 14	Triticum aestivum (wheat)	Grain	Lipid Transfer Protein

As Table 31.1 shows, some substances in foods (PR-10 protein, 2S Albumin, etc.) that cause allergies or different types of immunity are associated with genetics, excessive contact with allergens, and disorders in the inhibitory system in the small intestine (Baysal, 2008). The most common food allergies are given in more detail below.

Milk Allergy

A milk allergy is most associated with cow's milk. Milk allergy is an immunological reaction to cow's milk. Milk allergy may be IgE or non-IgE mediated. After a certain age, individuals may develop sensitization to different proteins (αs1, αs2, β, κ-casein, α-lactalbumin and β-lactoglobulin) depending on perceptual, nutritional and climatic conditions. It is observed primarily in children when they are introduced to cow's milk because β-lactoglobulin is present in cow's milk but not in breast milk, and they can tolerate it after 5 years of age. Estimating its prevalence is complex (Malik & Kaul, 2023; Vandenplas et al., 2024). An alternative therapeutic approach is to heat-treat dairy products to denature the proteins so that symptoms are reduced or absent. An example of this is the production of bakery products (Upton et al., 2024). The importance of intestinal mucosal immunity in allergic symptoms and that the use of probiotics can increase tolerance was highlighted at the end of the study examining the gut flora of children with cow's milk allergy in Japan (Shibata et al., 2024). Similar results were found in a study conducted in Poland (Cukrowska et al., 2021). In the same year, milk allergy was found to be improved by a mixture of Dutch probiotics and prebiotics. Probiotic microorganisms are fragile, so the amount administered may not be maintained as it passes through the gastrointestinal system. This is especially true in the kitchen, which is a very stressful environment for microorganisms. It can be challenging to preserve them until they reach the people who will consume the food. For this reason, it is more logical to use postbiotics, which are the metabolites of probiotics, which have recently taken their place in the literature. There is a study showing that postbiotics can be studied in milk allergy (Yammoto-Hanada et al. 2023).

Egg Allergy

Egg allergy is an IgE-mediated immunological response. It is more common in atopic individuals. This allergy is thought to be genetically transmitted. It is common in children. The most effective treatment method is avoidance of egg consumption. However, this may interfere with adequate nutrition in young children. Therefore, there are studies (Dana et al, 2021; Karisola et al, 2021; Palosuo et al, 2021). showing that an oral immunotherapy protocol can be used to eliminate or alleviate egg allergy. In addition to these treatment methods, an alternative treatment approach is to denature the proteins by subjecting the egg to heat treatment. Krawiec et al. point out that the ability to tolerate the egg varies according to the degree to which the egg has been cooked. They also suggest that the basophil activation test is the best diagnostic method for egg allergy. When heat-treated, the absence or mild observation of egg allergy symptoms is most functional in gastronomy when making bakery products (Krawiec et al., 2023; Upton et al., 2024; Malone & Daley,2024).

Peanuts

Peanut allergy is caused by IgE-mediated hypersensitivity. As a result of sensitizing IgE receptors, IgE receptors on basophils and mast cells cross-link with peanut-specific IgE antibodies whenever peanuts are consumed, triggering an allergy. About 20 % of children are allergic to peanuts (Patel & Koterba, 2023). Several studies aim to reduce this allergy rate, the most important of which is Learning Early About Peanut Allergy (LEAP). LEAP is designed to reduce the risk of allergy by introducing peanuts to high-risk babies aged four to six months. This study showed that the early introduction of peanuts to infants prevented the development of peanut allergy (Du Toit et al., 2015). There has been another recent study in support of this study, and the researchers found similar results to the results of the previous study (Logan et al., 2022).

The effective method for individuals with peanut allergy is to exclude it from the diet, as with other allergic foods. Another alternative is an immunotherapy protocol. Researchers mainly focus on the immunotherapy method (Cronin et al., 2023; Ferslew et al., 2023; Voskamp et al., 2023), but according to the study conducted by Kidon et al. suggests that the immunotherapy protocol is more effective when consuming heat-treated peanut (Kidon et al., 2024).

Fish and Shellfish

Fish and shellfish allergy is thought to be permanent. A fish allergy occurs in infancy. Shellfish allergy occurs in adolescence (Ebisawa et al., 2015). Seafood allergy has similar symptoms to other allergies. The difference is that seafood allergy can show symptoms up to eight hours after ingestion, whereas regular allergies show symptoms within two hours of ingestion. Some seafood poisonings (scombroid poisoning, marine algae toxins, paralytic shellfish poisoning, diarrhetic shellfish poisoning toxins, ciguatera, etc.) can be confused with allergic reactions. Many parts of fish have been described as allergens, and parvalbumin, aldose A, beta-enolase, vitellogenin, and tropomyosin proteins have been described as fish allergens by the WHO/International Union of Immunological Societies (IUIS) allergenic classification (Ruethers et al., 2018; WHO/IUIS allergenic classification Home Page, May 2024). According to a clinical study in Hong Kong, fish allergy occurs in childhood and most people with fish allergy claim to be able to tolerate fish with β-parvalbumin levels (Leung et al., 2023). Caution should be taken with seafood allergens. The parvalbumin proteins found in fish are heat stable. The fact that the parvalbumin structure is heat resistant suggests that some fish allergies are permanent (Dong & Raghavan, 2022). Therefore, care should be taken in kitchens or food packaging.

Wheat

Wheat allergy is usually caused by its gluten content. Wheat allergy can be an IgE-mediated allergy or a non-IgE-mediated allergy. Wheat allergy is more common in children than in adults. It has been reported that the allergy usually resolves after 12 years of age. Wheat allergy affects 0.33–1.17 % of the world population and is most associated with celiac disease (non-IgE mediated). Celiac disease is an inherited disease. It is characterized by various histological changes in the small intestine. The only proven treatment for this disease is the elimination of gluten from the diet (Cabanillas, 2019; Patel & Samant, 2023). Recent studies have suggested that immunotherapy and treatment with omalizumab may be an alternative treatment option (Chinuki et al., 2020; Nagakura et al., 2020). For this disease, which has no clear treatment alternative, it is necessary to be sensitive.

Food Allergy Management in Mass Nutrition Systems

Food allergies are becoming a growing health concern worldwide. Organizations, especially those offering group nutrition services, must be informed about and ready to address food allergies. This chapter covers the significance of managing food allergies and the necessary policies and procedures in large-scale nutrition systems (Buldimir et al., 2019).

Food allergies are conditions that occur when the immune system overreacts to certain foods, leading to serious health problems. Allergic reactions can vary from mild symptoms to life-threatening conditions such as anaphylaxis. A study conducted in the United States of America found that approximately 8% of children have food allergies. The management of food allergies, whose prevalence is increasing, in large-scale food service systems is crucial for public health. Below are some recommendations for managing food allergies in public food systems:

- **Education and awareness:** Public food system personnel should receive food allergy training. Training should cover allergen recognition, prevention of cross-contamination, and emergency procedures. There is a need for a greater focus on food allergy education, particularly for catering students, and an improvement in training content. The main problems in training are a lack of time and high staff turnover (Soon, 2020).
  A study conducted in Turkey aimed to measure the level of food allergy knowledge in the kitchen department of a hospitality organization. The chefs

were highly knowledgeable about the definition of food allergy, symptoms, and potential causes of allergens. However, they lacked knowledge about proper food handling and preparation (Eren et al., 2021).

• **Menu planning:** The menu must clearly indicate all foods containing allergens. Alternative options should be provided, and measures should be taken to prevent cross-contamination during their preparation. Allergen information must be prominently displayed on menus and in food service areas (Food Allergy Research & Education, 2020). It would be better for the staff to show sensitivity to this issue and ask the customers whether they have food allergies without telling them that they have food allergies. In this case, it is already necessary to request this information in the check-in process of accommodation establishments to ISO 22000 Food and Safety system.

• **Monitoring for allergens:** Public food systems are required to monitor all food processes for image and advertising and meet current allergen labeling legislation (European Parliament, 2011). These establishments should pay special attention to prevent cross-contamination from food contact surfaces and possible contamination after cleaning and to check the effectiveness of cleaning processes. In addition, allergen management should be embedded in the Hazard Analysis and Critical Control Point (HACCP) system, which is a systematic approach to identify, evaluate, and control each food safety hazard. According to these systems, specific working procedures and cleaning plans need to be implemented for allergen control. Furthermore, cleaning procedures must be validated initially and periodically, as visual inspection alone is insufficient for this purpose. (Galan-Malo et al., 2019). It's essential to store allergenic products separately from other items to prevent cross-contamination. Specifically, keeping allergenic dry foods in closed cabinets is essential. Additionally, it's crucial to rinse tools like knives and cutting boards before handling allergenic foods. It's also crucial for food workers to wash their hands frequently as a preventive measure.

• **Labelling:** During the purchasing process, it is essential that the supplier food company matches the information on the label with the content. When considering FSA warnings, we understand that the most common reason for product withdrawals and recalls is incorrect allergen labeling on the packaging. Unfortunately, this is quite common in this case. Checking the picture or on-pack information against ingredient specifications is vital to the allergen management process. To minimize this risk, it is critical to have a process in place that includes the inspection of both the supply and bulk feeding systems by the responsible authorities (Stein, 2015).

- **Emergency procedures:** Emergency procedures to be applied in case of an allergic reaction must be determined and all personnel must be trained in this regard (Sicherer & Sampson, 2018).

Results

Allergies, usually mediated by IgE and T-helper (Th)2 cytokines, are abnormal body immune responses to foreign substances. Allergy symptoms can be mild (atopic dermatitis, rhinitis) or severe (anaphylaxis). Food, medicines and insect stings are the most common allergens. All allergic inflammation stages require vitamins (A and D), minerals (zinc, iron), fiber, fatty acids, and phytochemicals. Following industrialization, the incidence of food allergy has increased worldwide, and food allergy management is complex and focused. Diet influences the development and course of allergic diseases. Diets high in energy, protein, saturated fat, and simple sugars and low in fiber, vegetables, fruits, and vitamins increase the risk of allergy. Effective treatment for food allergies is the elimination of allergenic foods from the diet. Alternative treatments are still under investigation. In conclusion, effective food allergy management in congregate nutrition systems should aim to prevent allergic reactions through proper labeling and segregation of allergen-containing foods and to provide safe and healthy nutrition environments by increasing the level of staff education and awareness.

References

Baysal, A., Aksoy, M., Besler, H. T., Bozkurt, N., vd. (2008). Diyet El Kitabı. 8. Baskı, Hatipoğlu Yayınevi, Ankara, Türkiye: pp. 445–453.

Budimir J, Mravak-Stipetić M, Bulat V, Ferček I, Japundžić I, Lugović-Mihić L. Oral ve perioral hastalıklarda alerjik reaksiyonlar - alerji cilt testi sonuçları ne gösterir? Oral Surg Oral Med Oral Pathol Oral Radyol. 2019 Ocak; 127 (1):40–48.

Blázquez, A. B., & Berin, M. C. (2017). Microbiome and food allergy. *Translational Research, 179*, 199–203.

Cabanillas, B. (2019). Gluten-related disorders: Celiac disease, wheat allergy, and nonceliac gluten sensitivity. Critical Reviews in Food Science and Nutrition, 60(15), 2606–2621. https://doi.org/10.1080/10408398.2019.1651689

Chinuki, Y., Yagami, A., Adachi, A., Matsunaga, K., Ugajin, T., Yokozeki, H., Hayashi, M., Katayama, I., Kohno, K., Shiwaku, K., & Morita, E. (2020). In vitro basophil activation is reduced by short-term omalizumab treatment in hydrolyzed wheat protein allergy. Allergology International, 69(2), 284–286. https://doi.org/10.1016/j.alit.2019.09.006

Chun, Y., Lee, J. H., & Bunyavanich, S. (2024). Epigenomic and epigenetic investigations of food allergy. Pediatric Allergy and Immunology, 35(1). https://
doi.org/10.1111/pai.14065

Cronin, C., Salzburg, N., Woon, Y., & Wurttele, J. T. (2023). Primary, secondary
and tertiary prevention of food allergy: current practices and future directions. Allergologia Et Immunopathologia, 52(2), 32–44. https://doi.org/
10.15586/aei.v52i2.1023

Cukrowska, B., Ceregra, A., Maciorkowska, E., Surowska, B., Zegadło-Mylik,
M. A., Konopka, E., Trojanowska, I., Zakrzewska, M., Bierła, J. B., Zakrze-
wski, M., Kanarek, E., & Motyl, I. (2021). The Effectiveness of Probiotic
Lactobacillus rhamnosus and Lactobacillus casei Strains in Children with
Atopic Dermatitis and Cow's Milk Protein Allergy: A Multicenter, Randomized, Double Blind, Placebo Controlled Study. Nutrients, 13(4), 1169. https://
doi.org/10.3390/nu13041169

Dana, V. G., Fallahpour, M., Shoormasti, R. S., Nabavi, M., Bemanian, M. H.,
Fateh, M., Zaker, Z., Torabizadeh, M., Aghapour, S. A., & Arshi, S. (2021). Oral
Immunotherapy in Patients with IgE Mediated Reactions to Egg White: A
Clinical Trial Study. Immunological Investigations, 51(3), 630–643. https://
doi.org/10.1080/08820139.2020.1863979

Dong, X., & Raghavan, V. (2022). A comprehensive overview of emerging processing techniques and detection methods for seafood allergens. Comprehensive Reviews in Food Science and Food Safety, 21(4), 3540–3557. https://doi.
org/10.1111/1541-4337.12987

Dougherty, J. M., Alsayouri, K., & Sadowski, A. (2023, July 31). Allergy. Stat-
Pearls - NCBI Bookshelf. https://www.ncbi.nlm.nih.gov/books/NBK545237/

Du Toit, G., Roberts, G., Sayre, P. H., Bahnson, H. T., Radulovic, S., Santos, A. F.,
Brough, H. A., Phippard, D., Basting, M., Feeney, M., Turcanu, V., Sever, M.
L., Lorenzo, M. G., Plaut, M., & Lack, G. (2015). Randomized trial of peanut
consumption in infants at risk for peanut allergy. New England Journal of
Medicine/˜the œNew England Journal of Medicine, 372(9), 803–813. https://
doi.org/10.1056/nejmoa1414850

Ebisawa, M., Ballmer-Weber, B. K., Vieths, S., & Wood, R. A. (2015). Food
allergy: Molecular basis and clinical practiceIn Chemical immunology/
Fortschritte der Allergielehre/Progress in allergy/Chemical immunology and
allergy. https://doi.org/10.1159/isbn.978-3-318-02341-1

Eren, R., Çetin, M., Eren, A., & Çetin, K. (2021). Food allergy knowledge, attitude, and practices of chefs in resort hotels in Turkey. International Journal of Gastronomy and Food Science, 24, 100345. https://doi.org/10.1016/
j.ijgfs.2021.100345.

European Parliament, Directive - 2011/83 - EN - consumer rights directive - EUR-Lex. (May, 2024). http://data.europa.eu/eli/dir/2011/83/oj

Ferslew, B. C., Smulders, R., Zhu, T., Blauwet, M. B., Kusawake, T., Spence, A., Aldridge, K., DeBerg, H. A., Khosa, S., Wambre, E., & Chichili, G. R. (2023). Safety and immunopharmacology of ASP0892 in adults or adolescents with peanut allergy: two randomized trials. Allergy, 79(2), 456–470. https://doi.org/10.1111/all.15931

Conrado, A. B., Patel, N., & Turner, P. J. (2021). Global patterns in anaphylaxis due to specific foods: A systematic review. the Journal of Allergy and Clinical Immunology/Journal of Allergy and Clinical Immunology/the Journal of Allergy and Clinical Immunology, 148(6), 1515–1525.e3. https://doi.org/10.1016/j.jaci.2021.03.048

Food Allergy Research & Education. (2020). Food Allergies: A Growing Public Health Issue. Retrieved from https://www.foodallergy.org.

Galan-Malo, P., Ortiz, J. C., Carrascon, V., Razquin, P., & Mata, L. (2019). A study to reduce the allergen contamination in food-contact surfaces at canteen kitchens. International journal of gastronomy and food science, 17, 100165. https://doi.org/10.1016/j.ijgfs.2019.100165

Jefferson, A. A., Davidson, L., Scurlock, A. M., & Stern, J. (2024). Food insecurity and health inequities in food allergy. Current Allergy and Asthma Reports, 24(4), 155–160. https://doi.org/10.1007/s11882-024-01134-0

Karisola, P., Palosuo, K., Hinkkanen, V., Wisgrill, L., Savinko, T., Fyhrquist, N., Alenius, H., & Mäkelä, M. J. (2021). Integrative transcriptomics reveals activation of innate immune responses and inhibition of inflammation during oral immunotherapy for egg allergy in children. Frontiers in Immunology, 12. https://doi.org/10.3389/fimmu.2021.704633

Kaur, S., & Kaur, M. (2022). Image of Local cuisine in Emerging Gastronomic Destinations: scale review, development, and validation. International Journal of Hospitality & Tourism Administration, 25(1), 153–201. https://doi.org/10.1080/15256480.2022.2092247

Kidon, M. I., Shavit, R., Levy, Y., Yahia, S. H., Machnes-Maayan, D., Frizinsky, S., Maoz-Segal, R., Offenganden, I., Kenett, R. S., Nancy, A., & Hovav, R. (2024). Peanut oral immunotherapy using an extensively heated and baked novel composition of peanuts. Pediatric Allergy and Immunology, 35(5). https://doi.org/10.1111/pai.14146

Krawiec, M., Radulovic, S., Foong, R., Marques-Mejias, A., Bartha, I., Kwok, M., Jama, Z., Harrison, F., Ricci, C., Lack, G., Du Toit, G., & Santos, A. F. (2023). Diagnostic utility of allergy tests to predict baked egg and lightly cooked egg allergies compared to double-blind placebo-controlled food challenges. Allergy, 78(9), 2510–2522. https://doi.org/10.1111/all.15797

Lee, A. S. E., & Ramsey, N. (2024). Climate change and food allergy. Immunology and Allergy Clinics of North America, 44(1), 75–83. https://doi.org/10.1016/j.iac.2023.07.003

Leung, A. S. Y., Wai, C. Y. Y., Leung, N. Y. H., Ngai, N. A., Chua, G. T., Ho, P. K., Lam, I. C. S., Cheng, J. W. C. H., Chan, O. M., Li, P. F., Au, A. W. S., Leung, C. H. W., Cheng, N. S., Tang, M. F., Fong, B. L. Y., Duque, J. S. R., Wong, J. S. C., Luk, D. C. K., Ho, M. H. K., . . . Leung, T. F. (2023). Real-World sensitization and tolerance pattern to seafood in Fish-Allergic individuals. Journal of Allergy and Clinical Immunology. In Practice/the Journal of Allergy and Clinical Immunology. In Practice. https://doi.org/10.1016/j.jaip.2023.09.038

Logan, K., Bahnson, H. T., Ylescupidez, A., Beyer, K., Bellach, J., Campbell, D. E., Craven, J., Du Toit, G., Mills, E. N. C., Perkin, M. R., Roberts, G., Van Ree, R., & Lack, G. (2022). Early introduction of peanut reduces peanut allergy across risk groups in pooled and causal inference analyses. Allergy, 78(5), 1307–1318. https://doi.org/10.1111/all.15597

Lopez, C. M., Yarrarapu, S. N. S., & Mendez, M. D. (2023, July 24). Food allergies. StatPearls - NCBI Bookshelf. https://www.ncbi.nlm.nih.gov/books/NBK482187/

Malik, R., & Kaul, S. (2023). Cow's milk protein allergy. Indian Journal of Pediatrics/Indian Journal of Pediatrics, 91(5), 499–506. https://doi.org/10.1007/s12098-023-04866-5

Malone, J. C., & Daley, S. F. (2024, January 9). Elimination diets. StatPearls - NCBI Bookshelf. https://www.ncbi.nlm.nih.gov/books/NBK599543/

Nagakura, K., Yanagida, N., Sato, S., Nishino, M., Takahashi, K., Asaumi, T., Ogura, K., & Ebisawa, M. (2020). Low-dose-oral immunotherapy for children with wheat-induced anaphylaxis. Pediatric Allergy and Immunology, 31(4), 371–379. https://doi.org/10.1111/pai.13220

Nutrition, C. F.F.S. a. A. (2024, April 12). Food allergies. U.S. Food And Drug Administration https://www.fda.gov/food/food-labeling-nutrition/foodallergies

Palosuo, K., Karisola, P., Savinko, T., Fyhrquist, N., Alenius, H., & Mäkelä, M. J. (2021). A randomized, Open-Label trial of Hen's egg oral immunotherapy: efficacy and humoral immune responses in 50 children. Journal of Allergy and Clinical Immunology. In Practice/the Journal of Allergy and Clinical Immunology. In Practice, 9(5), 1892–1901.e1. https://doi.org/10.1016/j.jaip.2021.01.020

Patel, N., & Samant, H. (2023, June 25). Wheat Allergy. StatPearls - NCBI Bookshelf. https://www.ncbi.nlm.nih.gov/books/NBK536992/

Patel, R., & Koterba, A. P. (2023, July 4). Peanut allergy. StatPearls - NCBI Bookshelf. https://www.ncbi.nlm.nih.gov/books/NBK538526/

Ruethers, T., Taki, A. C., Johnston, E. B., Nugraha, R., Le, T. T., Kalic, T., McLean, T. R., Kamath, S. D., & Lopata, A. L. (2018). Seafood allergy: A comprehensive review of fish and shellfish allergens. Molecular Immunology, 100, 28–57. https://doi.org/10.1016/j.molimm.2018.04.008

Sakihara, T. (2024). Regular consumption following early introduction of allergenic foods and aggressive treatment of eczema are necessary for preventing the development of food allergy in children. Current Opinion in Allergy and Clinical Immunology. https://doi.org/10.1097/aci.0000000000000983

Shibata, R., Itoh, N., Nakanishi, Y., Kato, T., Suda, W., Nagao, M., Iwata, T., Yoshida, H., Hattori, M., Fujisawa, T., Shimojo, N., & Ohno, H. (2024). Gut microbiota and fecal metabolites in sustained unresponsiveness by oral immunotherapy in school-age children with cow's milk allergy. Allergology International, 73(1), 126–136. https://doi.org/10.1016/j.alit.2023.10.001

Sicherer, S. H., & Sampson, H. A. (2018). Food allergy: a review and update on epidemiology, pathogenesis, diagnosis, prevention, and management. *Journal of Allergy and Clinical Immunology*, *141*(1), 41–58.

Soon, J. M. (2020). 'Food allergy? Ask before you eat': Current food allergy training and future training needs in food services. *Food Control*, *112*, 107129.

Stein, K. (2015). Effective allergen management practices to reduce allergens in food Handbook of Food Allergen Detection and Control Flanagan S. https://doi.org/10.1533/9781782420217.1.103

Sudharson, S., Kalic, T., Hafner, C., & Breiteneder, H. (2021). Newly defined allergens in the WHO/IUIS Allergen Nomenclature Database during 01/2019-03/2021. *Allergy*, *76*(11), 3359–3373.

Tercanlı, E., & Atasever, M. (2021). Besin alerjileri. Academic Platform Journal of Halal Lifestyle, 3(1), 31-53.

Türker, N., & Süzer, Ö. (2022). Tourists' food and beverage consumption trends in the context of culinary movements: The case of Safranbolu. International Journal of Gastronomy and Food Science, 27, 100463. https://doi.org/10.1016/j.ijgfs.2021.100463

Upton, J. E., Wong, D., & Nowak-Wegrzyn, A. (2024). Baked milk and egg diets revisited. Annals of Allergy, Asthma, & Immunology, 132(3), 328–336.e5. https://doi.org/10.1016/j.anai.2023.12.024

Vandenplas, Y., Meyer, R. M., & Huysentruyt, K. (2024). Food allergy: Prevention and treatment of Cow's milk allergy. Clinical Nutrition ESPEN, 59, 9–20. https://doi.org/10.1016/j.clnesp.2023.11.007

Voskamp, A. L., Khosa, S., Phan, T., DeBerg, H. A., Bingham, J., Hew, M., Smith, W., Abramovitch, J., Rolland, J. M., Moyle, M., Nadeau, K. C., Lack, G., Larché, M., Wambre, E., O'Hehir, R. E., Hickey, P., & Prickett, S. R. (2023). Phase 1 trial supports safety and mechanism of action of peptide immunotherapy for peanut allergy. Allergy, 79(2), 485–498. https://doi.org/10.1111/all.15966

WHO/IUIS Allergen nomenclature home page. (May 2024). https://www.aller gen.org/

WHO/IUIS Allergen Nomenclature Sub-Committee. (2021). Allergen Nomen-clature. Retrieved from http://www.allergen.org.

Yamamoto-Hanada, K., Sato, M., Toyokuni, K., Irahara, M., Hiraide-Kotaki, E., Harima-Mizusawa, N., Morita, H., Matsumoto, K., & Ohya, Y. (2023). Com-bination of heat-killed Lactiplantibacillus plantarum YIT 0132 (LP0132) and oral immunotherapy in cow's milk allergy: a randomised controlled trial. Beneficial Microbes, 14(1), 17–29. https://doi.org/10.3920/bm2022.0064

Yazicioğlu, I., Keskin, E., & Sezen, N. (2022). Relationships between Cuisine Qual-ity, Food Image, Feelings, Recommendation and Revisit Intention: Gaziantep Case. Journal of Culinary Science & Technology, 21(6), 903–921. https://doi. org/10.1080/15428052.2021.2024471

Zhang, P. (2023). The role of diet and nutrition in allergic diseases. Nutrients, 15(17), 3683. https://doi.org/10.3390/nu15173683

Ayşen Ertaş Sabanci[1] and Ekin Akbulut[2]

Chapter 32 Evaluation of Gastronomic Elements of Railway Travel Routes in Turkey

Introduction

Turkey has been home to various cultures and civilizations throughout history. Therefore, it has a rich gastronomic heritage. Turkey's gastronomic richness allows the discovery of different flavors and plays an important role in tourism. Train tourism, which has become a new trend in recent years, offers a pleasant journey in a special and unique atmosphere. The concept of train tourism has been shaped by the prominence of the train as a means of transportation used in touristic expeditions, short distances and private trips (Çontu, 2006). Traveling in the comfortable comfort and unique landscapes of the trains also provides the opportunity to taste various flavors of Turkey on the route.

Train tourism in Turkey first emerged through the Doğu Express and then diversified with different routes such as Izmir Mavi Train, Kars Express, Güney Kurtalan Express, Konya Mavi Train and Van Gölü Express (Bayraktar, 2020). It is thought that examining gastronomy elements such as geographically marked products, gastronomy festivals, food-themed museums on these routes and renewing the stops on the route accordingly will allow these routes to appeal to more tourists. From this point of view, this study aims to highlight the gastronomic dimension of train tourism in Turkey and to reveal its potential to offer an unforgettable flavor journey for travelers.

Gastronomy Tourism and Gastronomic Routes

Gastronomy tourism is defined as a type of tourism that aims to make the travel experience sustainable and to spread the tourism activity throughout the year (Çalışkan, 2013). Food and beverage culture is one of the basic elements of sustainable tourism and makes significant contributions to the local economy (Birdir & Akgöl, 2015). Therefore, the importance of gastronomy tourism

---

1   Research Assistant, Recep Tayyip Erdoğan University, Ardeşen Tourism Faculty, Department of Gastronomy and Culinary Arts, aysen.ertas@erdogan.edu.tr
2   Lecturer, Eurasia University, Eurasia University, Vocational School, Department of Hotel and Catering Services, ekin.akbulut14@hotmail.com

is increasing day by day. In recent years, with the change in the understanding of vacation, the importance of exploring the flavors of the traveled region has increased (Durlu-Özkaya et al., 2013). This change strengthens the prediction that the interest in gastronomy tourism will increase.

Gheorghe et al. (2013) define gastronomy tours as a system of holistic and thematic tourist experiences that include one or more routes in a specific geographical area. A gastronomy route is the presentation of activities such as trying new products, visiting traditional markets and shopping in local shops, etc., which include the determining elements of a certain route (Üzülmez & Akdağ, 2020). Kızılırmak et al. (2016) identified gastronomy tour routes in Turkey in their study. Madeira et al. (2017) stated in their study that there are prominent routes in the Lisbon region as gastronomy and especially wine routes, and that these routes can be used as a tool to attract more tourists to the region with the help of a model to be created. Özkaya et al. (2018) in their study on olive and olive oil routes; an "Zeytin Rotası" was created for tourists entering Turkey from Istanbul.

Evaluation of Railway Travel Routes

Different modes of transportation are used to pass between destinations on touristic routes. Today, people prefer trains as a means of transportation when exploring unique and cultural places. In addition, the fact that tourists meet their food, entertainment and recreation needs on the train, have the opportunity to travel with sleeper cars, provide internet access and increase train speeds have made rail transportation more preferred (Alkan, 2018). There are many train services with various concepts and routes in train tourism. These services, which are preferred by those looking for a different experience, those who want to watch the scenery or travel in a relaxed way, have recently attracted more attention, especially with the influence of social media. The Mavi Train, which runs between Cape Town and Johannesburg in South Africa and is famous for its luxurious restaurant, golden windows and romance; the Sky Train with three locomotives that travels from Xining, China to Lhasa, crossing the Tibetan Plateau and the Tangula Pass; Copper Canyon in Mexico; Palace on Wheels in India; and the Indo-Pacific Train in Australia are examples of special trains around the world (Cook et al., 2016).

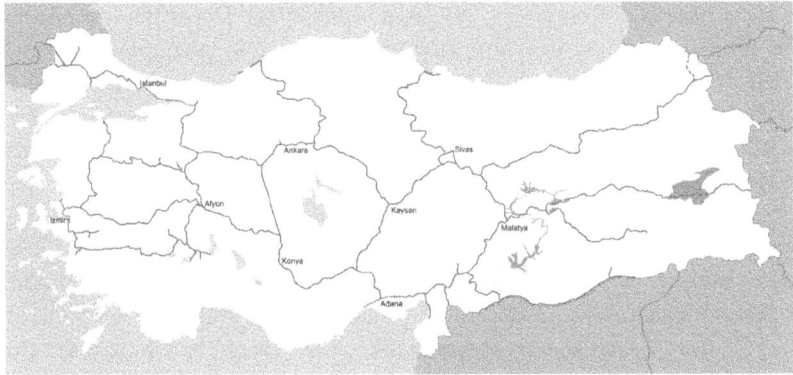

Figure 32.1. System Map of Turkish State Railways
Source: Wikipedia, 2024

The main line trains serving in Turkey are Doğu Express, Konya Mavi Train, Ege Express, Izmir Mavi Train, Pamukkale Express, 6 Eylül Express, 17 Eylül Express, Van Gölü Express, Güney Kurtalan Express, Erciyes Express, Ankara Express (TCDD Taşımacılık, 2024). Alkan (2018), in his study on train routes in Turkey, discussed the tourism destinations on the Kurtalan Express route, the points that can be visited in these destinations and the tourism activities that can be done in these destinations, and offered some suggestions for the Kurtalan Express to be considered as a touristic train journey.

When the literature is examined, it is suggested that local gastronomy values cannot be sufficiently promoted in most of the destinations and therefore it is recommended to create gastronomy routes for a solution (Nergiz, 2017; Çavuşoğlu & Çavuşoğlu, 2018; Bayraktar, 2021; Denk, 2021; Cabaroğlu, 2023). In this context, with the increasing popularity of train tourism, preparing gastronomic routes within this framework and addressing train tourism and gastronomy together can make a significant contribution to the field.

Evaluation of Doğu Express and Gastronomic Elements

Touristic train routes first started with the Doğu Express, and different routes started to emerge as the demand for train travel increased with the influence of social media. The Doğu Express completes its journey between Ankara and Kars in approximately 26 hours (TCDD Taşımacılık, 2024). Departing from Ankara, the touristic train route runs through Kırıkkale, Kayseri, Sivas, Erzincan, Erzurum and ends in Kars. Due to the natural beauties on the train route, it is one of the train routes that attract tourists, travelers and photographers. The peak season is summer (TCDD Taşımacılık, 2024). As gastronomic elements of the Doğu Express route, the geographically marked products of the cities on the route, gastronomy festivals and gastronomy museums can be evaluated. There are 33 geographically marked food and beverage products in Ankara, the first route, followed by 3 products in Kırıkkale, 28 products in Kayseri, 14 products in Sivas, 8 products in Erzincan, 52 products in Erzurum and 5 products in Kars (Turkish Patent and Trademark Office, 2024). It can be said that the Doğu Express is quite rich in geographically marked products.

Gastronomy-themed festivals organized in Ankara; Elmadağ Education, Science, Culture and Tirit Festival, Kutludüğün Gözleme and Ayran Festival, Beypazarı Carrot Festival, Beypazarı Traditional Historical Houses, Handicrafts, Carrot and Güveç Festival, Gastro Ankara Taste Feast, Breakfast Festival, International Çubuk Turşusu and Culture Festival, Gourmet Festival, Ankara Coffee Festival, International Kalecik Karası Grape Festival, International Bread Festival, Ankara Ice-Cream and Dessert Festival, Enfes Street Food Festival, Ankara Taste Festival, and Bir Yudum Grape Festival (Ekerim & Tanrısever, 2020; Festivals, 2024). The gastronomy-themed Yahşihan Yoğurt Festival and Sulakyurt Melon-Watermelon Festival are organized in Kırıkkale. The gastronomy-themed festivals organized in Kayseri are Walnut-Gilaburu Festival, Culture and Apricot Festival, Hasancı Pilav Festival and International Kayseri Pastırma, Sucuk and Mantı Festival (Ekerim & Tanrısever, 2020). The gastronomy-themed festivals organized in Sivas province are Sivas Güneykaya Municipality Wrestling, Börek and Külbez Festival, Traditional Ahmet Ayık Karakucak Wrestling and Honey Festival, Zara Honey and Culture Festival, Gemerek Culture, Art and Potato Festival, Akıncılar Culture, Art and Melon Festival and MERDER Honey, Yoğurt and Madımak Festival. These festivals are mostly held in summer (Ekerim & Tanrısever, 2020). In Erzincan province, the Nature-Culture and Tulum Cheese Festival and Refahiye Culture and Honey Festival are organized with a gastronomy theme. Traditional Gravyer and Kaşar Festival and Cultural Festival Feast are organized in Kars. In Erzurum province, the Traditional Plateau Festivals Cağ Kebap Festival is organized (Ekerim & Tanrısever, 2020). It is seen that the cities on the route have a wide variety of options in terms of gastronomy festivals. Updating the stops on the route from time to time according to the festivals and extending the break times a little longer will allow the route to be better utilized for gastronomy tourism.

The gastronomy museums on the Doğu Express route are Atatürk Orman Çiftliği Museum and Exhibition Hall, Wine Museum and Bread Museum in Ankara, Historical Erzurum Houses Restaurant Museum in Erzurum, and Zavot Cheese Museum-Eco Museum in Kars (Çekal et al., 2022). Activities such as taking breaks in the relevant cities to visit the gastronomy museums on the route and tasting local food culture and local products by visiting local guides will positively affect the satisfaction of the participants.

Evaluation of Mezopotamya Express (Ankara-Diyarbakır Train) and Gastronomic Elements

The train departing from Ankara takes a 3-hour break in Malatya; the return train departing from Diyarbakır takes a 3-hour break in Elazığ and Kayseri for sightseeing purposes (TCDD Taşımacılık, 2024). The cities and durations of the stops are sufficient to have various gastronomic experiences during the train journey. On the route of the Mezopotamya Express, there are 42, 55 and 11 geographically marked food and beverage products in Malatya, Diyarbakır and Elazığ, respectively (Turkish Patent and Trademark Office, 2024). Diyarbakır is particularly rich in geographically marked products. At the same time, local products and street flavors can be experienced at the stops along this route.

The gastronomy-themed festivals organized in Malatya can be listed as Yeşilyurt Cherry-Culture and Sports Festival, International Culture, Art and Apricot Festival, International Coffee and Culture and Art Festival, Arapgir Vintage Festivals and Doğanşehir Apple and Culture Festival (Ekerim & Tanrısever, 2020). The gastronomy-themed festivals organized in Elazığ are Coffee and Chocolate Festival, Ağın Leblebi, Mulberry and Molasses Festival, Keban Water and Trout Festival and Grape and Orcik Festival (Eryılmaz & Orhan, 2021). In Diyarbakır province, the International Diyarbakır Watermelon Festival and Diyarbakır Food and Local Flavors Fair are organized (Ekerim & Tanrısever, 2020). When the gastronomy festivals on the route are evaluated in general, it is a very rich train route especially in terms of local products. For this reason, it can be assumed that tourists who act with the motivation to experience gastronomy tourism will be satisfied, while tourists who participate in the train tourism experience will leave the tour satisfied because they taste different flavors.

In Malatya province, there is the Buğday Museum as a gastronomy museum (Çekal et al., 2022). For tourists who want to visit a gastronomy museum, a stop can be made in Diyarbakır, which has the only gastronomy museum on the route.

Evaluation of Izmir Mavi Train and Gastronomic Elements

Izmir Mavi Train runs regularly every day between Ankara and Izmir. Starting from Ankara, the train route follows Eskişehir, Kütahya, Balıkesir, Manisa and İzmir. With its natural beauties, culture, industry and port cities, this route offers its passengers an average experience of 13 hours and 40 minutes (TCDD Taşımacılık, 2024). There are 9, 18, 30, 26, 26, and 36 geographically marked food and beverage products in Eskişehir, Kütahya, Balıkesir, Manisa, and İzmir provinces respectively on the route of İzmir Mavi Train (Turkish Patent and Trademark Office, 2024). It can be said that Balıkesir, Manisa and İzmir provinces are very rich in geographically marked products and this richness should be utilized in the train route.

Gastronomy-themed festivals organized in Izmir province; March Nine Herb Festival, Izmir Chocolate Dessert Festival, Bornova Cherry Festival, Seferihisar Ata Bread and Armola Festival, Seferihisar Tangerine Festival, Cretans and Herb Festival, Alaçatı Herb Festival, Buca Municipality Cherry Festival, Urla Traditional Vintage Festival, International Urla Artichoke Festival, Urla Hohutalan Village Melon Festival, Gastro Fest, Boyoz Festival, Cocktail Fest, Coffe Fest, Agricultural and Local Products Festival, Tea Festival, Waffle Festival, Cuisine Konak: İzmir Flavors Festival, İrimağzı Pig Harvest Culture and Tourism Festival and Karşıyaka Anchovy Festival (Ekerim & Tanrısever, 2020). In Eskişehir province; Sivrihisar Dövme Sucuk Festival, Mihalıççıklılar Day and Cherry Festival and Eskişehir Lentil Festival are organized. In Kütahya province; Traditional Gediz Tarhana Festival, Tavşanlı Chickpea and Coal Festival and Broad Bean Festival are organized. In Manisa, Akhisar Olive Harvest Festival, Adala Peach Festival, Vintage Festival, International Manisa Mesir Macunu Festival, Cherry Festival, Kırkağaç Kavun Festival and Sarıgöl Sultaniye Grape Festival are organized. In Balıkesir province; Susurluk Ayran and Culture Festival, Bigadiç Meat and Milk Festival, Edremit Olive Harvest End Festival, Ayvalık Olive Harvest Festival and International Burhaniye Olive and Olive Oil Harvest Festival are organized (Ekerim & Tanrısever, 2020). It can be said that the İzmir Mavi train is one of the richest train routes in terms of gastronomy festivals. During the festivals, tourists can taste local flavors and street delicacies, as well as participate in activities and musical performances in the festival areas. Thus, they can have an unforgettable gastronomic train experience.

Gastronomy museums on the route of the Izmir Mavi train can be listed as Manisa, Egea Olive and Olive Growing Museum; Balıkesir Edremit Evren Ertür Historical Olive Oil Instruments Museum; İzmir Köstem Olive Oil Museum (Çekal et al., 2022). In terms of gastronomy museums, especially olive and olive oil themes stand out. This is a sufficient motivation factor for gastro tourists interested in olives and olive oil to prefer this route.

Evaluation of Konya Mavi Train and Gastronomic Elements

Konya Mavi Train serves passengers every day between Konya and Izmir provinces as a round trip and return route. Konya Mavi Train starts from Konya and ends in Afyonkarahisar, Uşak, Manisa and İzmir. This journey takes 12 hours on average (TCDD Taşımacılık, 2024). There are 73 geographically marked food and beverage products in Konya province, 42 in Afyonkarahisar province, and 7 in Uşak province on the route of Konya Mavi Train (Turkish Patent and Trademark Office, 2024). The high number of geographically marked flavors of Konya province on this route is quite remarkable. Konya Mavi Train offers the opportunity to try different flavors for tourist groups interested in local products.

The gastronomy-themed festivals organized in Konya are Strawberry Festival, Tahinli Pide Festival and Akşehir Cherry Culture and Art Festival. In Afyonkarahisar province; Dazkırı, Carpet, Rug and Haşhaş Festival, Sivrihisar Dövme Sucuk Festival, Bolvadin Kaymak and Eber Gölü Festival, Pea Festival, Karaadilli Cherry and Potato Festival and Flamingo and Egg Festival are organized. In Uşak province, the Cherry Culture, Art and Trade Fair is organized (Ünlü & Nizamlıoğlu, 2022). Provinces hosting festivals with different concepts are located on this train route. A stopover in Afyonkarahisar province for sightseeing purposes can provide passengers with an opportunity for festival experience.

Evaluation of Ege Express and Gastronomic Elements

Ege Express route starts from Izmir Basmane and goes to Manisa, Balıkesir, Kütahya and Eskişehir. The return route is operated with the same route. Ege Express completes a journey in approximately 11 and a half hours. Ege Express connects not only the cities on its route but also the cultures. This route is especially preferred by tourists in the summer months (TCDD Taşımacılık, 2024). The Ege Express is also one of the train routes rich in gastronomic elements. On this route, you can have a delicious break in Balıkesir.

Pamukkale Express and Evaluation of Gastronomic Elements

Pamukkale Express serves passengers between Denizli and Eskişehir. Pamukkale Express is a route starting from Denizli and ending in Afyonkarahisar, Kütahya and Eskişehir (TCDD Taşımacılık, 2024). There are 10 food and beverage products with geographical indications in Denizli province, 42 in Afyonkarahisar province and 7 in Uşak province, respectively, on the Pamukkale Express (Turkish Patent and Trademark Office, 2024). The gastronomy-themed festivals organized in Denizli province are as follows: Corn-Sunflower Harvest and Keşkek Day Festivities, Tripolis Culture and Turfanda Sultaniye Çekirdeksiz Grape Festival, Traditional Kale Pepper Festival and Yağlı Pehlivan Wrestling, Culture, Art and Leblebi Festival, Çivril International Apple-Agriculture Culture Festival, Çal Vintage Culture and Art Festival and Serinhisar Leblebi and Culture Festival (Ekerim & Tanrısever, 2020). The festivals on the Pamukkale Express route differ from other festivals in that they are combined with local products and events. For this reason, it can appeal to different tourist groups at the same time, allowing the majority to leave this journey satisfied.

Evaluation of Van Gölü Express and Gastronomic Elements

Van Gölü Express is one of the train routes running between Ankara and Tatvan (Bitlis). The route of the Van Gölü Express starts from Ankara and ends in Kayseri, Sivas, Malatya, Elazığ, Tatvan. This route takes approximately 26 hours and 30 minutes (TCDD Taşımacılık, 2014). Bitlis province, the last route of the Van Gölü Express, has 1 geographically marked food and beverage product (Turkish Patent and Trademark Office, 2024t). Bitlis Walnut Festival is organized as a gastronomy-themed festival in Bitlis province (Ekerim & Tanrısever, 2020).

Evaluation of Güller Express (Isparta-İzmir (Basmane) Train) and Gastronomic Elements

Güller Express is a daily reciprocal train line between Isparta and Izmir (Basmane). The routes of this route are Burdur, Isparta, Denizli, Aydın and İzmir. The average travel time of the train route is 8 hours and 30 minutes (TCDD Taşımacılık, 2024). There are 11 geographically marked food and beverage products in Burdur province, 14 in Isparta province, 10 in Denizli province and 25 in Aydın province on the Güller Express (Turkish Patent and Trademark Office, 2024). The gastronomy-themed festivals organized in Isparta are Seyyit Veli Baba Sultan Commemoration and Pilav Festival, Traditional Senirkent Culture, Art and Grape Festival and Isparta Rose Festival (Akturfan & Şen, 2023). In Burdur province, Karamanlı Marble and Walnut Festival and Kozağacılar Traditional Göce (Tarhana) Festival are organized. In Aydın province; Kuşadası Olive Festival, Arap Dede Keşkek Hayrı, Koçarlı Pine Nut Festival, International Fig Festival, Buharkent Fresh Fig Festival and Veg Fest (Didim) are organized

(Ekerim & Tanrısever, 2020). When the festivals on the Güller Express route are examined, it is noteworthy that there are festivals for keşkek and tarhana products, which are recognized dishes in Turkish cuisine culture. These products can enable the promotion of the country's culinary culture in international areas with the experience of foreign tourists participating in train tourism. The gastronomy museums in Aydın, Çine Beekeeping Museum and Oleatrium Olive and Olive Oil History Museum (Çekal et al., 2022).

Evaluation of Güney Kurtalan Express and Gastronomic Elements

Güney Kurtalan Express is a train line that starts in Ankara and runs through Kayseri, Sivas, Malatya, Diyarbakır, Sivas, Malatya, Diyarbakır and ends in Kurtalan (Siirt). Güney Kurtalan Express completes a journey in approximately 26 hours. It is one of the main line trains with a long duration (TCDD Taşımacılık, 2024). There are 6 geographically marked products in Siirt province (Turkish Patent and Trademark Office, 2024). At the same time, Egg Festival and Culture and Art Festival and Siirt Fıstığı Promotion and Honey Festival are organized as gastronomy-themed events in Siirt province (Ekerim & Tanrısever, 2020). The fact that the Egg Festival is similar to Easter in terms of time, name and content provides an extraordinary experience for Güney Kurtalan Express passengers.

Evaluation of Erciyes Express and Gastronomic Elements

Erciyes Express is one of the train lines operating between Kayseri and Adana every day. Erciyes Express follows a route from Kayseri to Niğde and Adana (TCDD Taşımacılık, 2024). There are 4 and 19 geographically marked food and beverage products in Niğde and Adana provinces respectively on the Erciyes Express (Turkish Patent and Trademark Office, 2024). The gastronomy-themed festivals organized in Adana province can be listed as Watermelon Festival, Culture, Art and Cherry Festival, Adana Taste Festival, Adana Kebap and Şalgam Festival, World Rakı Festival, Çiçekli Village Pomegranate Festival, International Ceyhan Watermelon and Agriculture Festival, Sarımazı Olive Festival and Karakışlakçı Honey and Strawberry Festival. Darboğaz Cherry and Art Festival and Hıdırellez and Potato Festival are organized in Niğde province (Ekerim & Tanrısever, 2020). It can be said that the participation of tourists in kebab, one of the important representatives of Turkish culinary culture, and raki festivals, the national drink, will contribute to the continuity and promotion of Turkish culinary culture.

6 Eylül Express—17 Eylül Express and Evaluation of Gastronomic Elements

6 Eylül Express is a passenger train that runs daily between Izmir (Basmane) and Balıkesir (Bandirma). Since the tourism sector is developed in these two cities, it is one of the most preferred train routes by summer tourists. The route of the 6 Eylül Express ends in İzmir, Manisa and Balıkesir (TCDD Taşımacılık, 2024). On the way back, there is a route starting from Bandırma and ending in Basmane with the 17 Eylül Express. The train completes its journey in 7 hours on average (TCDD Taşımacılık, 2024).

Conclusion

Addressing the gastronomic richness of train routes will help local and foreign tourists learn about the food cultures in different geographical regions of Turkey and discover flavor stops. In this context, Afyon Gastronomi Train, which was launched by the Association of Turkish Travel Agencies (TÜRSAB) in coop- eration with Afyonkarahisar Municipality to give a new impetus to tourism, is a special train tour organized to promote gastronomy tourism specific to Afyonkarahisar province of Turkey. This train route, which aims to introduce the rich culinary culture of Afyonkarahisar and offer passengers the opportu- nity to experience local delicacies, is the first project to combine gastronomy and train tourism. Afyon Gastronomi Train reveals the importance of enriching other existing train routes in Turkey with gastronomic elements. Geographically marked products, gastronomy festivals and gastronomy museums were evalu- ated as gastronomic elements of cities on different train routes.

Geographical Indication Products represent local products and local flavors that cities have. As a result of the registration of these products, their sustain- ability is ensured by standardizing and transferring them to future generations. For this reason, the number of geographically marked products owned by the provinces as a gastronomic element is also an indicator of gastronomic rich- ness. Each of the train routes considered in the study is very rich in terms of geographically marked products. For this reason, determining stopover places where gastronomic experiences can be experienced and renewing the routes by giving sufficient break times may positively affect the satisfaction status.

Festivals aim to attract the attention of many domestic and foreign tourists and increase the attractiveness of the region, making it a destination for gastronomy tourism (Lee & Arcodia, 2011). Gastronomy festivals include elements such as presentation, production, tasting, recipes, cultural food rituals and ceremonies, culinary cultures and traditions of foods specific to the region where the festival is held (Cömert & Çetin, 2017). Globally recognized coffee, chocolate, vintage, breakfast and gastronomy festivals will make these routes attractive for local and foreign tourists. At the same time, it will allow those participating in train tourism to have a different experience. Gastronomy-themed museums are one of the indicators of gastronomy development. Tourists whose purpose of travel is gastronomy visit these museums where they can learn about the gastronomic history, traditions and culture of the city they visit and taste local products (Aksoy & Sezgi, 2015). The presence of gastronomy museums in different cities along the train routes also contributes to the cultural and gastronomic richness of the routes.

Cities on the UNESCO Creative Cities Network and Train Routes with the theme of gastronomy; Afyonkarahisar (Konya Mavi Train and Pamukkale Express), Balıkesir (İzmir Mavi Train, Ege Express and 6 Eylül Express- 17 Eylül Express), Diyarbakır (Mezopotamya Express and Güney Kurtalan Express), Kayseri (Doğu Express, Van Gölü Express, Güney Kurtalan Express and Erciyes Express) and Konya (Konya Mavi Train) (UNESCO, 2024). It can be said that stops in these cities will provide different experience opportunities for passengers participating in the train route and will positively affect train routes in terms of diversity.

References

Aksoy, M., & Sezgi, G. (2015). Gastronomi Turizmi ve Güneydoğu Anadolu Bölgesi Gastronomik Unsurları. *Journal of Tourism and Gastronomy Studies*, 3(3), 79–89.

Akturfan, M. & Şen, A. (2023). Rekreasyon Turizmi Bağlamında Gastronomi Temalı Festivaller. *Journal of Humanities and Tourism Research*, 13(1): 230–244.

Alkan, A. (2018). Alternatif bir Turizm Rotası: Kurtalan Ekspresi. *Journal of Tourism & Gastronomy Studies*, 6(4), 1016–1038.

Bayraktar, Y. (2020). *Deneyimsel Turizm Bağlamında Tren Turizmi: Doğu Ekspresi ve Turistik Doğu Ekspresi Seyahatleri Örneği.* (PhD Thesis) Atatürk University Institute of Social Sciences, Erzurum.

Bayraktar, Z. A. (2021). *Gastronomi Turizmi Kaynağı Olarak Gastronomi Rotaları: Schleswig-Holstein Peynir Rotası Örneği Üzerinden Kars Peynir Rotası Model Önerisi.* (PhD Thesis). Atatürk University Institute of Social Sciences, Erzurum.

Birdir, K. & Akgöl, Y. 2015. Gastronomi Turizmi ve Türkiye'yi Ziyaret Eden Yabancı Turistlerin Gastronomi Deneyimlerinin Değerlendirilmesi, *İşletme ve İktisat Çalışmaları Dergisi*, 3(2), 57–68.

Cabaroğlu, T. (2023). Türk Şarapçılığının Durumu ve Sorunları. *Bahçe*, 52 (Special Issue 1), 269–275.

Cook, R., Hsu, C., & Marqua, J. (2016). *Konaklama ve Seyahat İşletmeciliği*. (M. Tuna, Trans.) Ankara: Nobel Akademi Publishing.

Cömert, M & Çetin, K. (2017). Gastronomi Temalı Yerel Festivaller Üzerine Bir Değerlendirme. *Uluslararası Sosyal Araştırmalar Dergisi*, 10(54), 1092–1101.

Çalışkan, O. (2013). Destinasyon Rekabetçiliği ve Seyahat Motivasyonu Bakımından Gastronomik Kimlik, *Journal of Tourism and Gastronomy Studies*, 1(2), 39–51.

Çavuşoğlu, M. & Çavuşoğlu, O. (2018). Gastronomi Turizmi ve Gökçeada Lezzet Rotası. *Güncel Turizm Araştırmaları Dergisi*, 2(1): 347–359.

Çekal, N., Doğan, E. & Aktürk, H. (2022). Türkiye'de Gastronomi Müzeleri ve Özellikleri. *Sosyal, Beşeri ve İdari Bilimler Dergisi*, 5(11): 1655–1673.

Çontu, M. (2006). *Alternatif Turizm Çeşitleri ve Kızılcahamam Termal Turizmi Örneği, (Unpublished Master's Thesis)*, Abant İzzet Baysal University Institute of Social Sciences, Bolu.

Denk, E. (2021). Türkiye'de Gastronomi Turizmi Açısından Coğrafi İşaretli Ürünler. *Journal of Silk Road Tourism Research*, 1(1), 51–61.

DTD Demiryolu Taşımacılık Derneği, (2024). https://dtd.org.tr/DTD-Sekt%C3%B6r-Raporu-25.08.2023.pdf (Access Date, 20.05.2024).

Durlu-Özkaya, F., Sünnetçioğlu, S. & Can, A. (2013). Sürdürülebilir Gastronomi Turizmi Hareketliliğinde Coğrafi İşaretlemenin Rolü, *Journal of Tourism and Gastronomy Studies*, 1(1), 13–20.

Ekerim, F., & Tanrısever, C. (2020). Türkiye Gastronomi Festivalleri ve Haritalandırılması. *Journal of Tourism & Gastronomy Studies*, 8(3), 2277–2297.

Eryılmaz, G. & Orhan, H. C. (2021). Elazığ İli Gastronomi Turizmi Potansiyelinin SWOT Analizi İle Değerlendirilmesi. *Turizm Çalışmaları Dergisi*, 3(2), 1–18.

Festivals, Go Türkiye, (2024). Ankara Festivalleri. https://festivals.goturkiye.com/tr/ankara-festivalleri (Access Date, 24.05.2024).

Gheorghe, G., Nistoreanu, B.G., & Filip, A. (2013). Traditional Products-Vectors of Sustainable Development on the Regional and National Markets. *Amfiteatru Economic*, 15(7), 645–658.

Kızılırmak, İ., Ofluoğlu, M., & Şişik, L. (2016). Türkiye'de Uygulanan Gastronomi Turları Rotalarının Web Tabanlı Analizi ve Değerlendirmesi. *Journal of Tourism and Gastronomy Studies, 4* (1), 258–269.

Lee, S. & Arcodia, C. (2011). The Role Of Regional Food Festivals For Destination Branding. *International Journal of Tourism Research,13*(4), 355–367.

Madeira, A., Correia, A., & Filipe, J. (2017). Wine and Gastronomy: Experiences and Routes in Lisbon. Proceedings Book, 313– 318.

Nergiz, H. G. (2017). Trakya Turizm Rotası. *Anatolia: Turizm Araştırmaları Dergisi, 28*(1), 200–202.

Özkaya, F. D., Özkaya, M. T., Tunalıoğlu, R., Bayar, R., & Tunalıoğlu, E. (2018). Anadolu'da Zeytin ve Zeytinyağlı Yemekler Rotası. *Journal of Tourism and Gastronomy Studies, 6* (3), 263–274.

TCDD, (2024). Ana Hat Trenleri. https://www.TCDD Taşımacılık,tasimacilik. gov.tr/tr/ana_hat_trenleri (Access Date, 20.05.2024). TCDD (Türkiye Cumhuriyeti Devlet Demiryolları / State Railways of the Republic of Turkey).

Turkish Patent and Trademark Office, (2024). Türkiye'nin Coğrafi İşaretli Ürünleri. https://ci.turkpatent.gov.tr/anasayfa (Access Date, 24.05.2024).

UNESCO, (2024). UNESCO Yaratıcı Şehirler Ağı. https://www.unesco.org. tr/Pages/88/129/UNESCOYarat%C4%B1c%C4%B1-S%CC%A7ehirler-Ag%CC%86%C4%B1 (Access Date, 26.05.2024)

Ünlü, Y. & Nizamlıoğlu, H. F. (2022). Gastronomi Festivalleri Kapsamında Konya Mutfağının Değerlendirilmesi. *Ankara Hacı Bayram Veli Üniversitesi Turizm Fakültesi Dergisi, 25*(1), 68–97.

Üzülmez, M., & Akdağ, G. (2020). Gastronomi Turizminde Yeni Tur Rotaları: 3A (Adana-Antep-Antakya) Lezzet Bölgesi. *Journal of Tourism and Gastronomy Studies, 4*, 51–63.

Wikipedia, (2024). System Map of Turkish State Railways. https://upload.wikimedia.org/wikipedia/commons/1/16/TCDD_System_Map.GIF (Access Date, 26.10.2024)

Sena Bakir[1] and Ayşe Gülnihal Altin[2]

Chapter 33 Sensory Analysis and Consumer Perception in Gastronomy

Introduction

Food science and technological expertise have advanced significantly in recent years. Several physical, chemical and microbiological tests are carried out to evaluate the conformity of foods produced in the food industry to assess quality criteria. The confirmation of food's quality criteria took the attention of the world's top chefs to learn about the physicochemical changes that culinary processes make to food, and the ability to blend flavors to create new tastes and textures. Furthermore, new product developments rely on new food processing techniques that ensure the quality of foods.

Quality measurements are essential for the multidimensional product evaluation before reaching the consumer. Sensory analysis methods are also among the food evaluation criteria (Miişoğlu et all., 2005). Sensory analysis has a critical function in measuring the effects of products on consumers appreciations, and the determinations of consumers at points where objective measurements, such as consumers' appreciation of the product, are incomplete (MEB, 2012). In the field of sensory analysis, people identify, provide, and elucidate the determining aspects of foods that correspond to the five senses (Miişoğlu et all., 2005), which are view, smell, taste, hearing and texture (Onoğur & Elmacı, 2011). With sensory assessments, the first impression of consumers have of foods and beverages is evaluated (Metin, 2021), and the level of liking (acceptance) of foods in terms of consumption can be determined (MEB, 2012).

Sensory analysis studies are carried out for many purposes such as determining the effect of shelf life of products on sensory properties, developing substitute products, developing products from the wastes of various vegetables and fruits within the scope of zero waste (Topkaya, 2017), and also performing the

---

1 Asist. Prof. Dr. Sena BAKIR, Recep Tayyip Erdogan University, Ardesen Tourism Faculty, Gastronomy and Culinary Arts, and Recep Tayyip Erdogan University, Blueberry Application and Research Center, sena.bakir@erdogan.edu.tr
2 Lecturer, Ayse Gulnihal ALTIN, MSc. Recep Tayyip Erdogan University, Ardesen Tourism Faculty, Gastronomy and Culinary Arts, aysegulnihal.kahraman@erdogan. edu.tr

improvement stages of the developed products and determining the consumer appreciation and preference on the improved products (Silici, 2005), and examining the effects of cooking techniques on sensory properties (Çıtak, 2023).

Gastronomy research often employs sensory analysis techniques that come across product development studies. Besides, restaurant managers are implementing the latest culinary innovations in their dining rooms to improve the customer experience. The creation of a new product that is intended to fill a market demand or the enhancement of an existing product by altering its func tion or content to suit a specific goal is referred to as new product development (Şahin & Arabacı, 2017; Öztürk & Onurlubaş, 2018). Organoleptic analysis tools are a crucial component of quality assurance and new product development, and they also aid in marketing and marketing research initiatives (Fuller, 2011). Alternative product developments for nutritional preferences like raw food (Uçan, 2021), vegan or vegetarian (Vatandost & İnce Karaçeper, 2024), various nutritional restrictions such as lactose or gluten intolerance (Sahin, 2021), probiotics, and functional ingredients with nutritional solid aspects (Onurlar & Durlu Ozkaya, 2018) are frequently encountered when the studies on new product development are examined. Studies on fusion cuisine products (Ercan, 2021) and the modernization of cultural dishes in terms of content or presentation and consumer acceptance levels (Uçuk et al., 2022) are conducted in addition to current methodologies like molecular cuisine in product development studies (Beyter & Yüceer, 2023).

Considering these facts, sensory analysis can be a valuable tool for creating new products, main courses, desserts and drinks in a restaurant. The way consumers respond to the sensory aspects of food (especially colour, aroma, smell, taste and texture) influences the success of new products.

Development of Sensory Characteristic

The combination of contemporary food processing technology and early universal processing methods created the technological groundwork for the development of prepared foods. The product's sensory attributes are crucial quality factors that affect the final product's position on the market and its chance that the target market will find the product appealing and purchase it. After all, eating food that tastes delicious is always necessary, in addition to the necessity for food safety.

Each cooking method produces unique changes in the physical and chemical properties, overall flavor profile, and component makeup, resulting in a variety of gastronomic experiences. Therefore, it is essential to balance taste preservation with desirable texture to produce the highest standard of dishes (Jia et al., 2023). The raw materials and completed goods are handled, processed, packed, and stored by the necessary standards, which is the primary responsibility of quality control programs (Giovannucci & Satin, 2001). Thermal treatments, which provide safer, longer shelf lives, have fewer spoiling bacteria (Augusto, 2020), also cause the degradation of food quality and because of that, the food industry looks for substitutes in cutting-edge food processing technology to lessen the potential harm (Rosenthal, Guedes, dos Santos, & Deliza, 2021). Newly produced food products by utilizing new techniques bring together the question of organoleptic qualities. The desired and wanted sensory characteristics of these products are tested with various methods before being unleashed on the market by researchers, academicians, and experts in fields.

The reheat treatment of products is a standard application in the food industry, which may cause an alteration in food quality. The best possible taste replication is guaranteed by employing efficient reheating methods. The main objective of developing the prepared dish business is to integrate industrial equipment with dish preparation processes, encouraging innovative industrialization to boost agricultural growth and highlight the different cuisines of other countries worldwide (Jia et al., 2023).

The industrial growth and technological development of culinary dishes through central kitchens are reflected in prepared products, a technological extension of traditional preconditioned foods and industrially formed culinary items (Li et al., 2022). Small and medium-sized businesses can still find opportunities to develop cutting-edge products that meet modern consumer demands (Cayot, 2007).

Sensory Analysis and Consumer Perceptions

The product's sensory qualities are crucial quality factors that affect the final product's position on the market. Because, in addition to physiological, socio-cultural and psychological factors, sensory elements are effective in consumers' purchasing decisions. The most effective way to describe a product's qualities in terms of perceived intensities and attributes is through descriptive sensory analysis (Karaman & Çetinkaya, 2020). Taste is the most decisive feature among the senses of individuals in their food and beverage consumption preferences. Sensory reactions to the taste, smell and texture of foods contribute to shaping food preferences and eating habits.

The findings of scientific studies have demonstrated that the quality and significant sensory attributes of a product can be determined and managed through descriptive analysis or through consumer testing, which allows for the examination of whether a modification has had an impact on the product's overall quality or a specific property (Bahamonde, Diez, Quevedo, Luaces, & del Coz, 2007; Grunert et al., 2008)

Gastronomy, sensory science, and history have all investigated food harmonization in order to develop novel flavor combinations and comprehend the factors that influence people's preferences for particular foods and drinks (Arellano-Covarrubias, Escalona-Buendía, G´omez-Corona, & Varela, 2022). The cutting-edge processing techniques, informed by scientific research, conducted by academic institutions and business executives, guarantee that fruits' full potential can be efficiently realized and distributed to all corners of the globe through gastronomic experiences (Leal, Sousa, da Silva, de Freitas, & de Souza Martins, 2023). For instance, Herawati et al. (2024) assessed the different techniques, formulas, and ingredient combinations to produce coffee brews, and they decided the best way to brew by sensory panels.

New technologies for tenderization, such ultrasound and/or ultra-high pressure treatment, have shown promise recently in terms of improving meat products' texture, tenderness, and sensory quality while minimizing the loss of nutrients (Dong, Zhang, Mei, Xie, & Shao, 2022), and these mentioned techniques are recommended for meat processing. Kaan, Tuna, Tepe, Zeren, and Küçükçetin (2024) demonstrated that the Lor cheese was successfully used to create a high-protein snack. In another study, Baylan and Badem (2023) created functional foods that support healthy nutrition by preserving the main characteristics of some traditional Turkish foods, adding purple-mix extract or purple flour, and developing products highly appreciated by panelists.

Regarding the use of lyophilized food in gastronomic products, recipes were included from molecular gastronomy restaurants for the lyophilization of some foods, like chicken breast, to produce light and durable substitutes (Babi´c, Cantalejo, & Arroqui, 2009). The ice cream business could benefit from using freeze-dried persimmon peel powder as an added-value ingredient to enhance the functional properties of their products, which were approved by sensory analysis participants (Yosefiyan, Mahdian, Kordjazi, & Hesarinejad, 2024). Moreover, aromatic herbs, namely parsley, peppermint, coriander, basil, and thyme, which are fragile to food processing techniques and have limited shelf-life, were utilized in the preparation of various dishes; both cooks and customers found these freeze-dried culinary goods to be acceptable based on sensory characteristics (Monsalve, Gaviria, & Correa, 2021).

The innovative meals developed by Rekdal et al. (2023) received positive ratings from consumers during consumer testing, suggesting that the utilization of

Nativa intermedia as a potent fermentation agent, has a wide range of sensory appeal in a variety of culinary applications and cultural contexts. The methods and procedures bring something new to the chef's repertoire and can increase the variety of foods that can be fermented in restaurants and other settings (Rekdal et al., 2023).

Some of the popular techniques for reheating include induction cooking, boiling, steaming, microwaving, oven baking, and open flame heating, which techniques produce a variety of physical and chemical changes that impact characteristics like color, texture, flavor, and overall sensory perception because of their unique heating principles (Song et al., 2022). In terms of flavor retention and sensory performance, microwave reheating fared better than other methods when it came to surimi gels (Luo et al., 2022) and Hongsu chicken (Wang, Zhang, Fan, Yang, & Fang, 2018), which is a technique recommended for last years to reheat leftovers or immediate product preparations in chef's kitchen.

However, it should be kept in mind that the gastronomy marketing programmes of companies and or restaurants target their consumers regarding their consuming behavior, not just on sensory analysis. A study conducted by Rojas-Rivas, Urbine, Zaragoza-Alonso, and Cuffia (2021) indicated the differences between Mexican and Argentine customers in the field of representation, the hierarchy of representations, and the cognitive and attitudinal relevance, based on consumer perceptions of both nations. Different cultures sought different perceptions.

Conclusion and Future Aspects

Given the fast-paced nature of the modern world and the booming take-out food sector, consumer preferences have evolved toward more convenient meal options. In order to achieve culinary perfection and worldwide well-being, food science must work in concert with industry, gastronomy, and science. Cooking techniques, preprocessing, and preconditioning significantly impact the sensory qualities, including texture and nutritional makeup, of prepared foods. Investigating new cooking techniques and cross-checking the results with consumer demands and expectations are essential to achieving the ideal texture and flavour. At this point, sensory analysis is a useful tool to understand consumer perception and market a new product in gastronomy science.

Refenrences

Arellano-Covarrubias, A., Escalona-Buendía, H. B., G´omez-Corona, C., & Varela, P. (2022). Pairing beer and food in social media: Is it an image worth more than a thousand words? International Journal of Gastronomy and Food Science, 27(100483). doi:10.1016/J.IJGFS.2022.100483

Augusto, P. E. (2020). Challenges, trends and opportunities in food processing. Current Opinion in Food Science, 35, 72–78.

Babi´c, J., Cantalejo, M. J., & Arroqui, C. (2009). The effects of freeze-drying process parameters on broiler chicken breast meat. Food Science and Technology, 42, 1325–1334. doi:10.1016/j.lwt.2009.03.020

Bahamonde, A., Diez, J., Quevedo, J. R., Luaces, O., & del Coz, J. J. (2007). How to learn consumer preferences from the analysis of sensory data by means of support vector machines (SVM). Trends in Food Science and Technology, 18, 20–28.

Baylan, İ. & Badem, A. (2023). Bazı Geleneksel Ürünlerin Mor Un ile Formüle Edilmesi ve Duyusal Analiz ile Değerlendirilmesi. Kültür Araştırmaları Dergisi, 17, 197–207.

Beyter, N. & Yüceer, M.B. (2023). "Moleküler Gastronomi Teknikleri ile Ürün Geliştirme Denemeleri: Türk Kahveli Süt Helvası Örneği". The Journal of Social Sciences. 10/66, 98–118.

Cayot, N. (2007). Sensory quality of traditional foods. Food Chemistry, 101(1), 154–162.

Çıtak, S. (2023). "Ekşi Mayalı Ekmeğin Saman Ateşinde Pişirilmesinin Lezzet Profili ve Dokusuna Etkisinin Araştırılması, Odun Ve Elektrikli Fırında Pişirilenlerle Kıyaslanması", İstanbul: İstanbul Okan Üniversitesi Lisansüstü Eğitim Enstitüsü, Gastronomi Anabilim Dalı, Gastronomi Programı, Yüksek Lisans Tezi, Aralık, İstanbul, Türkiye.

Dong, Y., Zhang, H., Mei, J., Xie, J., & Shao, C. (2022). Advances in application of ultrasound in meat tenderization: A review. Frontiers in Sustainable Food Systems, 6(969503).

Ercan, M.O. (2021). "Gastronomi Turizmi Kapsamında Türk Tatlılarının Şefler Tarafından Değerlendirilmesi: Füzyon Mutfak Uygulamaları Kapsamında Ürün Geliştirme Çalışması" Nevşehir Hacı Bektaş Veli Üniversitesi Sosyal Bilimler Enstitüsü Gastronomi ve Mutfak Sanatları Anabilim Dalı. Yüksek Lisans Tezi. Nevşehir. Türkiye.

Fuller, G. W. (2011). What Is New Food Product Development? . In B. Raton (Ed.), New Food Product Development. Florida, USA: CRC Press Taylor and Francis Group.

Giovannucci, D., & Satin, M. (2001). Food Quality Issues: Understanding HACCP and Other Quality Management Techniques A Guide to Developing Agricultural Markets and Agro-enterprises. 2007; http://ssrn.com/abstract= 996762.

Grunert, K. G., Jensena, B. B., Sonnea, A. M., Brunsøa, K., Byrne, D. V., Clausen, C., . . . Scholderer, J. (2008). User-oriented innovation in the food sector: relevant streams of research and an agenda for future work. Trends in Food Science and Technology, 19(11), 590–602. doi:10.1016/j.tifs.2008.03.008

Herawati, D., Armawan, M. S., Nurhaliza, N., Mu'arij, F. A., Hunaefi, D., & Noviasari, S. (2024). Impact of bean origin and brewing methods on bioactive compounds, bioactivities, nutrition, and sensory perception in coffee brews: An Indonesian coffee gastronomy study. International Journal of Gastronomy and Food Science, 35(100892).

Jia, Y., Hu, L., Liu, R., Yang, W., Khalifa, I., Bi, J., . . . Li, B. (2023). Innovations and challenges in the production of prepared dishes based on central kitchen engineering: A review and future perspectives. Innovative Food Science & Emerging Technologies, 103521.

Kaan, I., Tuna, O., Tepe, A., Zeren, F. E., & Küçükçetin, A. (2024). Effect of drying temperatures and using prebiotics on the physicochemical and microbiological properties as well as consumer acceptance of probiotic-enriched Lor cheese snacks produced by vacuum drying. International Journal of Gastronomy and Food Science, 36(100929).

Karaman, E. E., & Çetinkaya, N. (2020). Gıda tercihinde duyuların rolü: tat duyusunun tat testi ile demografik özelliklere göre farklılığının tespiti. Atatürk Üniversitesi Sosyal Bilimler Enstitüsü Dergisi, 24(2), 883–898.

Leal, G. F., Sousa, H. M. S., da Silva, R. R., de Freitas, B. C. B., & de Souza Martins, G. A. (2023). Fruit-derived products: A parallel between science, industry and gastronomy. Food and Humanity, 100218.

Li, W., Zheng, L., Xiao, Y., Li, L., Wang, N., Che, Z., & Wu, T. (2022). Insight into the aroma dynamics of Dongpo pork dish throughout the production process using electronic nose and GC× GC-MS. LWT - Food Science and Technology, 169 (113970).

Luo, X., Xiao, S., Ruan, Q., Gao, Q., An, Y., Hu, Y., & Xiong, S. (2022). Differences in f lavor characteristics of frozen surimi products reheated by microwave, water boiling, steaming, and frying. Food Chemistry, 372 (131260).

MEB (2012) .Duyusal Kontrolleri Yapma, Gıda Teknolojisi Alanı, Ankara. https://megep.meb.gov.tr/mte_program_modul/moduller_pdf/Duyusal%20 Kontrolleri%20Yapma.pdf

MEB, Duyusal Kontrolleri Yapma, Gıda Teknolojisi Alanı, Ankara. www.megep. meb.gov.tr (22.05.2024), 5.

Metin, E. (2021). İnovatif Bir Yaklaşım Olarak Yenilebilir Çiçeklerin Çikolatalarda Kullanımı, Balıkesir: Balıkesir Üniversitesi Sosyal Bilimler Enstitüsü Gastronomi ve Mutfak Sanatları Anabilim Dalı, Yüksek Lisans Tezi, 42.

Miişoğlu, D. & Hayoğlu, İ. (2005). Tat Eşik Değerlerinin Algılanması, Tanınması ve Derecelendirilmesi, Harran Üniversitesi Ziraat Fakültesi Dergisi, 9/2, 29.

Monsalve, J. R., Gaviria, L. J., & Correa, A. A. (2021). Use of freeze-dried aromatic herbs with quality organoleptic characteristics in gastronomic products. International Journal of Gastronomy and Food Science, 24(100341).

Onoğur, T. A. & Elmacı, Y. (2011). Gıdalarda Duyusal Değerlendirme, Sidas Medya, 2. Basım, İzmir, 9.

Onurlar, B. & Durlu Özkaya, F. (2018). "Moleküler Probiyotik Dondurma", Journal of Tourism and Gastronomy Studies 6/3, 154–168

Öztürk, D. & Onurlubaş, E. (2018). Gıda Sektöründe Yeni Ürün Geliştirme: Konya'da Bisküvi, Çikolatalı ve Şekerli Mamuller Alt Sektörü Üzerine Bir Uygulama, International Journal of Economic and Administrative Studies, 17, 551–568.

Rekdal, V. M., Rodriguez-Valeron, N., Garcia, M. O., Vásquez, D. P., Sörensen, P. M., Munk, R., & Keasling, J. D. (2023). From lab to table: Expanding gastronomic possibilities with fermentation using the edible fungus Neurospora intermedia. International Journal of Gastronomy and Food Science, 34(100826).

Rojas-Rivas, E., Urbine, A., Zaragoza-Alonso, J., & Cuffia, F. (2021). Cross-cultural representations of gastronomy among consumers in two Latin American countries. Food Research International, 140(109881).

Rosenthal, A., Guedes, A. M. M., dos Santos, K. M. O., & Deliza, R. (2021). Healthy food innovation in sustainable food system 4.0: integration of entrepreneurship, research, and education. Curr Opin Food Sci 2021, 42:215–223.). Current Opinion in Food Science, 42, 215–223.

Silici, Sibel. "Balda Duyusal Analiz", Gıda Mühendisliği Dergisi, (2005), 39.

Song, Y., Zhang, H., Huang, F., Li, X., Liu, J., Mehmood, W., . . . Zhang, C. (2022). Changes in eating quality and oxidation deterioration of pork steaks cooked by different methods during refrigerated storage. International Journal of Gastronomy and Food Science, 29(100576).

Şahin, A. ve Arabacı, O. (2017). Yeni Ürün Geliştirme Takımlarında Örgütsel Ortamın Proje Başarısı ve Proje Hızı Üzerine Etkileri. Journal of International Social Research, 10 (52), 1185–1204

Şahin, Aysel. (2021). Farklı Formlarda Geliştirilen Glütensiz Galetaların Besin Değerleri, Duyusal Analizleri Ve Satın Alma Niyeti Açısından Değerlendirilmesi, Kocaeli: Kocaeli Üniversitesi Sosyal Bilimler Enstitüsü, Turizm İşletmeciliği Anabilim Dalı, Gastronomi Ve Mutfak Sanatları Bilim Dalı, Yüksek Lisans Tezi. Ekim.

Topkaya, Cansu (2017). "Nar Kabuğu Tozu İlavesinin Keklerin Besinsel, Duyusal ve Mikrobiyolojik Özelliklerine Etkisi", Pamukkale Üniversitesi Fen Bilimleri Enstirüsü Gıda Mühendisliği Anabilim Dalı, Yüksek Lisans Tezi. Denizli.

Uçan, Berre Zeynep. (2021). Farklı Baharat Kombinasyonları ile Hazırlanan Raw Food Ürünlerinin Duyusal Analiz Yöntemi ile Değerlendirilmesi, Balıkesir Örneği, Balıkesir: Balıkesir Üniversitesi Sosyal Bilimler Enstitüsü, Gastronomi ve Mutfak Sanatları Anabilim Dalı, Yüksek Lisans Tezi.

Uçuk, Ceyhun, Özdemir, S.S & Kahraman, A.G. (2022). "Tabak Prezantasyonunun Kötü Görünümlü Yiyeceklerin Kabulüne Etkisi: Şırdan Örneği", Journal of Tourism and Gastronomy Studies, 10 /1, 171–192.

Vatandost, E.G. & Ince Karaçeper, E. (2024). Gastronomi Çalışmalarında Alternatif Reçete Geliştirme: Vegan, Vejetaryen ve Laktozsuz Panna Cotta. Sosyal, Beşeri ve İdari Bilimler Dergisi. 7(1), 31–42.

Wang, J., Zhang, M., Fan, K., Yang, C. H., & Fang, Z. (2018). Effects of reheating methods on the product quality of Hongsu chicken dish. Journal of Food Processing and Preservation, 42(11), e13823.

Yosefiyan, M., Mahdian, E., Kordjazi, A., & Hesarinejad, M. A. (2024). Freeze-dried persimmon peel: A potential ingredient for functional ice cream. Heliyon, 10(3). Heliyon, 10(3), e25488.

Soner Özyalçin[1] and Mete Ünal Girgen[2]

Chapter 34 Evaluation of Viticulture in Northern Cyprus in Terms of Gastronomy Tourism

Introduction

Cyprus has been an island nation known throughout history for its rich cultural heritage, unique natural beauty and delicious cuisine. Viticulture has a long history on this magnificent island. In this context, local wines form an important part of the island's cuisine. However, viticulture in Cyprus is not limited to wine production; it has also become an important element of gastronomic tourism. Viticulture creates a perfect combination and opens the doors to a world full of delicious wines when combined with the unique soils, climate and local grape varieties of Cyprus. The viticulture tradition of Cyprus dates back to ancient times and has been combined with modern techniques today. The island is known for its local grape varieties, especially 'Verigo' and 'Mavro', which allow the production of wines with unique characteristics (Kostrzewa, 2010).

Cyprus wines are enriched with special flavors from the island's climate and soil, making them a sought-after flavor worldwide. Viticulture in Cyprus is not limited to wine tasting and production. At the same time, experiences such as tours of the vineyards, grape harvesting events and wine production tours are also offered. Such events offer visitors the opportunity to discover the local viticulture tradition and delve deeply into the local culture. In addition, wine and food pairing events organized in harmony with the rich cuisine of Cyprus have become an important part of gastronomy tourism. This research will focus on the evaluation of viticulture in Cyprus in terms of gastronomy tourism and the island's potential in this area. The aims of the research are to explain the importance of viticulture tours and wine tasting events to discover the unique flavors and cultural riches of Cyprus and why this magnificent island is an ideal destination for gastronomy tourism.

---

1   Res. Asst. Soner ÖZYALÇIN Gastronomy Program, School of Tourism and Culinary Arts, Final International University. ORCID ID: https://orcid.org/0009-0004-1068-7579 HYPERLINK "mailto:soner.ozyalcin@final.edu.tr"soner.ozyalcin@final.edu.tr
2   Assoc. Prof. Dr. Mete Ünal GİRGEN Tourism Program, School of Tourism and Culinary Arts, Final International University. ORCID ID https://orcid.org/0000-0003-2709-5639 HYPERLINK "mailto:mete.girgen@final.edu.tr"mete.girgen@final.edu.tr

Literature Review

Viticulture is an agricultural activity and is a field related to the cultivation of grapes and the production of beverages such as wine from these grapes (McGovern, 2013). By establishing vineyards or managing existing vineyards, different grape varieties are grown. This diversity is used in the production of various beverages such as wine, raki, grape juice (Jackson, 2016). In this way, viticulture is not only grape cultivation, but also the basis of an important economic sector such as the wine industry. The origin and history of viticulture is quite old and is a widespread agricultural activity throughout the world. It has been determined that the plant known as grapevine or vine (Vitis sp.) grew in many geographical regions millions of years ago. Grape seeds found in press residues dating back 10,000 years reveal that viticulture has a deep-rooted history in human history. Viticulture developed in Europe under the influence of the Roman Empire and was carried out under the auspices of monasteries in the Middle Ages. Despite the damage caused to viticulture areas by the Thirty Years' War and other events, viticulture has survived as an important industry in Europe to this day (Karabat, 2014).

Viticulture generally refers to a society's grape growing, wine production, and traditions related to these processes. This culture may vary depending on the geographical characteristics, climate, and soil of the region, and generally reflects a society's relationship with beverages throughout history (Algün, 2016). Viticulture may include a society's interest in wine production, the value placed on vineyards, and rituals and celebrations associated with wine. Viticulture may also reflect the social, cultural, and economic importance of wine and is often considered an important part of a region's identity. This culture is passed on to future generations and maintained through activities such as wine tourism (Charters, 2006).

Viticulture tourism is a type of tourism that is usually associated with the wine industry and where tourists visit vineyards and experience the wine production process. This type of tourism is quite popular in wine-producing regions and includes local viticulture, wine tasting events and vineyard visits. Viticulture tourism offers visitors the opportunity to walk in vineyards, visit wineries, taste wine, experience local cuisine and participate in wine-related events. This type of tourism contributes to both the wine industry and the local economy by offering tourists a unique experience. In addition, viticulture tourism can contribute to the preservation of natural and cultural resources when combined with sustainable tourism practices (Soare et al., 2010; Carrasco et al., 2019).

There is plenty of evidence that viticulture tourism makes positive contributions to the regional economy. For example, Robinson, Harding and Vouillamoz (2013) explain the economic impact of viticulture tourism on the region as follows: "Viticulture tourism encourages tourists to the region and contributes to the development of the local wine industry." In addition, McGovern (2013) shares a similar view, stating that viticulture tourism "contributes to the regional economy and the income it provides to local service and supply industries." Viticulture tourism has a strong relationship with local gastronomy and they support each other. This type of tourism offers visitors the opportunity to experience the rich wine culture of the region and taste local wines. Activities such as visiting vineyards, participating in wine tasting tours and learning about the wine production process allow visitors to get to know the viticulture tradition of the region. In addition to these experiences, there is also the opportunity to taste delicious food, often paired with regional dishes (Hall and Mitchell, 2001).

Visitors can taste local wines made from grapes grown in the region, and they can also try regional dishes at local restaurants and wineries. This provides an unforgettable experience for tourists and contributes to the local economy by increasing the income of local businesses. Viticulture tourism can also increase the interest of local people in local gastronomy. The flavors that tourists experience in the region emphasize the importance of local products and food culture, and encourage local people to take a greater interest in their own cuisine. As a result, this relationship between viticulture tourism and local gastronomy provides unforgettable experiences for tourists and contributes to the economic and cultural development of the region (Getz and Brown, 2006).

Research Methods

The study investigated the potential of viticulture in Northern Cyprus and the evaluation of local products obtained from grapes produced in this region in terms of gastronomy tourism. The qualitative method was used as the research method in the study. The research method section and the findings section were developed with the contributions of 16 research participants who are experts in their fields. The semi-structured interview technique was applied as the research method and answers were sought to open-ended questions. The studies of international organizations that evaluated viticulture in Northern Cyprus in terms of gastronomy tourism and/or encouraged and supported local gastronomy will be examined and their positive and negative effects will be determined and explained. The regions to be examined in the academic research were determined after the literature review. The research participants were selected from among the field professionals who are stakeholders in viticulture and tourism from different regions in Northern Cyprus. The method used in the study of Özgül Katlav et al. (2019) and applied to a similar research participant profile was preferred. The participants answered open-ended questions and expressed their opinions on various topics. The evaluation of viticulture in terms of gastronomy tourism, these concepts; qualitative method was used to determine and examine the geography and businesses that define it, to determine the supporting organizations and to investigate the policies they carry out (Karataş, 2015). The main question of the study is addressed in the first question in its most general form and is a question seeking an answer to the research problem. The sub-questions of the study are between the second question and the fifth questions (both included). The research questions are as follows:

1. What do you think about the current situation of the viticulture sector in Northern Cyprus?
2. How do you evaluate the future development of the viticulture industry in Northern Cyprus?
3. What are the main problems facing the viticulture sector in Northern Cyprus?
4. What are the contributions of local products of viticulture in Northern Cyprus to the economy?
5. What are the events organized regarding viticulture in Northern Cyprus?

Findings Research Participants

The 16 people who participated in our research as research participants are including 5 women and 11 men and were individuals with at least 10 years of experience in their fields and known for their expertise, carefully selected from grape growers in vineyards located in every region of the island. Research participants represent different areas as 4 from Kyrenia, 7 from Nicosia, 2 from Famagusta, 1 from Akıncılar, 1 from Mehmetçik and 1 from Yeni Erenköy - Yalusa. The education level of research partcipitants differs as, 3 of the participants have PhD, 5 from MSc and 8 from B.Sc. education. Table 34.1 gives detailed information about demographics.

Table 34.1. Demographic Data of Research Participants

No	M/F	Age (n)	Education	Field	District	Years of Experiences by Sector
R1	F	48	M.Sc.	Agricultural Engineer	Kyrenia	25 years
R2	M	39	B.Sc.	Agricultural Engineer	Kyrenia	13 years
R3	M	41	B.Sc.	Agricultural Engineer	Nicosia	15 years
R4	F	49	B.Sc.	Agricultural Engineer	Nicosia	19 years
R5	M	58	Ph.D.	Agricultural Engineer	Kyrenia	25 years
R6	M	69	B.Sc.	Politician	Nicosia	20 years
R7	M	45	M.Sc.	Politician	Nicosia	10 years
R8	M	41	M.Sc.	Wine Connoisseur	Kyrenia	20 years
R9	M	58	B.Sc.	Gastronomy	Famagusta	40 years
R10	F	45	Ph.D.	Academician	Kyrenia	10 years
R11	M	60	B.Sc.	Politician	Kyrenia	18 years
R12	F	59	Ph.D.	Businessman	Kyrenia	30 years
R13	M	47	M.Sc.	Businessman	Lurucina	10 years
R14	M	39	M.Sc.	Agricultural Engineer	Nicosia	12 years
R15	F	71	B.Sc.	Farmer	Galatya	50 years
R16	M	51	B.Sc.	Farmer	Yalusa	30 years

Responses from Participants

According to the majority of participants (n=9), when we look at the current situation of viticulture in Northern Cyprus, we see that there is an increase compared to previous years. However, this increase is very slow. Today, thanks to developing technology, viticulture has become easier and an increase is observed in the current situation.

The participants of the research on the current status of the viticulture sector stated that the viticulture sector in Northern Cyprus is a sector that is increasing compared to previous years. However, this progress is slow due to current problems. According to the participants (n=3), citizens interested in agriculture tend to focus more on olive cultivation than other agricultural activities. Despite this, there is a certain potential increase in viticulture. The current status of the viticulture sector in Northern Cyprus has been positively increasing in recent years in North Cyprus. This increase is generally seen in the viticulture sector. However, citrus and olive cultivation are more preferred.

> One of the reasons why viticulture in Northern Cyprus has not shown a significant increase in its current situation is that the agricultural and soil structure of the northern region is not very suitable. Therefore, our citizens are forced to turn to other agricultural activities. (R5)

The current state of viticulture in Northern Cyprus is increasing compared to the past thanks to technology. However, this increase is limited due to the unsuitability of the soil structure. If we talk about the future of the viticulture industry, it should be noted that it has a very large potential. If we can use this potential correctly, we can become one of the world's leading quality wine production centers (n=5). If we evaluate the development of the viticulture industry in Northern Cyprus, the island of Cyprus has a very old history in viticulture. In fact, while viticulture used to be done by the Turkish people, marketing belonged to the Greeks. There was such a tradition in the history of the island. However, if the current administration on the island does not improve, the viticulture sector is a sector that could suffer serious damage. If the current political order continues, this situation could have negative consequences for the viticulture industry (n = 5).

Some of the participants (n = 3) think that the viticulture industry is at a very high quality level. However, opposing views are of the opinion that positive developments will only occur if the necessary investments are made in this regard (n = 9). Viticulture is seen as a very special field. According to the answers given by the participants, if we consider the current status of the viticulture industry, its future seems quite bright and has the potential to add great value to North Cyprus. However, it is difficult to say anything definite about the future, because the current order on the island (political—implemented embargoes, lack of experts in the field, infrastructural deficiencies, etc.) is very complicated. Unfortunately, this situation makes the future of the viticulture sector uncertain. The viticulture industry has great potential. If the right steps are taken, the island of Cyprus can become a world-renowned wine production center. However, improving the current political situation is of critical importance for this potential to be realized.

Social, Cultural and Environmental Problems

The main problems are the instability of the current political order and political uncertainties that can affect the stability of our businesses. Such uncertainties negatively affect our businesses in an environment where security and stability are not ensured (n = 3). The main problems faced by the viticulture sector are the lack of sufficient government interest in the sector, which hinders the development of the viticulture sector and limits farmers' access to technical support and resources (n = 4).

> The main problem of the viticulture sector is the lack of necessary appointments. This causes a lack of expertise in the sector and reduces efficiency and quality standards. (R5)

In particular, the current agricultural problems, poor soil quality and conditions that are not suitable for viticulture, can negatively affect the productivity. Factors such as climate change and drought seriously affect viticulture production, which can reduce harvests and damage infrastructure (n = 4).

Economic Problems

The main problems in the viticulture sector are that agriculture is generally facing economic difficulties. This makes it difficult for the viticulture sector to be financially sustainable because costs are increasing and incomes are decreasing. Insufficient agricultural lands and lands that are not suitable for viticulture hinder growth and competition in the sector, which makes it difficult for farmers to market their products and earn income (n = 3). Although there is a standard support provided by the state, the amount and scope of this support is generally insufficient. Although the support provided per root in particular provides a certain amount of income for farmers in the sector, more support and incentives are important to encourage development in the sector in general (n = 4). It is stated that the supports provided by the state are outdated and no longer suitable for today's conditions. Therefore, the state needs to review and update its support policies for the viticulture sector. It is important to encourage innovative projects and provide support that will better meet the needs of the sector (n = 7). It is clearly accepted that the current supports are insufficient and the sector is lagging behind. Therefore, the state needs to provide more effective and comprehensive support to the viticulture sector. This will ensure that the sector develops in a more sustainable way and will allow farmers to produce under better conditions (n = 5). The state attaches importance to investing in the viticulture sector and providing support to farmers. In this context, various supports and incentives are provided to contribute to the development of the sector. Support is provided to farmers in areas such as supporting projects, providing technical consultancy services and organizing training programs for the sector (n = 2).

North Cyprus is developing various policies and programs to increase the sustainability and competitiveness of the viticulture sector. Through these programs, farmers
are provided with opportunities to learn and apply modern agricultural techniques.
In addition, farmers are supported economically with various financial supports and
incentives. (R11)

Feedback about Local Products

Viticulture and local products associated with viticulture are very important in
Northern Cyprus. Special grape varieties grown in the region form the basis of
a rich cultural heritage and gastronomic diversity. Local businesses and producers are making efforts to promote the products obtained from these grapes and
evaluate them within the scope of gastronomic tourism (n = 10). The naturalness
and organic structure of local products increase the gastronomic tourism potential of the region. The geographical indication and registration of these products
are of great importance in terms of their protection and promotion to a wider
audience. Local products associated with viticulture, especially local flavors such
as pekmez, köfter, and sucuk processed with products obtained from their own
vineyards, are offered to guests both in local restaurants and hotels. These products are the most prominent products in this context (n = 6).

Efforts are also being made to promote and increase awareness of these products through organizations such as grape harvest events. The fact that these flavors are not known by the new generation and the lack of promotion prevents
these products from receiving the necessary attention. Our government, municipalities, hotel and restaurant businesses need to take a more active role in the
dissemination and promotion of these products. The rich viticulture tradition
and local products of Northern Cyprus are on their way to becoming an important part of the cultural and gastronomic diversity of the region. The promotion
and protection of these products can contribute to the economic development of
the region by increasing its tourism potential (n = 10).

Local products in Northern Cyprus attract the attention of local and foreign
tourists visiting the region. Tourists especially want to visit the areas where these
products are made and be involved in the production process. However, unfortunately, there is a lack of businesses or areas in the region that can meet this
demand. Existing businesses are generally unable to meet this demand and are
unable to offer tourists the opportunity to promote local products. Hotel visitors
want to taste and buy the local flavors of Northern Cyprus. However, the fact
that tourists are not fully aware of these products and the lack of businesses in
the region that produce and sell these products make it difficult to meet this

demand. Local businesses and producers need to make an effort to meet tourists' interest in local products. Special areas or businesses can be created to promote local products and show the production process to tourists. In this way, the
interest of tourists visiting the region in local products can be increased and the
tourism potential of the region can be further developed.

> The Turkish Cypriot community has a strong attachment to its local products and a
> traditional structure. However, it currently faces significant difficulties in passing on this
> valuable heritage to future generations and lives in fear of being forgotten. (R5)

Traditional local products constitute an important part of Turkish Cypriot culture and are a heritage that has been passed down from the past to the present.
However, due to the impact of modern life, difficulties arise in preserving and
transferring these values. The decreasing interest of future generations in traditional local products and the forgetting of the production methods of these
products indicate that the cultural heritage is at risk of being lost. The contribution of local products to the economy, such as local wines, grape molasses, rai-
sins, and grape sausage, attract the attention of tourists. In addition, the support
of local producers by purchasing these products by the local people contributes
to the island's economy (n = 5).

> In the marketing of products and tourism promotion activities, inadequacies are
> observed regarding Cyprus grapes and viticulture. The cultural heritage and local prod-
> ucts of the region are not used effectively in tourism. Although small businesses carry
> out promotional activities with their own efforts, more comprehensive and effective
> work can be done with state support. (R15)
> Marketing local products is of great importance. However, due to lack of promotion,
> many people are not aware of the existence of these products. (R9)
> Some events organized specifically for viticulture in Northern Cyprus, such as the
> Galatya Vineyard Festival, can be given as examples. (R8)

Some examples of events organized for viticulture include some restaurants
organizing their own vineyard and wine events. There are also grape harvest
events organized by the vineyard owners themselves. These events usually have
limited participation from locals or tourists (n = 13).

Conclusion

Evaluating viticulture in terms of gastronomy tourism has important advantages such as increasing the tourism potential of Northern Cyprus, contributing
to the local economy, introducing cultural richness and encouraging sustainable tourism practices. Similar studies have shown that evaluating viticulture

in Northern Cyprus in terms of gastronomy tourism is of great importance in terms of increasing the tourism potential of the region, contributing to the local economy, introducing cultural richness and encouraging sustainable tourism practices (Kim and Kim, 2002; Liu, 2003; Ioan-Franc and Istoc, 2007; Cohen and Ben-Nun, 2009; Fountain and Tompkins, 2011; Kocaman and Kocaman, 2014; Tafel and Szolnoki 2020; Çavuşoğlu, 2023; Sinha, 2023; Messina et al., 2024). Associating local products and local tastes with tourism can increase tourist interest in Northern Cyprus. Integrating viticulture activities with tourism can contribute to increasing tourism revenues in the region and the development of the tourism sector. In addition, tourism activities related to viticulture can increase the income of local producers and help create jobs. This can support economic development in Northern Cyprus and stimulate the local economy. Viticulture and local products are an important part of the cultural heritage of Northern Cyprus and these activities can provide tourists with the opportunity to experience the local culture by promoting the cultural richness of the region. Combining viticulture with gastronomy tourism can help promote sustainable tourism practices. This can contribute to the implementation of sustainable tourism principles such as preserving natural resources, supporting local communities and reducing environmental impacts.

The recommendations of participants are as follows:

• The appointment of experts in the field of viticulture in the country in the right positions
• More active support from the state and private institutions the businesses related to viticulture.
• Improving state policies and ensuring sustainability & better promotion should be done.
• Interest should not be the priority (not negatively affecting the development of the state for the sake of personal gain)
• The country should not bow to the current conditions due to the embargoes and restrictions applied. Despite all these negativities, the sector must be protected.

References

Algün, V. (2016). *Gastronomik bir öge olarak üzümün görsel sanatlardaki biçimleri: Sosyo-kültürel ve tarihsel bir inceleme* (Master's thesis, Sosyal Bilimler Enstitüsü).

Carrasco, I., Castillo-Valero, JS ve Pérez-Luño, A. (2019). Kültürel ve yaratıcı bir endüstri olarak şarap turizmi ve şarap tatili: Bullas şarap rotası örneği. *Kültürel ve Yaratıcı Endüstriler: Girişimcilik ve Yeniliğe Giden Yol* , 181–195.

Charters, S. (2006). *Wine and Society. Routledge,* London: Routledge.

Cohen, E., & Ben-Nun, L. (2009). The important dimensions of wine tourism experience from potential visitors' perception. *Tourism and Hospitality Research, 9*(1), 20–31.

Çavuşoğlu, M. (2023). Yöresel Cıttaslow Şehir Lezzetlerinin Gastronomi Turizmi Açısından Önemi: Kuzey Kıbrıs Örneği. *Gastroia: Journal of Gastronomy And Travel Research, 7*(2), 407–418.

Fountain, J. M., & Tompkins, J. M. (2011). The potential of wine tourism experiences to impart knowledge of sustainable practices: The case of the Greening Waipara biodiversity trails.

Getz, D., & Brown, G. (2006). Critical Success Factors for Wine Tourism Regions: A Demand Analysis. Tourism Management, 27(1), 146–158.

Hall, C. M., & Mitchell, R. (2001). Wine Tourism and Regional Development: A New Tourism That Supports Agriculture. Tourism Management, 22(5), 297–306.

Ioan-Franc, V., & Istoc, E. M. (2007). Cultural tourism and sustainable development. *Romanian Journal of Economic Forecasting, 1*(2007), 89.

Jackson, R. (2016). Shelf life of wine. In *The Stability and Shelf Life of Food* (pp. 311–346). Woodhead Publishing.

Karabat, S. (2014). Dünya ve Türkiye Bağcılığı, *Apelasyon e-Dergi,* Ocak 2014 Sayısı.

Karataş, Z. (2015). Sosyal bilimlerde nitel araştirma yöntemleri. *Manevi temelli sosyal hizmet araştırmaları dergisi, 1*(1), 62–80.

Kim, M. K., & Kim, S. H. (2002, April). Economic impacts of wine tourism in Michigan. In *Proceedings of the 2002 Northeastern Recreation Research Symposium* (pp. 140 146).

Kocaman, M., & Kocaman, E. M. (2014). The importance of cultural and gastronomic tourism in local economic development: Zile sample. *International Journal of Economics and Financial Issues, 4*(4), 735–744.

Kostrzewa, S. (2010), Cyprus Wine Destinations Wines of Cyprus: Nectar of the Gods. Retrieved from https://web.archive.org/web/20201118055906/https://www.winemag.com/2010/05/05/wines-of-cyprus-nectar-of-the-gods/

Liu, Z. (2003). Sustainable tourism development: A critique. *Journal of sustainable tourism, 11*(6), 459–475.

McGovern, P. E. (2013). *Ancient Wine: The Search for The Origins of Viniculture.* Princeton University Press.

Messina, G., Nicosia, E., & Porto, C. M. (2024). Vineyard tourist routes as a factor of regional development: the case of Sicily in a path methodology. *Preliminary Reports and Negative Results in Life Science and Humanities*, (1).

Özgül Katlav, E., Yönet Eren, F., & Tuna, M. (2019). Kapadokya'da bağcılığın gastronomi turizmi açısından değerlendirilmesi.

Robinson, J., Harding, J., & Vouillamoz, J. (2013). *Wine Grapes: A Complete Guide to 1,368 Vine Varieties, İncluding Their Origins and Flavours.* Penguin UK.

Sinha, G. (2023). Exploring the Culinary Symphony: A Comprehensive Literature Review on the Interplay of Gastronomy and Viticulture, Investigating the Cultural, Social, and Economic Impacts of Food and Wine Pairing in Contemporary Perspectives. *International Journal for Multidimensional Research Perspectives*, 1(4), 27–40.

Soare, I., Otilia, MAN, Costachie, S. ve Nedelcu, A. (2010). Romanya'da bağcılık potansiyeli ve asma turizmi. *Revista de turism-studii si cercetari in turizm*, (10), 68–74.

Tafel, M., & Szolnoki, G. (2020). Estimating the economic impact of tourism in German wine regions. *International Journal of Tourism Research*, 22(6), 788–799.

Beysun Güneri[1] and V. Ruya Ehtiyar[2]

Chapter 35 A Qualitative Study on the Implementation of the Cross-age Peer Tutoring Model in Culinary Lessons

Introduction

In recent years, the increase in interest in gastronomy has led to a rise in the number of businesses providing food and beverage services, consequently increasing the demand for qualified professionals in the field of gastronomy. To meet this demand, the number of programs opened at both secondary and higher education levels in our country has increased over time. However, issues regarding the quality of education provided alongside the increase in the number of programs have been noted. Evaluations in the literature indicate the inadequacy of practical training, particularly in the culinary field (Öney, 2016; Arslanhan & Özdemir Yaman, 2020; Babaç & Önçel, 2018; Topal & Gök, 2020).

Keeping up with the continuous advancements in the dynamic gastronomy sector has been challenging for teachers and instructors (Arslanhan & Özdemir Yaman, 2020; Akmeşe et al., 2020; Öney, 2016). Additionally, these innovations are not easily adapted into the current educational curricula (Cankül, 2019). Moreover, due to the large class sizes, teachers sometimes struggle to meet all students' learning needs. Active involvement in the sector is highly effective in helping students gain up-to-date knowledge and techniques in vocational training at secondary education institutions (Akın, 2018; Babaç & Önçel, 2018). Students gaining sector-specific experience in different establishments learn various techniques and acquire diverse skills and knowledge according to the characteristics of the establishment. Furthermore, they have the opportunity to reinforce their education. At this point, the cross-age peer tutoring model comes into play to support the teaching-learning environment.

The cross-age peer tutoring model can help students, especially those who are encountering culinary courses for the first time, adapt to the kitchen and assist

---

1   Ph.D., Akdeniz University, Goynuk Culinary Arts Vocational School, Department of Hotel, Restaurant and Catering Services, beysunguneri@akdeniz.edu.tr
2   Prof., Akdeniz University, Tourism Faculty, Department of Hospitality Management, ehtiyar@akdeniz.edu.tr
* This study is derived from the author's doctoral dissertation.

the teacher with the help of well-trained peer tutors in a crowded classroom environment. Practical culinary training is extremely important as it positively enhances students' practical competencies Therefore, it is essential that practical training in culinary education is sufficient in terms of both quality and quantity. To ensure this adequacy, the education provided by teachers in schools should be supported by various teaching methods, which can have positive effects on the quality and sufficiency of practical training (Orhaner & Hussein Tunç, 2007). Peer tutoring, defined as a concept where students of the same age or different age groups share similar knowledge and learning experiences (Topping & Ehly, 1998), can be used as a method to support the learning-teaching environment in practical culinary training (Oakley et al., 2017; Shin & Kim, 2020; Pillay, 2017).

Peer tutoring is an instructional strategy that offers numerous advantages such as enhancing students' practical skills, improving self-confidence and communication abilities (Topping, 2005), facilitating more comfortable questioning (Demirel, 2013), promoting social interaction and collaboration, providing opportunities to learn from different perspectives, and developing mentoring and leadership skills (Topping & Ehly, 1998; Mynard & Almarzouqi, 2006). This system is seen as a method that increases social dynamics within the educational context by allowing students to interact with their peers (Mynard & Almarzouqi, 2006). Furthermore, peer tutoring shows that students tend to solve their issues by asking their peers when they hesitate to ask their teachers (McCleary & Weaver, 1990; Boud et al., 2001). In this context, peer tutoring is considered an effective method that facilitates individual learning and enhances educational quality.

The purpose of this study is to reveal the contributions of the peer tutoring model to the basic culinary course at the secondary education level, based on the opinions of the students involved in the research, to identify the challenges encountered in the process, and to draw conclusions on whether the peer tutoring model can be an effective method for acquiring basic culinary skills. Accordingly, a peer tutoring model was developed for the Basic Food Production course included in the culinary education provided at the secondary education level, and the contributions of cross-age peer tutoring to the learning environment in practical culinary courses and the challenges encountered in cross-age peer tutoring practices were explored.

Method

This research is designed as a case study, one of the qualitative research methods. The research is limited to students taking the Basic Food Production course in the 10th grade of the culinary branch of a Vocational and Technical Anatolian

High School located in Küçükçekmece, Istanbul, during the second semester of the 2016–2017 academic year. The study group of the research included 15 peer tutees selected from 10th grades and 7 peer tutors selected from the 11th grades of the same school. The peer tutees and peer tutors were selected by random selection among the volunteers, considering their academic success. Since the practical training of the Basic Food Production course was conducted in groups, the students for each group in the peer tutoring program were determined by a simple random method and divided into 5 groups of 3 students each.

Semi-structured interview forms were used to collect the data in the research. To examine the participants' views on the peer tutoring practice in-depth, three questions were posed to each student, and the interviews were recorded (Yıldırım & Şimşek, 2016). The interview transcripts were thoroughly analyzed, with each word, sentence, or paragraph coded. During the phase of theme and category creation, similar narratives were grouped into general categories, and theme analysis was conducted (Miles & Huberman, 1994; Creswell, 2005). For internal reliability, the consistency review technique was used, and the Kappa consistency coefficient was found to be 0.821 between the coding made by two independent researchers. To increase external validity, detailed descriptions were provided, and purposive sampling was used (Yıldırım & Şimşek, 2016). For external reliability, the confirmation review technique was used. The data obtained and the conclusions reached were evaluated by an expert researcher in the field of Tourism Education using the expert review technique.

The peer tutoring program was designed in three stages by the researcher. In the first stage, preparation and planning were carried out, and the cross-age peer tutoring model was determined. In the second phase, the participants were selected based on volunteerism using by random selection. In the third stage, implementation and evaluation phases were carried out. Peer tutors were given information on teaching techniques, and the curriculum content was conveyed. The program was implemented for 6 weeks, with each group managed by a peer tutor. In the first weeks, basic topics such as hygiene, vegetable chopping, and cooking techniques were covered, while in the following weeks, the focus was on stock preparation, soup making, and egg cooking techniques. Throughout the program, the course teacher provided guidance to ensure the successful completion of the process.

Findings

In this study, the views of students in the roles of peer tutor and peer tutee regarding the contributions of peer tutoring and the challenges experienced in the process are specified as main themes and sub-themes in Tables 35.1 and 35.2, with quotations included in the tables.

Table 35.1. Contributions of Peer tutoring According to Peer Tutees and Peer Tutors

Category	Subcategory	Quotation
Contributions of peer tutoring to the Course	Cultivation of a Positive Attitude Towards the Course	***TE* 4 (Group 2, F**):** *"I was especially scared of the cutting techniques, but now I feel more comfortable."*
	Enhancement of Motivation for the Course	**TE 10 (Group 4, M***):** *"I became more curious when I saw what my peers explained and how they had developed themselves. They talked about their internship, which inspired me. I started to like the course and the department."*
	Execution of Effective and Efficient Lessons	**TE1 (Group 1, M):** *"They spent an entire lesson giving me one-on-one attention for things I couldn't do… It was good because they are more experienced than us."*
	Advance Preparation and Review of Course Material	**TR3 (Gorup 3 M):** *"We learned each practice we taught in advance, which reinforced our previous knowledge… Also, we refreshed and reviewed our old knowledge, which was beneficial for us."*
Contributions to Learning	Acquiring Task Distribution Skills	**TR****2 (Group 2 F):** *"I can explain the recipe to them myself. While explaining, I delegate tasks by saying 'you will do this' and 'you will do that."*
	Maintaining Classroom Discipline	**TR5 (Group 5 M):** *"Last year, there were many absences. This year, there is more seriousness in the kitchen. Also, when a peer tutee goes somewhere for a long time, we ask where they are, which adds a sense of seriousness."*
	Assisting the Teacher in Crowded Classrooms	**TE1 (Group 1, M):** *"The class is more orderly; there is noise and unruliness in a crowded setting. Working with a group of three was better. Also, having a tutor was effective in maintaining this order."*

Table 35.1.   Continued

Category	Subcategory	Quotation
	Enhancing Academic Achievement	TE2 (Group 1, M): *"I found the course difficult. My first exam was already low, but thanks to peer tutoring, I improved my score on the second exam."*
	Enhancing creativity	TR3 (Group 3, M): *"The potato salad allowed me to create something original, and it was highly appreciated. I decided on the quantities myself. I found the opportunity to reflect something of myself, which I really liked. I was very pleased that my taste was appreciated."*
Contributions to Professional Skills	**Enhancing Professional and Technical Skills**	TE 5 (Group 2, F): *"I struggled a lot with julienne cutting. But the peer tutor gave us enough explanation, showed it a few times, and I learned to cut correctly."*
Interpersonal Relationships Among Peers	**Feeling Comfortable in the Presence of the Peer Tutor**	TR4 (Group 4, F): *"At least when they have a question, they can ask us without any hesitation before asking the teachers."*
	Strengthening Peer Relationships	TR1 (Group 1, M): *"Our relationships with the learners became more sincere. Our communication improved. We established good dialogue. We became like older and younger siblings."*
Behavioral Contributions	**Enhancing Students' Self-Confidence**	TE6 (Group 2, F): *"I have low self-confidence but am ambitious. However, my peer tutor helped me overcome my lack of self-confidence."*
	Developing Empathy Skills	TR4 (Group 4, F): *"Peer tutoring made me more empathetic. We understood how our teachers feel."*
	Improving Communication Skills	TR3 (Group 3, M): *"I gained the ability to address individuals. It greatly improved my communication skills, which is very important for me in the future."*

(continued on next page)

Table 35.1.   Continued

Category	Subcategory	Quotation
	Exhibiting Leadership Behaviors	TR6 (Group 4, F): *"I had the opportunity to reflect my leadership spirit. I felt like I was the head chef of a hotel, teaching new interns. It was a wonderful feeling."*

*TE: Tutee; **M: Male; ***F: Female; ****TR: Tutor

According to Table 35.1, the contributions of peer tutoring, based on the views of peer tutees and peer tutors, are categorized into four main categories: contributions to the course, contributions to learning, contributions to professional skills, and contributions to peer relationships.

Codes such as the desire to repeat peer tutoring, encouragement to become a peer tutor, effective and efficient learning in the course, and feeling comfortable alongside the peer tutor indicate students' satisfaction with peer tutoring and their desire to experience this method again. Additionally, contributions such as the enhancement of professional and technical skills, increased motivation for the course, assisting the teacher in crowded classrooms, and boosting the self-confidence of peer tutees demonstrate the broad and positive impacts of this method on students.

Table 35.2. Challenges Encountered during the Peer tutoring Process According to the Perspectives of Peer Tutees and Peer Tutors

Category	Subcategory	Quotation
Educational and Pedagogical Challenges	Limited Authority During the Lesson	TE5 (Group 2, M): *"They should not do all the applications themselves; they should explain the rights and wrongs to us. Some applications were like this."*
Participation and Interaction Issues	Difficulty in Teaching Disinterested Students	TR3 (Group 3, M): *"It's difficult to teach a disinterested student."*
	Inability to Monitor the Activities Conducted by Other Groups	TE9 (Group 3, F): *"Also, we can't follow the applications done by other groups."*
	Inability of the Instructor to Closely Engage with Students	TE15 (Group 5, F): *"Our teacher cannot engage with us more closely. The teacher of other classes placed them in good internships."*

Table 35.2. Continued

Category	Subcategory	Quotation
Social and Behavioral Challenges	Fear of Being Belittled	**TE11 (Group 4, M)**: *"But they might look down on us… Since they are only a year older than us, they might see us as inexperienced."*
	Difficulty in Peer Tutor's Adaptation	**TE14 (Group 5, F)**: *"In the first weeks, it was not very comfortable, it seemed a bit hesitant…"*

These findings reveal various challenges encountered during the peer tutoring process. Educational and pedagogical difficulties include issues such as students wanting to take a more active role and the lack of participation in practical education. These challenges highlight important areas that need to be considered to enhance the effectiveness of peer tutoring programs. Measures such as ensuring greater student participation, providing more support from teachers to students, and improving social dynamics can make the peer tutoring process more successful.

Results

This study identified significant benefits and challenges associated with the peer tutoring model in culinary education. The key contributions include improvements in students' attitudes, motivation, and the effectiveness of lessons. Students developed a more positive attitude towards the course and felt more comfortable with practical tasks. Observing their peers' development and hearing about their internships inspired students, thereby increasing their interest in the course. Peer tutors provided one-on-one attention, enhancing the effectiveness of lessons due to their experience. The research conducted by Shin and Kim (2020) supports these findings, indicating that students developed a more positive attitude toward cooking classes, which contributed to increased self-confidence, enhanced learning awareness, and greater encouragement.

In terms of learning, peer tutors effectively learned how to distribute tasks, which is crucial in professional kitchens. Peer tutoring created a more disciplined and serious learning environment in the classroom. Studies by Piepmeier (1998) and Rao and DiCarlo (2000) also demonstrate that peer tutoring is effective in maintaining classroom discipline. The results indicate that peer tutors help maintain order and focus in crowded classrooms, thereby facilitating the learning process. Additionally, students improved their culinary skills through detailed explanations and demonstrations from peer tutors. Pillay (2017) found that peer tutees primarily learned technical skills and only slightly improved their management skills, a finding that aligns with the results of this study. Relationships among peers were strengthened through peer tutoring. Students felt more comfortable asking questions and seeking help from peer tutors before approaching teachers. This model fostered closer relationships and better communication among students. The positive contributions of peer tutoring to students' communication skills are supported by various studies (Sin et al., 2019; Roseth et al. 2008; Pillay, 2017; McKinstery & Topping, 2003). Mckinstery and Topping (2003) concluded that peer tutoring is effective in enhancing communication and interaction among peers. Behavioral contributions include increased self-confidence among students due to peer tutoring. Peer tutors developed empathy and communication skills, which are crucial for their future success. Sin et al. (2019) and Sainz et al. (2024) and Durán and Vázquez (2021) also noted that peer tutoring positively affects students' empathy skills. Moreover, peer tutors had the opportunity to develop and demonstrate leadership qualities (Pillay, 2017; Secomb, 2008).

In addition to the benefits, several challenges were identified. Peer tutors sometimes struggled to balance their authority, leading to incomplete or rushed explanations, and found it difficult to engage disinterested students. Large class sizes prevented teachers from giving individual attention, affecting education quality (Shin & Kim, 2020). Some students felt belittled by authoritative peer tutors and experienced minimal learning, viewing the instructors as overly authoritative and inexperienced (Pillay, 2017). Peer tutors also reported feeling hesitant and uncomfortable in their new roles, spending excessive time, feeling underestimated, and lacking understanding of peer tutoring (Shin & Kim, 2020). They suggested that more training on peer tutoring and handling difficult students would be beneficial (Pillay, 2017).

To enhance the effectiveness of the peer tutoring model, several recommendations are proposed. Providing extensive training on technical skills and pedagogical methods to ensure tutors are well-prepared is essential (Topping 1988; Topping 1996). Continuous support and guidance from the course instructor with regular check-ins and feedback sessions can help tutors refine their teaching approaches. Developing a structured curriculum that outlines specific roles and responsibilities of peer tutors ensures they have clear guidelines on conducting lessons and handling different classroom situations.

Encouraging active participation from all students by incorporating interactive and engaging activities can help maintain interest and motivation among students. Implementing regular monitoring and evaluation of the peer tutoring program to identify areas for improvement and collecting feedback from both tutors and tutees is crucial. Promoting a supportive and respectful classroom culture where all students feel valued and comfortable is also necessary. Addressing instances of belittling behavior promptly and ensuring peer tutors maintain a positive and encouraging attitude can make the peer tutoring process more successful.

By addressing these recommendations, the peer tutoring model can be refined to maximize its benefits for students' practical competencies, professional development, and interpersonal skills in culinary education.

References

Akın, A. (2018). "Gastronomi Turizminde Staj Eğitiminin Önemi: Gaziantep Üniversitesi Örneği" *Iğdır Üniversitesi Sosyal Bilimler Dergisi*, (16).

Akmeşe, K. A., Özata, E. & Sormaz, Ü. (2020). "Gastronomi Sektörü Meslek Uzmanlarının Çalışanlardan Mesleki Beklentileri ve Gastronomi Eğitimi İle İlgili Düşünceleri" *Journal of Yasar University*, 15(58).

Arslanhan, Y. & Yaman, Z. Ö. (2020). "Gastronomi ve Mutfak Sanatları Bölüm Mezunlarının Eğitime İlişkin Memnuniyet Düzeyleri ile İstihdam Özelliklerinin Belirlenmesine Yönelik Bir Araştırma" *Journal of Tourism and Gastronomy Studies*, 8(3), 2013–2028.

Babaç, E. & Önçel, S. (2018). "Anadolu Üniversitesi Gastronomi ve Mutfak Sanatları Bölümü Öğrencilerinin Öz yeterliklerine Yönelik Nitel Bir Araştırma" *Journal of Tourism and Gastronomy Studies*, 6 (2). 282–298.

Bekar, A., Arman, M. S. & Sürücü, Ç. (2017). Turizmde çekicilik unsuru olarak gastronomi müzeleri: Marmaris bal evi örneği. The Journal of Academic Social Science, 42(42), 468-477. Bekar, Arman, and Sürücü (2017)

Boud, D., Cohen, R. & Sampson, J. (2001). Peer Learning in Higher Education: Learning from and with Each Other, Clays Ltd, St Ives plc, London

Boud, D., & Cohen, R. (2014). *Peer learning in higher education: Learning from and with each other.* Routledge.

Cankül, D. (2019). Assessing The Quality Of Gastronomy Education: Turkey Case. *Elektronik Sosyal Bilimler Dergisi*, 18(70). 986–1001.

Creswell, J. W. (2005). *Educational research: Planning, conducting, and evaluating, Quantitative and Qualitative Research*, NJ: Merrill Prentice.

Durán Gisbert, D., & Vázquez Rivas, A. (2021). Implementing peer tutoring for the development of empathy in nursing education. *Investigacion y Educacion En Enfermeria*, 39(2).

Demirel, F. (2013). Akran eğitiminin matematik dersinde kullanımının öğrenci tutumu, başarısı ve bilgi kalıcılığına etkisi. *(Publication No. 330441) [Master's thesis, Ulusal Tez Merkezi]. Ulusal Tez Merkezi.*

McCleary, K. W., & Weaver, P. A. (1990). High involvement peer-based education (HIPE). *Hospitality Research Journal,* 14(2), 199–208.

McKinstery, J., & Topping, K. J. (2003). Cross–age Peer Tutoring of Thinking Skills in the High School. *Educational Psychology in Practice,* 19(3), 199–217.

Miles, M. B. & Huberman, A. M. (1994). *Qualitative Data Analysis.* 2ⁿᵈ Ed., Thousand Oaks, Sage, Ca.

Mynard, J., & Almarzouqi, I. (2006). Investigating peer tutoring. *Elt Journal,* 60(1), 13–22.

Oakley, A. R., Nelson, S. A., & Nickols-Richardson, S. M. (2017). Peer-led culinary skills intervention for adolescents: Pilot study of the impact on knowledge, attitude, and self-efficacy. *Journal of nutrition education and behavior,* 49(10), 852–857.

Orhaner, E. & Hussein Tunç, A. (2007). *Ticaret ve Turizm Eğitiminde Özel Öğretim Yöntemleri.* Siyasal Kitabevi, Ankara

Öney, H. (2016). "Gastronomi Eğitimi Üzerine Bir Değerlendirme" *Selçuk Üniversitesi Sosyal Bilimler Enstitüsü Dergisi,* (35). 193–203.

Piepmeier Jr, E. (1998). Use of conceptests in a large lecture course to provide active student involvement and peer teaching. *American Journal of Pharmaceutical Education,* 62(3), 347.

Pillay, C. (2017). Peer teaching: Applying interactive initiatives in preparation for the workplace in the culinary sector. *In New Zealand Association for Cooperative Education 2017 Conference Proceedings* (pp. 31–34).

Rao, S. P., & DiCarlo, S. E. (2000). Peer instruction improves performance on quizzes. *Advances in physiology education,* 24(1), 51–55.

Roseth, C. J., Johnson, D. W., & Johnson, R. T. (2008). Promoting early adolescents' achievement and peer relationships: the effects of cooperative, competitive, and individualistic goal structures. *Psychological bulletin,* 134(2), 223.

Sainz, V., Maldonado, A., & Calmaestra, J. (2024). The TEI Program for Peer Tutoring and the Prevention of Bullying: Its Influence on Social Skills and Empathy among Secondary School Students. *Social Sciences,* 13(1), NA-NA.

Sarı Gök, H. & Şalvarcı, S. (2021). Türkiye'deki gastronomi temalı müzelere yönelik çevrimiçi ziyaretçi deneyimlerinin incelenmesi. Seyahat ve Otel İşletmeciliği Dergisi, 18(1), 120–140.

Secomb, J. A. (2008). Systematic review of peer teaching and learning in clinical education. Journal of Clinical Nursing, 17,703–716.

Shin, S.-H., & Kim, C.-W. (2020). A Study on Subjectivity of Underachievers on Peer Assisted Learning in Culinary Skills related Subject. *The Journal of the Korea Contents Association*, 20(1), 562–572. https://doi.org/10.5392/JKCA.2020.20.01.562

Sin, D. Y. E., Chew, T. C. T., Chia, T. K., Ser, J. S., Sayampanathan, A., & Koh, G. C. H. (2019). Evaluation of constructing care collaboration-nurturing empathy and peer-to-peer learning in medical students who participate in voluntary structured service learning programmes for migrant workers. *BMC Medical Education*, 19, 1–13.

Topal, H. & Gök, İ. (2020). "Fine Dining Restoranların İstihdam Politikalarına Gastronomi Eğitiminin Etkisi" *Journal of Tourism and Gastronomy Studies*, 8 (4). 2883–2897.

Topping, K. J. (1988). The Peer Tutoring Handbook Promoting Co-operative Learning. Croom Helm, Brookline Books, Cambridge.

Topping, K. J. (1996). "Effective Peer Tutoring In Further and Higher Education: A Typology and Review Of The Literature". *Higher Education*, 32(3): 321–45.

Topping, K., & Ehly, S. (1998). Peer-assisted learning. Routledge.

Topping, K. J. (2005). "Trends in Peer Learning". *Educational Psychology*, 25(6): 631-645.

Yıldırım, A. & Şimşek, H. (2016). *Sosyal Bilimlerde Nitel Araştırma Yöntemleri*, 10. Baskı, Seçkin Yayıncılık, Ankara.

Yılmaz, H., & Şenel ,P. (2014). Turistik Bir Çekicilik Olarak Gastronomi Müzeleri. 15. Ulusal Turizm Kongresi. Engelsiz Turizm Kongre Kitabı. 1615 s. (pp. 499–510)..Ankara.

Milton Keynes UK
Ingram Content Group UK Ltd.
UKHW021627121224
452348UK00022B/458